The Anti-Journalist

The Anti-Journalist

KARL KRAUS AND JEWISH SELF-FASHIONING
IN FIN-DE-SIÈCLE EUROPE

Paul Reitter

The University of Chicago Press   CHICAGO & LONDON

The University of Chicago Press, Chicago 60637
The University of Chicago Press, Ltd., London
© 2008 by The University of Chicago
All rights reserved. No part of this book may be used or reproduced in any manner whatsoever without written permission, except in the case of brief quotations in critical articles and reviews. For more information, contact the University of Chicago Press, 1427 E. 60th St., Chicago, IL 60637.
Published 2008
Paperback edition 2020
Printed in the United States of America

29 28 27 26 25 24 23 22 21 20   1 2 3 4 5

ISBN-13: 978-0-226-70970-3 (cloth)
ISBN-13: 978-0-226-75457-4 (paper)
ISBN-13: 978-0-226-70972-7 (e-book)
DOI: https://doi.org/10.7208/chicago/9780226709727.001.0001

Library of Congress Cataloging-in-Publication Data

Reitter, Paul. The anti-journalist : Karl Kraus and Jewish self-fashioning in fin-de-siècle Europe / Paul Reitter.
p . cm.
Includes bibliographical references and index.
ISBN-13: 978-0-226-70970-3 (cloth : alk. paper)
ISBN-10: 0-226-70970-1 (cloth : alk. paper)
1. Kraus, Karl, 1874–1936—Political and social views. 2. Jews—Identity—Europe—History—19th century. 3. Antisemitism in the press—Europe—History—19th century. 4. German literature—Jewish authors—History and criticism. 5. Jewish press—Europe—History—19th century. 6. Jewish journalists—Europe—History—19th century. I. Title.
PT2621 .R27Z765 2008
838'.91209—dc22

2007020594

CONTENTS

Acknowledgments vii
Abbreviations xi
A Note on Editions xiii
A Note on Translations xv

Introduction • All That Is Solid Melts into Ink 1
1 • German Jews and the Writing of Modern Life 31
2 • Karl Kraus and the Jewish Self-Hatred Question 69
3 • Mirror-Man 107
4 • Messianic Journalism? Benjamin and Scholem Read *Die Fackel* 137
Conclusion • The Afterlife of Anti-Journalism 175

Notes 183
Bibliography 241
Index 249

ACKNOWLEDGMENTS

At the risk of driving away readers with my first sentence, let me be candid, right up front, about the provenance of this book: *The Anti-Journalist* began as a dissertation. It had, as such, a committee. And I remain grateful to the members of its committee—Robert Holub, Hinrich Seeba, and Judith Butler—for their generous encouragement and challenging feedback, and for interweaving those two things so beautifully. I am also grateful to them for continuing to play a role in shaping the project after signing off on the Ph.D. thesis version of it. Bob Holub's role was particularly important. Throughout the years, he has been a wonderfully supportive mentor.

As a graduate student at UC Berkeley, my work profited from the input of many excellent scholars. Some were in my home department, the German department: Anton Kaes, Bluma Goldstein. Some were not: Martin Jay, Hans Sluga. Still, the German department deserves special thanks. With Bob Holub and then W. Dan Wilson as its chairperson, the department provided me with a series of fellowships and more support for research trips and conference travel than I requested. It was, after all, the late 1990s.

At the same time, the core research for my dissertation could not have been done without a residential fellowship from the German National Literature Archive in Marbach am Neckar. There I had the good fortune to have as my institutional "host" Friedrich Pfäfflin, a leading expert on my subject, Karl Kraus; and in conversation with Dr. Pfäfflin I learned a great deal about our mutual interests. Happily, this experience would become part of a pattern. The community of established Kraus scholars proved to be genuinely welcoming. And I am duly grateful to it for that. I especially want to thank Gilbert Carr and Edward Timms for inviting me to their 1999 conference on the reception of Kraus's work, and for their valuable commentary on the talk I gave.

Ohio State University, where I have spent the past six years, magnanimously supported my research, both with sabbatical quarters for writing and with funding for trips to archives in Vienna and Jerusalem. Furthermore, Ohio State colleagues in an array of disciplines read parts of the book and gave me useful feedback. They are, in no particular order, Robin Judd, Nina Berman, Brian Rotman, Jenny Siegal, and Steve Kern. Galey Modan, Matt Goldish, and Gregor Hens offered wise thoughts on the process of book writing. Galey and Gregor also helped by being good friends, as did Robin and Nina.

A number of colleagues and colleague-friends from around the fields of German and Jewish studies commented on *The Anti-Journalist* in ways that mattered: Willi Goetschel, Noah Isenberg, Michael Stanislawski, Amir Eshel, Peter Gordon, David Brenner, Helmut Walser Smith, David Myers, Scott Spector, Michael Rohrwasser, Liliane Weissberg, Richard Levy, Anson Rabinbach, Michael Brenner, Ulrich Baer, Daniel Boyarin, Christoph König, Steven Beller, Ritchie Robertson, Azade Seyhan, and Wilhelm Vosskamp. It is an honor to be able to say that Paul Mendes-Flohr, a shaping force in German-Jewish studies, was steadfast in his support and encouragement. Mark Anderson insightfully reviewed the manuscript for the press. He also took the time to go over his criticisms with me. That my book challenges parts of his work rather roughly makes his gesture all the more gracious. The main point, however, is that in revising the manuscript I acted on all of his suggestions and am thus indebted to him. I benefited, as well, from the advice of a reviewer who chose to remain anonymous.

My editors at the University of Chicago Press, T. David Brent, Elizabeth Branch Dyson, and Kate Frentzel, did an exemplary job of guiding this project through the publication process. Richard Allen edited the manuscript with a degree of rigor and intelligence that struck me as being extraordinary. Indeed, his incisive, broad-ranging commentary helped make the book better on every level, and I feel very fortunate to have had the opportunity to work with him.

It is, of course, for readers to decide whether or not *The Anti-Journalist* is a good book. But I will presume to say that without the help of two people it would be a shadow, a hapless, anemic shadow, of the book it has become.

Practically speaking, Leo Lensing and Brett Wheeler were collaborators on this project. Leo's work on Kraus combines exegetical brilliance with scholarly circumspection and enormous erudition. In helping me improve my book he generously—and tirelessly—mobilized all those resources. An admirably close reader and my closest friend, Brett identified many problems in the manuscript and spent countless hours talking through possible solutions to them.

My father, Robert Reitter, was born in prewar Budapest, into a family of acculturated Germanophile Jews, and he was always willing to share with me an experiential knowledge of issues that have a critical part in my project. He was also an enthusiastic, discerning reader whose feedback helped make *The Anti-Journalist* more engaging. I thank my wife, Maria, for providing all those things that someone writing a book hopes for from a partner: patience, loving support, good editorial advice, etc. This book is dedicated to her and to our daughter Cecelia.

A compressed version of chapter 2 appeared as "Karl Kraus and the Jewish Self-Hatred Question" in *Jewish Social Studies* 10, no. 1 (Fall 2003): 78–111.

ABBREVIATIONS

F   Karl Kraus, *Die Fackel*. Available online at the Fackel Gate, Austrian Academy Corpus, http://corpus1.aac.ac.at/fackel/.
KZ   Karl Kraus, *Eine Krone für Zion,* in Kraus, *Frühe Schriften,* vol. 2, ed. J. J. Braakenburg, 298–314. Munich: Kösel Verlag, 1979.
"HC"   Karl Kraus, "Heine und die Folgen" ("Heine and the Consequences"), 1910. Reprinted in *Die Fackel in 1911* (F 329–30:6–33).
"HF"   Karl Kraus, "Harikari und Feuilleton," in *Untergang der Welt durch schwarze Magie,* ed. Christian Wagenknecht, 140–51. Frankfurt/M: Suhrkamp, 1989.
"LS"   Karl Kraus, "Die letzten Schauspieler," in *Untergang der Welt durch Schwarze Magie,* ed. Christian Wagenknecht, 152–56. Frankfurt/M: Suhrkamp, 1989.

BB   Walter Benjamin, *Briefe,* ed. Christoph Gödde and Henri Lonitz. Frankfurt/M: Suhrkamp, 1995–2000.
BGS   Walter Benjamin, *Gesammelte Schriften,* vol. 2, ed. Rolf Tiedemann. Frankfurt/M: Suhrkamp, 1977.
"KK"   Walter Benjamin, "Karl Kraus" (1931), in Benjamin, *Illuminationen,* sel. Siegfried Unseld, 353–84. Frankfurt/M: Suhrkamp, 1977.
"DJ P"   Moritz Goldstein, "Deutsch-jüdische Parnaß," *Der Kunstwart: Halbmonatsschau für Ausdruckskultur auf allen Lebensgebieten* 25, no. 11 (March 1912): 281–94.

"JIB" Theodor Gomperz, "Über die Grenzen der jüdischen intellektuellen Begabung," in Robert Kann, ed., *Theodor Gomperz: Ein Gelehrtenleben im Bürgertum der Franz-Josephszeit*, 384–92. Vienna: Verlag der österreichische Akademie der Wissenschaften, 1974.

KB Franz Kafka, *Briefe 1902–1924*, ed. Max Brod. Frankfurt/M: Fischer, 1966.

SB Gershom Scholem, *Briefe*, vol. 1: *1914–1947*, ed. Itta Shedletzky. Munich: Beck, 1994.

ST Gershom Scholem, *Tagebücher*, vol. 1: *1913–1917*, vol. 2: *1917–1923*, ed. Herbert Kopp-Oberstebrink et al. Berlin: Jüdischer Verlag, 1995, 2000.

"SF" Heinrich von Treitschke, "Der souveräne Feuilleton," in Treitschke, *Bilder aus der Deutschen Geschichte*, vol. 2, 147–82. Lepizig: Hirzel, 1908.

WGS *Richard Wagner, Richard Wagners Gesammelte Schriften*, vol. 13, ed. Julius Kapp. Leipzig: Hesse und Becker, 1911.

A NOTE ON EDITIONS

The current standard edition of Kraus's works, the *Schriften* or *Writings* edited by Christian Wagenknecht, was published between 1986 and 1994 in twenty volumes by Suhrkamp Verlag. This edition consists of all of the titles published by Kraus in his lifetime, many of which were anthologies of essays, satires, and the "glosses" that had appeared in *Die Fackel* up until 1918. The edition also includes two posthumously published works (*Die Sprache* and *Dritte Walpurgisnacht*), anthologies from later volumes of *Die Fackel*, and unpublished manuscripts that were the basis of Kraus's public readings of Shakespeare, Nestroy, and Offenbach. A CD-ROM version of the Suhrkamp edition is available from DirectMedia in Germany. The Suhrkamp edition does not include *Die Fackel*, which was first published in a complete edition by *Kösel* Verlag (Munich) from 1968 to 1976. An inexpensive reprint followed from Zweitausendeins in 1977 that included a volume containing the so-called "Act Edition" of *Die letzten Tage der Menschheit* [*The Last Days of Mankind*] and an invaluable index of names by Franz Ögg. A CD-Rom version of the journal, edited by Friedrich Pfäfflin, appeared with Sauer Verlag in 2003. The disk includes PDF versions of two essential bibliographical works: *Der Fackel-Lauf,* Pfäfflin's detailed bibliography of the journal and its imitators, as well as Wolfgang Hink's volume, which presents a complete table of contents of the journal, index of other contributors, etc. In January 2007, *Die Fackel* became available online from the Austrian Academy of Sciences in Vienna. It will also soon issue an updated, digital version of Ögg's index of names.

A NOTE ON TRANSLATIONS

Most of Kraus's corpus has not been translated into English (or any other language), and the renderings of it presented in this book are mine. I have also tended to rely on my own translations of writings by German-language authors whose works have been rendered into English. The reason why is not that I regard available translations as inadequate. I have, in fact, consulted standard translations and have generally found them to be helpful. But because one of my main concerns is to trace a particular set of terms and tropes through a network of texts, it was important to convey the original wording of those texts more exactly—or more literally—than most translations do. And so, unless otherwise indicated, all translations in this study are mine.

INTRODUCTION

All That Is Solid Melts into Ink

For journalism, in its most paradoxical form, is Kraus.
—Walter Benjamin

Journalism too had its modernist moments. Indeed, some of the most searching modernist criticism in Germany and Austria found expression in the feuilleton, or cultural journalism. As one scholar recently put it, "During the Weimar era the feuilleton took on an avant-garde function as the locus of a concerted effort to articulate the crisis of modernity."[1] The irony here is that in German culture journalism—and especially the feuilleton—had long been seen as a particularly vivid agent of the very crisis in question.

Journalism had been seen, that is, as having a key role in the accumulation of experience to which scholars have given the name "the crisis of modernity." Contemporaries often spoke in more evocative terms. Marx claimed that in industrialized societies daily life changed so quickly as to seem to be in a state of "permanent revolution." He also remarked that living in such societies therefore meant existing in an atmosphere of evanescence. "All that is solid melts into air," reads his description of the modern world. For Richard Wagner, nothing facilitated this becoming ethereal of what had felt solid as directly as did journalism, or at least nothing else did in the realm of culture. It was "journalism," according to Wagner, that "introduced" the disorienting "'modern'" into Germany's "cultural development."[2] Nietzsche too regarded journalism as bringing about a fundamental and dauntingly open-ended transformation of culture.[3] Writing in the late nineteenth century, and striking an appropriately grave tone, he counted "the press" among the few "premises whose thousand-year conclusions no one yet has wagered to draw." The press was a phenomenon whose ultimate consequences loomed so large that facing them was more than commentators could bear.

If Nietzsche's claim was ever approximately right, if there was ever a reluctance to consider the lasting impact of the press, that reluctance did not last long. What the effects of such powerful forces would be soon became a *leitmotif* in Central European thought. Between the fin de siècle and the Second World War, a parade of authors speculated about how new technologies and urban centers altered the perception of time and space and taxed the human sensory apparatus in an unprecedented manner, leaving people alternately isolated and de-individuated, hypersensitive and phlegmatic. The pointedness of Marx's line about the experience of modernity succumbed to the very condition he announced as thinkers like the philosopher Ernst Bloch and the sociologist Georg Simmel brought forth even more radical-sounding appraisals. Bloch's terms seem downright eschatological. For him, modernity's signature characteristic was a falling away of sequential limitations, or a new "simultaneity of the non-simultaneous." Simmel, for his part, believed that the unending "shocks" of the turn-of-the-century metropolis had yielded a whole new psychic make-up, an "individual" freer than its predecessors but also less capable of staying loyal to its defining identifications. Similar notions abound in the literature of the period. The narrator in Robert Musil's *The Man without Qualities* [*Der Mann ohne Eigenschaften*, 1930] famously tells readers that in 1913 time began to "move as fast as a riding camel." A shared confusion resulted. In "Kakania" circa 1913, "people no longer knew which way was up and which way was down."[4]

The historical moment conjured in Musil's novel witnessed the rise of a mass press in Berlin and Vienna. And many of the era's self-portrayals show this new mass press as adding greatly to what they, like *The Man without Qualities,* present as a dramatic sensation of instability. A bewildering number of daily editions, unbridled fear-mongering and scandal-mongering, relentless round-the-clock systems of production and distribution, ruthless competition among newspapers, the voices of whose "criers" made up a good part of the din in city streets as they trumpeted the arrival of more absolutely urgent news—these features led to visions of mass journalism as Moloch, as the embodiment of modern capitalism's volatile energy and rapacity. Yet journalism also came across as a special kind of commodity, one that had an uncanny power over its consumers.[5]

Kurt Tucholsky's vignette "The Newspaper Reader's Prayer" ("Das Gebet des Zeitungslesers," 1927) memorably conveys this idea. Looking at the "newspapers of all shapes and sizes" that are "piled, scattered and balled up on his furniture," Tucholsky's newspaper reader feels compelled to ask for divine help. "Dear God . . . I have to read them all, all of them," he pleads. As he lists the news items that interest him, it becomes clear that the prodigious newspaper clutter in his head is self-perpetuating. The stories he has read are jumbled together in such a way that they have no order of importance. "World's smallest bellybutton" comes just before, and appears to be as significant as, "Mussolini, black shirts." Impaired by a surfeit of news reports, the newspaper reader sees all the news as newsworthy. And so he must read it all. However, because there is now so much news, reading it all seems impossible, even to the benighted newspaper reader. Hence the newspaper reader's need to pray.[6]

At the same time, however, the crisis of modernity had also to do with the perceived loss of non-secular, relatively stable sources of meaning and structures of identity, with what Max Weber labeled "the disenchantment of the world."[7] As early as the beginning of the nineteenth century, Hegel attributed to journalism a salient part in that process. Indeed, he invoked for reading the newspaper nothing less than the status of "realistic morning prayer."[8] One had "oriented oneself" for the new day by reestablishing a faith grounded in a discrete body of timeless, sacred words: scripture. These words, Hegel's comparison implies, were supplanted by the eminently perishable, rapidly circulating, programmatically mundane "facts" of the daily edition.

Of course, the formulation "realistic morning prayer" hardly bespeaks disquiet. But as the journalism industry expanded, accounts of how it made culture more profane took on a tone of alarm. A little over a century after Hegel had commented on reading the newspaper, Walter Benjamin assailed the press for diminishing the value and obscuring the magic of language, whose mysteries he revered.[9] Not only did he propose that the "empty phrases" in "feuilletonism" represented the "linguistic expression" of that "arbitrary power" through which the "topicality in journalism" achieves its "dominance over the world of things" ("KK," 354). In 1931, Benjamin complained that, with the advent of the journalistic-feuilletonistic phrase, language was "transformed into an instrument of production" (355). So even during its Weimar apotheosis, when Benjamin himself was parsing the crisis of modernity in the avant-garde feuilleton section of the *Frankfurter Zeitung*, the feuilleton appeared to promote a harsh new order of cultural disenchantment. Tellingly, Hermann Hesse, who could not stop playing with the theme of reenchantment, had his last major narrator deride the interwar years under the heading "the age of the feuilleton."[10]

It was in 1929, moreover, that the philosopher Theodor Lessing declared "feuilletonist" to be "the meanest insult in the German language."[11] But why "feuilletonist"? What had made that word crueler than the appellation "journalist"? The feuilleton was a type of journalism, after all. And if the feuilleton and journalism were not interchangeable categories, the latter rubric was frequently attached to the former mode of writing. In fact, when Wagner vilified journalism as the bearer of the modern spirit, he probably had in mind feuilletonistic journalism. For where he levels this charge, Wagner's concern is the modern appropriation of German *culture;* and, as intimated above, the feuilleton of his day can be defined as "cultural journalism." It can be defined as a journalism that addressed all sorts of cultural topics, most often in a conversational and aesthetically engaging manner.[12] Having originated in the Parisian press around 1800, the feuilleton had become, by the time of Wagner's death in 1883, an established part of major German and Austrian newspapers. Yet only a little later could individual feuilletons be instances of "feuilletonism." Only around the turn of the century, amidst a flourishing post-*Gründerzeit* culture of coffeehouse literati, did a special feuilletonistic voice emerge as a widespread style of reportage.

That voice was itself a popular theme in fin-de-siècle feuilletons, which thus provide much in the way of self-portraiture. In a feuilleton from 1894, for example, Hugo von Hofmannsthal asserts that the "relation of feuilleton writing to the things in life" is "full of ironic precocity and overdeveloped skepticism, deeply untruthful and unspeakably seductive."[13] Hofmannsthal's reproach was hardly unique. For many commentators, feuilletonism amounted to verbal dandyism. It had the alluring, elaborately stylized emptiness that seemed so pervasive among its main producers. But given how diverse the prose published under the designation "feuilleton" was, it should not be surprising that other turn-of-the-century authors saw different features as the essence of feuilletonism. Alfred Polgar, himself an accomplished feuilletonist, emphasized what he perceived to be the bad hybridity of the Viennese feuilleton, specifically its "jocose mixture of ur-Jewishness and ur-Aryanness [*Urjudentum und Urariertum*], of synagogic melancholy and Grinzinger alcohol atmosphere [*Alkohollaune*]."[14]

A more plausible attempt to locate the distinguishing characteristic comes from a more scholarly source, the historian Carl Schorske. It too contains an element of censure. Discussing the place of the author's subjectivity in the fin-de-siècle Viennese feuilleton, Schorske observed: "In the feuilleton writer's style, the adjectives engulfed the nouns, the personal tint virtually obliterated the object of discourse."[15] Schorske might have been thinking of the following phrases, which the Vienna-based critic Rudolf Strauß used in 1896, in reviewing a book by a poet who was, at the time, relatively unknown: "One has to have beheld that pale, delicate face with its slightly dull gray eyes and its drooping reddish blonde mustache, one has to have heard that tired and inexpressibly mild person speaking, in order to be able to form a full and precise judgment of him."[16]

What explains this trend is, in Schorske's view, a collective narcissism. Disaffected by the failures of liberal politics, many fin-de-siècle Viennese intellectuals turned inward, to psychological exploration and radical self-reflection. According to Schorske, these affinities encouraged the highly "subjective response of the critic or reporter" that we see in the feuilleton.[17] Benjamin, by contrast, maintained that despite its suggestion of authorial intimacy, the "chatter" [*Geschwätz*] of such prose lacks precisely subjective content ("KK," 370). He portrayed the feuilleton as consisting of production-driven "empty phrases" that say more about language under "high capitalism" than about the feelings of feuilleton writers. In the turn-of-the-century screeds that made "feuilletonist" a superlatively mean "insult," we encounter in propagandistic form elements of both Schorske's and Benjamin's ideas. The feuilleton was generally anathematized as a decadent "versified journalism" and also as a commercial intrusion into the poetic realm. Critics accused feuilleton writers of attenuating and commodifying *Kultur*.

CULTURAL JOURNALISM AND THE JEWISH QUESTION

The rhetoric of cultural degeneration and commodification was also a central part of antisemitic discourse in fin-de-siècle Germany and Austria. There, according to the historian Peter Pulzer, "no profession" was "more completely dominated by Jews than journalism."[18] And the blights that were projected onto both the feuilleton and German Jews were often projected onto the feuilleton and German Jews *together*.[19] Attacks against the feuilleton and antisemitic invectives frequently dovetailed, thereby reinforcing each other.[20] It was actually "Jewish journalism" [*jüdische Journalistik*] that Wagner held responsible for bringing "'the modern'" into German culture. Consider, as well, the following lines from a 1913 essay that appeared in

Der Brenner, a reputable Austrian journal. The "mission of the Jews today," we are told, is "to strip all discipline from thinking, to commit sodomy with the word, to deflower, to *feuilletonize* the intellect, to turn it into a prostitute in the newspaper and market hall" (my emphasis).[21]

Or witness the more famous example of Heinrich von Treitschke (1834-96). Treitschke was one of the most prolific and colorful historians in Wilhelmine Germany—not by chance did W. E. B. DuBois sit in on his lectures during his stay in Berlin. Treitschke was also a nationalist who zealously supported the Hohenzollern Reich at a moment when internal struggles seemed to be imperiling both German political unity and the very notion of a coherent German cultural identity. German Jews, meanwhile, had in 1871 been granted full civil rights, and, thanks to some extraordinary success stories, they appeared to be quickly gaining influence within German society.[22] This was a fraught context that fostered new expressions of prejudice and new forms of scapegoating. Indeed, it was *the* context that saw the first antisemitic political parties take shape. And if Treitschke never belonged to an antisemitic organization, by the end of the 1870s he had joined, and had made more respectable, a swelling chorus of Jew-baiters.

Treitschke also did more than that. He helped cultivate the aggressive style of sloganeering that would prove to be among the most fateful legacies of Wilhemine antisemitism.[23] More specifically, he authored the imprecation: "The Jews are our misfortune!" Although the polemical character of this phrase would have been hard to miss, Treitschke went to some lengths to frame his line as a conclusion drawn from an actual historical diagnosis. In putting forth this diagnosis he relied heavily—and perhaps even primarily—on arguments about journalism. For instance, in 1879 Treitschke deemed the "overrepresentation of Jewish journalists" to be the "most dangerous" threat to Germany's political health.[24] Having subsequently blamed the German Jew Ludwig Börne for the corrosive "tone" of "our" political "journalism," Treitschke focused on the feuilleton.[25]

His article "The Sovereign Feuilleton" ["Das souveräne Feuilleton," 1891?] treats Heinrich Heine, another German Jew, as the father of German "feuilletonism." According to Treitschke, Heine founded a deleterious journalistic form. But rather than contributing to the divisiveness of German political discourse, it harmed German culture. Heine developed a superficial yet formally accomplished style whose easy-to-consume character resulted in its becoming "sovereign." He thus made dominant in Germany a writing that breaks with a core value of German letters: respect for substance. "With Heine, there appeared among us for the first time a virtuoso of form who did not care about the content of his words."[26]

Treitschke proceeds to sketch Heine's mixture of virtuosity and vacuity as being the equivalent of the sexual dissoluteness one learns in France.[27] That Heine began to forge an artful new style of urban reportage before leaving Germany seems to not have mattered.[28] Unconcerned with accuracy, and not one for subtle innuendo, Treitschke has Heine, who lived in Paris from 1831 until his death in 1856, take up the feuilleton by way of swallowing "the foam of this French passion-drink" in an "aroused" state ("SF," 154). This lubricious deed was evidently the opposite of an inspired moment. In fact, Treitschke depicts Heine's writing as being doubly derivative and therefore profoundly antithetical to the independent "German intellect." Heine's feuilletonistic style represents, for Treitschke, an imitation of "epigonic [French] literature" (154).[29]

But it would be misleading to imply that at the turn of the century the feuilleton was merely a beleaguered, "Jewified" form, that the projective mechanisms of nationalist discourse, along with anxieties about the fate of high culture in an incipient mass society, completely colored its meaning. There were writers who stuck up for the feuilleton. The novelist and critic Joseph Roth offered an eloquent defense, for example.[30] Moreover, quite a few German Jews with close ties to the genre commanded respect. They did so as prose stylists, as the authors of imaginative literary reportage, and as erudite commentators on the arts. As reviewers, the best German-Jewish feuilletonists—e.g., Alfred Kerr and Theodor Herzl—acted as authoritative mediators of German culture. If, as George Mosse has argued, *Bildung*, or self-refinement through cultural education, served among German Jews as a privileged vehicle for social integration, even taking on the status of a new "religion," then Kerr and Herzl were something like secular priests.[31] Stefan Zweig's memoir *The World of Yesterday* [*Die Welt von Gestern*, 1944] offers a nice illustration of this idea. In it Zweig recalls that his liberal Jewish father venerated the feuilleton section of the *Neue Freie Presse*—over which Herzl presided—as an "oracle."[32]

For Herzl himself, correlatively, high-end cultural journalism provided symbolic grounding. As Schorske pointed out, "It was fitting that, rather than devoting himself purely to belles lettres, he [Herzl] sought anchorage in journalism. Here he would have an outlet for his creative ambitions, acquire an audience, and become an arbiter in the area of culture without the risks of solitude which genius must endure."[33] Writing feuilletons for the

Neue Freie Presse was not the way to achieve the aura of "genius." But it did give one instant influence and the sacerdotal prestige that attended being an "arbiter" of culture in a culture-worshipping society.

That critics inveighed against Jewish feuilleton writers and "feuilletonism" so fiercely could reflect the importance of the form. Antisemitic rhetoric can be risibly counterfactual, to be sure. And no doubt Treitschke exaggerated in speaking of "the *sovereign* feuilleton." Yet the need to discredit the genre, to mark it as constitutively "other" or "fundamentally un-German," to use Treitschke's own phrase ("SF," 155), can be interpreted as a sign that the feuilleton had become an accepted discourse, part of the fabric of cultural life. After all, the *Neue Freie Presse* was the only newspaper in turn-of-the-century Central Europe with an international reputation. Thus the paper and Herzl's feuilleton section must have had a large number of non-Jewish readers.[34] Not only that, non-Jews too, it seems, regarded the paper as secular gospel. As one contemporary put it, the *Neue Freie Presse* was the "prayer book of *all* educated people" (my emphasis).[35]

The resonance Treitschke's diatribes found might further indicate that their target mattered. We can detect echoes of his criticisms, moreover, in places that were seminal in their own right, such as the writings of Adolf Bartels. Bartels was a highly successful, stridently nationalist literary critic whose work regularly appeared in the prestigious *Kunstwart* magazine. His campaigns against Heine and the feuilleton would eventually grow more expansive and more vitriolic than Treitschke's. But in the 1890s Bartels often sounded as though he were quoting Treitschke, who was decades older and, at the time of his death in 1896, the more famous of the two. In 1897, for example, Bartels warned: the Jews are the "chief representatives" of "a feuilletonism in Germany" that is "at bottom corruption" and "takes as its ideal French literature and the French journalistic model."[36]

There were analogous stereotypes. In his study *Jewish Self-Hatred* Sander Gilman tracks the notion that even the most precocious Jewish members of the community of German speakers are afflicted by linguistic problems. Their German is distorted by the background buzz of German-Jewish dialect, by their "hidden language," their *Mauscheln*. As a number of cultural theorists have stressed, because Germany did not become a unified nation state until 1871, German identity tended even afterward to be coded in cultural and linguistic terms rather than in political and territorial ones.[37] Hence, according to Gilman, the great significance of stereotypes about the *linguistic* defects of German Jews. Like the antisemitic trope of *Mauscheln,* anti-Jewish ideas about the "un-German" feuilleton functioned to mark Jews as being different where, in acting as *cultural* authorities, they appeared to have taken on a basic feature of German identity. Such ideas worked toward *preserving* Jews as one of the foils of cultural otherness against which German identity was defined.

But antisemitic stereotypes about the feuilleton did more than insist on the foreignness of the form. They did more, that is, than use established notions of Jews as Frenchifiers, formalists, mercenaries, and imposters to bolster decades-old fantasies about German culture, about its singular depth and autonomy. And the "more" in question here is not merely that antisemitic stereotypes about the feuilleton invoked the same established notions to blame Jews for the manifestly "un-German" tendencies in post-unification German culture and politics. What is different about the vocabulary of these stereotypes, what made them so resonant and so convoluted, is that they also spoke to a powerful new anxiety about the becoming less solid of crucial demarcation lines and, indeed, of culture in general. Otherwise put, anti-Jewish polemics against cultural journalism spoke to the experience of up feeling perilously like down.

By declaring that mobile new insider, the Jewish feuilletonist, to be the ultimate outsider, stereotypes about the feuilleton served to allay just that sort of anxiety. Yet they also went *well* beyond straightforward denial. In fact, antisemitic stereotypes about the feuilleton might have been first part of anti-Jewish discourse to *emphasize* the theme of an unsettling resemblance between opposites.[38] These stereotypes often contain a new pattern of argumentation, to the effect that in the feuilleton the uncreative Jewish mind brings about "deceptively similar" replicas of what its antipode, German creativity, produces. Late nineteenth-century stereotypes about the feuilleton thus made Jews and journalism into *the* iconic carriers of a debilitating semiotic confusion in which the difference between the original and the copy, and what is most sacred and most profane, gets lost. In Wagner's writings—and elsewhere too—it was precisely such disorientation that "Jewish journalism" engendered in German culture. There remained clear signs of Jewish alterity. But the problem of the "modern" was not so much that Jews had forced a foreignness upon Germans, as that Germans had begun to fashion themselves after utterly un-German models: the simulacra of Germanness that Jewish journalists made. For German idealist thinkers like Kant and Hegel, the great promise of modernity was the freedom of self-determination, or in a word, autonomy. At its most distopian, Wagner's thinking essentially negates this promise. Modernity makes for conditions in which an "other" determines the German collective self, an other that is itself derivative rather than self-determining. "Modern," for Germans, means living in a state of absolute heteronomy.

The explicit logic of Wagner's position was as follows. Lacking "solid sensibilities" and a Germanic stake in content, assimilated Jews have "an enormous talent" for mirroring and exploiting cultural accomplishments that are not of their own design. And so Jews possess a special aptitude for the protean, derivative, mass-produced language of journalism, where it can even be "a Jewish characteristic to have no Jewish characteristics."[39] Through their journalism Jews attempt to pass off their "counterfeit" writings as authentic German culture, meeting too often with success.[40]

For Treitschke, of course, the feuilleton became popular in the unsubtle manner of fast food. Tasty, easy to obtain, and cheap, it proved hard to resist. But Treitschke too worked with the motif of a copying that seemed to be spiraling dangerously out of control. Only after pages of discussion is he prepared, in "The Sovereign Feuilleton," to say how "the feuilleton reveals what the Frenchman and the Jew have in common" (155). So Treitschke does not always take the visibility of the feuilleton's otherness for granted. Furthermore, what the Frenchman and Jewish feuilletonists share is a disregard for substance that has as its chief concomitant an uncanny ability to foster imitation. French literature is "epigonic," and quite possibly a copy of the results of "Aryan creative might." Jews borrow this copy, but they then go a large step farther by managing to get the originators to copy a vacuous second-order replication of their own substantial achievements. For Jews have imitated the French copy and brought their copy-of-a-copy to Germany, where Germans appear to be copying it.[41]

In *Jewish Self-Hatred* Gilman's thesis is that the deprecatory trope of *Mauscheln*—that is, speaking with a Jewish accent—played a large part in *German-Jewish* constructions of Jewish identity. Certainly the same can be said of claims about the Jews' journalistic acumen. Turn-of-the-century German-Jewish culture sent forth more than a few calls for acculturated Jews to revitalize themselves spiritually, to free themselves from an eviscerating "half-ness" and regain their creative potency. Here too the figure of the Jewish journalist had a kind of emblematic status, very often operating as a symbol of where acculturated German-Jewish intellectuals stood and of what they lacked. It evoked, for some German Jews, their paradoxical situation apparently with unique force. This was the paradox of how Jewish intellectuals could exist simultaneously at the center and the margins of German culture. German-Jewish feuilleton writers administered a culture that, as the most conspicuously free-floating or deracinated modern minds, they did not have the resources to help transform.[42] Their vocation was a culture whose deepest levels were seen as lying beyond their reach.

A famous fin-de-siècle article, which blasted Jewish "assimilation" and which was authored by a German-Jewish Germanist, maintains that "the voice of the feuilleton Jew does not move the German people."[43] In 1904, the Jewish classicist Theodor Gomperz meditated on "the limits of the Jewish intellectual gift," coming to the conclusion that the best German-Jewish playwrights can only be "dramatic feuilletonists."[44] If Herzl's role at the *Neue Freie Presse* gave him symbolic "anchorage," during his Zionist phase he connected his activities there with the Jews' inability "to bring something real into the world." He believed that deeds of such an order require single-minded dedication, that greatness entails putting down roots. Producing feuilletons, with their constantly shifting themes, was therefore a symptom of Jewish inadequacies. Herzl lamented: "We [Jews] still need to learn what unconditional commitment means; and even today I myself have not yet learned it, for I continue to write feuilletons."[45]

Jakob Wassermann's essay in *On Judaism* [*Vom Judentum*, 1913], an important anthology of cultural Zionist writings, treats a figure closely related to the feuilletonist, the "literatus" [*Literat*], as a concentrated cipher for the losses that result from the Jews' integration into the modern Western societies.[46] "The Jew as a European, as a cosmopolitan, is a literatus; the Jew as an Oriental, not in the ethnographic sense, but rather in the mythic sense . . . can be a creator."[47] Wassermann adds that this Jewish literatus "represents *the* person who has been separated from myth" (my emphasis). By extension, the Jewish literatus is *the* antipode of "the Jew as an Oriental," of the creative Jew.

These ideas did not go unchallenged. But even where they underwent modernist revaluations and reversals, their basic elements tended to remain provocatively intact.[48] For example, while Wassermann, a well-known novelist, was making the literatus into a negative model of Jewish identity, a young student named Walter Benjamin was doing otherwise with similar associations. Benjamin acknowledged how common views like Wassermann's had become. Then he proposed that the "serious mission" of European Jews consists in their being "those literati" who with a religious "earnestness" occupy themselves with the "affairs of today" and extract "Geist" from "the art they cannot make" (*BB* 1:61). In Benjamin's countermodel precisely the cultural journalism of Jewish nonartists is the place best suited for a powerful assertion of Jewishness.[49]

So it is fair to say that in fin-de-siècle Germany and Austria prominent journalistic practices and forms were widely characterized as mirrors of German Jewry's inner condition. Shrouding certain practices and forms was a discourse about Jewish acculturation and intellectuality that was diverse yet, for the most part, organized around the theme of crisis. This point raises questions about formidably innovative moments in German and Austrian culture. How might the charged semantic value of journalistic forms, their "Jewish content," have helped produce the new styles of journalism that German Jews created? How might the thick discursive links between journalistic writing and "Jewishness" have helped shape the meaning of those styles?

The main argument of this book is that bringing these questions to bear on fin-de-siècle Vienna's most explosive journalistic style will deepen our understanding of both its development and its striking significance.[50] "Striking," because here journalism was not simply framed, with some irony, as being the devotional literature of secular society. Rather, it was accorded the status of an exalted spiritual act of unmatched ardor. I am thinking of the journalistic "dialectics" to which Benjamin once referred as "the hottest prayer for redemption that passes over Jewish lips today": Karl Kraus's "journalism in its most paradoxical form," his vaunted "anti-journalism."[51]

Given the remarkable place of journalism in discussions of German Jewry's intellectual and existential state, it should not be all too surprising that Kraus, a German-Jewish satirical journalist, purported to be "perhaps the first case of an author who simultaneously experiences his writing as an actor."[52] And, indeed, I will claim that the most daring features of the style Kraus called his "neuer publizistischer Form" ["new journalistic form"] can be read—and in notable cases were essentially read—as being part of a radical enactment of German-Jewish identity.[53] In doing so I will be entering into an old debate about Kraus's oeuvre, which a number of critics have associated primarily with the problem of Jewish self-hatred. As I map out my argument, I will say how I intend to work through this debate and also what conceptual gains I hope to make along the way. But first let me introduce the figure at its center.

KARL KRAUS

Kraus was born on April 28, 1874. Like a quite a few other luminaries in fin-de-siècle Vienna, he spent the very beginning of his life in the provinces. When he was three, his father, an affluent paper manufacturer, moved the family from Bohemia to the imperial capital. It would be Kraus's home until he died of heart failure in 1936.

Kraus alluded to his childhood frequently but without providing a general evocation of it. His reminiscences tell mostly of specific mental and bodily sensations, and seldom of the life circumstances in which he felt them. Kraus's writings offer few insights, for example, into the nature of his relationships with the members of his family. With other sources of information being scarce, many questions have remained open.[54] Not the least of them is that of Kraus's encounter with Jewish tradition in his acculturated parents' house. How much exposure was there? How deeply did it affect him? What we do know is that Kraus, the eighth of nine siblings, was often physically unwell. Some of his problems apparently had to do with a scoliotic condition whose symptoms were and would stay visible—caricaturists would later mock Kraus's abnormality. In any event, his health was bad enough that he had to be held out of grammar school for long periods of time, during which he was tutored privately. Hence, perhaps, the theme of solitude that runs through his recollections of his youth.

At the Franz-Josefs-Gymnasium in the Hegelgasse, Kraus was an uneven student and at times a difficult one. Early on, then, Kraus showed himself to be willing to run afoul of authority figures. But no evidence suggests that he was exhibiting anything more than teenage obstreperousness, or something other than glimmerings of the principled oppositional stands for which he would gain renown, e.g., his stand against the First World War. Commentators have long argued that an adolescent inclination for making scenes troubled Kraus's home life much more severely, doing permanent harm to his relationship with his siblings.[55] Such claims might seem as though they should be part of the biography of a wrathful satirist, and thus they have a certain appeal. Yet they remain hard to support. For example, an 1891 letter that is supposed to illustrate how bad the familial tensions had become hardly points to dire conflicts. Kraus's younger sister Marie strikes a teasing tone in the body of the missive. In its postscript his older sister Emma follows her lead, adverting playfully to Kraus's ambition of becoming a great actor. Even her "children's children" will know of his feats on the stage, she jokes.[56]

It would be hard to think of an author more feud-prone than Kraus. It would be even harder to think of one who did as much boasting about the size of his various "hatreds." But for all Kraus's rancor—with some justification, he has been described as having the "energy of a demonic Woody Allen"—he appears to have become a largely gentle and warm presence in the private sphere. That, at least, is the image his correspondence with his most intimate companions yields (Kraus never married or had children).

His overwhelmingly, sometimes insipidly, tender love poetry reinforces this impression. And so does the loyalty with which he supported friends like Peter Altenberg, turn-of-the-century Vienna's bedraggled master of the verbal sketch or "Skizze." Still, as Leo Lensing has deftly shown, a number of signs indicate that as a young adult Kraus clashed with his father.[57] Expressing the classic discontent of the fin-de-siècle writer born to bourgeois parents, Kraus states, in an 1897 missive to his brother Richard, that their father claims "not to want a son with a literary education." Kraus then adds to the archetypal character of his anger by faulting their father, Jakob Kraus, for not displaying "emotional warmth."[58] But Jakob Kraus was evidently no Hermann Kafka. The former father was not a combative or domineering person. For what it is worth, in the only extant photograph of him, a portrait taken in his dotage, he comes across as "kindly." More important, when his son quit studying law in order to devote himself fully to a career in cultural journalism, he accepted that decision graciously, or so it would seem. It was just a few years later that Kraus founded his own newspaper, and his father greatly facilitated the undertaking by giving him paper and loaning him money.

The first issue of *Die Fackel* [*The Torch*], Kraus's satirical, not-quite weekly, appeared on April 1, 1899. By then, Kraus had established himself as a critical voice in fin-de-siècle Vienna. He had done so mostly through his cultural and political reportage, which he had been publishing in and beyond the city's preeminent journalistic organs, and through two pamphlets. One of those pamphlets sends up a series of even more established literati, for example, Hermann Bahr and Felix Salten. In the other Kraus ridicules Theodor Herzl's fledgling Zionist movement. But *Die Fackel* did not become an instant success on the strength of Kraus's name. Kraus, after all, was not exactly famous, yet his newspaper's initial circulation could have been as high as 30,000 copies. Indeed, *Die Fackel* is supposed to have "turned Vienna red," the color of its cover, when its excited ur-readers stood around devouring and discussing it where they had bought it.

What struck a chord was Kraus's combination of wit and earnest muckraker's outage. These two qualities come together in the "battle cry" sounded on the first page of the first *Fackel*. Kraus's line "was wir umbringen" ["what we decimate"] is a colloquial expression that cleverly plays off of the phrase "was wir bringen," which literally translates as "what we deliver" and which was used as a newspaper motto, much like "All the News That's Fit to Print." Yet at the same time this mock-motto loomed as a real threat because Kraus, sharp-tongued and now fully independent, had put himself in a position to go after the objects of his scorn with minimal restraint. Also at work in the immediate appeal of *Die Fackel* was the Luther-like drama of Kraus's gesture. Here was a young and talented journalist, a journalist who had been on his way to making a comfortable career for himself within a mighty journalistic establishment, breaking with that establishment and saying, in effect, "I cannot do otherwise."

The explanation Kraus gives in his debut issue centers on the interlocking problems of "alliances" and "hypocrisy." When Kraus founded his newspaper, the influencing of reporters and the leveraging of editors were still open secrets in Austrian journalism.[59] Hence, for example, Herzl's need to insist throughout his diaries that no one had ever bought his opinion. Hence too Herzl's complaint about the "base subservience" of the *Neue Freie Presse*, as a result of which he was "not allowed" to have his "own opinion."[60] Yet Herzl, as we know, had oracular status. And he had it partly because at the high end of Austrian journalism corruption was becoming much less flagrant than it had been in previous decades. No doubt the better newspapers felt pressure to distance themselves from an emerging boulevard press. Thus those papers had begun to make efforts to present themselves as dispassionate, "fair-and-balanced" sources of news and of political and cultural commentary. But, again, the same newspapers continued to further the interests of political allies and financial backers. It was this contradiction that Kraus found so insidious as to be a kind of calling. Sounding a lot like Oscar Wilde, whom he admired, Kraus wrote in 1899 that "there are two beautiful things in the world: to be part of the *Neue Freie Presse,* or to despise it."[61]

His more practical point was this: if one wanted to speak honestly about the journalistic malfeasance that mattered most, one would have to give up the symbolic "anchorage" that went along with writing for a respected organ. For respected liberal newspapers were not about to unmask their own hypocrisy and accuse themselves of artfully spreading false consciousness. One would have to secure a high degree of autonomy by starting a newspaper that had no "party affiliation" and, because it would support itself through subscription revenues, would not answer to companies that bought advertising space. One would have to start a newspaper like *Die Fackel*.[62]

During the paper's long run—it lasted until 1936, with Kraus acting as the owner and sole writer and editor from 1911 on—Kraus reported on local events like trials, egregious arrests, and corruption in Vienna's police force. However, the paper's substance consisted of meta-reporting. Above all, Kraus covered the Viennese press's coverage of news.

But there would be several shifts of emphasis. Most notable is the "cultural turn" that *Die Fackel* took around 1906, when Kraus began to concern himself more intensively with the problem of form and, concomitantly, to dedicate more of his energy to formal experimentation. He started to compose aphorisms and, soon thereafter, fictional dialogues and dense verbal montages. Several years later, he began working on an epic multimedia drama about the First World War. These developments help explain why Kraus's readership got smaller, and also why he could eventually count among it a gallery of modernist innovators: Franz Kafka, Ludwig Wittgenstein, Oskar Kokoschka, Arnold Schönberg, Bertolt Brecht, Alban Berg, Fritz Lang, Alfred Döblin, and Thomas Mann, to name a few. But exposing journalistic turpitude was always a central part of *Die Fackel*. Unsurprisingly, this pursuit did not only earn Kraus adulation. His targets, in fact, often counterattacked.

One of the more prominent counterstrikes occurred in 1900 and ended badly for Kraus. Its impetus was the suspicious praise that Hermann Bahr, a critic, playwright, and frequent contributor to the *Neue Freie Presse*, heaped on the theater director Emrich von Bukovics. In the past, Bahr had been dismissive of Bukovics's work, going so far as to call it that of "an illiterate." But when Bahr and Bukovics became friendly, Bahr's public tone toward Bukovics changed. Worse still, not long before Bahr's encomium appeared, Bukovics had given Bahr a desirable plot of land. Having learned of these dealings, Kraus remarked that Bahr had good reason to laud the director and now also "good grounds for building a villa." Bahr responded by suing and met with success—a lot of it. The settlement he won was large enough, according to Edward Timms, to make Kraus's quip into "one of the most expensive puns in literary history."[63]

But even at its start *Die Fackel* was far from monothematic. Kraus printed poems as well as theories of poetry during its first years. And he offered both intricate analyses and "glosses" of all manner of topics. They include theatrical productions, industrial strikes, academic controversies, and political scandals. Yet if Kraus addressed large events, he might have also agreed with Siegfried Kracauer's axiom that "unassuming surface-level phenomena are of more help in determining the historical significance of an epoch than are the epoch's explicit attempts to evaluate its position."[64] For Kraus often tried to show how such things as the clichés in personal ads revealed what he came to see as his age's signature calamity: the dulling of the popular imagination at a moment of rapid technological progress. Indeed, Kraus's concern about the fate of the imagination in modern society unites his coverage of many disparate subjects, from adultery trials to comma use.

He was particularly concerned about the fate of the mind in his own society. We might regard turn-of-the-century Vienna as an extraordinarily dynamic place, one teeming with figures like Freud, Robert Musil, Gustav Mahler, Arthur Schnitzler, and Egon Schiele.[65] But, for Kraus as for Hermann Broch, that Vienna was the waltzing, stultifying "world capital of kitsch."[66] The situation looked as bleak in the rest of Austria. And this characteristic cultural impoverishment was being made worse by a local journalistic industry that was, of course, especially bad. "No language is spoken and written as poorly as the German language, and in no region is it spoken and written as poorly as it is in Austria," Kraus maintains in an article that seeks to expose how Austria's press has leveled the difference between speech and writing.[67] The press's attempt to sound conversational has created, he asserts, "our Babel of one language." Readers are now qualified to write for newspapers they cannot understand because journalists now write like their readers speak. Soon readers will speak like journalists write, at which point communication will break down completely, or so Kraus grimly predicts.

With as much hyperbole and "negative chauvinism," he castigated the press for indulging a Viennese tendency to ruin both art and life by coupling art objects with use objects: "Vienna's streets are paved over with culture, the streets of other cities with asphalt," he once wrote.[68] So "when a traffic accident occurs in Berlin," reporters at least manage to convey a few facts, while in Vienna they discuss "the essence" of traffic, the essence of accidents, and the question, "what is man?" yet say nothing about how many people were hurt. In the scenario Kraus sketches, pretentious ornament has taken the place of practical instrument, with the result that the job of conveying the news goes undone.

Kraus was not the only one to suggest that local extravagances left the Viennese feuilleton uniquely marred. His friend and fellow literatus Alfred Polgar shared his opinion, as did his enemy Bahr. More recently, scholars have taken up, and have continued to advance, part of Kaus's point. A number of literary scholars have argued that regional peculiarities thoroughly informed the style of cultural journalism in fin-de-siècle Vienna. They have tended to do so, however, in flattering tones. In a further twist, they have cited that nemesis of the Viennese feuilleton, Kraus himself, as evidence of what they claim is the Viennese feuilleton's unrivaled mordancy, its singularly "biting wit."[69]

But, like so many of Kraus's attitudes, his views on the extent to which Viennese traits mattered in the production of "feuilletonism" are at once strident and ambiguous. Kraus's indictment of feuilletonists did not stop at the city limits, after all. Quite a few of his main offenders were Berlin-based non-Viennese, e.g., Maximilian Harden and Alfred Kerr. And when, in reckoning with the feuilleton, Kraus skewered its practitioners for denaturing imaginative discourse, for making art into "not-art" and thus "heaven into a hell," he seemed to have in mind all German-speaking cultural journalists. Broad ideas about the state of bourgeois culture underlie his attack on the feuilleton, just as they underlie much of his critical reportage. Indeed, while Kraus presented these ideas as aphoristic insights rather than as parts of an integrated theory, some bear affinities with important theoretical work on the constitutive features of modern culture—for example, with Georg Simmel's analysis of the relationship between modern culture and the modern individual. The moment in this analysis that most readily invites comparison with Kraus's work is Simmel's reading of fashion.

Simmel thought that the power of fashion lay in its ability to meet two enduring—and opposing—psychological needs simultaneously: the need to fit in and the need for distinction. Writing in 1895, he also stressed that fashion did not always have its current significance.[70] What enabled the rise of the fashion *trend* as a social phenomenon is the plight of the modern individual. Fashion's "dominant" place in the social landscape has to do with the loss of a "metaphysical grounding." The allure of the fast-moving fashion cycle corresponds both to a modern "hunger for the new" as well as to the speed with which fashions of all kinds spread and lose their exclusivity in industrialized urban centers. It corresponds, more fundamentally, to an internal unmooring, to the needs and also the possibilities that attend our "emptiness of the soul."[71]

Clothes really do "make the man" only in those settings in which the chief mechanisms of identification and distinction have been relocated outward and are no longer tied to the content of beliefs that "justify our existence." One of the defining aspects of the fashion trend is, in fact, its lack of expressive value. How we dress might say a lot about our psychological investments and how sophisticated we have become, but in the age of the fashion trend clothes say little about our inner convictions and emotional states. In Simmel's theory the whole system of the fashion trend breaks down when we call on our clothes to convey genuine sentiments. His preferred example is the negation of the system's restless movement in the fixity of funeral attire.

Feuilletonism, for Kraus, speaks to similar needs in analogous ways. Yet it also poses a much greater social threat. Whereas Simmel tended not to hazard strong evaluative claims about the developments he charted, Kraus, "the apocalyptic satirist," made them freely, especially when dilating on the ills of feuilletonism. As Kraus conceived of it, feuilletonism is a language of people who "stretch themselves toward the ceiling." It is a language of bourgeois strivers, one born of a new mobility and characterized by both conformity and showing off. Otherwise put, feuilletonists deal in the paradox of a formulaic individualism. Because they want to be "recognized by the best society" rather than to communicate their own perspective, feuilletonists eagerly hold to a "tone" that has proven consumable and popular. And that, in turn, is why they "all taste alike." But since what makes the feuilleton appealing to the "best society" is its veneer of imaginative verbal impressionism and literary grace, feuilletonists just as eagerly put their "talent" on display at the expense of reporting the news.[72] Another condition of possibility for this phenomenon is, according to Kraus, a vacuum of belief. Only in an era in which "journalistic sales clerks" can be treated as "holy men" will the feuilleton have the requisite prestige to function as a vehicle for social advancement.[73]

At the same time, however, the feuilleton brings about its own enabling circumstances. That "journalistic manure is pushed through the minds of readers twice a day" helps those increasingly enfeebled readers accept the mass-produced verbal "trinkets" of the feuilleton as *Bildung*. Cultural journalism thus helps make *Bildung* into little more than a hollow fashion statement. Indeed, Kraus wrote of how "*Bildung* hangs on the body" like "clothes on a mannequin."[74] He emphasized, in addition, that cultural journalism has led to a general cheapening of culture in Vienna *and* Berlin. Kraus bemoaned how the writers Stefan Zweig, a Viennese, and Emil Ludwig, a German with ties to Berlin, could aspire to be authors of "world literature" by "cozily decorating the holes that comprise the *Bildung*" of "the newspaper reader." Having switched around his figures, Kraus also stated that "in the manner of an elevator" Zweig and Ludwig lift the "contemporary reader" to false heights. Here "all" the reader "has to do is enter below in order to be up top."[75]

The essay that makes these claims begins with an analysis of a single grammatical error. It is a typical procedure for Kraus. In his "criticism of language," or *Sprachkritik*, he often attempts to show how the smallest linguistic missteps can reveal large failures of the imagination. Since, in his thinking, our ability to feel sympathy depends on our imaginative faculties, and since Kraus also believed that deliberating carefully over words is the best practice for ethical deliberating, he frequently tried to have his *Sprachkritik* serve as a moral mirror. At stake in his *Sprachkritik*, then, was more than proper language use. As Erich Heller put it, Kraus saw a "connection between mistreated words and mistreated bodies." And if Kraus sometimes lost control of his pedantry—Oskar Kokoschka's memoirs recall him quizzing friends on the topics covered in the latest *Fackel*—he was never the narrow, conventionally elitist advocate of "good German" that he has been repeatedly made out to be.[76]

It is true that Kraus on occasion acted as though language were a natural resource that should be shielded from pollutants. But not only was he friendlier to dialects and foreign terms than were many other critics, his disquisitions on mixed metaphors, false archaisms, and neglected syllables generally seek to identify *symptoms* of hazardous mental developments. Furthermore, these developments had to do with cognitive indolence among highly educated bourgeois readers and writers. What really dismayed Kraus was the misuse of language among would-be cultural authorities, among people who, like Zweig, presented themselves as experts in language and who were equipped to do better. In fact, the people on whom Kraus focused tended to commit their solecisms precisely in trying to appear as ultra-proficient, while hastily instrumentalizing language in the manner of feuilletonists. Parsing Zweig's misappropriation of an antiquated verb-form, Kraus wrote that "only a would-be author of world literature" would have such a problem.[77]

Thus for a number of reasons it seems wrong to say, as well-known scholars have, that Kraus considered *all* grammatical mistakes to be "coextensive" with moral rot.[78] Just as misleading is the assertion that Kraus's insistence on typographical correctness makes him the father of today's "zero tolerance" approach to sloppiness in print culture.[79] No doubt Kraus was obsessed with keeping his *Fackel* free of the minutest errors. But he also emphasized in various ways that he applied this standard only to his own writing. Rather than being a practical component of his *Sprachkritik*, Kraus's demand for typographical perfection was a modernist conceit that served as a means of stressing how special, how *singularly* intense and reverential his relationship to language was.

Kraus might have venerated language as a force that can help us ripen into mature ethical agents, and he might also have consistently warned against political appeals to the irrational. Yet it is not right to portray him, as some critics have done, as one of those Viennese whose goal was to defend the ideal of the rational self at just the moment when psychoanalysis and Ernst Mach's attack on mind-body dualism seemed to be making that ideal "unsalvageable."[80] For Kraus had neo-romantic leanings, and also eroticist ones—he was an early and ardent supporter of Frank Wedekind's work who even organized a private performance of *Pandora's Box* in 1905, when public stagings were forbidden. And Kraus often spoke out against attempts to administer rationally the emotional and mental experiences that he prized, in large part, for being untamed. "Deviant" or "perverse" sexual activities between consenting adults could be good for the soul. Allowing the developing study of sexual pathologies and Austria's "ethics laws" to regulate them was the real perversity, Kraus argued.[81] Similarly, he disdained psychoanalysis not so much on account of the size and strength of irrational energies in its model of the mind, but because it subjected these mysterious energies to systematic scrutiny. Psychoanalysis, he once repined, "analyzes the dreams into which the disgust it elicits tries to flee."[82] Elsewhere he made a related point less darkly. Kraus quipped: "Psychoanalysis is a rabbit that was swallowed by the boa constrictor whose insides it wanted to see."[83]

In quite a few places, moreover, Kraus treats language as an erotic, mythic power, as an anonymous genius that demands and should receive our submission. "I have not mastered language, but it has mastered me completely," he avowed, adding that language "does with me whatever it wants to."[84] It may be that Kraus acted on such beliefs in cultivating a stage style for his public readings, of which he gave over seven hundred. According to Elias Canetti's "eyewitness" recollections, Kraus presented himself there as a kind of shamanic emissary of language. Canetti's testimony implies that Kraus sought to cast a spell over his audience with his imperious demeanor and the mesmerizing "vibrations" of his voice. Kraus was, in Canetti's view, successful in this pursuit. The title of the second volume of Canetti's autobiography, *Die Fackel im Ohr* [*The Torch in My Ear*], is clearly an allusion to how Kraus's words reverberated in his, Canetti's, head. And at some length the book describes both an atmosphere of slavish worship at Kraus's readings and the difficulty of breaking Kraus's spell.[85]

Audio recordings and film footage of Kraus's performances suggest that Kraus was, indeed, a charismatic and effusively forceful presence.[86] In parts of the film footage, which was taken in 1934, his general appearance and his dithyrambic bearing might even remind some viewers of the title figure in Fritz Lang's Mabuse films. Canetti's ultimate criticism is that this style of intellectual leadership left no room for active intellectual responses among

Kraus's followers. Kraus's behavior thus did not jibe with his own admonitions about the need for such engagement. For Canetti, Kraus's cult-of-the-self comportment was a galling form of hypocrisy. But other listeners came away with different impressions. Benjamin regarded Kraus's preternatural fervor as being only fitting, as being commensurate with the injustices that Kraus wanted to bring to light. His Kraus is paradoxical in many ways, and one of them, as we will see, is that Kraus's "non-human" characteristics make him a particularly compelling "messenger" of "real humanism."

This humanist message eventually became one of the main sources of Kraus's appeal. Some of his most popular satires had as their goal to reveal eager exploitation of human suffering on the part of would-be sensitive and refined journalistic observers. That is, Kraus tried to expose how feuilletonists embraced the worst catastrophes as fodder for their literary reportage. During the Balkan war, for example, he wrote: "The face of the feuilleton has smeared itself with blood. Ornaments on worthless prose now mock endless human hardship. . . . Inexpressible misery serves miserable description." As was so often the case, his preferred technique for laying bare iniquity was citation. Here is Kraus quoting what was, for him, a brutally precious dispatch from the war-ravaged Balkans: "General Fitschew is a stocky man of average height; he has a full round face whose skin has something rosy about it and seems almost diaphanously delicate. There are but a few white strands in his dark mustache, and his astonishingly fast-moving little eyes dart back and forth without pause, as though they wanted to resist having a fixed place, as though they wanted to look inward and outward at the same time."[87]

Kraus's most famous stage appearance, moreover, took place in November 1914, and in it he delivered a stirring condemnation of Austrian enthusiasm for the First World War. Breaking the silence he had kept since August, he made the fate of the imagination in the "age of the feuilleton" responsible for the collective euphoria over events that could only lead to colossal suffering: "That which one can no longer imagine must happen, and if one could have imagined it, it would not have happened," he intoned.[88] He also claimed that the war would not have happened if the press had not wanted it to happen. In Kraus's reading the press did not simply pave the way to disaster by selling—through the feuilleton—pre-packaged imaginative responses to the news, thus causing the popular imagination to atrophy. Having established itself as an omnipresent filter between the popular imagination and the external world, the press was literally in a position to "dictate" reality. And it used its position to bring about a sensational, horrific reality that would sell a lot of newspapers. So more than the authority of a prayer book, in Kraus's view the press's words have powers traditionally ascribed to the word of God. Accordingly, he eventually put his pioneering analysis of mass media in biblical terms: "In the beginning was the press / And then the world appeared."

ANTI-JOURNALISM AND JEWISH SELF-FASHIONING

If my introduction to Kraus qualifies as useful, then it is possible to develop a useful overview of Kraus's oeuvre while barely touching on "Jewish issues." Yet it is also possible to read almost every element of Kraus's work as interacting with those issues in some significant way. This interaction is often hard to miss. *Die Fackel* contains what has been labeled as a "gigantic discourse" on Jews and Jewish culture, much of which is clamorously hostile.[89] According to his first biographer, Kraus "located in the Jewish problem the fulcrum of the general process of cultural annihilation," and that is not really an overstatement.[90] For Kraus vituperated against Jewish journalists in apocalyptic language. He accused them of playing a special role in bringing about "the destruction of the world" through the "black magic" of newspaper ink.

Kraus's campaign against journalism was not aimed exclusively at its Jewish practitioners, to be sure. One of his preferred targets was Bahr, a non-Jew with *völkisch* antisemitsm in his background. But Kraus also implied that "the Viennese" he abominated somehow had been influenced by Jewish affections. In fact, he once defined this "Viennese" as a "mixture of Viennese and Jew," who, as such, represented "an inexplicable answer to our race question."[91] Quite a few of Kraus's remarks underline more conventional antisemitic ideas. He sometimes even made Jews out to be the driving force behind all the greediest and most invasive modern institutions: "They control the press; they control the stock exchange; and now they control the unconscious too."[92]

Kraus, furthermore, laced many of his barbs with less playful appropriations of antisemitic scurrilities. He railed against "Jewish corruption" in "Jewish newspapers," for example. Among his motives for doing so was, as one might imagine, the belief that as a group Jews were particularly guilty of the worst journalistic abuses. The "Jewish press" was "more talented" and therefore "more dangerous" than the "antisemitic press," he insisted.[93] Antisemitic journalists at least made no secret of their biases. Jews convincingly acted as though they were covering the news in a cosmopolitan spirit, while they duplicitously advanced "Jewish interests." Or as Kraus put it, "The way from the reporter to the rabbi is never far" (F 339:2). This ethnic collusion had, he thought, a number of pernicious effects. They included antisemitism. It was "Jewish solidarity" that elicited so much animus toward the Jews. And it was this sort of theory and rhetoric that gained Kraus a reputation for exhibiting "Jewish self-hatred." He once prompted as circumspect an observer as Arthur Schnitzler to exclaim: "His [Kraus's] attitude toward the antisemites is the most repulsive thing I have ever seen."[94]

Most notorious of all has been Kraus's polemic against Heine, "Heine and the Consequences" ["Heine und die Folgen," 1910]. Here Kraus begins by sounding a series of familiar and thoroughly loaded insults. He declares that the feuilleton is a "French sickness" (F 329-30:7) which Heine picked up in Paris and brought back to Germany.[95] Kraus also associates the feuilleton with decadence, with both the rich French diet and with Parisian sexual depravity. The Heine he initially constructs is a diseased sexual cripple who has recourse to a hollow feuilletonistic style because "the German language only thinks and sings for someone who can give her children" (F 329-30:8). Going beyond innuendo, Kraus directly couples Heine's Jewish heritage with his affinity for the feuilleton. In Kraus's reading Heine is a dandified "Moses." Heine is a Moses who provides his people with "Eau de Cologne" rather than water, yet one whose model of literary journalism they, the Jewish "consequences," have followed into the promised land of German culture, making it their foundational text (F 329-30:33).

Kraus argues in other directions as well. Only a few years before he published the essay, he had dismantled a series of antisemitic stereotypes about the "feminine character" of the "Jewish race," calling them "groundbreaking in the realm of idiocy."[96] And in addition to embracing Heine's late poetry, "Heine and the Consequences" eventually undermines the logic of the very sexualized taunts that Kraus invokes at its beginning. But the damage had been done, it seems. Unpopular in its own day, "Heine and the Consequences" has become a privileged object of scholarly opprobrium in ours. The book-length studies devoted to it—both written in German and not translated—are decidedly censorious.[97] Moreover, the essay has fared no better among Germanists working in other languages. Gilman summarized it in the following terms: "This attack on Heine using the rhetoric of the anti-Semitic views on the nature of the Jews' language is meant by Kraus to be a defense of 'good' language, language that does not blur the line between ornament and philosophy, and an attack on the 'bad' language attributed by Kraus . . . to the Jew."[98] Similarly, the Kafka scholar Mark Anderson has proposed that "Heine and the Consequences" establishes anti-Jewish "oppositions" coextensive with those that structure Otto Weininger's much-maligned *Sex and Character* [*Geschlecht und Charakter*, 1903].[99] Jacques Le Rider, a leading theorist of Viennese modernism, has gone farther still, stating that Kraus's text "can only really be understood as yet another symptom of *jüdischer Selbsthaß* [Jewish self-hatred]."[100]

But the story of Kraus's "relation to Jewish things" and his "Jewish reception" hardly ends there. In various ways Kraus identified with Jewish culture. He liked, for example, to present himself as an irascible modern-day Old Testament prophet. And if he underestimated the impact of Austrian antisemitism early on, he eventually became one of its more notable critics. Thus in addition to being repeatedly lionized as a "great Jew," Kraus has been defended against the charge of self-hatred by eminent German-Jewish thinkers, e.g., Walter Benjamin, Gershom Scholem, Hannah Arendt, and Theodor Adorno. Their defenses tend to be short, even epigrammatic. As we might expect of such attempts to deal with a paradox-laden mass of material, they are sometimes misleading.

Take the case of Adorno. His remark, "What Kraus could not forgive the Jews against whom he wrote was that they ceded mind [*Geist*] to the sphere of circulating capital," ignores both significant shifts and major themes in Kraus's writings.[101] It would be more accurate to say that Kraus could not get past his sense that an overdetermined desire for *symbolic* capital led German Jews to be especially active in producing the fateful stylistic excess of the feuilleton, or to be especially likely "to sing" where they should "report" the facts. When Kraus wanted to explain why his arch-rival Maximilian Harden, a prominent German-Jewish journalist, tried so garishly to display a mastery of German, he ascribed to Harden a burning need to "distinguish himself from a Schmock [i.e., from a vulgar or disreputable Jewish journalist]" (*F* 234–35:10).[102] Kraus's critique of German-Jewish culture does come across in places as a neo-Marxist assault on the links between Jews and capitalism. Yet more often it evokes Franz Kafka's famous thoughts on how the pressures of assimilation resulted in "hyperactive" writing "hands" among German-Jewish authors, thoughts in which Kraus, as we will see in the body of this book, plays a crucial role (*KB* 337).

There are some thorough, differentiated analyses of Kraus's enigmatic "Jewish Question." Harry Zohn, Robert Wistrich, and Edward Timms all conscientiously survey the inconsistencies in Kraus's utterances about German-Jewish culture.¹⁰³ But these readings have clear limitations. They are primarily biographical, their concern being to determine: How did Kraus really feel about Judaism? To what model of Jewish identity does he conform?¹⁰⁴ No doubt those are worthy topics. However, discussions of them often rely without much critical probing on "native" categories, on categories that were applied to Kraus in his own day. Zohn, for example, wants to know whether Kraus was a "'self-hater'" or an "'arch-Jew.'" As Zohn investigates this question, others go unexamined, including the issue of how Kraus's "gigantic" critical response to his fellow German-Jewish literati helped shape the formal features of his work.¹⁰⁵

Not only that, the scholars I mentioned above have tended to interpret even the most blustering of Kraus's statements about German-Jewish authors as Gilman, Anderson and Le Rider do, i.e., literally, or as reliable expressions of actual beliefs. The problem is that while Kraus seems to have employed certain grotesque stereotypes because he subscribed to them, he also appropriated antisemitic rhetoric in a willfully contradictory process of self-fashioning. Much like Nietzsche, of whom he was sometimes an enthusiastic reader, Kraus used paradoxical self-stylization as a vehicle for asserting a place beyond recognizable intellectual and generic categories. Moreover, he was clearly interested in the semantic plenitude of anti-Jewish discourse. Kraus once commented: "Antisemitism is the mentality that takes seriously about a tenth of the charges leveled by Jewish stock-market humor against its own blood."¹⁰⁶ And he at times worked with antisemitic language ironically and *strategically,* in a manner that approximates what Shulamit Volkov has called "antisemitism as a cultural code." That is, by playing hyperbolically with antisemitic tropes, Kraus created some of the spectacular paradoxes through which he bolstered his aura of critical idiosyncrasy and independence.¹⁰⁷ "In dealing with Kraus's relation to Jewish issues," Scholem aptly observed, "one can only commit errors, something for which Kraus himself made sure there would be plenty of scope."¹⁰⁸

Kraus's investment in independence—and in the appearance of it—had a number of sources. He believed that his critical voice and stylistic gifts were unique, utterly so. As Canetti's profile of him emphasizes, Kraus felt that his mission was to stand fundamentally apart in a milieu full of merely talented writers.¹⁰⁹ Another factor was credibility. Kraus, as we know, saw even the best Viennese newspapers as being massively compromised by their ties to various power interests. Again, these connections and their effects are one of the chief themes of *Die Fackel,* and one of the main reasons why he founded the journal in the first place. In Kraus's opinion his ethical superiority in the world of journalism depended on his near-total institutional autonomy.

Furthermore, and as Kraus never tired of pointing out, fin-de-siècle Austria offered him little in the way of attractive modes of collective identification. He wrote, for example: "If a man of letters could feel any desire to engage in politics, he would in Austria always wind up between parties. The first thing he would learn is the necessity of defending an idea against those who claim to stand for it. Every party would drive him to a different one. Were he an honest antisemite, upon hearing the exaggerations of the Imperial city's mayor [Karl Lueger], he would become a fanatical philosemite. Were he a convinced Zionist, the sight of a private box at the *Volkstheater* would make him into a follower of Herr Bielohlawek [a well-known antisemitic politician]" (*F* 190:15).[110] From the perspective expressed here, contradiction in the public arena is a logical necessity. Anything else would lead to self-misrepresentation, especially, it seems, with regard to the "Jewish issues" that were on Kraus's mind so often.

But what is ultimately at stake in tracking the different patterns in and functions of Kraus's antisemitic discourse? Beyond challenging the dominant paradigm in the study of Jewish self-hatred, this analytic move enables us to reckon effectively with the question of how ideas about Jewish identity and journalistic forms figured in the development of Kraus's "new journalistic form." For if Kraus's "strategic" use of anti-Jewish tropes generally has an ironic flavor, it accompanies a serious critique. It accompanies a critique of the German-Jewish literati in which Kraus engages in innovative and formative ways with that large discourse linking Jewishness and journalism. And the substance of this critique has been obscured by the looming precept that it represents little more than a ventilation of "internalized" antisemitism.[111]

I want to argue that in the most infamous "symptom" of his Jewish self-hatred, "Heine and the Consequences," Kraus operates with anti-Jewish discourse mostly for strategic purposes, while offering a seminal formulation of his boldest stylistic principles. In effect, Kraus sets his maverick journalistic practices in opposition to foibles that he perceived to be especially rampant among Jewish journalists. Here Kraus does, indeed, connect their feuilletonistic style to the process of German-Jewish acculturation, but he does so without drawing on categories like the innately "'bad' language" of "the Jew." Instead he extends the line of analysis he had begun in his early account of Zionism, which excoriates Herzl for borrowing the logic of German antisemitic ideology.[112] More specifically, Kraus charges Heine and his journalistic "consequences" with accepting ideals that were often used against them and that he, Kraus, regards as dubious, chauvinistic, and unethical. These ideals—which, in an act of paradox-flaunting, Kraus himself deploys and then abjures—equate linguistic mastery with achieving a phallic authority over language, as well as with autogenetic originality.[113]

To such attitudes Kraus counterposed something like an alternative notion of cultural authenticity. In a later text he *valorizes* his being "one of those epigones who dwell in the old house of language" (*F* 443-44:28). He also offered as a sort of credo the line that "the imitator is often better than the originator."[114] In "Heine and the Consequences" Kraus stresses that our thoughts exist before us in language: "A thought is something found, something found again and again" (*F* 329-30:30). The real writer thus turns out to be a slow and deliberate "gatherer" of linguistic "thought particles" rather than an avatar of mental virility.

Our highest goal, Kraus goes on to mandate, should be to quote language creatively. Hence after mocking Heine's inability to impregnate language, Kraus reproaches him for adopting an aggressive, heterosexist model of linguistic success, and for applying it to journalism in a distinctively Jewish attempt to reach the center of the German public sphere.[115] Around the same time, or in 1911, Kraus extolled the "revelatory" power of the effectively "repeated word," attributing this mimesis to the unassimilated culture of Eastern Jewry.[116] Far more typical is the 1913 essay in which Jakob Wasserman finds among "oriental" Jews the mythic creativity that deracinated Western Jews were supposed to lack. Kraus, by contrast, prized in a group of Eastern Jews a capacity for extreme mimicry. He embraced in them the very thing that both critics of assimilation—like Wassermann—and self-proclaimed assimilationists—like Walther Rathenau, who wanted Jews to be genuine producers of German culture and not "imitated Germans"—strove to overcome.[117] With its celebrated quoting, montages of citations, and "acoustic mirroring," the style that Kraus had begun to cultivate shortly before he wrote "Heine and the Consequences" makes good on these *counter*principles.

But there is also a larger point to be put forth here. In developing his anti-journalism Kraus directly subverted major markers of Jewishness with a consistency that seems highly overdetermined. Indeed, as he lays out his "new" journalistic style in texts like "Heine and the Consequences," he focuses on, and dramatically disrupts, the *governing* associations in the discourse that made journalistic writing into a privileged emblem of the

German-Jewish intellect. These associations include but, as I will show, are not limited to the pairing of imitation with superficiality and of originality with authenticity.[118] It is as if the way to establish a truly radical position as a Jewish journalist was to take an avant-garde stand, *in both theory and practice,* on precisely these issues. It is if establishing a truly radical position as a Jewish journalist had to entail what amounted to a radical performance of German-Jewish identity.[119]

By contextualizing Kraus's style in this manner, I hope to illuminate further not only its evolution but also how it came to be understood as such a performance, how Kraus's anti-journalism became, for Benjamin and Scholem, the most Jewish writing in the German language. For their readings of Kraus's style belong to the same general context of discussion in which I will be placing it. As young men, Benjamin and Scholem rejected what they saw as mainstream German-Jewish assimilationism. But they also rejected the alternative that had generated the most excitement among intellectuals of their ilk, Martin Buber's cultural Zionism. Actually, they went well beyond rejection. Put off by what they regarded as Buber's cult of elemental authenticity and mythic originality, they scorned his Zionism, both wittily and violently. Scholem spoke of young German-Jewish intellectuals being in "Buberty." Benjamin cudgeled Buber for using "the terminology of "National Socialism." More importantly, Benjamin and Scholem sketched out further, more drastically dialectical models of Jewish identity. Both thinkers deprecated journalism in the most withering terms. Yet both also experimented with making the medium into the unlikely locus of the most vital and salutary Jewishness, a fact that powerfully underscores the significance of journalistic writing in the process of German-Jewish self-fashioning. Their interpretations of Kraus's style unfolded largely within this framework. Benjamin's most comprehensive essay on Kraus—which embraces above all Kraus's quoting—picks up on his, Benjamin's, early thoughts on the literatus who is at once incapable of making art and deeply Jewish. For his part, Scholem speculated about how unoriginal journalistic writing signaled the decline of modern Jewish culture and yet, in an extreme form, could be a kind of redemption. Enthusing about the "messianic" Jewishness of Kraus's style, Scholem contended that Kraus "never had an original thought in his life." He added that his observation "is meant here infinitely more as a compliment than as a criticism."[120]

So the present book is about the meanings German-Jewish journalism took on at a moment when both German Jews and journalism were together deeply implicated in the "crisis of modernity." It is also about how those meanings helped give rise both to modernist journalistic forms and innovative thinking about German Jewry's predicament. Indeed, in the final part of the book I will show that Benjamin's and Scholem's neglected ruminations on the Jewishness of *Die Fackel* occupy a significant place in what might be their most probing thoughts on German-Jewish culture and its manifold discontents.

I will begin broadly. Chapter 1 examines a variety of fin-de-siècle couplings of journalism and Jewish identity, including some of the antisemitic texts to which "Heine and the Consequences" is frequently likened. In chapter 2 I track Kraus's critique of the German-Jewish literati, ultimately situating it within the discursive context that my first chapter evokes. My focus is the particular phase of Kraus's critique that coincides—quite strikingly—with the emergence of his mature style. This phase began around 1907 and lasted until the outbreak of the First World War.

After bringing to light how "Heine and the Consequences" opposes a discourse of "Jewish journalism" that makes "a fetish of creativity," to use a phrase from the notes for Benjamin's "Karl Kraus" (1931) essay (*BGS* 2:3:1106), I establish a more positive reference point. Chapter 3 takes up revealing affinities between Kraus and Kafka, some of which Kafka himself gestures at in his epistolary account of the "Mauscheln" that "scarcely anyone in the little world of German-Jewish literature can avoid." Here my aim is to extend and deepen my analysis of how Kraus framed his style in critical relation to certain tendencies in German-Jewish culture. Then, without reducing that style to a sustained engagement with "Jewish issues," I consider how key formal features of *Die Fackel* connect with Kraus's radical authorial self-fashioning. I examine how Kraus's mimetic practices reinforce his fashioning of his anti-journalism against *two* foils. These are the foils of German-Jewish feuilleton writers *and* the dominant values in largely antisemitic discussions of the German-Jewish feuilleton. Finally, chapter 4 takes up Benjamin's and Scholem's interpretations of Kraus's "journalism in its most paradoxical form," reading them against the discursive context with which I begin, and to which I now want to turn.

CHAPTER ONE

German Jews and the Writing of Modern Life

If I am someone who writes a lot, and someone for whom every letter is the mark of a wound, who could say that I am a journalist? It would have to be a Jewish characteristic to have no Jewish characteristics. —Karl Kraus

"Why are there so many Jewish journalists?" Among other places, we find this question at the center of "The German-Jewish Parnassus" ["Deutschjüdischer Parnaß"], a brooding essay on German-Jewish assimilation that appeared in 1912 and promptly elicited much debate.[1] Its author continues: "A journalist is a mirror that catches the images of the day and throws them back." Here it seems that Jews have a special proclivity for journalistic writing: there are "so many Jewish journalists." And this affinity indicates a further one for ephemeral copying, for "the other" of original, deep, edifying cultural production. After all, in "The German-Jewish Parnassus" a journalist is a flat surface that merely "catches the images of the day and throws them back," leaving both itself and its material untransformed. These points belong at the center of the text because Moritz Goldstein, the young Jewish scholar who wrote it, uses "true creativity" as his main criterion in assessing German Jewry's psychic health. According to him, Jews will enjoy spiritual well-being only where they have "the productive character," or only where they can do much more than "be a mirror."[2] In Goldstein's account the success of German Jews as journalists emblematizes the failure of Jewish assimilation.

Bad assimilation, unhealthy mirroring, journalism: This nexus of themes should be familiar to anyone who has even a passing acquaintance with

German antisemitic discourse. Think, for instance, of that "classic" of anti-Jewish literature, *Mein Kampf* (1925). In it Hitler repeatedly combines those motifs as he fulminates against the Jews and speaks of the dangers they pose.

If he finds brutal solace in the notion that "a 30 centimeter shell has always hissed more than a thousand Jewish newspaper vipers," Hitler also deems Jewish journalists to be a seminal factor in Germany's interwar malaise.[3] It was a press "of chiefly Jewish origins and journals," he seethes, that "knew how to make palatable to our people the nonsense of 'Western Democracy.'" He quickly adds: "Did it [the press] not ridicule our morals and customs, interpreting them as old-fashioned and hum-drum, till our people finally became 'modern'? Did it not, by continued attack, undermine the fundamentals of State authority for so long till a single blow was sufficient to cause the building to collapse?"[4] Updating a canonical anti-Jewish motif, Hitler has the "chiefly Jewish" press promote "'Western Democracy'" in Germany with singular effectiveness. At the same time, that press kills off traditional "morals," enabling an un-German "'modern'" culture to spread throughout the Weimar Republic. But Jewish journalists did not simply seduce intelligent Germans into assimilating themselves to foreign models. First these journalists had to reproduce "the tone of decency" to which such Germans were accustomed. They had to mirror German culture convincingly. Only then could the coordinated messages of the Jewish press resonate widely and have the desired, destructive impact. Or as Hitler sums up his theory, "thus the poison could penetrate into and work in the system of our people."[5]

In "The German-Jewish Parnassus" Jewish journalists imperil only their own cultural development. Jews might be caught up in a modern existential struggle, but they are not the primary carriers of a modern culture in which all that is solid and of enduring value melts into journalistic imitation. Jews, in Goldstein's view, make vital contributions to German art. Most often they do so as critics or cultural administrators. Yet some German Jews have brought forth epochal artistic accomplishments, to which Goldstein adverts proudly. Still, as the surfeit of Jewish journalists makes clear, German Jewry's imaginative powers have been dulled. Where he discusses this problem, Goldstein assigns much of the blame to the afflicted. He laments the willful blindness and abject ethos of assimilated German Jews, and he stresses that these attitudes stand in the way of a creative efflorescence. But he also contends that German-Jewish servility is at bottom a response to inveterate antisemitism. Ultimately it was the pressure of anti-Jewish sentiment that flattened Jews into mirror-like journalists. In effect, Goldstein both appropriates a popular antisemitic trope and rewrites its causal logic. Antisemites' nonacceptance of Jews is held to be responsible for a Jewish tendency that antisemites often cited to justify their nonacceptance.[6]

Of the readers who voiced an opinion about Goldstein's self-diagnosis, most were unenthused. Certainly the majority of the German Jews who reacted to his text did so combatively. But the tenor of their response does not necessarily mean that Goldstein's position was marginal. For quite a few of the Jewish participants in the debate about "The German-Jewish Parnassus" seem to have been more aggrieved over the essay's provocative wording and very public setting than over its substance. Others Jews, like Walter Benjamin, disputed Goldstein's grim forecast yet agreed with some of his central insights, such as the one whereby German Jewry's attachment to journalistic forms bespeaks something crucial about its cultural condition. And Goldstein and Benjamin were hardly alone with this thought. We find variations of it, in fact, in writings by an array of German-Jewish critics.[7]

Let me offer two examples. Having once alluded to the label "feuilletonist" as the mother of all German insults, the philosopher Theodor Lessing proceeded, in 1930, to treat Karl Kraus's choice of medium as the most illuminating sign of Jewish self-hatred. Lessing's reasoning begins with the idea that whenever Jews attempt to integrate into a society that despises them, they will locate in themselves causes for the hostility under which they suffer. Thus Jewish self-contempt emerges, casting over Jewish intellects a web of misanthropic emotion that prevents them from ascending to the ranks of great *Dichter und Denker*. Instead, self-loathers produce works whose significance quickly fades, as is the case with journalistic works. All that will remain of Kraus's journalistic opus is "a mountain of printed paper," Lessing conjectured.[8] It follows that there cannot be a more telling symptom of self-hatred. Otherwise put, it follows that German Jewry's torment will come to light most vividly in newspaper ink. And, indeed, Lessing stated about Kraus: "In no other form in contemporary Germany does the self-hatred of an ethical being reveal itself so clearly as in this irredeemable tragedy, because here a beautiful and pure natural talent wasted itself on utterly fruitless work [journalism]."[9]

By contrast, Gershom Scholem apostrophized Kraus as a "messianic movement of language." But, for Scholem as for Goldstein and Lessing, the journalistic activities of acculturated German Jews compellingly symbolized an existential crisis. Not long after "The German-Jewish Parnassus" had appeared, Scholem wrote a series of diary entries and essay fragments in which he too asks why there is such an abundance of Jewish journalists.

His answer is as slashing as Goldstein's. Remarking on the structural similarities between journalism and Musivstil, a quotation-oriented genre of medieval Hebrew writing, Scholem hypothesizes that when Jews became spiritually empty or "perverted," they naturally turned to, and thrived in, unoriginal journalism (*ST* 2:486).[10] This idiosyncratic and damning proposition contains a twist, which Scholem himself makes explicit. If journalistic prose connects with medieval Hebrew literature, specifically with the Musivstil, then through the unlikely vehicle of journalism modern Jewry might enact an old and deep literary Jewishness. In pondering Kraus's style Scholem maintains: "Both: Journalism and Kraus are children of the medieval Jewish culture" (486).[11] Kraus, however, is a "worthy and therefore unhappy child."[12] Moreover, it is Kraus who "discovers the most unexpected Jewish provinces in this [German] language" (486).

The first part of this chapter traces the often unexpected, frequently paradoxical, mostly dolorous ways in which German-Jewish authors framed journalistic writing as a privileged emblem of acculturated German Jewry's spiritual plight. All of the thinkers whose ideas I will consider were prominent figures; all of them lived and wrote during Kraus's lifetime; all of them are mentioned in *Die Fackel*. So while necessarily small, my survey should take meaningful steps toward evoking an immediate and underexamined context of discussion, a context that will help us to understand better a major aspect of Kraus's criticism. To be sure, Kraus's relentless coupling of Jews and journalism—"Without Heine, no feuilleton" is one of his most famous lines—has attracted interest. But, as I stressed in my introduction, scholars have tended to equate that coupling with antisemitic platitudes and to reduce it to a "symptom of Jewish self-hatred."[13] My hope is that bringing to light the complexity of utterances about Jewishness and journalism, which German Jews put forth around Kraus, will help us to look with a new openness at how and why he himself linked those themes. In addition, the analysis I undertake here will enable us to situate historically, and thus to recognize the radicality of, Kraus's critique of Jewish journalists, the topic that I take up in chapter 2.

I have a further motive for working closely with texts like Goldstein's. At issue in chapter 4 is the question of how Kraus's style came to be signified within German-Jewish circles as a profoundly Jewish phenomenon. As Lessing's and Scholem's comments about Kraus show, that moment in his reception connects *directly* with fin-de-siècle claims as to why there are "so many Jewish journalists." Tracking those claims will therefore help us to come to terms with Kraus's "Jewish significance." Finally, since the complexity of such claims has to do both with their imaginative leaps—journalism as the child of medieval Jewish culture?—and with how they interact with larger discourses, I have extended the scope of the present chapter. In its second part I turn to the anti-Jewish motifs that Goldstein accepted and unsettled in designating journalistic copying to be a mirror of German Jewry's inner disrepair, and that, for different reasons, Kraus at once dramatically reinforced and exploded.

AN "ENORMOUS TALENT FOR JOURNALISM"

Known for his liberal convictions and for being a stalwart opponent of antisemitism, Rabbi Adolf Jellinek was Viennese Jewry's "spiritual leader" during the 1870s and 1880s.[14] In the same period—a period that witnessed the number of Vienna's Jewish inhabitants increase rapidly, as well as the advent of political antisemitism in Austria—Jellinek hazarded several definitions of Jewish ethno-cultural identity.[15] One of them suggests that the "Jewish intellect" possesses female qualities. A "literary femininity" [*literarische Weiblichkeit*] runs through Jewish culture, according to Jellinek's *Jewish Ethnicity* [*Der jüdische Stamm,* 1869].[16] Like the idea that the Jews' journalistic precocity corresponds to their cognitive shortcomings, the motif of Jewish mental effeminacy occupies considerable space in turn-of-the-century anti-Jewish discourse.[17] But if antisemites could accuse Jews of lacking "male" intellectual and artistic potency, or the autonomous *Schöpfungskraft* of the male genius, perhaps the alternative gendering of the Jewish mind could be celebrated as a Jewish strength. This sort of logic appears to be at work in *Jewish Ethnicity,* which *exalts* the Jews' "literary femininity." It seems that Jellenik tried to resist antisemitism by selectively adopting and revising antisemitic tenets.[18]

Given that the stereotypes of Jewish mental effeminacy and the Jews' journalistic acumen both served to distance Jews from such qualities as cultural originality and existential authenticity, we should not be surprised to encounter these stereotypes coming together in anti-Jewish writings. Here, for instance, is a passage from *Sex and Character,* the widely discussed study of male and female "principles" by the Viennese philosopher and suicide Otto Weininger: "The congruity between Judaism and femininity becomes exact as soon as we begin to reflect on the Jew's endlessly protean nature [*unendliche Veränderungsfähigkeit*]. The Jew's enormous talent for journalism, the 'mobility' of the Jewish mind, the dearth of solid and original sensibilities—isn't all that as true of women as it is of Jews: They are nothing, and for that reason they can become anything?"[19] Several decades before Weininger cited "the Jew's enormous talent for journalism" in support of his propositions about the "congruity between Judaism and femininity," Jellinek had compiled an analogous set of Jewish traits, investing them, however, with brighter meanings. Indeed, Jellinek followed his claims about Jewish "literarische Weiblichkeit" with an argument to the effect that journalistic writing neatly matches, and thus helps us to grasp, the Jewish intellect.

"The journalist," Jellinek writes in *Jewish Ethnicity in Sayings* [*Der jüdische Stamm in Sprichwörtern,* 1881], "must be mobile, quick, enthusiastic; he must break down [*zersetzen*], combine, and summarize; he must enter *in medias res;* he must always have in front of his eyes the core of the question of the day and the key point in every debate; he must outline his objects with precise strokes; his writing must be epigrammatic, dialectical, and poignant; in short, pithy sentences he must give his topics a certain pathos; through esprit he must give them color, through piquancy, spice."[20] Jellinek describes journalistic writing as a substantial pursuit that entails artistic qualities, like poignancy and pithiness, and various acuities, such as "dialectical" analysis. Perhaps, then, he felt genuine pride upon enumerating what he perceived to be the connections between Jewish intellectuality and "the journalist."[21] Still, if Jellinek intended to deliver a thorough, unequivocal endorsement of journalism, he fell short of his goal. His text sketches journalists and, by extension, Jewish minds, as moving restlessly and fast. The first adjectives we see in his passage are "mobile"—a form of the same term that Weininger used derisively in a very similar context—and "quick."[22] And so although the prose of journalists/Jews is "precise" and "epigrammatic," it can have little sensitivity to nuances and contours. "Breaking down" and "summarizing," focused narrowly on "key" themes, this writing pushes forward by bracketing and, readers reasonably might infer, at the price of trenchant contemplation and subtlety. How else could a journalist keep step with an unending procession of new questions "of the day"? As Jellinek depicts it, the journalism that illustrates the Jews' mental disposition bears some resemblance to a mass product.

It also resembles the fatally topical "mountain of printed paper" that Lessing had Kraus build, as well as the journalistic writing that Kraus himself, the most famous Jewish journalist in turn-of-the-century Vienna, evoked as a core feature of Jewish identity. In 1913, Kraus avowed: "If I am someone who writes a lot, and someone for whom every letter is the mark of a wound, who could say that I am a journalist? It would have to be a Jewish characteristic to have no Jewish characteristics."[23] What separates Kraus from conventional journalists is the extreme particularity that language has for him. If both write "a lot," only Kraus experiences each one of language's smallest units—letters—as something sensuously singular, as the "mark of a wound." With its contrastive structure, moreover, Kraus's partial syllogism implies that most journalists cultivate the opposite relation to language, exploiting language as the abstract, fungible resource that, on the surface, it seems to be. To operate with language in this journalistic manner must be a Jewish characteristic, since Kraus, the anti-journalist, could be called a journalist *only* if it were a "Jewish characteristic to have *no* Jewish characteristics." In short, Kraus suggests that because he takes linguistic particularity seriously, he is not a journalist, and that because he is not a journalist, he cannot have any Jewish qualities.

A further aspect of Kraus's elliptical equation warrants mentioning, namely, a paradox that will bring us back to Weininger's and Jellinek's conjoining of journalism and Jewishness. Read without reference to Kraus's context, the lines—"who could say that I am a journalist? It would have to be a Jewish characteristic to have no Jewish characteristics"—come across as a hyperbolic yet ultimately stable disclaimer. When the rhetorical dust settles, Kraus's point seems to be that his modernist journalism-beyond-journalism has no Jewish characteristics. Recalling the passage I cited from *Sex and Character* complicates his message. For there not only is having no Jewish characteristics a very basic Jewish characteristic, but the Jewish characteristic of having no Jewish characteristics manifests itself precisely in the Jews' "enormous talent for journalism." According to Weininger, Jews have a distinctive property, i.e., limitless mirroring, that does not allow for self-identical expressions of their distinctiveness. Jews have an "endlessly protean nature" and are therefore destined to model themselves after—to quote and to cover in journalism—what *others* produce. Thus in *Sex and Character* Jews "can become anything," except themselves.[24]

Doesn't Jellinek's more sanguine account of the Jewish-journalistic imagination contain at least some of the same ideas? After all, how could Jewish minds insinuate themselves into the center of "every debate" if they were grounded in "sensibilities" more "solid" than unimpeded changeability? And would those minds be so much oriented toward incessant "summarizing" and "breaking down" if they could create positive representations of their own peculiarities? Would the parallel between journalists and Jews work if Jews could achieve the kind of self-representation without which, by Weininger's standards, there is no self, but rather only the "nichts" of Judaism and femininity?

Of course, not everyone accepted those standards. Certainly Jellinek, who claimed to prize the femininity of Jewish culture, subscribed to different ones. We will see, furthermore, that Kraus embraced the dependence of his own journalism on the very mimetic practices (e.g., citation), which, *Sex and Character* implies, make the Jews' prodigious journalistic exploits a sign of existential nullity. Kraus also challenged the sorts of premises about linguistic originality, cultural production, and authentic selfhood that lie behind Weininger's disdain for "protean" journalism. In an essay entitled "Self-Mirroring" ["Selbstbespiegelung," 1909], for example, Kraus argues that the self should transform itself completely after the object it represents.[25] Correlatively, he intimates that the process of mirroring is more important than the self that mirrors: "Self-mirroring is allowed when the self is beautiful; it becomes a duty when the mirror is good."[26] Jellinek did not go as far. Although no doubt the more determined critic of antisemitism, when he tried to cast a favorable light on the stereotype that Jewish intelligence is journalistic, Jellinek reformulated a series of anti-Jewish tropes. He stressed the "mobile" nature of Jewish minds without contesting an established association between the mobility of "rootless" Jews and the Jews' cognitive and ontological inadequacies. Nor did Jellinek directly confute that system of cultural values by which "the word feuilleton" could be termed "the meanest insult in the German language," and to which Lessing appealed in bemoaning Kraus's prolific journalistic output.

Despite Weininger's vitriolic excess, the links he drew between the Jews' "talent for journalism" and their hollowness stood closer to the mainstream than Jellinek's sunnier assessment of the Jews' capacity for "summarizing." For a guiding value in nineteenth-century German high culture, and especially in German-Jewish high culture, was *Bildung*. And, according to a foundational conception of it, we develop into mature persons deserving of full cultural enfranchisement through *autonomous* self-forming.[27] (The German verb *bilden* denotes "to form.") Laying out the demands of *Bildung*, Johann Herder, an architect of the ideal, enjoined his readers to acknowledge: "You are your own creator" [*Du bist dein Schöpfer selbst*].[28] In *Sex and Character* Weininger seems to extrapolate from such thinking while at the same time inverting the Enlightenment ethos of social inclusion that had helped to make *Bildung* so popular among German Jews. First he denies Jews the possibility of self-authorship. With no "solid sensibilities" after which to form themselves, they shape and reshape themselves in the image of foreign cultures, of cultures that reflect someone else's sensibilities. Jews cannot begin to undertake the lofty assignment given to Goethe's Faust: "Become what you already are." *Bildung*, or really, Herder's prerequisite for it—i.e., the ability to strive ceaselessly after a properly actualized self—lies out of reach. From there Weininger proceeds to offer a drastically worded version of this point. Jews are "nothing," he concludes.

Elsewhere in the text Weininger intones, "the real Jew will lack for all eternity . . . the oak tree, the trumpet, the Siegfried motif, self-creation [*die Schöpfung seiner selbst*], the words: I am."[29] Jellinek clearly thought otherwise. He regarded modern Jewish identity as grounded in a weighty ethno-cultural tradition. But, again, by emphasizing the Jews' journalistic, apparently noncreative faculties, Jellinek lent credence to doubts about Jewish self-authorship and thus to doubts about the authenticity of the Jewish self. Moderate antisemites could and did *approvingly* quote Jellinek's work on Jewish identity. Consider the high-profile example of Werner Sombart's study *The Jews and Economic Life* [*Die Juden und das Wirtschaftsleben*, 1911]. Here too the most "specifically Jewish property" clashes with the imperatives of *Bildung*, because having "no Jewish characteristics" [*nichts Nationaljüdisches*] is once more a Jewish characteristic. And journalistic writing, or more precisely Jellinek's portrait of it, effectively evokes this paradoxical identity. Sombart writes, "that gifted Jews so often appear to have nothing Jewish about them has been adduced, strangely enough, as evidence that there exists no specifically Jewish property [*Eigenart*], yet it actually constitutes definitive proof of such a property, insofar as this property manifests itself in an abnormal ability to assimilate [*in einer übernormalen Anpassungsfähigkeit*]."[30] Shortly thereafter Sombart cites Jellinek's list of journalistic/Jewish traits, adding to it only the verbal nod: "All typically Jewish" [*Alles Judenart*].[31]

THE LANGUAGE OF ASSIMILATION

The Jews and Economic Life responds to late Wilhelmine-era exchanges about how both Zionist emigration and the dissolution of Jewish identity would affect Germany.[32] In it Sombart argues that German "economic life" would suffer if—in one way or the other—German Jews disappeared.[33] That contention prompted further debate, thanks in part to the author's own efforts. A well-known "national economist" and would-be expert on the "Jewish Question," Sombart went on a multi-city lecture tour dedicated to discussing his monograph.[34] He thus managed to attract attention from a number of luminaries. Among them was Heinrich Mann, who published his famous and eloquent caveat about how the loss of the Jews would impoverish German culture in an anthology that Sombart's book inspired.[35]

Sombart and Mann took similar positions for very different reasons. Unlike Mann, Sombart hardly esteemed the Jews' cultural contribution. Modifying Max Weber's thesis about Protestantism and the capitalist mind-set, Sombart limns "the Jews" as being the true spirit of capitalism, as being self-serving practicality embodied: "The questions that interest him [the Jew] most are: Why? To what end? What will it get me?"[36] On the other hand, Jews have no artistic vision. "The Jew sees sharply but not deeply," Sombart observes.[37] The common source of these features is the "specifically Jewish property" of "abnormal" assimilatory "gifts." Since what drives modern capitalist economies is ceaseless practical adaptation, or the activity at which Jews naturally excel, Jews are a dynamic force in the *Wirtschaftsleben*. But, again, though a crucial economic asset, the Jews' prosaic mentality and orientation toward adapting have a major drawback. They prevent the Jews from being seminal producers of culture: "Closely related to that quality [Jewish adaptability] is a certain lack of creative power." So, for Sombart, the Jews' tremendous "Anpassungsfähigkeit" has a Janus-faced result, namely, commercial prowess and cultural superficiality. In support of his point, he repeatedly links Jews and journalism.[38] This is the context in which Sombart cites Jellinek's passage on "the journalist." Sombart quotes Jellinek's ideas about the connection between the Jewish intellect and journalistic writing to make tangible both the paradox of the Jews' distinctive indistinctness and the cultural effects of that paradox.

Now it is one thing to assert that the Jews' "talent for journalism" betrays their deep-seated assimilatory characteristics. It is quite another to propose that the chief *consequences* of Jewish assimilation reveal themselves in a special affinity for ephemeral journalistic mirroring. The first claim can easily flow into the second, to be sure. Indeed, that happens in *The Jews and Economic Life*. There the Jews' outsized assimilatory capacities, which are *repeatedly* portrayed in terms of a journalist's attributes, lead Jews, as they integrate into host societies, to pursuits that cohere with those capacities, like journalism. Sombart's book thus suggests that the Jews' journalistic calling provides insights into *both* the Jews' permanent cognitive apparatus and their immediate historical situation. But it is also possible to develop the latter idea without laying down general principles about the Jews' "Veränderlichkeit" and "Anpassungfähigkeit." Lessing, for example, treated Kraus's attachment to journalistic prose as a singularly apt emblem of Jewish assimilation gone horribly wrong. Yet he wrote nothing about how Kraus's journalism corresponds to unchanging components of the Jewish intellect.

JOURNALISM AND "THE GERMAN-JEWISH PARNASSUS"

One of the most poignant examples of this sort of thinking entered the German public sphere while the debate about Sombart's book was in full swing. I am referring to Goldstein's article "The German-Jewish Parnassus." Having been rejected by various liberal organs, it appeared in the conservative cultural review *Der Kunstwart* and, as I mentioned above, quickly generated a hot exchange of its own.[39] As Scholem later commented, Goldstein violated an unwritten prohibition against speaking in "mixed company" of the large Jewish influence in German letters.[40] Such remarks were threatening because they could easily be seen as arrogant. They could also be used and, in fact, were used to lend weight to antisemitic stereotypes about the "victory of Jewishness" over German culture.

But it was hardly the issue of Jewish self-aggrandizement alone that made "The German-Jewish Parnassus" so incendiary. Goldstein put forth a whole series of provocative points, phrasing them as though he wanted to elicit critical rejoinders. He insisted that Germans would never regard German Jews as Germans; that the way in which assimilated German Jews answered this rejection left them culturally debilitated, or unlikely to create many works of genius in the German language; that of antisemites and assimilated Jews, assimilated Jews are the "worse enemy"; that by willfully blinding themselves, these Jews had allowed their predicament to harden into intractability; and that German Jews are Germans, in the end, and should not immediately try to found a culture of their own outside Germany.[41] Judging from the response it yielded, Goldstein's essay pressed on deep-seated anxieties and sensitivities among his German-Jewish readers. For that reason, and because the views Goldstein lays out bear directly on our main themes, I will discuss the text at some length.

With its admonitory, bitter tone, "The German-Jewish Parnassus" probably will not strike today's readers as unduly, or even remotely, boastful. Yet in setting up the gravamen of his case Goldstein starkly emphasizes German Jewry's cultural importance. For example, he avers that Hugo von Hofmannsthal "invented a new poetic style to replace Schiller's exhausted classicism" ("DJP," 286). Instead of gratitude, Goldstein complains, Germans show Jews wariness. Germans do not embrace Hofmannsthal as they would a "more German" author. A certain heartiness is missing from the applause (286). Worse still, Germans distort the aesthetic accomplishments of German Jews, marginalizing their efforts as somehow alien and un-German. To underpin this charge, Goldstein cites Richard Wagner's notorious lines about how Jews inevitably speak the language of the country they inhabit as a foreign language (284). He then documents the purchase Wagner's ideas have in the German imagination. And he locates in that purchase grounds for despair. Given all that German Jews have done, and that, as their productivity increases, the misrepresentations of their value only intensify, how could anyone hope for the kind of acknowledgment Jews would need to live with dignity as *German* Jews? By pretending that having a Jewish background does not matter in enlightened German society, assimilated Jews forego their self-respect. Indeed, they debase themselves. Hence the accusation that assimilated Jews are "our worst enemy." Hence too Goldstein's desire to give his fellow German Jews a wake-up call. It reads: "We Jews administer the intellectual property of a people who deny both our right and our ability to do that" (283).

But the phrase "administer the intellectual property" also heralds a shift in Goldstein's argument, as do a number of terms in the part of the text I just adumbrated. One of the chief premises there is that Jews, e.g., Hofmannsthal, have infused German culture with new life. That Germans *still* "detect in us something 'Asiatic'" ("DJP," 287) and generally find the best efforts of German Jews threatening volubly bespeaks the futility of the Jews' longing for acceptance. However, if German Jews have revitalized German culture, why state that they merely "*administer* the intellectual property" of the German "people"? And why might Goldstein start his sketch of the Jewish role in German culture with that same administrative function? He writes at the beginning of his text: "No one doubts the Jews' power in the press. At least in major cities and their newspapers, criticism is about to become a Jewish monopoly" (283). Finally, why announce, a few pages later, that the "voice of the feuilleton Jew does resonate with the German people" (286–87)?

The reason is that, notwithstanding his strident rhetoric, Goldstein's position turns out to be highly ambivalent, and the substance of his essay is ultimately more searching than it is polemical.[42] His essay evokes Hannah Arendt's famous remark about the "reckless magnanimity" with which Jews let host cultures take credit for their works. But it also anticipates Kafka's equally famous, largely countervailing claim about how the German of acculturated German Jews is the "tortured appropriation of foreign property."[43]

Often Goldstein focuses on what he believes to be the crippling consequences of German Jewry's delusion. Heine's status as "the only Jewish poet of significance throughout Europe" is, for him, a notable "symptom"("DJP," 289) of assimilated German Jewry's insalubrious "half-ness" [*Halbheit*] and "hermaphroditic nature" [*Zwitterwesen*] (290). At the same time, however, Goldstein remonstrates in a very different direction, faulting Germans for their unwillingness to give credit to *great* German-Jewish artists. Here, and elsewhere in his text too, he subverts the dichotomy of robust German art versus effete Jewish administrating and imitating, or a dichotomy on which he also heavily relies.

For example, Goldstein attaches to Christoph Wieland just the sort of deprecatory language that was frequently used to belittle Heine. He writes that Wieland, an esteemed contemporary of Goethe, could be "slippery in his works," and that Wieland "was merely a poet-imitator" [*Nachdichter*]. According to "The German-Jewish Parnassus," moreover, Wieland "was for the most part clever and formally adept [*formgewandt*], and without trace of authentic originality [*ohne eine Spur von echter Originalität*]" ("DJP," 289). Shortly thereafter Goldstein proposes that Jews helped to engender modern German cultural life. More specifically, he asserts, "*To no small degree German culture is Jewish culture*" (291). Heine's poetic rank might be an aberration, and Jews might generally act as mere cultural administrators, but Hofmannsthal is not an isolated occurrence. As Goldstein puts it, "For all the denying of Jewish genius . . . there is still a list of Jewish names that have become an irrevocable part of Germany's and Europe's development" (291). Despite their creative difficulties, Jews—a whole "list" of them—belong among the seminal figures in German and European culture.

But elsewhere in the essay those creative difficulties appear to be more formidable. Indeed, at its center Goldstein maintains: "Perhaps those who deny us true creativity are right; perhaps we lack great works—not because we lack great men, but because we lack the conditions under which the genius personality and the productive character are possible. . . . Why are there so many Jewish journalists? A journalist is a mirror that catches the images of the day and throws them back. That is its nature. Is it Jewish to be only a mirror and not to create? You assert that; many believe it. But I say: No! Rather, whoever was nothing but a mirror, smooth and polished, whoever knew how to concede and accept, he advanced in our half-Jewish situation" ("DJP," 288). The German Jews' vaunted "power in the press" looks almost like an entry in Goldstein's account of their stellar cultural feats. Yet ultimately journalistic mirroring, catching ephemeral images and throwing them back, symbolizes German Jewry's spiritual crisis. For the journalistic facility of German Jews reveals that they have had to press themselves into mirrors, into "polished," two-dimensional beings, in order to get ahead in a hostile environment. Again, "whoever was nothing but a mirror, smooth and polished, whoever knew how to concede and accept, he advanced in our half-Jewish situation."

Though less apodictically than Weininger, Goldstein too contends that along with a talent for journalism go existential and creative deficiencies. Mirror-like German Jews lack "great works," "the genius personality," and "the productive character." So while German Jews flock to cultural pursuits in wildly disproportionate numbers—soon they will have a "monopoly" on criticism—they cannot use culture as a vehicle for social and spiritual improvement. Ironically, their manic attempt to achieve acceptance through *Bildung*, through administering and copying German high culture, involves a mental foreshortening that precludes real *Bildung*. As in *Sex and Character*, in "The German-Jewish Parnassus" Jews do not have the existential fullness necessary for what counts as substantive self-cultivation. German Jews are not "nothing" in Goldstein's text, of course. But without the urgent desideratum of "the productive character," neither are they whole. Compromised by an abject variant of assimilation, Jews can only "catch images" and "throw them back." They have the potential to change: "Is it Jewish to be only a mirror and not to create? No!" Still, in their present condition German Jews cannot effectively form—and transform—themselves through art and cultural learning.

Goldstein goes on to advance a theory of art by whose standards German Jews have been faltering badly. Rejecting as outdated, or as "grandfatherly," the liberal ideal of cultural cosmopolitanism, he stresses instead that all major aesthetic accomplishments are grounded in a national consciousness: "The national [*das Nationale*] is not the end and the goal, to be sure, but the root of every great achievement; and from Homer and the Bible to Tolstoy and Ibsen the greats were, above all, great in their people [*Volk*] and for their people" ("DJP," 290). Since, as an assimilated Jew, Hofmannsthal, did not have "the national," it follows that even his creative power was somehow limited. It also follows that if German Jews are to thrive artistically, they must have their own cultural base. And, indeed, Goldstein writes: "For a people [*Volk*] as for art, the condition of real development is having one's own territory, and thus we apply the modern ideas of national individualism to the Jews: for the people—Zionism, for art, the revitalization of Hebrew language and poetry" (290).

Yet Goldstein cannot bring himself to advocate unequivocally either political Zionism or the sort of cultural Zionism at which his essay gestures. For the "leap into modern Hebrew literature," which would land Jews in a realm of "infinite creative possibilities," is simply too far. Its untenability rivals that of Jewish resettlement. "We German Jews, we who are *living today,* we Jews have just as little chance of becoming modern Hebrew poets as we do of emigrating to Zion" ("DJP," 291). But the trouble with political and cultural Zionism extends well beyond logistics. The key problem is that because *"German culture is to a large degree Jewish culture,"* Jewish culture must to a significant degree be German culture. Thus Goldstein asks: "Were we able, finally, to turn our backs on the German people—with newly awakened masculine pride [*Mannesstolze*]—could we ever cease to be German" (292)? He has already answered his question, with the statement: "However much we might want to separate culturally the Jewish-German from the not-Jewish-German, in order to break free from the compromise, from the half-ness, from the indignities to our humanity and manliness, it seems impossible, at least for the foreseeable future" (291). A Jewish pulling away from German culture would only result in another form of existential "half-ness" and, presumably, in the diminished creative potential that attends it. Under such circumstances how could Jews do what Goldstein demands of them: produce their own culture?

Even amidst this perplexing double bind, the necessity of a certain course of action is beyond doubt. Jews must not persist in "pining" after a love interest that spurns them. In a sentence that casts as effeminate the two objects of his disdain, i.e., Germans who refuse to accept Jews and German Jews who refuse to accept that rejection, Goldstein exhorts the latter to be "manly enough" to "rip the [female] loved one" [*die Geliebete*] from their "heart." Once again, however, there is a catch. This move will yield more splitting. Acknowledging that his injunction will be hard to carry out, Goldstein grimly suggests that "a piece of [*Jewish*] heart" might "remain hanging" ("DJP," 292) on Germany.

But what can German Jews do, in the here and now, to make themselves whole? As he concludes his piece, Goldstein admits that he has no real "solution." Yet he does purport to have thought out some "palliatives." Through them Goldstein outlines an alternative German-Jewish symbiosis, a symbiosis that differs profoundly from the one he believes to be an inimical German-Jewish fantasy. He describes how Jews could contribute to German and European culture "as Jews." Accordingly, Goldstein both calls for Jewish national self-consciousness and warns against an "exaggeration of the national principle." Only by tapping into the richness of "the national" will Jewish artists truly effloresce; and only if most Germans and some Jews stop "treating Germans and Jews as opposites" ("DJP," 293) will cultural cooperation be possible. Meeting the one goal might even help to bring about the other, Goldstein surmises. For once Jews have become less subaltern and "hermaphroditic," they will no doubt be more attractive to the European *Völker* among whom they live. "If Jews have come so far as to want to be nothing other than Jews, perhaps Europe will reach that place where it takes us to be nothing other than Jews. Then it will realize that it needs us—as Jews" (293).

Paradoxically, by renouncing their current project of assimilation and erecting a Jewish national consciousness, German Jews might integrate into their cultural environment successfully, or to everyone's benefit. The Jews will profit because with their new access to "the root" of all great art, i.e., "the national," they will be more productive. And European culture at its best represents just the merging or integration of unique, individual national cultures: "Almost all cultural phenomena in Europe have long been international." Thus Europe "*needs* us—as Jews." Goldstein adds, "in the end we all build on the same work, and we all can find ourselves in this work, even if we all add to it in our own way, precisely because we all add to it in our own way."

The main "palliatives" that will help Jews toward a salutary self-awareness, and thus toward a real German-Jewish symbiosis, are as follows: first, Goldstein underlines the need for a special kind of journal or "organ." What he has in mind is a journal that "unifies all creative Jews [*schaffenden Juden*] as Jews, an organ that does not serve religious and political aims, or those of individual parties, and that does not put a good Jewish sentiment before a good accomplishment, but rather is nothing other than a gathering place [*Sammelstätte*] for the best that Jews in Germany achieve" ("DJP," 292). In the absence of an actual homeland, the "Jewish earth" that is so desirable and so distant, Jews can claim for themselves a virtual, intellectual space, a "gathering" space for Jews from all over Germany. By showcasing their abilities "as Jews," "creative Jews" will help build up the wilted pride of assimilated German Jewry. The sight of redoubtable writing by self-identifying Jews will strengthen the "masculine pride" of Jews who feel ashamed of their Jewish heritage, of the Jews who hide behind "names that sound German," trapping themselves in a debilitating "half-ness." It is therefore of primary importance that the Jews who contribute to the journal shine. "A good accomplishment" should be regarded more highly than "a good Jewish sentiment."

Generally speaking, Goldstein's plan resembles W. E. B. DuBois's famous and roughly contemporaneous notion of a "talented tenth." DuBois hoped that the example of an extraordinarily gifted group within the black population, i.e., the "talented tenth," would, among other things, raise black self-esteem, which centuries of racism had damaged. Similarly, Goldstein speculates that upon seeing "the best Jews in Germany" excel "as Jews," uncreative assimilated Jews might feel better about taking the crucial step of "identifying themselves as Jews" [*sich als Juden bekennen*] ("DJP," 292). Such self-identification would bring Jews closer to "the national," to the ethnic self-awareness that in his view allows for cultural and imaginative productivity and thus for substantive inner development.

But as he proceeds through his list of "palliatives," Goldstein once again shifts the trajectory of his argument. It turns out that Jewish authors need to do more than simply be creative "as Jews." Goldstein asks of them that they provide Jews with model Jewish characters. The "Jewish" content of their work does matter. Quite literally, Goldstein imagines Jewish writers as the authors of a "new" Jewry. "For although much has come about, the Jewish drama, the Jewish novel remains unwritten. At stake, above all, is the creation of a new type of Jew, new not in life but rather in literature. And it is well known that we all see life—people, landscapes—as our artists envision them for us [*wie unsere Künstler sie uns vorsehen*]" ("DJP," 293).

This ending—only several short paragraphs of signing-off follow the passage I just cited—comes as a twist for another reason too: Goldstein's self-authorship idea clashes with much of his rhetoric. Where he enjoins Jews to participate in European culture in their "own way," Goldstein implies that there already exists a specifically Jewish mode of intellectuality and that it can flourish even outside of the Hebrew language. He reinforces this implication with the claim: "Jewish art is not at all identical to the treatment of Jewish themes [*jüdischem Stoff*]" ("DJP," 293). To be sure, throughout his essay Goldstein makes it clear that he wants Jews to be "modern, educated [*gebildet*], 'European'" (292). His goal is a true European-Jewish symbiosis, not a flight into Jewish tradition. But a real *symbiosis*, a proper merging of German and *Jewish* culture, would entail the mobilization of Jewish particularities. Indeed, in discussing the "nationality principle" Goldstein maintains that "the Jewish element [*das Jüdische*] is the best thing about a Jew" (290).

Goldstein omits to specify, however, what "the Jewish element" might be. At the conclusion of "The German-Jewish Parnassus" we learn why. There "the Jewish element" does not have to do with an indefinable and enduring "Jewish spirit," or with religious practice. Such ideas play no role in Goldstein's text. Rather, "das Jüdische" remains to be created along with its carrier, "the new type of Jew." Despite all his talk about the exigency of an organic rootedness in "Jewish soil," and of a solid cultural grounding in "the national," Goldstein ends on a note that in one respect coheres, albeit loosely, with something very different. Part of his conclusion coheres with poststructuralist thinking about the ungrounded, citational character of identity formation.[44] After all, he wants Jewish identity to be *enacted* in accordance with a literary model, with a fiction. And since "the new type of Jew" does not return to an ur-Jewishness but rather represents something new, it seems fair to say that Goldstein envisages those writers who will author the new Jew as the authors also of the "best thing" about their model Jewish figure, namely, "the Jewish element."[45] But while Goldstein's final gesture entails what might be called a slippage, it also serves to bolster his chief theme: the need for Jews to be elementally creative, or much more than journalistic mirrors. That need never seems greater, in fact, than when Goldstein points to a kind of radical *Bildung,* or self-formation through self-authoring, as the answer to German Jewry's identity crisis.

THE FEUILLETON AS A COGNITIVE LIMIT

The texts I have been discussing have noteworthy qualities in common. They all intervene into very *public* debates about Jewish identity, for example. Unsurprisingly, then, each author develops his claims with a certain argumentative brio and dramatic force. And no doubt rhetorical exigencies played a role in determining how they formulated their respective positions. Where Goldstein levels *all* journalists into mirrors, for instance, he is engaging in a kind of strategic simplification. He accentuates the saturnine content of his message by putting it so starkly. Would the suggestion that *some* journalists, and *some* German-Jewish journalists, *might* be regarded as mirrors have as much oratorical power, or the feel of a desperate spiritual warning?

This question raises another one. What if Goldstein did not believe that journalists in general, and German-Jewish journalists in particular, merely and uniformly reflected "images of the day"? At the very least his terminology would remain instructive. For however disingenuous it might have been, Goldstein's sketch of Jewish journalists, coming as it does at a crucial moment in a key text, helps demonstrate the cultural importance of the trope. Still, in order to track the full significance of the stereotype that Goldstein used, we need to pursue it into more intimate discursive settings. So let us consider Theodor Gomperz's posthumously published, seemingly candid essay "On the Limits of the Jewish Intellectual Gift" ["Über die Grenzen der jüdischen intellektuellen Begabung," 1904], which makes an analogous case in a different tone.[46]

Gomperz belonged to a prosperous German-Jewish family whose social circle included both Mendelssohns and Rothschilds. During his long and fruitful life, which began in 1832 and ended in the very year in which Goldstein's article appeared (1912), Gomperz won renown as both a classicist and as a liberal member of the imperial parliament. As might be expected of a friend and admirer of John Stuart Mill, Gomperz was a religious skeptic. Yet he regularly went to hear none other than Adolf Jellinek preach in Vienna's Seitengasse temple. In addition, in 1878 Gomperz stated a desire to spend his last years studying Hebrew and the Talmud. And he once wished that his sons would "with God's help, and despite whatever views they might have about religion, ritual, etc., go to temple wherever it be . . . on the anniversary of my death to say Kaddish, although this seems to go against the grain of the Enlightenment."[47] But his stance shifted with the rise of political antisemitism. Gomperz's will of 1887 urges his children to convert to Christianity. Moreover, he eventually campaigned for the abandonment of Judaism and against Zionism, though without ever disavowing his stake in his Jewish heritage. Late in his life, Gomperz emphasized the fact that the first Jewish graduate of a German *Hochschule* was a Gomperz. He was buried, in full ritual, in the Jewish section of Vienna's Central Cemetery.

Thus Gomperz too experienced a kind of "German-Jewish Parnassus." Like Goldstein, furthermore, he drew tight boundaries around the creativity of German Jews. In "On the Limits of the Jewish Intellectual Gift," Gomperz writes: "One encounters the question: Why is it that despite the Jews' no doubt marked gift for producing artistic and, above all, scientific accomplishments, we find very few Jewish names next to accomplishments of the very first order" ("JIB," 384). Taking up a familiar theme, he adds: "Clearly, in the arts that involve reproduction [*reproducierenden Künste*], acting and musical virtuosity, the Jewish gift displays no relative inferiority" (386). Gomperz then lists successful Jewish artists who are not actually artists. More precisely, he opines that these Jews are "feuilletonists" rather than true *Dichter und Denker:* "[Ludwig] Fulda und [Oskar] Blumenthal are thoroughly intelligent playwrights, however, one is not really wrong in designating them to be highly gifted dramatic feuilletonists" (386).

Gomperz applies to Fulda and Blumenthal the "meanest insult in the German language" in a way that is consistent with the term's function as an insult. For he uses the appellation to challenge Fulda's and Blumenthal's status as "real artists." Yet the word "insult" does not accurately describe the semantic value of "feuilletonist" in Gomperz's assessment of his fellow German Jews. There is a measured quality, even a politeness, to his prose. Whomever he might have intended to address, Gomperz did not plan to move his audience with professions of dismay. And by stating that "one is not *really* wrong about" Fulda and Blumenthal in labeling them "dramatic feuilletonists" ["man hat nicht ganz unrecht, wenn sie dramatische Feuilletonisten nennt"], Gomperz leaves open the possibility that one might be a little wrong, that maybe they do have artistic qualities, after all. Indeed, twice in a single sentence he notes how very "gifted" [*begabt*] the two playwrights are.

Perhaps Gomperz's judgment about their art is worth sharing. If Fulda and Blumenthal managed only to deal deftly in their works with contemporary themes, then the rubric Gomperz attaches to them would make sense. They would be "dramatic feuilletonists." That Fulda's and Blumenthal's writings receive little notice today could be adduced in support of this idea. But the important point here is not whether Gomperz evaluates his examples fairly. What warrants emphasizing is that he presents second-tier German-Jewish writers, a couple of "dramatic feuilletonists," as *the* limit cases of Jewish intelligence. For doing so suggests that Jewish writers cannot hope to transcend journalism. And the Jews' imaginative ceiling clearly represents a source of frustration for Gomperz. At the end of his text, in fact, he counterposes to Jews' journalistic talents a romanticized ideal of primordial creativity: "Although the Jews evince a high degree of critical understanding, incisive judgment, and brilliant wit, they appear to lack the opposite of these gifts: the unconscious, originary, dream-like, oracular" ("JIB," 389). Like Weininger and Goldstein, Gomperz defines the Jews' cognitive condition not only as the "opposite" of a more profound state but also in terms of an essential absence. Each author has the Jews "lack" what Weininger sees as "self-creation" and Goldstein calls "the genius personality."[48] In each case Jews lack the "Siegfried motif" and "dream-like," "oracular" productivity; they lack the means through which to generate their own myths.

However, in contrast to Weininger and Goldstein, Gomperz passes quickly over the problem at which his rhetoric gestures: that, cut off by their "limits" from the deepest mental activity, contemporary Jews lack spiritual depth and wholeness as well. While Weininger and Goldstein regard the Jews' "enormous" aptitude for journalism as a symptom of modern existential hollowness, Gomperz's utterances about "dramatic feuilletonists" and their "Jewish intellectual gift" are largely free-standing. He does not tie his remarks to condemnations and exhortations, to a vague yet ardent cultural politics, as those other thinkers do. Despite their decorous tone, Gomperz's claims come across as the personal reckoning of a German Jew who worried about the future value of his own intellectual labors. More than Goldstein's admonishing statements, Gomperz's observations resemble the *self-doubting* theories of Jewish creativity that Ludwig Wittgenstein expresses in his notebooks, and to which Ray Monk, Wittgenstein's biographer, applies the modifier "confessional."[49] "Amongst Jews," Wittgenstein asseverates, "'genius' is found only in the holy man. Even the greatest of Jewish thinkers is no more than talented. (Myself, for instance.) I think there is some truth to the idea that I really only think reproductively. I don't believe I have ever *invented* a single line of thinking. I have always taken one over from someone else.... What I invent are new similes."[50]

Troubled by Wittgenstein's ruminations on "Jewishness," Monk tries to locate behind some of them a logic other than anti-Jewish prejudice. Monk asks whether with the lines I just cited Wittgenstein might have been trying to safeguard himself against the perils of intellectual hubris. Because of how Wittgenstein stresses his distance from "genius," this speculation seems plausible. But Wittgenstein complicates matters by noting that he can "invent new similes." If simile and metaphor are the living, dynamic elements of language—and they certainly are that in Wittgenstein's philosophy—then invoking some responsibility for their creative evolution does not represent an avowal of modesty. What interests me, however, is not so much the psychological use to which Wittgenstein puts stereotypes about Jewish intelligence as his specific idiom. In appropriating the trope of Jewish "reproductiveness," and in associating Jewish assimilation with an estrangement from the highest mental activity ("amongst the Jews, 'genius' is found only in the *holy man*"), Wittgenstein repeats the very terms and themes we have been tracking. His use of them in introspections implies that they actually took root among eminently "gifted" German Jews. And the wealth of additional evidence only deepens this impression. There are suggestively self-doubting passages in Arthur Schnitzler's diaries, for instance.[51]

Thus we arrive at the issue of how ideas about the Jews' "reproductive" intelligence and journalistic facility might have become entrenched in powerfully critical minds. So I will now turn to the discursive force that drove such precepts into the German and Austrian public spheres: antisemitic ideology.[52]

MIRRORING MODERNITY

What does it mean to be a "mirror of modernity"? In 1975, the historian Gerson Cohen coined that phrase to make vivid the special dynamism he attributed to German-Jewish culture. "It was German Jewry," Cohen wrote, "that provided Jews everywhere with mature alternative models of Jewish response to modernity, from radical assimilation to militant Zionism and neo-orthodoxy, as well as a fresh rediscovery of the Jewish past and a reformulation of Jewish identity and commitment."[53] If *the* seminal "models of Jewish response to modernity" originated among German Jews, the experience of modernity must be compellingly reflected in German-Jewish cultural and political strivings. Hence Cohen's mirror figure. For Cohen, then, German Jewry's mirroring of modernity has to do with German Jewry's great innovations. German Jews "provided Jews everywhere with mature models of response" with which to negotiate a basic challenge of modern life: eroding traditional structures of identity. While Cohen might not have endorsed all the "models" he names, e.g., "radical assimilation" or "militant Zionism," his list eventually becomes resoundingly affirmative. Indeed, in an essay that emphasizes the value of studying Jewish history, he credits German Jews with "a fresh rediscovery of the Jewish past."

But there are darker variations on Cohen's theme. Witness, for instance, Max Horkheimer and Theodor Adorno's "philosophical" reading of antisemitism. It argues that Jews retained an archaic, "undisciplined mimesis,"[54] or something of the mimetic defense mechanisms found in nature. Transmitted through a "process of imitating," this mimesis was "inherited" by "generations" of Jews, from the "Jewish vagabond" [*Trödeljuden*] to the "banker." As a result, Jews were the group that most conspicuously "mirrored"—*zurückspiegeln* is the word Horkheimer and Adorno employ—the horrors of modern capitalism, of the "new system of production." Jews thereby elicited the rage of all those who needed to "repress their own suffering" under that system "in order to survive."[55]

As they try to explain how Jews became victims of a disastrous related problem, the "dialectic of Enlightenment," Horkheimer and Adorno also offer less idiosyncratic arguments. One of them is that antisemites associated

Jews with daunting, exploitative features of Western modernity, such as the capitalist "sphere of circulation."[56] I call this position less "idiosyncratic" because the idea that Jews often operate, in anti-Jewish ideology, as ciphers of modernity, and as "scapegoats" for modernity's ills, looms large in theories of German antisemitism.[57] Thinkers as different as Saul Friedländer and Jean-François Lyotard have speculated about how nineteenth- and early twentieth-century German antisemites projected onto Jews new sources of anxiety and discontent.[58] This topic is vast, and I cannot address it comprehensively, of course. But even a brief account of how the stereotypes about Jews and journalism at issue here emerged out of a perverse "response to modernity" should help us to understand their function and their power in fin-de-siècle Germany and Austria. For German and Austrian antisemites not only disparaged journalism as an emblematically Jewish, "reproductive" mode of writing, they also vilified "Jewish journalism" as a privileged and destructive mirror of modern culture.[59]

Consider the influential "case of Wagner." Richard Wagner became a prominent commentator on German and Jewish identity soon after the Revolution of 1848 had ended in political failure and, for him personally, Parisian exile. It was as an émigré, in fact, that Wagner published perhaps the most famous of the texts that I will examine below: "Jewishness in Music" ["Das Judentum in der Musik," 1850]. But before I get to Wagner's essays on Germanness and Jewishness, I want to outline Wagner's path to them. That is, I want to discuss the attitude he took into the post-Revolution era.

What seems to have excited Wagner in 1848 was the hope that revolution would have a cleansing, uplifting effect—that revolution would lead to nothing less than the spiritual emancipation of humanity. Indeed, Wagner's belief in progress and his anticapitalist leanings brought him close to the Young Hegelianism of some of his intimate friends and conversation partners, e.g., August Röckel.[60] But Wagner also tried to interpret the revolutionary moment as laden with religious significance. He agitated in a theological, or at least in a theosophical, key. For example, Wagner wrote: "I am Revolution. I am the ever-fashioning Life. I am the only God. . . . The millions, the embodied Revolution, the God become Man . . . proclaim to all the world the new Gospel of Happiness."[61] Rather than campaigning for constitutional reform or a unified German state, as did many of his fellow insurrectionists, Wagner openly dreamed of achieving spiritual redemption through political revolt.

Defeat left him as bitter as ever about the capitalist avarice and logic of exchange that he thought were compromising European culture. "And in the manner of a hideous nightmare, the demonic idea of Money will vanish from us with its loathsome retinue of open and secret usury, paper juggling, percentage and speculation," Wagner had effusively and erroneously prophesied in June of 1848.[62] Yet both during and after his exile he continued to envision redemptive scenarios. Only now redemption would be gained through *cultural* renewal, through an "artwork of the future." Tellingly, Wagner wrote the essays that introduce that theme, "Art and Revolution" and "The Artwork of the Future," in 1849 and 1850, respectively. Like the artworks of the distant Greek past, the artwork of the future will proceed from—and help to galvanize—a *national* community. More precisely, redemption through cultural renewal will take place as a German phenomenon. For Germans stand nearest to the ancient Greeks; and they are therefore most likely to overcome a "new culture" that unscrupulously reproduces original artistic and intellectual accomplishments for the sake of profit.[63] In this "new culture," art, which Wagner described as the "juice of life" [*Lebenssaft*], is commodified and concomitantly reified, as is the labor that creates it. By contrast, Germanness has at its core autonomous productivity. Germanness has to do with pursuing activities as ends in themselves and embracing the particular, nonexchangeable, sensuous value, "the joy," of those activities. "Being German means doing a thing for its own sake and for the joy of doing it; whereas utilitarianism, i.e., the principle whereby a thing is done because of an external personal objective, is un-German," Wagner asserted in 1865 (*WGS* 178). So during the post-1848 period he began to define "being German" as a mode of cultural production and in opposition to an emergent mass culture, to a culture that he eventually subsumed under the heading "Modern."

The same years witnessed further shifts in Wagner's writings. Among the most dramatic of them is, as numerous scholars have pointed out, an intensification of his antisemitic discourse.[64] Whatever else might have prompted this change, his more vicious way of talking about Jewishness corresponds to his new understanding of "being German." For Wagner, Jews had been the agents of a soulless capitalism before 1848. They remained that, while becoming the bearers of the modern cultural tendencies that clashed so saliently with, and represented the greatest threat to, Germanness. Jews became the embodiment of the modern cultural tendencies against the foil of which he formulated German identity.

According to Wagner, however, the new forces that attenuate art—and suck dry the "juice of life"—are not the doing of the Jews alone. In "'Modern'" ["'Modern,'" 1878] he writes: "In order to examine my topic more closely, I must refer to the difficult fate with which our language long met, and also to how the genius instincts of our great poets and sages had only just succeeded in giving it back its unique productivity, when, in concert with the literary and linguistic processes that I have been following here, frivolous epigones, who sensed their own unproductive inclinations, decided to jettison the gravity of their predecessors and to announce themselves as 'moderns'" (*WGS,* 179). The "epigones" whose frivolity imperils German culture are themselves German. They are the writers of "Young Germany," Wagner reveals, alluding to a movement that enjoyed prominence during the 1830s and, among other things, turned away from the recondite, occasionally morbid aestheticism of the German romantics and toward accessible, life-affirming art. Wagner contends that these authors began their careers promisingly but ended up dealing in a treacherous literary un-Germanness. Yet the key propagators of epigonic, "modern" culture belong to a different "folk": the Jews. Wagner's mildly paradoxical suggestion is that the Jews' lack of responsibility for inventing the "modern" both reflects how thick their alliance with that culture is and points to their responsibility for its spread. After all, modern culture is antithetical to a "unique" German "productivity" in Wagner's texts. Thus when he has the Jews *not* create the "'modern,'" when he maintains that "they found it as a growth on the field of German literature," Wagner evokes the Jews' affinity with the derivative "new culture." He also evokes the heady opportunism that helps explain the Jews' success in promoting the "modern" (179).

This explanation did not develop all at once. "Jewishness in Music" laments the general "Jewification of modern art." But, as the title of the text intimates, Wagner argues here that Jews have thrived primarily "in music." Offering another paradox—one that clearly foreshadows the idea that having no Jewish characteristics is a Jewish characteristic—Wagner makes the following claim: the Jewish composer Giacomo Meyerbeer has sheer un-Germanness to thank for his resemblance to German culture. Meyerbeer's music relies on mimetic abilities that emerged along with the Jews' alienation from artistic "feeling." These mimetic abilities therefore differ from the exalted mimesis of true art, which Wagner defined conventionally, or as "the mirror of nature." Jews copy the sound of German music with "deceptive accuracy." They do so, however, in the same way "parrots reproduce human words," and with just as little understanding (*WGS,* 17). A long history of rootless, diasporic living has taken from the Jews the sort of deep, productive ferment that, according to Wagner, can be had only through remaining grounded in a communal ur-language (16–18). Practiced at assimilating and unburdened with primordial profundity, Jews simply and unthinkingly "throw back" the sounds they pick up. The Jews' un-German cognitive-emotional superficiality—their artistic emptiness—enables them to echo German music with misleading precision. Jewish musicians like Meyerbeer have become popular not in spite their of distance from originality and genius, but rather because of it.

Such a dynamic operates only in the realm of music. "In more bountiful fullness than any other art form, music offers the possibility to speak without really saying anything. Once something has been said, it can be easily aped," Wagner writes (*WGS*, 17). Still, elsewhere too Jews copy. As emissaries of an unproductive, un-German modern culture, all they can do is mime and mine what others have engendered: "In this language, in this art, the Jew can only imitate and copy [*nachsprechen, nachkünsteln*]. He can create neither a poem nor a work of art" (13). Yet notwithstanding the Jews' animal-like mimetic talent, their cultural otherness is often painfully apparent. Wagner repeatedly cites the example of "Jewish speech." He states: "Particularly repellent to us are purely sensuous expressions of the Jewish language" (13). Touching on how Jewish culture might experience a renewal of its own in Hebrew, the Jews' ur-language, Wagner notes that even when Jews have a European language as their mother tongue, it remains "foreign" to them (12). Accordingly, the German spoken by German Jews, their "blabber," seems strange to Germans (19). And so does "Jewish music," at some points in the text. Not only are Jewish artists "least convincing" in the medium of "song" [*Gesang*], the Jews' difference often palpably manifests itself in their musical compositions (15). Here, then, Wagner writes against the grain of his own claims about "deceptively accurate" Jewish parroting. "Works of Jewish music," he declares, "produce in us the kind of effect we would derive from hearing a poem by Goethe, for example, translated into that jargon we know as Yiddish" (20–21).

Goethe returns toward the end of "Jewishness in Music," where Wagner once again reinforces the opposition of Jews and authentic art. The Jews "have not brought forth a true poet," he announces, and proceeds to impart a mini-narrative of decline. When "Goethe and Schiller wrote poetry," Germans "knew of no Jewish poet" (*WGS*, 28). How did Jews eventually gain notoriety in the sublime medium of poetry? That Jewish writers first achieved success just as "our [German] poetry became a lie" is no coincidence. Indeed, Wagner contends that the most famous German-Jewish would-be *Dichter,* Heinrich Heine, exploited this climate of mendacity. Heine "lied his way to the status of poet" [*sich zum Dichter log*], he asserts

(28). And like most of the forms of cultural inauthenticity that endanger Germanness, the poetic prevaricating in question is a "modern" phenomenon. Wagner ascribes the demise of German poetry to "modern self-deception" [*moderner Selbstbelügung*] (28).

Since Wagner has Jews infiltrate the German poetic sphere contemporaneously with its corruption, we might expect him to blame them for that state of affairs. But Wagner's causal chain turns out to be less straightforward. Despite his own dissembling, Heine's "office" [*Amt*] is actually to "expose" modern lies. Far from being a welcome repository of truth, however, Heine is full of "mockery" [*Spott*], and he criticizes with nihilistic abandon. Wagner sees Heine as having been "controlled by a demon of negation." Putting a further twist into his argument, he suggests that Heine's "negation" is both Jewish and directed against Jews.[65] "Heine," Wagner avers, "was the conscience of Judaism, just as Judaism is the bad conscience of our modern civilization" (*WGS*, 29). If Heine's calling is to lay bare "modern self-deception," and if he acts as "the conscience of Judaism," Jews must have "modern self-deception" on their collective conscience. Judaism is, in short, an agent of modern lying. At the same time, Judaism works to "expose" that very blight among other peoples. For Judaism is to "modern civilization" what Heine is to Judaism. In "Jewishness in Music" Judaism both fosters the fraudulence of "modern civilization" and makes modern society pay for its fraudulence in the deleterious manner of a "bad conscience."

Thus Jewishness manages to run counter to Germanness in several directions. Whether as profiteering imitators or through negation, Jews push back autonomous, joyful, German creativity. But Jews can change and even enter the ranks of "true humans." Heine's Jewish rival Ludwig Börne did that, though it cost him "sweat, privation, fear, and a fullness of suffering and pain," Wagner writes at the end of his essay (*WGS*, 29). Of course, this final part of "Jewishness in Music" is mostly continuous with the preceding sections. Jewishness in German culture remains a problem that must be solved. And in keeping with his general manner of discussing identity, Wagner describes "ceasing to be a Jew" and becoming human as a mode of artistic production. He proposes that Börne made himself into a "fertile work of redemption" [*widergebärenden Erlösungswerk*] (29). Börne's radical "self-destruction" [*Selbstvernichtung*] actually represents a creative moment. Out of it emerged a "work" that possesses a redemptive "fertility," a fertility that, Wagner conjectures, could help deliver Germans from their partially self-imposed cultural bathos. If only Jews would follow Börne, and not Heine and Meyerbeer, both Germans and Jews would blossom artistically and existentially in a culture manned by Germans and by Jews who have shed their Jewishness.

In much of "Jewishness in Music" Wagner moves on well-trodden ground. Over a half century prior to the text's publication, Herder had exhorted Jews to abandon Judaism completely, so that they might develop into full human beings. In the 1830s, Gustav Pfitzer condemned Heine's "linguistic fraudulence" [*Sprachfälscherei*] as well as the "polemical-acidulous doggedness" of Heine's "Judaization of literature."[66] Heine himself warned about how modern society unleashed an abstract, demonically negating "critical spirit" that is inimical to joyful "sensualist" art.[67] What Wagner's essay does with particular, if not novel, directness is formulate a paradox about Jewish assimilation. According to Wagner, Jews are at their most un-German where they appear to have integrated into German culture, since their vehicle for integration is opportunistic copying, and the governing principle of German identity is noninstrumental originality. This is the aspect of "Jewishness in Music" that mattered to Goldstein and Weininger, for example. Recall how Goldstein frames the text as a classic expression of the feeling that German Jews can neither produce nor appreciate German culture, of the feeling that their investment in *Bildung* will not get them admitted into the German *Kulturnation*. In addition to the passages he cites directly, Goldstein might well have had in mind lines like: "Alien and apathetic stands the educated Jew [*gebildeter Jude*] in the midst of a society he does not understand, with whose tastes and aspirations he does not sympathize" (*WGS*, 16). For his part, Weininger repeatedly invokes Wagner's claims about Jewish imitation and vacuity as he dismisses the merits of Jewish culture.

It is just the motif of vacuous Jewish mirroring that Wagner most conspicuously extends and amplifies in his later antisemitic writings. Take "'Modern,'" for example. There he ponders how Jewish hyper-epigones—"hyper" because they copy the work of German epigones—might drain the Germanness out of the German language, which he considered to be one of a few shared practices that unite the "German peoples" (*WGS*, 166). "What is German?" ["Was ist deutsch?"], an essay written in 1865 and first published in 1878, asks whether Germans will survive a newly dizzying onslaught of opportunistic Jewish replication. "It is as if the Jew wondered why so much intellect and genius served no purpose here, except to foster a lack of success [*Erfolgslosigkeit*] and poverty. . . . The Jew corrected this mistake on the part of the Germans by taking on German intellectual labor

[*Geistesarbeit*]. Thus we see today a repulsive distorted image [*Zerrbild*] of the German intellect being held up to the German folk as its putative mirror image [*Spiegelbild*]. We should fear that in time the folk will believe that it recognizes itself in this mirror image. Should that happen, one of the most beautiful dispositions of the human race would be extinguished forever [*für immer ertötet*]" (166). By inserting himself into the mentality that he imputes to Jews, and apostrophizing "one of the most beautiful dispositions of the human race," i.e., German autonomous productivity, as "a mistake," Wagner gives the passage an ironic inflection. But the tone of its last sentence is closer to elegiac. In it, after all, Wagner warns of how a "beautiful disposition" might be "extinguished forever."

What explains the new immediacy of this sad prospect? No longer do Jews imitate only German music with "deceptive" precision. Now their mirroring applies to all German "intellectual labor" [*Geistesarbeit*]. Of course, since Jewish copying is the antipode of German originality, of "the mirror of nature" that is German art, the "mirror image" [*Spiegelbild*], which the Jews construct, can only be a "distorted image" [*Zerrbild*] of Germanness. Yet the Jewish simulacrum must have the confusing "accuracy" of Meyerbeer's music, because German "original minds" are liable to mistake it for their own culture. The "German folk" might think that "it recognizes itself" in its epigonic Jewish opposite. All that is solid, or what is most authentic and most vital, i.e., productive "German intellectual labor," might melt into a Jewish "mirror image," and after that, into nothingness, "forever."[68]

"SHADOWS THROW BODIES"

Notwithstanding the many differences between Wagner and Kraus—Kraus *proudly* proclaimed himself to be "one of those epigones who dwell in the old house of language" (*F* 443-44:28)—Wagner's "distorted image" that doubles as a "mirror image" evokes a key anxiety in Kraus's critique of the press. The press, Kraus maintains, offers warped representations of the world that pass for real and thus alter reality. With their unshakable "belief in the printed word," readers understand their environment and transform it after flawed journalistic reports. In the scenario Kraus describes, journalists determine the shape of the events that are supposed to determine the content of their writing. Journalists, "who should report," have become "creators" [*Schöpfer*] (*F* 363-65:22). Here "shadows throw bodies" (23).[69] Wagner too accused journalists of destabilizing the relation of all that is solid and that which is shadowy. More precisely, he accused *Jewish* journalists of doing that. Anticipating Sombart's use of Jellinek, Wagner begins "'Modern'" by agreeing with a German-Jewish rabbi who had emphasized both how journalism helped mold "the new culture" and that Jews seem "directly or indirectly" to "control" the journalistic organs of note. "How true!," Wagner exclaims (*WGS*, 177). Shortly thereafter he writes that the "linguistic fraudulence" [*Sprachverfälschung*], which "we must hold responsible" for the "introduction of the 'modern' into our cultural development," was "transmitted by Jewish journalism" [*der jüdischen Journalistik*] (178). This "linguistic fraudulence" results in part from the Jews' "unripe knowledge of [the German] language." Jewish journalists sully German with their dialect or "jargon" [*Jargon*], according to Wagner (178). Even worse, "Jewish journalism" undermines the signature productivity of German minds. While discussing the waning "originality" of the "German world," Wagner grimly forecasts that "under the corrosive influence of Jewish journalism" German "scholars" will "lose what remains of their beautiful and thoughtful writing" (180). Indeed, he observes that German thinkers have already taken on some of the stultifying verbal mores of the "modern literary machine," which "liberal Jewry" runs (180).

If selective consumers of German culture (i.e., scholars) fashion their speech after the style of "Jewish journalism," then, for all its insufficient ripening, that style must appear as something other than immediately detectable foreignness. And so it seems that "Jewish journalism" is the linguistic form that best instantiates the Jewish "mirror image" of which Wagner had written a decade earlier. "Jewish journalism" is a "distorted" replica that somehow confuses its audience into mistaking it for the real thing. In the manner of a body-throwing shadow, Wagner's "Jewish journalism" involves an uncanny remodeling of originality (German culture) after imitation (Jewish culture). Accordingly, "'Modern'" hedges on the famous assertions about the Jews' cacophonous linguistic alterity that "Jewishness in Music" contains. The later essay still marks the German of Jews as inferior or "unripe." But Wagner moves the accent away from the theme of recognizable difference. His penultimate paragraph even suggests that Jews are shaking off the sibilant "Semitic hissing sounds" [*Zischlaute*] (*WGS*, 182) that had distinguished their speech from genuine German. Should "liberal-modern Jews" persist in acquiring a misleading similarity to Germans, the results will be catastrophic, Wagner speculates. The culmination of this process would seal what he elsewhere in the text calls "the victory of the modern Jewish world" (*WGS*, 181).

Between 1850, when "Jewishness in Music" appeared, and 1878, when "'Modern'" was published, a burgeoning of German antisemitic culture took place. Not only did Wagner read and admire some of the main figures in this development, for example, Paul Lagarde, but his line about the "victory of the modern Jewish world" resembles the leitmotifs and language of Wilhelmine antisemitism.[70] Consider its proximity to the title of Wilhelm Marr's pamphlet, *The Victory of Jewishness over Germanness* [*Der Sieg des Judenthums über das Germanenthum*, 1879], or to Heinrich von Treitschke's well-known phrase, "The Jews are our misfortune!" In short, "What is German?" and "'Modern'" draw on a larger trend. They are also part of that trend. For the factors with which we can see Wagner's texts engage helped prompt the general sharpening of anti-Jewish rhetoric in Germany and Austria. These factors include the very visible role played by German Jews in a dramatic, post-1848 transformation of the German press.

Of course, the German press already had undergone several dramatic transformations, and it underwent further ones long after Wagner's death. At the beginning of the nineteenth century, Hegel stated, as I noted in my introduction, that reading the newspaper had become a mode of self-orienting comparable in importance to morning prayers in earlier eras.[71] The 1830s and 1840s witnessed the taking root of the German feuilleton as a popular genre. And in his recent study *Reading Berlin: 1900*, the historian Peter Fritzsche convincingly argues that a truly mass press, a press that bombarded urban dwellers with multiple daily editions and created "a catastrophe of phrases," as Kraus put it, emerged only in the twentieth century.[72] Yet the most explosive moment of change in German and Austrian newspaper culture is the period between 1850 and 1880. With censorship reduced in the post-Metternich era, and major cities and their bourgeois public spheres expanding rapidly, dozens of major newspapers came into being. Among them were the great liberal dailies published by German Jews: *Die Frankfurter Zeitung* (1856), *Das Berliner Tageblatt* (1872), *Die Neue Freie Presse* (1864), and the *Neues Wiener Tageblatt* (1867).[73] So while Wagner unabashedly exaggerated the power of "Jewish journalism," as well as the Jews' responsibility for commercializing German culture, his critique does loosely correspond to an actual historical occurrence. Indeed, it was in trying to account for "the rise" of Wilhelmine-era political antisemitism that the historian Peter Pulzer asserted: "There was no profession that was more completely dominated by Jews than journalism."[74] For Pulzer, in other words, the Jews' new journalistic power helps us to understand why the time in which Wagner wrote "'Modern'" saw the birth of new forms of antisemitic agitation.

But the prominence of German Jews in journalism was a longstanding phenomenon, and anti-Jewish responses to it were not always so shrill. A ribald, satirical current runs through this strand of discourse, from Alexander Sessa's send-up of Moritz Saphir, *Our Company* [*Unser Verkehr*, 1813], through Gustav Freytag's play *The Journalists* [*Die Journalisten*, 1852], to numerous caricatures of and by Kraus. Furthermore, when we look closely at attacks on "Jewish journalism," we find significant differences among those of them that appear to be quite similar. We find differences between Wagner's philippics and Marr's, for instance. And since one of the points I have been trying to make here is that stereotypes having to do with Jews and journalism vary in important respects, I want to note some of these disparities. Through the "Jewish press," according to Marr, Jews "monopolize" the "free exchange of opinions in the daily press."[75] Using their own press, that is, Jews invade and *shut down* a wide swath in the German public sphere. After all, a "free exchange of opinions in the daily press" that someone "monopolizes" is no longer free. Thus journalism serves as a weapon of choice in the Jews' "victory over Germanness."

Wagner's essay "'Modern'" puts forth an analogous argument. Again, Wagner begins with an approving reference to an account of the Jews' "control" of the press, and he then portentously discusses the "victory of the modern Jewish world" over the "German world." In Wagner's case, however, the trope of "Jewish journalism" connects with—and derives its meaning from—a nexus of ideas about Germanness, Jewishness, originality, and modern replication that is missing from Marr's text. Wagner portrays "Jewish journalism" as more than an instrument of Jewish might. He presents it as an expression of Jewish intellectuality. But I am not implying that we should treat Wagner's statements about "Jewish journalism" as some kind of idiosyncrasy. To the contrary, I have examined them because of their influential and broadly representative character. Certainly Wagner's thematic constellations, where Jewish journalistic copying stands over against authentic art and existential fullness, should remind us of the ideas we encountered in the first part of this chapter. In addition, Wagner's antisemitic ideology resonates with a whole array of later anti-Jewish, antimodern claims about the corrupting superficiality of journalistic writing. It resonates, for example, with Wilmont Haacke's *Feuilleton Handbook* [*Handbuch des Feuilletons*, 1953]. Haacke stresses how the "Jewish feuilleton" is a "product of the Jews' fanatical enthusiasm for civilization" and means by "civilization" more or less what Wagner meant by "modern": the opposite of a deep German culture that creates joyously and for the sake of creating.[76]

Kraus once insisted that neither Wagner nor Heine had affected his thought. Late in his career, that is, he called both Wagner and Heine "childhood illnesses," which he had somehow managed to avoid.[77] It is a curious remark. For the idea of Heine as an "illness" evokes "Heine and the Consequences," the essay by Kraus that deems Heine's writing to be a "French sickness," and "Heine and the Consequences" thus evokes Wagner's portrayal of Heine as a cultural contaminant. But the antisemitic language in Kraus's polemic exhibits a more immediate likeness to the virulent Heine-baiting of two other conspicuous figures in the history of German cultural chauvinism: Heinrich von Treitschke and Adolf Bartels. An early reader even went as far as to respond to "Heine and the Consequences" by labeling Kraus "Bartels II."[78] My aim in the next chapter will be, among other things, to offer a very different interpretation of Kraus's text. I want to show that Kraus used Treitschke's and Bartels's styles of antisemitic discourse in a complicated and, ultimately, *critical* way. Since the critical content of Kraus's essay will be more accessible if we are acquainted with its object, I will conclude this chapter with brief sketches of Treitschke's and Bartels's diatribes against Heine and his feuilletonistic style.

HEINE-BAITING, PART ONE

As Kraus once pointed out, Treitschke was not particularly consistent in his discussions of Heine. Citing from Treitschke's five-volume *German History* [*Deutsche Geschichte*, 1879–95], Kraus noted that Treitschke characterizes Heine as a capable poet who articulated "true German feeling" in one place and as an un-German Jew in another (*F* 88:20–21). About Heine's famous work, *Germany: A Winter's Tale* [*Deutschland: Ein Wintermärchen*, 1844], Treitschke wrote: "Just this poem showed the German what separates him from the Jew."[79] Elsewhere Treitschke maintained that Heine's style of literary journalism "was all un-German from the bottom up" ("SF," 155). Epistolary evidence complicates the picture further still because some of Treitschke's personal letters convey an appreciation for Heine's poetry.[80] But Treitschke's correspondence also indicates that certain elements of his antisemitic tirades against "the Jewish press," as he often put it, were earnestly meant. Indeed, shortly before his essay "Our Prospects" ["Unsere Aussichten," 1879] appeared in a respected journal and ignited the "Berlin antisemitism debate," Treitschke had complained about Jewish journalists in less public settings. In letters he castigates the "Jewish press"—and particularly the *Berliner Tageblatt*—for exacerbating the divisive *Kulturkämpfe*, and for thereby undermining what he regarded as a great feat: German unification under Prussian leadership.[81]

"Our Prospects" contains similar claims. Having listed various threats to German political and cultural health, Treitschke advances the following diagnosis: "most dangerous of all is the unfortunate overrepresentation of Jewish journalists."[82] Historically, he explains, Jews have proven to be unpatriotic and have used their journalistic power to impede the progress of the German state. Hence Treitschke's preoccupation with liberal Jewish critics, as well as his phrase, "The Jews are our misfortune."[83] Like most antisemitic polemicists, Treitschke's made specific Jews into tangible symbols and agents of this general "misfortune." "It was Börne," he contended in 1880, "who introduced into our journalism the tone that speaks derisively of our fatherland—without even a semblance of respect."[84]

In "Our Prospects" Treitschke credits Heine with co-authoring this irreverent journalism. But his indictment of Heine extends considerably farther. For Treitschke also charged Heine with attenuating the strengths of German literary culture in new ways. His essay "The Sovereign Feuilleton" ["Der souveräne Feuilleton," 1891?], for example, proposes: "With Heine, there appeared among us for the first time a virtuoso of form who did not care about the content of his words" ("SF," 154). Treitschke goes on to depict Heine's experience in Paris, and the circumstances in which Heine invented his feuilletonistic style, as the mental analogue of sexual self-abasement: "Without resistance, Heine's receptive, dependent mind gave itself over to the confused thoughts that he [Chateaubriand] feverishly aroused in him, and that actually came from old, epigonic literature. Heine greedily drank down the foam [*Schaum*] of the Parisian passion-drink" ("SF," 154). Treitschke's Heine has a promiscuous, effeminate, mental character. "Without resistance," Heine's "receptive, dependent" essentially passive intellect "gave itself over" to the jumbled thoughts "aroused" in him by a French male author whose ideas themselves are "epigonic" and thus lacking in creative virility. By imagining that Heine "drank down" French triviality in a substance ("foam") that evokes not only Champagne bubbles but also semen, Treitschke further associates Heine's feuilletonistic style with aberrant and unproductive sexuality. And because he frames this reading with remarks about "the superior [creative] might of Aryans" (149), and about all that "the Jew and the Frenchman have in common" (155), his portrait of Heine has an explicitly anti-Jewish coloration.

Decades earlier, Wolfgang Menzel had pictured Heine traveling through Italy in 1822 as a "Jew boy standing impudently in front of the Italian paintings of the Madonna with his hand down his pants."[85] Alluding both to the belief that Heine had contracted syphilis in Paris and to Heine's ties to the Young Germany movement, Menzel had later written: "The physiognomy of the Young Germans was that of a dissipated Jewish youth who has just returned from Paris, stinking of musk and garlic, and dressed after the latest trends, but also rendered completely blasé by his own lasciviousness."[86] By taking such utterances into account, we can see that Treitschke availed himself of established motifs in antisemitic Heine criticism. But, in contrast to Menzel, Treitschke gave the theme of Frenchified-Jewish, sexual-literary debauchery a *special* application to literary journalism. For Treitschke develops his Menzel-like claims about Heine in an essay that focuses on the feuilleton and its cultural consequences in Germany. Beyond having Heine's feuilletonistic style decadently invert the proper, Germanic relation of form and content, Treitschke has Heine's manner of feuilletonistic writing "replace with obscenity" the healthy "passion" of German literature and "indulge in lubricious dreaming" ("SF," 154).

Otherwise put, in Treitschke's texts Heine remains what he is in "Jewishness in Music" and Menzel's screeds: a sexually suspicious defiler of culture, a poetic fraud, and a propagator of modern, anti-German negation. But the Heine whom Treitschke ultimately constructs is different in that he vitiates the creative energies and ethical values of German society *primarily* through the feuilleton. Treitschke writes of how the feuilleton that Heine brought to Germany "dissolves all art forms" and "undermines all ideals" ("SF," 153). As we will see, Kraus's dictum, "Without Heine, no feuilleton," might describe Treitschke's objections to Heine in "The Sovereign Feuilleton" better than those that Kraus himself expresses in "Heine and the Consequences."

Bartels inveighed against Heine more prolifically than did either Treitschke or Kraus. In fact, Bartels may well have inveighed against Heine more prolifically than anyone. It would be difficult, moreover, to find "Heine hatred" more influential than Bartels's. To be sure, Bartels was notorious for his toxic ranting. He once derided Heine's "prattle" as "Judenpiß,"[87] which is no doubt why Kraus drew a verbal caricature of Bartels micturating on Heine's grave.[88] Yet many readers considered Bartels, who reviewed books regularly for the "distinguished" *Kunstwart,* to be a competent literary critic.[89] As was the case with the historian Treitschke, Bartels's appeal stemmed in part from his ability to confer scholarly authority and respectability on crude antisemitic stereotypes. Bartels's works certainly sold well: many of his books went through multiple editions, which generally amounted to the printing of thousands of copies. But perhaps an even more striking measure of Bartels's success is that by 1910 his name could stand as a metonymy for a larger body of antisemitic literary criticism. That is how Kraus uses "Bartels" in "Heine and the Consequences," for example.[90] Thomas Mann later employed the word in a very similar way.[91]

The magnum opus of Bartels's campaign against Heine appeared in 1906, fifty years after Heine's death. As its title suggests, *Heinrich Heine: Also a Monument* [*Heinrich Heine: Auch ein Denkmal*] was meant as an intervention into debates about how to memorialize Heine, in whose memory monuments had been unveiled in the Bronx and on Corfu but not in Germany. Having filled close to four-hundred pages with assorted barbs, Bartels wagers a succinct answer to the question at issue. He concedes that a Heine-monument should stand on German soil while stipulating that it bear the inscription: "To Heinrich Heine / Their great poet and champion [*Vorkämpfer*] / From the German Jews." Bartels then specifies that a monument bearing the words, "To Heinrich Heine / From the German People [*Volk*]," is impermissible.[92]

Though they lack the rancorous tone in which he couched so many of his utterances about Heine, these pronouncements exemplify the familiar main theme of Bartels's sprawling polemic. I call this theme—i.e., the theme of the Jews' foreignness to German culture—"familiar" because Bartels had been making such pronouncements for years. In 1897, for instance, he wrote that Jews are the "chief representatives" of "a feuilletonism [*Feuilletonismus*] in Germany" that is "at bottom corruption" and "takes as its ideal French literature and the French journalistic model."[93] Eventually Bartels published an entire monograph on the Jews' essential literary difference: *Jewish Heritage and Literary Criticism* [*Jüdische Herkunft und Literaturwissenschaft*, 1925]. In it he contends: "Jewish literature can be recognized on the basis of its linguistic and phonetic essence [*Wesensart*]." Yet he also cautions that "Jews have always been able to copy everything." Thus some "weaker Germans have come under Jewish influences."[94] Indeed, like Wagner, Bartels wrote in ominous tones about how Germans could mistake the Jews' distorted replica of German culture for the original. With his broad popularity, Heine represented precisely such a threat. Hence Bartels's driving need to expose the Jewish "otherness" of Heine's work.

"One should not think," Bartels claims in *Heinrich Heine*, "that I want to deny Heine all poetic qualities. No, he is a poet, but a poet of a sort different from that of our German poets. He is a poet-virtuoso who conforms to the contemporary Jewish nature."[95] Bartels's attempt at clarification is misleading. For he proceeds to insist that Heine's virtuosity has little to do with real poetic accomplishment—even with Jewish poetic accomplishment. Bartels "reveals" Heine to be a virtuoso only in the effete manner of a "Jewish dancing master." And the medium of which Heine was the true "master" turns out to be the artistically bankrupt "Jewish feuilleton." According to Bartels, "The really bad thing is the incalculable damage that the feuilleton industry has done to our Germanic soul . . . the moral values of the widest circles have their origin in the Jewish feuilleton. The same can be said of their bad German, which we find already in the great [feuilleton] master Heinrich Heine, because it is naturally a fable that he wrote with stylistic excellence. Heine is nothing more than a Jewish dancing master. There is no trace of German linguistic spirit [*Sprachgeist*] in his writings."[96] Did Kraus earnestly appropriate such rhetoric in his campaign against the feuilleton? Does he deserve the epithet "Bartels II"? Let us now examine Kraus's writings and find out.

CHAPTER TWO

Karl Kraus and the Jewish Self-Hatred Question

I despise above all two kinds of people: Jews and journalists. Unfortunately, I am both.[1]
—Ferdinand Lassalle

One knows that my hatred of the Jewish press is exceeded only by my hatred of the antisemitic press, while my hatred of the antisemitic press is exceeded only by my hatred of the Jewish press. —Karl Kraus

Has anyone been accused of Jewish self-hatred more often and more emphatically than Karl Kraus? Otto Weininger, Kraus's fellow fin-de-siècle Viennese, appears to be the only real competition. In fact, studies of German-Jewish culture frequently make Kraus and Weininger stand by themselves under headings like "Self-Rejection and Self-Hatred" and "Prophets of Doom."[2] Kraus receives such treatment because his *Fackel* reverberates with antisemitic clamor.[3] He demonized "all-too clever" Jewish intellectuals as a "life-threatening force."[4] He bragged that the "aversion" most antisemites felt toward "Jewish things" was "child's play" next to his.[5] He pilloried the "Jew boys" at the "Jewish press."[6] And he admonished Jews to give up Judaism completely and seek "redemption through total assimilation," to cite one more of the many examples that come to mind (*F* 23:7).[7]

Thus it shouldn't be all too surprising that Theodor Lessing, the author of the first book about Jewish self-hatred, saw Kraus as "the most revealing instance" of his topic.[8] Other influential contemporaries, e.g., Martin Buber, Arthur Schnitzler, Franz Werfel, and Max Brod, described Kraus in similar terms.⁹ And, again, so have more recent critics.¹⁰ Walter Kaufmann, Mark Anderson, Steven Lowenstein, Jacques Le Rider, and Sander Gilman all have portrayed Kraus as an ardent Jewish self-hater.¹¹ In well-known works Anderson and Lowenstein underline the parallels between Kraus and Weininger, that famous suicide who relentlessly disparaged Jewish culture.¹² Le Rider goes farther where he maintains that antisemitism alone motivated "Heine and the Consequences," Kraus's notorious polemic against Heine. This essay, he insists, "can really be understood only if it is seen as yet another symptom of jüdischer Selbsthaß [Jewish self-hatred]."¹³ While Gilman points to ambiguities in Kraus's claims about Jews and Judaism, soon afterward he makes a more dramatic gesture in the opposite direction, likening Kraus's rhetoric to Hitler's.¹⁴

This approach has an obvious problem. The murkiness that Gilman notes actually pervades *Die Fackel*. For Kraus also embraced his Jewish heritage, at times quite forcefully.¹⁵ He even avowed: "Above all things, I love, and am grateful to, the holy, uncompromising natural power of Judaism" (*F* 890–905:38). Such statements do not populate Kraus's writings as densely as do antisemitic obloquies, to be sure. But neither are they isolated second thoughts. Tellingly, some of Kraus's most astute readers believed that he showed his true face in formulations like the one I just quoted. They include Walter Benjamin, who once wrote that he wanted "to draw" Kraus's "Jewish physiognomy,"¹⁶ and Gershom Scholem, who vigorously defended Kraus against the charge of Jewish self-hatred.¹⁷ Berthold Viertel, Werner Kraft, and Erich Heller all viewed Kraus as a "great Jew."¹⁸ Theodor Adorno expressed much the same perception more poignantly—by apostrophizing Kraus as an inverted, self-immolating "Shylock" who "sacrifices his own blood" out of altruism.¹⁹

What critic today would attach the phase "great Jew" to Kraus? By contrast, Jewish self-hatred has become an established theoretical category. And so its side has prevailed in the debate about Kraus's Jewish identity.²⁰ Yet there are notable exceptions to this trend. For example, Edward Timms has given an even-handed account of Kraus's utterances about Jewish culture.²¹ Harry Zohn, Robert Wistrich, and Leo Lensing have tracked these rhetorical vacillations just as carefully.²² But even here conceptual difficulties persist. In analyzing Kraus's Jewish self-hatred, the scholars I mentioned have proceeded from a single hermeneutic point of departure. Those who assert that Kraus offered dichotomous answers to the "Jewish Question," as well as those who focus on his more draconian ones, have pursued, for the most part, literal readings of Kraus's antisemitic writings.²³ That is, they regard Kraus's anti-Jewish outbursts as reliable indications of an inner torment. Le Rider makes this logic clear when he tells us that we can comprehend Kraus's attack on Heine "*only*" as a "*symptom* of jüdischer Selbsthaß" (my emphasis).[24]

Of course, much of the anti-Jewish rhetoric in *Die Fackel* conforms to the definition of Jewish self-hatred that underlies Le Rider's argument. Certainly Kraus "accepted," or attributed truth to, some antisemitic stereotypes.[25] How else to explain the venomous language in so many of his reckonings with German Jewry? But why must Kraus's anti-Jewish remarks have only one sort of impetus and only one meaning? When addressing the theme of Jewish culture, Kraus was hardly wedded to a single register. We have observed him moving from rebarbative antisemitism ("Jewish corruption") to solemn philosemitism ("I have always loved the holy, uncompromising natural power of Judaism"). Why should we expect consistency from his antisemitic discourse? Furthermore, Kraus was an arch-satirist. Couldn't he have used antisemitic rhetoric ironically? Couldn't his antisemitic bluster have had causes beyond heartfelt internecine loathing?

Shulamit Volkov has made a strong case for the idea that in turn-of-the-century Germany antisemitism often operated as a "cultural code."[26] Instead of employing anti-Jewish discourse to articulate a deep-seated animus, or to assault Jews verbally, many Germans did so in order to align themselves with the conservative cultural values that were associated with antisemitism. Anti-Jewish discourse functioned "symbolically," as an effective "shorthand," as a convenient, even fashionable set of markers with which Germans and Austrians positioned themselves on their map of German culture. Now people who appropriated antisemitism in this way might actually have subscribed to antisemitic stereotypes. An antisemitic illocution easily could have served multiple purposes: ventilating genuine racist hostility *and* identifying its author as part of a non-liberal group. However, admitting these possibilities hardly diminishes the significance of Volkov's insight. For she has located examples of anti-Jewish language whose *primary* aim seems to be the cultural self-stylization of Germans who were not convinced antisemites. And Volkov's own primary aim is to illuminate the complexity of German antisemitic discourse rather than to find absolutely distinct strains of it.

But what about the complexity of Jewish antisemitic discourse?[27] Several critics have addressed this issue. For instance, Allan Janik has pointed out that when one sees Jewish authors who used anti-Jewish language simply as pathological self-haters, interpretive foreshortenings tend to occur.[28] Yet to the best of my knowledge no one has asked about the functional variety of such usages. No one has taken up Volkov's insight and investigated the different things antisemitic discourse does, and that it seems constructed to do, in writings by German Jews. There are good reasons for the disparity between theories of German and Jewish antisemitism. German antisemitism is a larger, more fateful phenomenon. It has attracted more scholarly interest, and the study of it has advanced farther. In addition, the structural differences between these antisemitisms necessitate different historiographical models. German and German-Jewish antisemitism vary with regard to psychological composition, for example.[29] As critics from Lessing to Gilman have stressed, a riven, masochistic quality runs through the lives and works of the most prominent German-Jewish antisemites, while their German counterparts more frequently come across as demagogic dissemblers.[30] Compare Kraus and Weininger to Heinrich von Treitschke, who despised Heine in public and privately adored him,[31] and also to the antisemitic politician Karl Lueger, who, when queried about having Jewish friends, cynically riposted, "I decide who's a Jew."[32] But antisemitism became a cultural code among both Germans and German Jews. Indeed, I want to argue that notwithstanding his more fervent anti-Jewish pronouncements, Kraus used antisemitic discourse for strategic purposes in just that place where we are supposed to have the surest signs of "internalized" stereotypes: "Heine and the Consequences."[33]

Examining the strategic value of this text means asking why and how Kraus exploited the symbolic power of antisemitic language. I will therefore situate "Heine and the Consequences" within the context of the relevant cultural pressures that Kraus felt around 1910, or during the time in which he wrote the essay. I will proceed intertextually as well, for when we survey Kraus's antisemitic rhetoric, we see diverse patterns, and that "Heine and the Consequences" bears affinities with only some of them. Here, then, I hope to explicate how "Heine and the Consequences" differs from Kraus's most bigoted antisemitic moments; how the text belongs to another order of his antisemitic discourse; and what factors, outside of a "genuine" Jewish self-contempt, prompted Kraus to mobilize anti-Jewish stereotypes against Heine. Let me add that Kraus was not alone with his complex Jewish antisemitism. Many German Jews—for example, Weininger—availed themselves of antisemitic language with evident and grim sincerity. However, others, including Heine himself, used provocatively anti-Jewish tropes as Kraus did, at least some of the time: in an ugly yet often trenchant mode of self-representation that remains to be integrated into *our* map of German culture.[34]

Between 1898 and the beginning of the First World War, Kraus cultivated two types of antisemitic discourse. In one he worked with antisemitism strategically, spicing with anti-Jewish stereotypes his invectives against well-known liberal Jewish feuilletonists, e.g., Heine, Theodor Herzl, Felix Salten, Maximilian Harden, and Alfred Kerr, while often subverting those same stereotypes. Through such paradoxes Kraus signaled his distance from mainstream liberal Jewish letters *and* from mainstream antisemitic stereotypes about liberal Jewish letters, without aligning himself with a recognizable cultural position. He thereby bolstered a feature he clearly cherished: his aura of maverick critical singularity and independence.[35] Witness his claim: "According to the census, Vienna has 2,030,834 inhabitants, that is, 2,030,833 souls and me" (*F* 315–16:13).

Yet Kraus's "strategic Jewish self-hatred"—by which I mean his strategic use of antisemitic discourse—was more than a rhetorical vehicle for asserting autonomy in a journalistic environment that could feel oppressively sectarian. Kraus wanted to dissociate himself from liberal Jewish feuilletonists in part because he had serious reservations about their writing. And these reservations played a dynamic role in the evolution of Kraus's own linguistic principles and practices. Indeed, we encounter alongside Kraus's strategic deployment of antisemitic language key formulations of his stylistic principles, or more precisely of *counter*principles that respond to what he perceived to be the fateful stylistic excesses of Jewish feuilletonists. So it strikes me as no coincidence that "Heine and the Consequences," the most spectacular, most controversial example of Kraus's strategic antisemitism, has been designated to be one of only two "breakout" texts in which Kraus "became himself."[36] By pursuing the question of Kraus's "Jewish self-hatred," we will come to see how thoroughly Kraus worked with—and also critically through—ideas that link Jewish identity and journalism as he laid out his journalistic project.

I say that Kraus "worked critically through" these ideas because his critique of German-Jewish feuilletonists is simultaneously a critique of stereotypes *about* German-Jewish feuilletonists. Again, in framing his anti-journalism, Kraus went beyond playfully invoking and undermining such tropes; he went beyond paradox-flaunting, that is. He also went beyond setting up incisive, if not always judicious, oppositions between his style and that of German-Jewish feuilleton writers. In "Heine and the Consequences" he develops some of his signature stylistic commitments against another foil too. Kraus volubly activates—then reinscribes in innovative and formative ways—the governing tenets and values in precisely the discussions that made journalistic writing into a privileged marker of Jewishness. It is as if establishing a truly radical authorial position as a Jewish journalist had to entail intervening radically into those discussions, into the discussions that I analyzed in the previous chapter. It is as if, as I suggested in the introduction, establishing that kind of authorial position in fin-de-siècle Vienna had to entail what amounted to a radical performance of German-Jewish identity.

Kraus also focuses on journalism in his other pattern of antisemitic discourse, but generally without entering into any sort of ironic play. Here his broadsides often appear to be animated by conspiracy theories about the partisan machinations of the "Jewish press."[37] These attacks are, in addition, appreciably more violent and apparently more earnest than what we find in "Heine and the Consequences," as ingenuous as that latter modifier might sound. Still, if Kraus's varieties of antisemitic language are different enough to warrant a basic distinction, they do sometimes intertwine. Although putting them into separate categories does not involve working with counterfactual "ideal types," some qualifying and refining will therefore be necessary. Moreover, Kraus's anti-Jewish rhetoric shifted throughout his career. At the beginning of the First World War, for which Kraus occasionally held the Jews responsible, the bipartite character of his anti-Jewish utterances abated somewhat.[38] Straightforward accusations became more prominent.[39] Yet that mode had not been the core of Kraus's antisemitic discourse. It was not even the first part to take shape.

VARIETIES OF JEWISH SELF-HATRED

In 1898, Kraus was twenty-four and a rising star in Vienna's journalistic firmament. For five years, he had been writing incisive, often humorous theater and book reviews for cultural weeklies and liberal dailies, such as *Die Gesellschaft* and the *Neue Freie Presse*. But these works dimly resemble his essays in *Die Fackel*, which have more stylistic daring and satirical bite and a greater thematic scope. What had gained Kraus notoriety, even before he founded his own newspaper, were two pamphlets: *Demolished Literature* [*Die demolierte Literatur*, 1897] and *A Crown for Zion* [*Eine Krone für Zion*, 1898]. In *Demolished Literature* Kraus parodies several journalistic champions of Viennese modernism, for example, Felix Salten and Hermann Bahr, whose beloved Café Griensteidl was about to be torn down.[40] Kraus does not emphasize that most of these writers were Jews. Rather, he dwells on the triviality of their coffeehouse existence and on their linguistic foibles.

The thrust of his criticism is that these would-be iconoclasts form a coterie whose members have the same affected feelings and opinions, which they write about in the same affected way. In short, Kraus charged them with an extravagant form of hypocrisy. And by implication he foregrounded his own critical autonomy, placing himself beyond even the cutting edge of Viennese modernism. For unlike the movement's conservative opponents, Kraus endorsed its vaunted break with tradition. He skewered modernist critics like Salten and Bahr because, in his opinion, they lacked the very radical energy that they themselves celebrated.

A Crown for Zion too can be understood as a step toward, and harbinger of, the journalistic independence that Kraus acquired with the founding of *Die Fackel*. Here, as Kraus's title announces, the "Jewish question" plays a leading role: *A Crown for Zion* is basically a critique of Zionism. Yet Kraus continues to berate the object of his opprobrium in *Demolished Literature*. More precisely, he couples the problem he speaks to there, i.e., the fecklessness of Vienna's coffeehouse literati, with his new theme, namely, the hazards of German-Jewish assimilation. Thus the literary-journalistic culture from which Kraus wanted to distance himself took on a Jewish character in his work.

This development does not represent a passage into self-hatred. Nowhere in *A Crown for Zion* does Kraus ascribe the linguistic weaknesses of Jewish literati to an inherited cognitive flaw or to an unbridgeable cultural alterity. And that, according to Gilman, is just the antisemitic stereotype that self-hating German-Jewish authors "accepted."[41] Throughout much of the text, Kraus simply claims that Jewish assimilation has led to certain kinds of cultural excess, including Jewish antisemitism. But he criticizes this phenomenon in typically incendiary fashion, liberally deploying antisemitic stereotypes as he proceeds. A paradox results. Kraus states his opposition to Jewish antisemitism in antisemitic terms. If we read that act as a way in which Kraus could achieve bold satirical effects and separate himself from both conventional critics of antisemitism and from conventional antisemites, then the paradox becomes less bewildering.

Of course, Kraus *wanted* to achieve the effect of bewilderment. We are dealing with a writer who, for instance, openly renounced religion in 1899 and secretly converted to Catholicism in 1911, only to declare, in 1922, that he had left the Catholic Church "out of antisemitism."[42] We are dealing with a writer who was, moreover, intensely and literally concerned with his image. Kraus printed in *Die Fackel* a professional photographic portrait of himself, using it, after he had been caricatured, as a kind of visual refutation.[43]

Furthermore, although Kraus alienated more than a few of his high-profile allies (e.g., Harden), thus solidifying his status as an irascible and uncompromising *Einzelgänger,* he routinely communicated to his readers that his work had support. He even provided them with full bibliographical information for literature that treated him favorably. Given the care with which Kraus fashioned his public appearance, as well as the ubiquity and dense layering of his paradoxes, it seems improbable that the difficulty of characterizing him emerged by chance. That Kraus's subsumptive challenges have flustered the most resourceful critics only adds to this impression.

Did Kraus bring forth a "rare interplay" of "reactionary theory and revolutionary praxis," as Benjamin maintained ("KK," 360)? Benjamin's phrase has substance as well as symmetry: Kraus often couched apocalyptic messages in wildly innovative prose. Yet many of his theoretical essays defend his more radical formal techniques, such as his *pre*-Dada photomontages and his attempts to reproduce "all the noises" of modern life in an epic style addressed "to the cosmos."[44] And the very fact that Kraus wrote theoretical essays warrants stressing, since, as Max Horkheimer observed, such a "radius of action" extends beyond the categories into which commentators often tried to place him, e.g., "polemicist and satirist," to use Horkheimer's examples.[45]

Although Kraus's politics sometimes drifted toward the right, the rubric "reactionary modernist" is misleading.[46] Not only did Kraus explicitly abjure the attitude to which it refers,[47] but his hostility to reactionary modernist key terms, such as "authenticity," and his allergic response to nationalism, or "irrationalism," as he liked to say, put him in another cultural-political camp.[48] But which one? In his recent answer to this question, Carl Schorske describes Kraus as a "modernist of the spirit" and as a modernist "puritan."[49] While Schorske's analysis of Kraus is characteristically learned, his general heading seems inadequate. Kraus did occasionally demand an austere separation between art and practical life, or between "ornament and instrument." But his own *literary* journalism exhibits a more libertine aesthetics, as do his many aphoristic tributes to unbridled eroticism.[50] In them, it is worth noting, Kraus often expresses an unbridled misogyny—"Because it is illegal to keep wild animals, and pets give me no pleasure, I will remain unmarried"—even though he fought against sexism in Austria's legal system.[51] We know from Kraus's utterances about his Jewish identity, and from the bemusement they elicited, that, with impressive results, Kraus flaunted his contradictions in this most sensitive area too. Hence Scholem's claim: "In dealing with the question of Kraus and his relationship to Jewish issues, one can in my opinion only make mistakes, something for which Kraus himself made sure there would be plenty of scope."[52] The willful ambiguity that Scholem registered abounds in *Die Fackel*. Down to the very genre status of his writing, Kraus's important features resist meaningful categorization.

Kraus calls himself a "journalist" and *Die Fackel* a "newspaper" [*Zeitung*] in its first issue (*F* 1:1).[53] A decade later, he spoke of his prose as "a new journalistic form" [*einer neuen publizistischen Form*].[54] Later still, Kraus stopped applying this sort of epithet to his work. Yet his "newspaper" retained the formal trappings of journalism. *Die Fackel* appeared as a periodical,[55] and although Kraus published in it aphorisms, poems, and dramas, he dedicated much of his space to reporting on cultural and political events.[56] Thus quite a few readers—for example, Benjamin, Scholem, and Thomas Mann—considered Kraus's literary undertaking to be journalistic in nature.[57] More recently, Pierre Bourdieu suggested that Kraus was a journalist who turned against his colleagues. As such, according to Bourdieu, Kraus was "well-placed" to analyze the perils of investigating one's "immediate neighborhood."[58]

Certainly Kraus did turn against the press. If *Die Fackel* has a main theme, it is the ills of modern journalism,[59] on whose stultifying "empty phrases" Kraus blamed "the destruction of the world."[60] "To have no thoughts and to be able to express them—that makes a journalist," he once wrote.[61] Because of such remarks, and also because *Die Fackel* deviates from the stylistic norms of turn-of-the-century literary journalism, there is something profoundly awkward about labeling Kraus a journalist.[62] Moreover, when he wanted to set off his writing against a negative foil, Kraus tended to use types of journalism, from Maximilian Harden's purplish prose to the garrulous "Sunday paper," as his points of contrast. What complicates these distinctions, however, is that their meaning depends on Kraus's *proximity* to the "neighborhood" of the journalism from which they distance him. Rather than proclaiming his *Fackel* to be absolutely incommensurate with journalism, Kraus stressed that he disrupts journalistic conventions. And, as Kraus generally acknowledged, disrupting journalistic conventions entails operating on or around the field of journalism. He asserted, for instance: "My readers believe that I write for the day because I write about the day. So I will have to wait until my works have become old. Then they might have actuality."[63] Like other journalists, Kraus writes "about the day." But his "works" also run counter to those of other journalists, who discuss the day "for the day," and whose efforts therefore have only ephemeral relevance. After all, Kraus surmises that his writings "about the day" will *gain* "actuality" over time. They did, according to some accounts. It may be that by achieving enduring newness Kraus became, for Benjamin, "journalism in its most paradoxical form."⁶⁴

With the appellation "anti-journalist," another critic pithily described Kraus's oppositional attitude toward his medium. But while generally apt, this neologism says little about Kraus's formal creativity, and it fails to separate Kraus from the crudely reactionary, journalistic critics of journalism from whom he is so different, and with whom he is often made to coconspire. Perhaps Heinz Politzer best evoked Kraus's generic intractability when he compared Kraus to Franz Kafka's enigmatic figure "Josephine the singer." Josephine's "Pfeifen," or whistling, is apparently identical to the everyday *Pfeifen* through which her fellow "mouse folk" communicate with each other, and yet it is something utterly and arrestingly apart. Josephine has cultivated a paradoxical *Pfeifen*-beyond-*Pfeifen*. And she clings to her singularity within mouse culture.⁶⁵

Reviled by Elias Canetti as an intellectual tyrant, adulated by Aharon Appelfeld as an incorruptible Jewish voice,⁶⁶ Kraus was an irreducibly idiosyncratic writer who strove to represent himself as such.⁶⁷ At times, he tergiversated on the theme of Jewish culture because he had countervailing views about it. At other times, however, Kraus's rhetoric appears less confessional and more like a means of creating colorful paradoxes—paradoxes with which he flagged his position outside the journalistic cliques and types that he insistently derided.⁶⁸ Consider the second of the two epigrams that introduce this chapter: "One knows that my hatred of the Jewish press is exceeded only by my hatred of the antisemitic press, while my hatred of the antisemitic press is exceeded only by my hatred of the Jewish press" (*F* 557-60:63). Kraus's chiasmus makes his animosities seem even more paradoxical than they are as it taunts his readers into puzzling over his place in German culture. For Kraus assumes familiarity and comprehension on the part of his readers, "one knows," where they cannot know, since what they are supposed to know is logically impossible: that his hatreds simultaneously exceed each other. But the coming together of these antipathies was not an off-the-charts occurrence. Under the editorship of two Jewish contemporaries, Victor Adler and Friedrich Austerlitz, the Viennese *Arbeiter-Zeitung* railed against the same "Jewish press," or liberal newspapers owned and edited by Jews, and also against the antisemitic press, on the grounds that both disseminated bad ideology.⁶⁹ Kraus's trope turns a similar combination of rage into something intransigently particular, into an emblem of his rancorous critical independence. It prompts his readers to ask, "Where does

Kraus stand?," while obscuring the answer behind rhetorical contrivance and heady illogic.

The antisemitic discourse in *A Crown for Zion* often advances the same aims. Criticizing Jewish antisemitism in antisemitic terms, Kraus casts his paradoxes beyond the pale of recognizable cultural positions. Yet at various moments in the text the significance of Kraus's anti-Jewish stereotypes changes. They become part of a conspiracy theory: Kraus intimates that tribal loyalties prevent Jews, even thoroughly acculturated Jews, from pursuing goals that would benefit all humanity.[70] Still, more often than not here antisemitism functions strategically or as a cultural code. Let us examine how this process works.

Kraus sets up *A Crown for Zion* as his response to Zionist soliciting. He states that a Zionist official has just asked him for a donation to the second Zionist Party Congress in Basel. Then he opines that giving money would contribute to the institutionalization of the fledgling Zionist Party under Herzl, its regal founder.[71] Hence Kraus's title. It refers both to the amount requested—the "crown" or *Krone* was an Austrian unit of currency—and to the end to which the crown would be put: Herzl's coronation as the "king of Zionism." But Herzl is not Kraus's sole point of attack. In *A Crown for Zion* Kraus impugns the basic agenda of Zionism by asserting that antisemitism is the essence of "the Zionist idea." He also calls Zionist aims "antisemitic" and the Zionists "Jewish antisemites" (*KZ*, 298–99). Kraus's explanation for these charges is that Zionists want what "Aryan antisemites" seek, namely, the expulsion of the Jews from European culture. The gold coins sent to the Zionist Congress will become so many new "yellow stars," which, in getting one's name on the list of delegates, land one in "the new ghetto" (299).[72]

Kraus's list of grievances extends much farther. For example, he blasts Zionist "nationalist propaganda." It is risible, he maintains, and most of it could have come from "the mind of an antisemitic librettist" (*KZ*, 301). Similarly, he lampoons the Zionist slogan, "Europe is the land of servitude" (301). Such maudlin extravagance only shows how ill-equipped the Zionists are to make good on their plan to "create a Jewish culture." Kraus also finds cultural destitution in the Zionist newspaper *Die Welt*. Citing its accounts of the first Zionist Congress, he condemns what he perceives to be its propagandistic tone and intellectual vapidity. He proceeds to seize upon a peculiar concern, which he finds particularly revealing: the newspaper's attentiveness to the "hand movements" of the speakers at the congress (302). Not only is the general Zionist "party plan" antisemitic, Zionists stand on common ground with their ostensible antipodes elsewhere too. That the stillness of Jewish orators is a major news item indicates, according to Kraus, that antisemitism has colored Zionist thinking about Jewish speech. If they did not believe that Jews tend to gesticulate when talking, why would Zionists need to disprove this crude bias—among themselves—by incessantly adducing counter-evidence? In further supporting his claim Kraus adverts to "Mauschel" (1897), an essay by Herzl. There Herzl works with a series of antisemitic stereotypes and excoriates the bad manners, faulty German, and the general depravity of the type of Jew, i.e., "Mauschel," that he detests (299).

But Kraus himself characterizes Herzl and Zionists of his cultural ilk—highly literary, haute-bourgeois Germans and Austrians—in stereotypical terms, or more precisely, as incorrigible Jewish dandies. "Tired of thinking only about their nerves," the Jewish coffeehouse writers of "Young Vienna" turn to Zionism for ready semblances of "social feeling" and spiritual depth. Underneath it all, however, Herzl and his closest followers remain what they have been. Zionism is another fashion statement for them, another means of indulgent self-stylization. Making a point he would repeat in *Die Fackel*, Kraus writes that such Zionists remove the "exotic ties that could ruin the image of 'exceptional melancholy'" and then order their desert costumes "from the best tailor." When "they ask themselves what is missing from the outfit, they can only answer: a homeland!" (*KZ*, 305). Such sacerdotal posturing will fail, he conjectures, because it does not have the ethical weight necessary to undergird a true collectivity.

Yet Kraus does not simply depict Zionists as Jewish decadents who indiscriminately employ large concepts like "servitude" and "homeland" and carelessly endorse antisemitic ideas. He interprets their Zionism as a complex and problematic new form of Jewish acculturation. Indeed, he accuses some Zionists of being fixated with "stupid" German stereotypes about the Jewish body, or with "bodily stigmas," as he puts it. Kraus thinks that these Zionists evince the same nationalistic "pride" as German antisemites and work with racist discursive structures in trying to recast such stigmas as marks of nobility. Playing off the German colloquialism "high-nosed" [*hochnäsig*], which means arrogant, he writes: "To own a hooked nose is now a great achievement, and one cannot carry it high enough" (*KZ*, 306). This elitism will be hard to stomach, Kraus contends. Indeed, he predicts that "fanatical" Zionists who speak the corporeal language of racist antisemitism will make antisemites out of "Christians who have had no taste for it" (306). Those Zionists might celebrate *Jewish* particularities. However, they do so in the idiom of *German* nationalism and insist, Kraus stresses, that

Europe's "intellectual achievements of the last centuries" be "assimilated completely to the Jewish mind" (307).[73] What presents itself as an attempt to assimilate German culture to Jewish culture does the opposite, because "fanatical" Zionists derive their demands for assimilation from German nationalist discourse. As they talk about making European culture conform to the "Jewish mind," Zionists reveal how thoroughly they have modeled their new Jewish culture after German ideology.

In laying out the paradox of an assimilationist Zionism, Kraus enlists antisemitic stereotypes. But whether or not we agree with his criticisms, we should acknowledge that he appropriates these stereotypes in the service of a reflective polemic against a controversial movement in Jewish culture, and with quite a bit of irony. Witness his sketch of Herzl buying his desert outfit at an expensive tailor. Kraus has taken up a key figure in turn-of-the-century antisemitic discourse: the trope of the Jewish dandy.[74] Yet he does not use this conceit in the traditional way, which would entail suggesting that Jews incline to a sterile, narcissistic dandyism because they have no aptitude for productive cultural activities. Above all, Herzl looks ridiculous in his designer ethnic gear. And within the context of an essay that clearly seeks to perform a rigorous, if also humorous, critique of ideology, Kraus's satirical images of Herzl hardly come across as hard-edged antisemitic caricature.[75]

There is also irony in the text's most famous line, which travesties a well-known poem by Wilhelm Müller and implies that nature assimilates more smoothly than the Jews. Having framed *A Crown for Zion* as a cultural dispatch from Bad Ischl, a vacation site that was popular among Vienna's Jewish bourgeoisie, Kraus reports: "I heard a brook speak *Mauscheln* [*Ich hört' ein Bächlein mauscheln*], and when, astounded, I yelled into the forest, my echo answered me with a question" (*KZ*, 307). To speak *Mauscheln* is to speak a Yiddish-inflected, and for many contemporaries, a Yiddish-infected, German. So through a small orthographic shift Kraus makes an innocent bucolic musing, "Ich hört' ein Bächlein rauschen" [I heard a brook flowing], into a deprecatory mock observation. However, he does not propose that the German of the Jewish guests at Bad Ischl has an indelible Yiddish coloration. The scenario Kraus presents us with is, moreover, obviously fantastic. A brook talks. Again, Kraus's point seems to be that even nature can assimilate better than the Jews, whose assimilation he has been decrying as tangled with contradictions. Nature, by contrast, speaks Jewish dialect fluently, or at least fluidly. It also exhibits Talmudic mores. In accordance with the Talmudic custom, the forest answers with questions.

Here Kraus employs an antisemitic stereotype, *Mauscheln,* to give bold expression to his provocative critique of Jewish assimilation, though without necessarily having "accepted" an antisemitic idea. In fact, he believed that *Mauscheln* could be sublime. As Kraus wrote in 1912, in a panegyric to his favorite Yiddish theater troupe, "What matters in art is *who* speaks *Mauscheln*" (*F* 343–44:12). Nonetheless, he managed to find credibility in various other antisemitic tropes. Where they occur in *A Crown for Zion,* his critical discourse shifts, becoming shriller and flatter.

Although much of the text sends up assimilationist absurdities, Kraus too lobbies for assimilation. He wants total integration, since only the utter "dissolution" of Judaism will end the "thoroughly corrupt Jewish society" (*KZ,* 298). By "corrupt Jewish society," Kraus means the Jews who played such an important role in the liberal Viennese press.[76] These Jews promote "Jewish interests," he contends, especially the interests of the "money Jews" [*Geldjuden*] who finance their newspapers, while feigning objective nonpartisanship. Newspapers like the *Neue Freie Presse,* which was owned by a Jew, and whose cultural pages none other than Herzl edited, are much more insidious than manifestly propagandistic publications.[77] The former newspapers dupe their readers with false pretenses about journalistic integrity and disinterested information and thus deform the Viennese public sphere. The latter present themselves as nothing other than what they are, "party organs." Insofar as Kraus finds in the work of liberal Jewish intellectuals enduring and parochial "ghetto tendencies" (312), he appears to advance a kind of conspiracy theory. While such comments stand on the margins of *A Crown for Zion,* they soon occupied a more central place in Kraus's writings.

"JEWISH CORRUPTION IN "JEWISH NEWSPAPERS"

If Kraus thought that his satirical pamphlets would drive a wedge between himself and the journalistic establishment, he was wrong. In 1897, shortly after *Demolished Literature* had appeared, Moriz Benedikt, the Jewish publisher of the *Neue Freie Presse,* offered Kraus the position of chief feuilletonist at his newspaper. This act represented a great display of faith in Kraus's abilities. The position had gone unfilled since 1893, awaiting someone equal to the legacy of its previous occupant, Daniel Spitzer, a longtime Viennese institution. In short, Benedikt wanted to give Kraus a dream job. But Kraus already had decided that working for the *Neue Freie Presse* would be a nightmare. There he would be caught in a web of "Jewish corruption." Indeed, after founding *Die Fackel,* Kraus accused Benedikt of trying to hire him in order to preempt his campaign against the *Neue Freie Presse* (*F* 5:11). Kraus's reading imputes to Benedikt too much perspicacity. After all, *A Crown for Zion* merely insinuates that the *Neue Freie Presse* colludes with "Jewish interests." Only in *Die Fackel* does Kraus explicitly vituperate against Benedikt and his newspaper, and no one could have foreseen the intensity of his screeds, not even Kraus himself, since powerful *new* influences pushed him toward a more radical critique of "Jewish journalism."

Houston Stewart Chamberlain might be the most important of them. His main work, *The Foundations of the Nineteenth Century* [*Die Grundlagen des neunzehnten Jahrhunderts,* 1899], appeared almost contemporaneously with the first issue of *Die Fackel,* and Kraus did not take long in recommending it to his readers. As his claims about "Jewish corruption" in the press, and about how the "biggest problem with the *Neue Freie Presse*" is that it is a "Jewish newspaper" (*F* 5:17), began to elicit praise from antisemites, Kraus felt moved to explain his stance. Throughout his career, Kraus thought poorly of organized antisemitism and of self-identifying antisemites. He did not want to be associated with their ideology, however energetically he might have partaken of it. But it was not Kraus's style to achieve this end by toning down his analysis of Jewish culture or by lucidly outlining his position. Kraus's attempts at autobiographical clarification generally brought little clarity. And given his desire to evade any sort of cultural typologizing, obfuscation was almost certainly one of his aims. Yet when, in November 1899, Kraus instructed an antisemitic reader to familiarize himself with *The Foundations of the Nineteenth Century,* strategic concerns were not his only motivation. Kraus seems to have genuinely esteemed Chamberlain. Not only did he invite Chamberlain to fill an entire issue of *Die Fackel* with his vitriol, but earlier he had asserted that from Chamberlain "one learns what the coming of Jews into Western culture has meant" (*F* 21:31). Moreover, many of Kraus's utterances about Jewish culture resonate with Chamberlain's writings, which pit Germanic culture and Jewish culture against each other in a world-historical struggle.[78]

But Kraus did not inhabit Chamberlain's *Gedankengebäude* uncritically. He rejected Chamberlain's German nationalism, for example. Kraus also directed his anti-Jewish reader to another "authority" on the "Jewish Question," namely, Herder, whose thought does not jibe very well with Chamberlain's. Seconding Herder, Kraus posits that Judaism is inimical to enlightened cosmopolitanism, an ideal that had little value for Chamberlain

(*F* 21:31). Still, the Chamberlain-like note rings louder in Kraus's complaints about the *Neue Freie Presse*. The "biggest problem with the *Neue Freie Presse*" is that it is "a Jewish newspaper," because as a *Jewish* newspaper, the *Neue Freie Presse* stands on the wrong side of the great culture war and reports the news from a warped and warping perspective. How serious was Kraus here? It was at just this time, or in the fall of 1899, that he took formal steps to extricate himself from the bad effects of ethno-religious loyalties—by leaving Austria's "Jewish community." While he had not been observant, Kraus had been listed as Jewish on official documents that required a confessional designation. He became "confessionless."

Kraus's arguments about the bonds among assimilated Jews are, of course, self-subverting. After all, his own antisemitic biases are most painfully apparent where he discussed the need to overcome Jewish biases, which he did often. During the debates about whether to retry Alfred Dreyfus, the French-Jewish officer who, in 1895, had been convicted of espionage, Kraus insisted that the "Jewish press" supported Dreyfus for all the wrong reasons. Rather than weighing the evidence, it slandered anything and everything faintly redolent of antisemitism. Dreyfus was the beneficiary of a retrograde, hypocritical parochialism. Kraus called the "spirit" in which German correspondents—many of whom were Jewish—covered the Dreyfus Affair "Leopoldstadt in Paris," Leopoldstadt being the Jewish section of Vienna. By applying the term to reportage, Kraus suggested that German-Jewish journalists in Paris had not advanced beyond primitive neighborhood solidarity. These reporters, he lamented, "misrepresent, falsify, and smear" (*F* 27:24).[79]

That Kraus singled out the *Neue Freie Presse* through his conspicuously expansive criticisms of it should come as no surprise. More specifically, Kraus expatiated on the troubles that Berthold Frischauer, the Paris correspondent for the *Neue Freie Presse*, had with the French government. In his most comprehensive essay on this topic, Kraus writes: "the French immediately inferred from his [Frischauer's] gesticulating prose just how uncultured he is" (*F* 27:25). Notwithstanding his "gaudy displays of knowledge," Frischauer remains a ghetto figure and has no place in a conversation among civilized, enlightened Europeans. To belong there, a Jew would have to be fully assimilated. The French government did well in sending away Frischauer and his Jewish commitments, or so Kraus concludes.

The *Neue Freie Presse* became Kraus's preferred target because it was Vienna's most successful, and probably its best, liberal daily.[80] Indeed, Kraus argued that the better a "corrupt" newspaper seemed to be, the more deleterious it was. While actually feeding their audience propaganda, good newspapers like the *Neue Freie Presse* could lead intelligent readers to think that they were getting unbiased news. Hence Kraus's claim that he concentrated his critical energies on the "Jewish press" out of respect for it: "The Jewish press is more talented, and therefore more dangerous, than the antisemitic press" (*F* 168:16). These remarks seem almost generous compared to Kraus's more aggressive attempts to malign the "Jewish press." Elsewhere Kraus likened what he regarded as its exsanguination of *Geist* for the sake of profit to the mythical crime of Jewish ritual murder, writing, for example: "And the blood that they [the Jews] have was not siphoned from the body of a Christian, but rather, from the human intellect" (*F* 389–90:40). To be sure, Kraus was using the word "blood" figuratively, but in assessing the belligerence of his formulation we need to take into account that when he published these lines, ritual murder trials still took place. Leopold Hilsner, a Jewish shoemaker from Polna, had, in fact, just been convicted of killing a Christian girl—for her blood—and was sitting in an Austrian prison.[81]

About Hilsner's trial itself, or rather about the *Neue Freie Presse*'s coverage of it, Kraus argued: "This hideous, inane feeling of Jewish solidarity. None other than our liberal press sustained and nurtured it and always understood how to use the feeling successfully" (*F* 59:2). The "Jewish press" exploits a "feeling of Jewish solidarity," a particularistic narrowness, despite its liberal airs. In his essay Kraus wants everyone to be aware of this blight because, unfortunately, most people are unable to see that "Jewish solidarity is preached between the lines on every page of the *Neue Freie Presse*" (*F* 59:2). Yet antisemites pick up on the Jewish media cabal. Kraus goes on to assert that the persistent "ghetto tendencies" in the "Jewish press" encourage antisemitism, among other social ills. He even warns that antisemitic newspapers "live from this journalistic corruption." Kraus might well have worried about the extent of turn-of-the-century antisemitism. But that does not make his diagnosis of it any less antisemitic.

Kraus's ideas about a Jewish cultural conspiracy have an antisemitic appearance not least because they owe so much to, and therefore resemble, Chamberlain's seminal anti-Jewish thinking. Of course, we cannot know whether Kraus believed what he said about the *Neue Freie Presse*'s subtextual proselytizing. But since he stated the charge often, mostly without irony, in very sensitive places (e.g., during the horrific Hilsner Affair), and after earnestly asseverating that he had "learned" from a writer who thought that Jews were at war with German culture, it seems reasonable to surmise that he did.[82] Moreover, Kraus did not formulate his response to the spectacle of

Jewish journalists defending Hilsner in the heat of a single, charged juridical moment. A year earlier, or just after Hilsner's arrest in 1899, he decried what he saw as the *Neue Freie Presse*'s narrow reaction to the first stages of the Hilsner Affair (*F* 25:31).

No doubt Kraus's published utterances about the "Jewish corruption" in "Jewish newspapers" had some strategic value as well. They mark Kraus as being very different from the liberal Jewish journalists at whom he aimed his polemics. After all, the *Neue Freie Presse* did react defensively to antisemitic discourse in Austrian culture, though its position on such matters was hardly as straightforward as Kraus makes it out to be. And certainly Benedikt's newspaper would not have printed anything close to the anti-Jewish diatribes that Kraus published in his *Fackel*. My goal, however, is not to show that Kraus's writings on the "Jewish press" are verbalized contempt and nothing else. What matters is that Kraus's fears about "Jewish corruption," which he expressed with apparent sincerity, seem to have been driven by antisemitic stereotypes. So whatever Kraus's additional motives might have been, Jewish self-hatred, as Gilman defines it, was likely a major factor.[83] At the same time, there are significant tonal shifts within this strand of Kraus's antisemitic discourse. Even his fight against Benedikt's ethnic partisanship occasionally took on an ironic flavor.

In seeking to demonstrate the Jewish biases of the *Neue Freie Presse*, Kraus orchestrated elaborate hoaxes that have a damning message but a prankish character. Kraus's own censorious rhetoric created the conditions that prompted him to employ gentler instruments of humiliation. For the fervor he brought to his attacks on Benedikt led Benedikt to enact an extreme policy. By 1907, not mentioning Kraus, or "silencing him to death," as Kraus put it, had become an editorial stricture at the *Neue Freie Presse*. It was this development that resulted in Kraus's recourse to trickery, to trickery that involved sneaking into Benedikt's newspaper.

Posing, in February 1908, as a civil engineer and avid reader of the *Neue Freie Presse*, Kraus wrote a letter to the editor full of obsequies ("your highly esteemed paper") and false statements about the small earthquake that had just rattled Vienna ("we experienced here a so-called telluric, rather than a cosmic, earthquake"). The *Neue Freie Presse* published Kraus's report, presenting it as a legitimate news item. When he exposed the ruse, as well as just how much speciousness his missive contained, Kraus suggested that the newspaper would have scrutinized his observations more critically had he not attached to them a name that sounds Jewish, "J. Berdach." Kraus writes: "I told the *Neue Freie Presse* to watch out. One of those letters it receives from Leopoldstadt, after an elemental occurrence, could be from me" (*F* 245:21). The charge here is that Jewish names, the names of Jews who *might* live in Leopoldstadt, go into a special category at the *Neue Freie Presse*. J. Berdach did not, in fact, give a Leopoldstadt location as his address. In addition to making apocryphal observations—e.g., that during the earthquake one room in his apartment shook violently while another remained still, to cite a further example—Kraus wrote that all this happened at Glockengasse 17, but Glockengasse 17 did not exist.

A few years later, Kraus engaged in the same sort of heuristic mischief under a similar name, "Gabriel Bardach." This time the *Neue Freie Presse* complained that Kraus's trick amounted to a kind of libel, whereupon Kraus again reproved the *Neue Freie Presse* for giving preference to Jews. "One must ask him [Benedikt], what he understands under 'falsification': the plain invention of a credibly Jewish name, which the *Neue Freie Presse* unfailingly believes out of pious feeling for Berdach in the Glockengasse? Or the stupid-impudent contention that the 'falsification of a listing in the apartment directory' has been committed, even if the listing is not in the apartment directory" (*F* 431-36:122-23). According to Kraus, the *Neue Freie Presse* treated Jewish names with too much piety and, as a result, the basic standards of journalism with too little respect.

HARDEN AND THE CONSEQUENCES

Kraus's response to what he perceived to be assimilationist linguistic excess developed more slowly than his ideas about ethnic biases in the press. Indeed, during the early years of *Die Fackel* Kraus identified with two writers who became, for him, purveyors of the worst German-Jewish writing: Maximilian Harden and Heinrich Heine. Harden's Berlin-based independent cultural weekly, *The Future* [*Die Zukunft*], had even served as the model for *Die Fackel.* And Kraus had publicly made Harden out to be his main mentor. In one of the first issues of *Die Fackel*, for example, Kraus printed an open letter in which Harden gives him avuncular advice and encouragement (*F* 2:1). As to Heine, between the founding of his journal and the publication of "Heine and the Consequences," Kraus repeatedly defended him. So did some of Kraus's enemies. Born in 1797, Heine died in 1856, and the anniversary dates 1897 and 1906, as well as the surrounding years, witnessed much discussion about how to memorialize Germany's most famous German-Jewish writer.[84] When agitation for a Heine monument met with antisemitic resistance, the *Neue Freie Presse* came to Heine's aid. Its publisher, Benedikt, venerated Heine, and the paper championed Heine's cause. For instance, Benedikt ran front-page articles, some of which he wrote himself, that exhorted the Viennese to honor Heine in a fashion befitting his literary stature.[85] Kraus did not question the premise that Heine deserved a monument. Rather, he denounced the Jewish journalists who, as he saw it, had sanctimoniously gotten behind the effort to commemorate Heine with a statue. As late as 1906, Kraus argued that these journalists had turned Heine into the reified icon of a cultural establishment that Heine himself would have found repellent. In effect, Kraus suggested that Heine had been made into a cultural code. Heine's putatively devoted admirers were using his name as a symbol of their own mawkish cultural values. Hence in the essay "Around Heine" ["Um Heine," 1906] Kraus claims that Heine's supporters do not appreciate his real critical merits and that their gushy Heine worship has made it difficult for others to do so. One must get past the image of Oskar Blumenthal, a well-known German-Jewish journalist and playwright, in front of the Heine monument on Corfu, Kraus laments, before one can enjoy Heine (F 199:1).[86]

Shortly before Kraus printed this piece, he had dropped the almost reverential tone in which he had been addressing Harden. By 1907, he had begun to ridicule the turgidity of Harden's writing. And over the next few years Kraus published several installments of a "Harden Dictionary," the joke being that Harden's German tries to be so loftily Germanic that it ceases to be German.[87] It becomes another language, a "Desperanto," which Kraus undertakes to translate into German. These facetious renderings make clear that Harden spins out long and obscure statements to say what can be said more economically: Kraus often translates whole passages with a single laconic phrase. In other places Harden's high-falutin language is utterly impenetrable. To make the contrast between himself and Harden as graphic as possible, Kraus identifies such problems as concisely as possible, putting a question mark opposite Harden's text in the space where his mock renderings should be.

What caused the swelling in Harden's style? Why did Harden go so far in his quest to appear to be intimate with the German language, to the point where his readers could not follow him? Kraus located the answers to these questions in Harden's assimilationism. For Harden had taken acculturation to an extreme level. He changed his name, from Felix Witkowski, to a cognomen that evokes Prussian military values (i.e., hardness).[88] He cultivated a friendship with Bismarck, the Iron Chancellor, himself. He inveighed against the German spoken by most German Jews while presenting himself as an avatar of *Bildung* and as a vast repository of cultural knowledge.[89] He adorned his writing with recondite words, elaborate rhetorical figures, and mythological references, thereby gaining the status, in some circles, of a master German prosaist, much to Kraus's chagrin. And notwithstanding the dissenting ethos of *The Future*—the magazine was known for its combative treatment of Wilhelm II—Harden subscribed to conservative cultural values. Indeed, when he helped expose the homosexuality of Count Philip Eulenberg, a close advisor to Wilhelm II, he did so with *Schadenfreude* and in moralizing tones.

The Eulenberg affair broke in 1906. Kraus, meanwhile, had been trying to reveal the pernicious effects of Austria's ethics laws or *Sittlichkeitsgesetze*. In a series of essays written between 1902 and 1908, he asserts that the enforcement of these laws is pervasively biased in favor of heterosexual men and that ethics laws are generally harmful to ethical life. Regulating sexual behavior among consenting adults, Kraus argued, prevents us from making decisions in the very sphere in which our most intimate interactions with others take place. According to him, ethics laws shut down the process of ethical deliberation where we can best practice it. And so Kraus chafed against Harden's invasive prudery. His "Harden Dictionaries" record this friction. On almost every page we find the rarefied formulations with which Harden tried to sanitize gay sex and through which he superciliously expressed his distaste for it. For example, Kraus cites Harden's term "Männerminne," a composite of "men" *(Männer)* and the Middle High German word for "love" *(minne)*.

The rift between the two critics seems to have opened up, furthermore, over a bigamy trial. In 1904, Donna von Hervay, the wife an Austrian district governor in remote Leoben, was charged with the crime of having more than one husband. Because of Hervay's Jewish heritage, the right-wing press could and did frame her alleged transgressions as instances of Jewish immorality. Appalled by this racist scandal-mongering and by how it compromised the judicial process, Kraus wrote several angry articles about the case, one of which he entitled "The Witch Trial of Leoben" ["Der Hexenprozess von Leoben," 1904].[90] Here, strikingly, Kraus heaps scorn on remarks much like those that he had put forth during Hilsner's trial. More specifically, he condemns the antisemitic press for claiming that "'the Jewish press immediately took the side of the unscrupulous Jewish woman'" and for suggesting that "'Jewish solidarity'" is what led some people to sympathize with the accused. Kraus quotes—and takes umbrage at—uglier lines, such as those that cast Hervay as a "modern vampire," and as a "Jewish woman with satanic features."[91] Harden responded to the trial differently, joining the chorus of the more conventionally outraged. Not only did he disparage Hervay in *The Future,* but in the fall of 1904 Harden wrote to Kraus: "My dear Kraus, Donna Hervay was neither fine nor plain, but rather a hideous, slimy, lying, decadent, cold-hearted Jewish wench [*Judenmädel*] of the lowest sort."[92] This is the first sentence of the final letter in the Kraus-Harden private correspondence. Kraus, whose voluminous body of personal communication appears to be largely free of antisemitic language, never replied to Harden's assessment of Hervay.

In his first polemical exchange with Harden, Kraus flays Harden's "precious" neologisms and demonstrates that they are often ungrammatical, the reason being that Harden frequently created new words by removing the "s" that binds many compound nouns in German. Harden's procedure yields solecisms that sound bad, Kraus observes, rather than what Harden wanted: words that would sound archaic and ur-German. Illustrating his point, Kraus lists the opacities, "Monomachos" and "Molybdänomantie," neither of which he attempts to "translate." Particularly galling, for Kraus, was Harden's policy of making outside contributions to *The Future* conform to his ponderous personal orthography. Harden subjected even the "Jewish jokes" of a well-known humorist to such editing, Kraus notes. This example is suggestive. In singling out how Harden treats Jewish jokes, Kraus hints that Harden's stylistic problems are also somehow a Jewish problem.

Kraus's hint soon becomes an explicit accusation. He lambastes Harden's use of the dative case, then concludes that Harden stretches this grammatical principle as he desperately tries to solve the problem: "How can he [Harden] distinguish himself from a Schmock?" (*F* 234–35:10). What leads Harden to abuse language is his fear of being a "Schmock," a vulgar Jewish journalist figure. Overly zealous to become the Schmock's opposite, a Germanic cultural presence, Harden works greedily, even maniacally, with language, the medium through which he seeks to acquire symbolic capital.[93] He charges into the public sphere with his moralistic journalism and his fancy vocabulary. For reasons that have nothing to do with semantic necessity, Harden restructures the case-endings of the German language and loses himself and his readers in a "self-promoting," incomprehensible idiolect. Furthermore, Harden's assimilationist verbal bombast seems to have a direct relation to his dubious ethics. After he quotes Harden stating, "'That one is a murderer tells us nothing about his style,'" Kraus rejoins: "I go further in the evaluation of stylistic strengths and make them into a standard for moral values. That one is a murderer does not necessarily tell us something about his style. But his style can tell us that he is a murderer" (*F* 234–35:6).

As Kraus was feuding with Harden, he entered into a dispute with Alfred Kerr, originally Alfred Kempner, another eminent and highly acculturated German-Jewish journalist. Here too Kraus saw a troubling symbiosis of journalistic misconduct and stylistic overreaching—and an assimilationist dynamic—at work.[94] In fact, he called Kerr an "aesthetic schlemiel" and pronounced Kerr's style "dead" (*F* 324-25:50). Just as much as Harden, a would-not-be "Schmock," Kerr, the hapless "aesthetic schlemiel," is a pathetic Jewish figure. A similar "Jewish" need for symbolic capital fatally afflicts Kerr's style. Indeed, Kraus applied the term "schlemiel" to Kerr as a way of explaining why he too priggishly covered sex scandals. Kerr violated journalistic ethics, invading the private life of Berlin's police chief in order to penetrate more deeply into German culture—in order to achieve social "enrichment," as Kraus puts it. Yet Kerr already had formidable stature in literary Berlin. Significantly, like Kraus and also Harden, Kerr edited, and was the main contributor to, a cultural weekly, *Pan*. So in anathematizing Harden and Kerr, Kraus was holding up the differences between himself and perhaps the two journalists with whom he was most likely to be associated.[95] Also significant is the discontinuity between Kraus's analysis of Harden and Kerr and his ideas about "corruption" in the "Jewish press." No longer did Kraus rely on Chamberlain's antisemitic ideology. Neither did he intimate that the German of these German-Jewish journalists was inevitably deficient. Rather, Kraus proposed that their German became distended in perilous ways when they crassly instrumentalized language as a means of assimilation. Appropriately enough, then, Kraus did just the opposite as he denigrated Harden and Kerr. He employed epithets that have a Yiddish ring, i.e., Schmock and schlemiel.[96]

Kraus was especially fond of the former slight. In *The Journalists* (1852), a popular play by Gustav Freytag, the figure who emblematizes the untoward social ambition of Jewish journalists carries the name "Schmock," and Kraus repeatedly made reference to this character in using the word. According to Kraus, moreover, "everyone knows that in the world of appearances there cannot be forms more convoluted than a Christian who is a Schmock and a Jew who is stupid."[97] Schmocks, as Kraus—and apparently "everyone"—views them, are supposed to be Jewish. Nothing is "more convoluted" than a non-Jewish Schmock. Thus it is possible to argue that with their use of the terms "Schmock" and "schlemiel" Kraus's polemics against Harden and Kerr reinforce hackneyed ideas about *Jewish* cultural types.[98] It is also possible to argue, and it was argued, that Kraus was hasty in attributing stylistic excess to a Jewish Schmock complex. If Adorno endorsed

Kraus's related "judgment" of Heine, as mentioned in the introduction to this study, he also complained about the alacrity with which Kraus consigned ambitious writing by Jews to "the Schmock sphere" [*der schmockanten Sphere*].[99] But in the exchanges I have been discussing Kraus analyzes Harden's and Kerr's journalism carefully while enlisting the categories "Schmock" and "schlemiel" loosely and seldom. Furthermore, these terms do not only serve to alert readers provocatively to the connections between the Jewish identities of Kraus's antagonists and their linguistic deformities. Perhaps the main function of Kraus's Yiddish-sounding locutions is, again, that they pithily mark his distance from Harden and Kerr, who avoided such ethnic flavorings in their attempts at stylistic gentility. Kerr, in fact, wrote derogatorily of Kraus's "Austrianisms."[100]

As in *A Crown for Zion,* where Kraus both plays with *Mauscheln* in a joke and censures Herzl's essay on the idea of "Mauschel," in the invectives he aimed at Harden and Kerr Kraus makes fun of assimilated Jewish critics *as* Jewish writers. But he does not question the possibility of Jews writing successfully in German. It was Harden and Kerr who came close to that. Harden's essay "Sem" (1892) sweepingly characterizes the language of German Jews as being defective; Kerr portrayed Kraus's style as under-assimilated, as sullied by its Jewishness. In a verbal caricature that Kraus reprinted in *Die Fackel,* Kerr describes Kraus's dialectical writing as "tinny and Talmudic" [*Talmi plus Talmud*] and as a cacophonous mixture of Yiddish and German.[101] For his part, Kraus had stopped admonishing Jews to redeem themselves through "total assimilation." During the years around 1910, in fact, he became an enthusiastic advocate of Yiddishy culture.[102]

Kraus's new attentiveness to the language of acculturation and his desire to set himself apart from it were products of large shifts in his criticism. In 1906, with the tenth anniversary of *Die Fackel* on the horizon, Kraus took a linguistic turn. He began to devote less space to exposing journalistic graft and to concentrate on journalistic language. As Kraus put it in 1912, "The corruption that brings the news reports into line with the advertisements is utterly insignificant next to the turpitude that tries to put poetry into every formulation."[103] What he means by the phrase "tries to put poetry into every formulation" is the conjoining of factual reportage and literary discourse in the German feuilleton, a genre that, the *Neue Freie Presse* had just decided, began with Heinrich Heine.[104]

Kraus's interest in the feuilleton intensified for a number of reasons. Among them was his friend Adolf Loos, who wrote his famous essay,

"Ornament and Crime" ["Ornament und Verbrechen"], in 1908 and caused a sensation with his ostentatiously unornamented "Haus am Michaelerplatz" in 1910 (*F* 313–14:5).[105] Kraus praised Loos's architecture and cites "Ornament and Crime" in his anti-feuilleton campaign. For Kraus regarded the would-be poetic component of the feuilleton as analogous to the ornamentation on use-objects, which Loos wittily decried (the "and" in Loos's title, "Ornament and Crime," is thoroughly conjunctive). Stressing his similarities with Loos, Kraus informs his readers: "All Adolf Loos and I have tried to show is that there is a difference between a chamber-pot and an urn."[106] This, however, is an understatement. Kraus and Loos also tried to show that most conflations of the practical and the artistic spheres ruin both.

By bringing together literature and reportage, the feuilleton licenses distortion and, even worse, preempts any kind of active response to news, according to Kraus. Its abundance of packaged "impressions" leaves no space for such engagement. Eventually readers become incapable of imaginative thought, at which point they become completely dependent on feuilletonistic cultural journalism. Unable to form impressions on their own, they must get them, ready-made, from the feuilleton. As Kraus put it in 1909, "Journalism, which drove minds into their stalls, now has control of their slop" (*F* 289:4). Cultural journalism, he therefore concluded, is a self-perpetuating commodity. The feuilleton creates a greater demand for itself through its effect upon the minds of its readers. During the long build-up to the First World War, Kraus worried that the coinciding of rapid technological progress and this spiraling critical regression would lead to a major disaster. In the essay that announces his linguistic turn, which he entitled "Apocalypse" ["Apokalypse," 1908], Kraus offers a grim prognosis: "Culture cannot catch its breath, and in the end a dead humanity lies next to its works, whose invention cost it so much *Geist* that it had none left to put them to use. We were complicated enough to build machines, and are too primitive to make them serve us. We operate a world-wide system of traffic along a narrow road in the brain" (*F* 261–62:1). The cause of this narrowing is to a significant extent cultural journalism, which has constricted the imagination so severely that "today one cannot imagine the frightful decimation the printing press wreaks" (*F* 241:14). Anticipating the culture industry argument of the Frankfurt School, Kraus confronted his readers with a problem that shuts off the very mechanisms through which they might solve it, namely, their imaginative faculties. "The newspaper destroys the power to imagine [*alle Vorstellungskraft*]," wrote Kraus in 1912, "directly, in that by serving up facts with fantasy, it spares the recipient any labor on his own; indirectly, in that it makes him unreceptive to art by taking stealing for itself art's surface-level appeal."[107]

Paradoxically, Kraus's own journalism became *more* literary around 1908. His logic is, in part, as follows: Exposing corruption would do little good if readers lacked the cognitive power to make use of this knowledge. Thus Kraus attempted to jump-start their imagination by writing in a more elliptical, intricately figurative style, a style whose syntax often poetically mimics the shape of the objects it represents. "Heine and the Consequences" might, in fact, be the first essay in which Kraus invokes for his "new journalistic form" the status of art. Furthermore, in the year of its composition (1910), Kraus began to read many of his writings on stage, which entailed putting even more emphasis on rhetorical qualities. And we should note that the effects of Kraus's linguistic turn were not purely linguistic. In an attempt to reveal how both visual and verbal propaganda compromised the imagination and dominated political culture, Kraus developed early, seminal photomontages, whose debut in *Die Fackel* dates back to 1911. With the emergence of this technique, Kraus's style reached a new level of formal inventiveness, as Burkhard Müller has persuasively argued.[108]

Consider just a few lines from "In this Great Time," Kraus's famous essay on the First World War, ". . . in this time in which just that happens, which one could no longer imagine, and in which that, which one can no longer imagine, must happen, and if one could have imagined it, it would not have happened; in this serious time, which laughed itself to death over the possibility that it could become serious . . ." (*F* 404:1). The explicit upshot here is that we are safe as long as we can imagine apocalyptic destruction. After all, only when we can imagine the worst can we take steps to prevent the worst from happening. Once we have lost our imaginative abilities, we are lost, even doomed: "that, which one can no longer imagine, must happen." But just as significant is what George Steiner has called the "serpentine" form of Kraus's sentence, which winds on and slithers back to its refrain, "in this time," for many more clauses.[109] Kraus pushes his readers and auditors toward heavy cognitive exertion as he produces the effect of grand oratory and reproduces in his syntax the convolutedness of the time that he is describing. As apodictic as this claim might sound, nothing Kraus published before 1908 approaches the figurative complexity, or phonetic and morphological artfulness, of the sentence with which "In This Great Time" opens.

So just as Kraus began to demonize literary journalism as the "black magic" that would "destroy the world," he stepped into a new structural proximity to literary journalism, and into a new need to distance himself from it. This is the context in which Kraus wrote "Heine and the Consequences," his most famous assault on the feuilleton. By *following* the *Neue Freie Presse* and casting Heine as the progenitor of the German feuilleton, Kraus could go after an entire journalistic genre with personal satire, his best polemical weapon.[110] But, as I have been suggesting, there were other factors involved in determining the particular ways in which Kraus distanced himself from the feuilleton. That is, other, "Jewish" factors affected how Kraus formulated his counterstyle, his anti-journalism.

Kraus scholars—for example, Edward Timms—have long recognized that Kraus developed his innovative literary journalistic style as a response to the limits and perils of feuilletonistic writing, or as an attempt to "explode the frame of the feuilleton."[111] Kraus's critics, such as Gilman and Le Rider, have stressed that Kraus's critique of the feuilleton contains a far-reaching indictment of German-Jewish culture. What has not been examined effectively is how these key points fit together. In his biography of Kraus, Timms analyzes the difficult "Jewish identity" of his subject in a chapter that says very little about stylistic and formal matters. The same is true of most Kraus scholars who deal with the topic of Kraus's relation to Jewish culture. They treat this issue as a vexed psychological problem that does not bear immediately on the evolution of his avant-garde critical techniques. On the other hand, Gilman asserts that Kraus conceived of his style in hackneyed, fundamentally antisemitic terms. He maintains that Kraus tried to create a "good" German as the "other" of the insidious "language of the Jew."

My reading of "Heine and the Consequences" breaks with both interpretive tendencies. Unlike Timms, I track the ways—the complex, paradoxical, innovative ways—in which Kraus fashions his anti-journalism in opposition to a feuilletonistic writing whose fateful excesses he links to Jewish acculturation. And, in contrast to Gilman, I show that in this process of radical self-stylizing Kraus works with antisemitic discourse strategically and even subversively. As we will see, for all his egregious rhetoric Kraus ultimately aligns his *Fackel* with linguistic values and practices that run dramatically counter to what Gilman calls "anti-Semitic views on the nature of the Jew's language."

Taking this point into account might help to explain why Benjamin and Scholem greeted "Heine and the Consequences" so approvingly. Benjamin went to far as to describe the text as the "high point" of Heine criticism.[112] Yet given the intense acrimony and complicated alliances in the essay's immediate context of reception, we should be careful about measuring our understanding of it against early responses.[113] Several of the authors who judged "Heine and the Consequences" harshly had been feuding with Kraus, e.g., Kerr; and in condemning the essay they might well have been exploiting an opportunity to impugn an enemy. In the end, the charged reaction to Kraus's polemic gives us one more reason to start looking closely at the text itself.

ANOTHER SYMPTOM OF JEWISH SELF-HATRED?

"Heine and the Consequences" begins provocatively. Kraus opens by announcing that Heine, an exile in Paris from 1831 until 1856, "brought back to us the French sickness" of the feuilleton.[114] The importation of a French malady is particularly harmful because German and French culture are governed by opposing principles: content and form, respectively. Each has its shortcomings. But Kraus much prefers the "reliable monotony of German cream cheese" to French culture, which, like "an old rind of gorgonzola," conceals its decay under its garish scent. "There," Kraus declares, "you bite in, and you have to run out—to the toilet" ("HC," 6). In both places "life is hard to digest." However, while German culture tends to be heavy, French culture is downright insalubrious.

Continuing his gustatory metaphors, Kraus writes: "But the romance diet beautifies disgust. . . . The German way is to make beauty disgusting, which poses the challenge: How do we create beauty once again? French culture turns everyone into a poet. There art is not art. And heaven a hell!" ("HC," 6). Kraus then comes back to the theme of cultural transfer. Thanks to Heine—"Without Heine, no feuilleton" (7)—the Frenchified feuilleton, in which one "sings" where "one should simply report," menaces German art. In fact, because of Heine the superficial ethos of the feuilleton threatens art everywhere: "In Paris one gathered not only material, but rather form. Form, this form, which is only an envelope of the intellect and not intellect itself, which is only clothing for the body and not the very flesh of mind, this form merely had to be discovered to become ubiquitous. Heinrich Heine saw to that" (9).

What are "the consequences"? One is that German literary culture has suffered. Now a "terrible equality" exists among talented writers, all of whom "produce the mood" of the feuilleton, and all of whom taste the same, "like so many rotten eggs" ("HC," 11). Meanwhile, the reading public has languished under a dangerous misapprehension. Fooled by Heine's "linguistic swindle" (9), they think that the feuilleton provides both reliable information and real aesthetic experience. But they get nothing of substance from it, only fiction where there should be fact and the formal trappings of literary language. The Viennese public tries to nourish itself with air, which is why the "Viennese poverty of the imagination" is such an urgent problem. As Kraus puts it, "To write a feuilleton is to pull the curls of a bald man" (9).

Kraus's corporeal figures are not always so mild. He compares Heine's feuilletonistic style to a wasting venereal disease, for instance. Indeed, the phrase "the French sickness" alludes to the syphilis that supposedly afflicted Heine in exile. "How easily one becomes sick in Paris! How the German language loosens its morals!" ("HC," 7). Extending this motif even farther, Kraus famously remarks: "Heine loosened the corsets of the German language, so that every little salesclerk could fondle her breasts" (11). A debauched character, Heine debauches the German language. However, "she" resists him and his dissipated ways. Kraus asserts that Heine's writing lacks content because the German language "thinks and sings only for a man who can give her children" (8). Thus "one must be a real man to have a chance with her" (7). Clearly, the diseased Jewish journalist Heine was something other than that.

This constellation of insults is, for Mark Anderson, unmistakably antisemitic and very much in sync with Weininger's understanding of culture. Anderson argues: "Like the author of *Sex and Character*, Kraus operates with stark oppositional pairs—form versus content, female language versus male creator, Romance versus Germanic cultures, life versus art, instrument versus ornament—in order to denounce the 'decadent' ornamentalism and 'feuilletonism' of contemporary German literature."[115] After emphasizing Kraus's affinities with Weininger's binarisms, Anderson accuses Kraus of antisemitism even more directly: "But a careful reading of Kraus's text ["Heine and the Consequences"] reveals that the French are merely a foil for the Jews, Heine's proximity to French culture serving as a cipher for his pernicious position as an outsider and foreigner, as a Jew within the German language. Kraus's real targets are the Jewish journalists of the *Neue Freie Presse*, the Jewish *Kaffeehausliteraten*, the largely Jewish members and clients of aestheticist movements and institutions in Vienna like the *Wiener Werkstätte*."[116] "Heine and the Consequences" is, in other words, a thinly disguised offensive against German-Jewish culture whose organizing ideas are antisemitic stereotypes, e.g., the "pernicious position" of the "Jew within the German language." Once we comprehend what the text's "cipher" stands for, we will recognize just how antisemitic it is.

Here Anderson and Gilman agree. For Gilman too suggests that in "Heine and the Consequences" Kraus lightly encodes his antisemitism. More precisely, Gilman writes that "Kraus is careful not to attack Heine directly as a Jew; rather, he uses the markers that for his audience pointed to the image of the Jews' language."[117] But why would Kraus carefully avoid castigating Heine "directly as a Jew"? Elsewhere, after all, Kraus freely uttered the most vulgar antisemitic slogans. So what might be the meaning of the *particular* critical register in which he works in "Heine and the Consequences"? And what about the text's disclaimer, which Gilman omits to mention? In it Kraus insists that his antipathy toward Heine "has nothing to do" with the antisemitic "Heine hatred" of Bartels ("HC," 31). Where Kraus rails against "Jewish corruption" in the press, he generally does not distinguish his approach from mainstream antisemitism. Might not his doing so here signal a discursive shift, despite certain appearances to the contrary? Not only does Gilman fail to acknowledge this possibility, he brackets the high regard Kraus expresses for Heine's late poetry, the poetry that Heine wrote *after* he had "rediscovered" Judaism, albeit in his own irreverent way. That part of the text separates Kraus's polemic from other orders of "Heine hatred." For the disconsolate self-hater Weininger, and for the programmatic antisemite Bartels, nothing Heine produced carries a trace of "deutscher Sprachgeist."[118]

Furthermore, if we are to understand the ciphers in "Heine and the Consequences," it is not only the text that demands a "careful reading." We must also reconstruct the cultural codes the essay activates in creating such loaded signs. Gilman does not undertake this hermeneutic labor. Instead of decoding, he merely equates suspicious terms and phrases with anti-Jewish tenets. Many of the text's central tropes do have an important place in antisemitic discourse, to be sure: Heine as a Frenchified, emasculated, essentially un-German cultural contaminant. But even straightforwardly anti-Jewish language could serve to articulate sentiments not at all coextensive with antisemitism. When we assess the semantic value of that language, we therefore should be on the lookout for twists and turns. Needless to say, we should be especially watchful if the troubling locutions come from authors with complex attitudes toward Jews and Jewish culture.

Take the case of Hermann Bahr. A *völkisch* antisemite as a young man, he eventually championed the works of Jewish modernists. By 1894, moreover, he had begun to agitate for tolerance toward Jews. Yet in a history of Vienna published just before "Heine and the Consequences" came out, he meditates dourly on the "Jewification" of the city, adding as he concludes, "it [Vienna] was already Jewified long before the first Jew arrived there."[119] In Bahr's text "Jewification" has a decidedly pejorative meaning. It has to do, as it often did, with cultural vacuity, with aesthetic and existential shallowness. So with his use of "Jewification" Bahr reinforces a common antisemitic trope. Yet in the same breath he thoroughly unsettles the stereotype— by intimating that the negative traits connoted by the term "Jewification" *are actually ur-Viennese qualities too.* The logic of Bahr's statement turns on this counterintuitive idea. Without it, after all, the proposition that Vienna was *both* Jew-less and Jewified would be outright nonsensical rather than arrestingly oxymoronic. And not only does Bahr break the immediate causal link between Jews and Jewification, he wishes that the "ur-Jew," to whom he ascribes great spiritual force, exerted some "power over the city." He thereby implies that *Vienna Jewified the Jews.* If Vienna was Jewified "long before the first Jew arrived there," and the Jews who have remained aloof from Viennese customs are not Jewified, then the city itself must have facilitated the cultural decline of its assimilated Jews. Wherever assimilation takes place, Bahr suggests, it renders Jews culturally superficial. But in Vienna Jews experienced a particularly unfortunate bathos, or a particularly extensive Jewification, for they became *Viennese.* Lashing out at Vienna, Bahr enlists against it the rhetorical power of an antisemitic slogan, though without launching into an anti-Jewish screed.

Like his rival Bahr, his friend Loos, and his admirer Hermann Broch, who labeled Vienna the "world capital of kitsch," Kraus often took aim at Viennese foibles. He does that in "Heine and the Consequences," where he writes: "In Berlin things are not so bad. . . . When a streetcar accident occurs there, the Berlin reporters describe the accident. They focus on what is particular about the accident and spare the reader a discussion of what is common to all streetcar accidents. When in Vienna a streetcar accident occurs, the reporters write about the essence of the streetcar, about the essence of streetcar accidents, and about the essence of accidents—with some commentary on the question: What is man?" ("HC," 12). Because of the prominence in Berlin of Jewish journalists (both Harden and Kerr were based in Berlin), and of newspapers owned by Jews, Kraus's Berlin-Vienna dualism simply makes little sense as an antisemitic opposition. "Heine and the Consequences" might be, in the end, largely about German-Jewish writing. However, it seems unfair to move as quickly as Anderson does from the observation that Kraus works with "stark oppositional pairs" to the surmise that the essay's very structure conveys a dark message about German Jews. Not only do certain dichotomies turn out to be less than bigoted; some destabilize others. Doesn't the framing of reportage in Berlin, a *Großstadt*, as a salutary alternative to journalism in Vienna, a smaller city, militate against the text's Wagner-like evocation of a corrupt culture of urban modernity ("How easily one become sick in Paris!") invading German letters?

Similarly eager to show that antisemitic precepts guided Kraus's thinking, Gilman overlooks the numerous complexities and eventual reversals in Kraus's essay. Gilman claims: "This attack on Heine using the rhetoric of the anti-Semitic views on the nature of the Jews' language is meant by Kraus to be a defense of 'good' language, language that does not blur the line between ornament and philosophy, and an attack on the 'bad' language attributed by Kraus and Herzl to the Jew."[120] With the phrase, "the rhetoric of the anti-Semitic views," Gilman binds together antisemitic rhetoric and antisemitic beliefs. He indicates that antisemitic rhetoric *belongs to* "anti-Semitic views." To use it is to have them. Since Kraus appropriates "the rhetoric *of* the anti-Semitic views," his "attack on Heine" must be an expression of such views. It must be "*meant*" as "an attack on the 'bad' language" that Kraus "attributed" to "the Jew."

Yet there is no such master key to the text's codes. After only a few pages, in fact, Kraus changes the locks. Anderson and Gilman enter into Kraus's antisemitic message through his binary pairs, which, again, they characterize as encrypted anti-Jewish discourse. But by the center of "Heine and the Consequences" most of these oppositions are no longer intact. Let us look at what happens with Kraus's most salient oppositions: uncreative, deviant, foreign, journalistic formalism versus Germanic intellectual content and fecundity.[121] It is, above all, this motif that represents antisemitic rhetoric "on the nature of the Jews' language," to borrow Gilman's phrase. For the motif does bear a palpable resemblance to what we encounter in, say, "The Sovereign Feuilleton," Treitschke's pillorying of Heine. "With Heine, there appeared among us for the first time a virtuoso of form who did not care about the content of his words," Treitschke proclaims, just before he sketches Heine guzzling—"without resistance"—the spermatic "foam of the Parisian passion drink."

But Kraus injects an ironic, playful note into his portrait of French decadence. For one thing, he extends his food metaphors into a farcical verbal buffet of pungent Italian cheese, its plainer German counterpart, and rotten eggs. He achieves a similar effect through other ribaldries, through bawdily dramatizing Heine's relationship with the German language, to the point where the language becomes a female figure whose corsets Heine loosens, and who likes "real men." With these images, in addition, Kraus offers a satire of the encomia to divine, feminine sources of artistic inspiration, e.g., Venus, that pervade Heine's early writings. *One* of Kraus's aims here—he no doubt had several—seems to be to send up cleverly Heine's actual work. By contrast, Treitschke's essay lacks Kraus's epigrammatic punch lines and immanent references. It simply tries to press on Heine's vulnerable points, the foremost of them being his Jewishness. Albeit in sexualized and colorful terms, Treitschke unwaveringly, even ploddingly, pursues the goal of discrediting Heine and his "feuilletonism" as a foreign body in German culture.

Kraus also forcefully distances himself from the discursive materials on which his initial figurations of Heine rely. That is, he distances himself from stereotypes that link sexual deviance and such linguistic defects as unoriginality. Taking issue with Heine's polemic against August von Platen, a known homosexual, Kraus asserts that imprecations of this kind are embarrassingly prudish and unimaginative ("HC," 25-26).[122] He criticizes Heine's general attitude toward language for the same reason. Unlike Heine, who defined linguistic "'mastery'" as "'seizing without making mistakes or hesitating,'" Kraus argues that the artist's "accomplishment" lies in his care and caution, in his linguistic "scruples" (32). Thus the "male creator" turns out not to be a dominating force. Indeed, notwithstanding all his talk about the phallic exigencies of writing in German, Kraus ultimately theorizes: "Thought is in the world, but one does not yet have it. It is refracted through the prism of material experience into linguistic elements. The artist gathers them into thought. A thought is something found, something found again and again. Whoever searches for it is a true discoverer, even when someone else had found it before him" (25). According to this scheme, all we can really do is quote language: The author's task is to "discover" and "gather" linguistic elements. If we are careful and inspired, we might be able to cite language creatively, "gathering" in novel ways what "someone else" has already "found." But anything like the notion of masculine "self-authorship" and originality that Weininger idealized is, by these standards, a false value, even a blueprint for serious linguistic trouble.[123]

In aphorisms and other essays too Kraus rejects the dream of heterosexual male domination over language. This tendency is worth noting because it further indicates that he was being less than sincere when he measured Heine's success in terms of linguistic virility. Kraus wrote, for example: "I have only mastered the language of others. Mine does with me whatever it wants to."[124] Far from being "mastered" by the male artist, language has its way with him. Not only that, Kraus exalted metaphors as the "perversities of language."[125] An illuminating figure, he enthused, will deviate from standard usages, just as perversion deviates from standard sexual behavior. So, again, we should be cautious in identifying parallels between "Heine and the Consequences" and the rigid linguistic moralism of Heine's antisemitic critics.

At the beginning of the text, Kraus borrows their strategy of sexualizing Heine's language in order to decry spectacularly the social effects of the feuilleton. After all, Kraus really did believe that this style corroded the foundations of ethical life. But his hostility to patriarchal conceptions of linguistic propriety soon becomes manifest. We first encounter the German language as a woman looking for "a real man." Not long thereafter, however, we find Kraus revering language in a different key. He treats language as a miraculous, active, creative source. Language responds to scruples and self-doubt, not to attempts at mastery through acquisitive, predatory "seizing." Rather than hunting and conquering, the true artist searches and harvests "linguistic elements" that he has no part in creating. Here language seems to be an autogenetic force, and the male artist is hardly in a position to impregnate it. He opens himself up to language, letting it do to him whatever it, or—because the word for language in German *(Sprache)* is feminine—whatever *she* wants to.

Exploding his own dualities once again, Kraus contends that his own "newspaper" has artistic, even prophetic vision: "What lives from content dies with content. What lives in language lives with language. . . . How easily we read the maunderings of the Sunday paper. . . . With what difficulty we read the sentences of *Die Fackel!* . . . The event was near, and the perspective reached far. It was all written out in advance. It was veiled so that the curious day would have to wait. Now the veils will be lifted" ("HC," 14). Standard journalistic writing might live from, and lose relevance with, the ephemeral events it covers, but Kraus's anti-journalism does just the opposite. It "lives with language," the German language. Like art, or as art, his style is always news. Kraus's *Fackel* reports, furthermore, with inspired perspicacity, "it was all written out in advance," and also with poetic indirection, "it was veiled." These ideals are very different from, and even antithetical to, the call for a separation of art and "instrument" in which both Anderson and Gilman see an anti-Jewish subtext.

In effect, then, the distancing movement in "Heine and the Consequences" is a double movement. Kraus sets his *Fackel* in opposition to the dangerously bedizened "Sunday paper." But he does more than lay out his key formal principles against this foil. He also does more than complicate matters by constructing paradoxes that obscure his position. Radicalizing his self-fashioning greatly, Kraus develops his stylistic commitments in such a way that they engage innovatively and critically with a whole nexus of important ideas about journalism and German-Jewish identity. Consider what he does with associations between the feuilleton and the otherness of the German-Jewish intellect, or its lack of originality and virile mastery over language. Kraus loudly *activates* these associations, only to reprove Heine for subscribing to the linguistic values that govern them. As he proceeds, Kraus posits *doubly* counter-ideals, ones to which his actual practices in *Die Fackel* had recently begun to correspond. They include the aim of having a self-consciously mimetic relation to language, of acknowledging that one "lives with language" by quoting it. *Die Fackel* becomes a maverick antijournalism over against *both* the "versified journalism" ("HC," 22) of Heine and his Jewish followers *and* established chauvinistic thinking about the limits of their minds and their journalistic prose.

Indeed, when Kraus wants to counterpose to Heine a positive example of satirical humor, he adduces a French Jew, the operettist Jacques Offenbach ("HC," 29).[126] This paradox should prompt us to rethink further the brazen premises that introduce the essay. For if we interpret its opening argument—that German and French culture are fundamentally different from each other—literally, then how are we to understand its invocation of Offenbach? Kraus himself warns us against literalism in a belated epilogue, which he wrote in 1911.[127] There he states that he does not want to make Heine alone responsible for the advent of feuilletonism. If we come away from "Heine and the Consequences" with this reading, we have misread him, he tells us. A year later, Kraus poked fun at those among his audience who saw his text as the act of a puerile antisemitic contrarian.[128] In a fictional dialogue Kraus has one such reader say: "The whole world is for Heine. He has to be against Heine. . . . The horrible antisemite!" ("HF," 145). So how should we understand "Heine and the Consequences"? Once more, Loos provides an illuminating analogy, this time with regard to the genre status of Kraus's satirical essay. "Ornament and Crime" facetiously recounts the origins of the ornament—all the way back to prehistoric times—while developing a sophisticated analysis of contemporary culture. "Heine and the Consequences" works in a similar mode. Kraus uses a hyperbolic genealogical conceit ("Without Heine, no feuilleton") as a framework for more provocative hyperbole and also for theories and exegesis that dramatically, and even poignantly, undermine its own over-the-top assertions. As Kraus informs his readers, one of his goals is to make them struggle: "How difficult were the sentences of *Die Fackel!*" The most famous sentences in "Heine and the Consequences" appear to be easy enough to comprehend (e.g., "Heine loosened the corsets of the German language"), but after finishing the essay it is often hard to know what to do with them.

First, Kraus evokes a Heine who resembles an antisemitic caricature. Then he spurns Bartels and his antisemitic "Heine hatred." In doing so he dismantles the biases on which his original image of Heine stands, e.g., that because Jews do not have access to the deeper regions of the German language, they resort to superficial formal "tricks." Toward the end of the text, in fact, Kraus implies that Heine himself became a true poet of the German language when he began to write about Jewish motifs. He lauds Heine's neo-Jeremian "Lamentations" and also *Romanzero,* the anthology that contains both "Lamentations" and the "Hebrew Melodies." Tellingly, he execrates Heine's most popular works, the poetry and journalism that Heine the cultural outsider used to "break into" the center of German culture. According to Kraus, those texts display an overdetermined patriarchal aggression toward language, a swaggering, driven presumption of mastery. Where German-Jewish writing seems to be caught up in a mercenary project of assimilationism and cultural advancement, Kraus treats it with extreme derision, polemically distinguishing himself from this writing. Witness, again, how he responded to Harden and Kerr. The real problem with Heine is not Jewish deviance and effeminacy, but rather something altogether different. When Heine finally embraced his own outsider status, he became, paradoxically, a linguistic insider for Kraus.

A similar logic lies behind Kraus's observation about how fast "every Itzig Witzig today rhymes *ästhetisch* [aesthetic] with *Teetisch* [tea-table]" ("HC," 16). What Kraus emphasizes is that they rhyme with such "speed." The journalists who write in Heine's style share his bad linguistic ethics. They too step on Kraus's linguistic scruples. After all, Kraus mandated care, doubt, hesitation, and even a certain passivity toward language. Moreover, through the crude label "Itzig Witzig" Kraus marks the hasty journalistic "talents" in question as being Jewish. "Itzig" is the Yiddish word for the name Issac; "Witzig" is a play on the German word for joke, *Witz.* The tag "Itzig Witzig" thus gives Kraus's statement additional meaning. It reinforces his analysis of the ethnic character of the feuilleton style, as well as his acerbic tone. But none of that necessarily betrays that Kraus "accepted" important parts of antisemitic ideology. Above all, perhaps, the expression "Itzig Witzig" performatively separates Kraus from the Jewish journalists whom he finds so suspect, even if it, like the "Teetisch" rhyme, also refers to a famous phrase in the poetry of their model, Heine.[129] Recall how the terms "Schmock" and "schlemiel" function in Kraus's polemics against Harden and Kerr. As it does in those cases, Kraus's vocabulary contrasts with the language that he is criticizing. Whereas the parvenu Jewish literati couple the words of refined society ("ästhetisch" and "Teetisch"), Kraus is happy to use rhymes that have the sound of Yiddish ("Itzig Witzig").[130]

At the conclusion of his text, Kraus makes the link between Jewishness and feuilletonistic language even more graphic by portraying Heine as a modern Moses. "Heine was a Moses who with his staff struck the rock of the German language . . . water did not flow out of the rock . . . but rather, Eau de Cologne" ("HC," 33). If Heine was a Moses, then, like Moses, Heine must have transformed Jewish culture. Otherwise, there would be little basis for the comparison. Yet, unlike Moses, who conjured life-sustaining forces and created a new culture out of his followers—Heine himself described Moses as an artist whose work was the Jewish people—Kraus's Heine is a dandy who could give his people only Eau de Cologne. Hannah Arendt famously regarded Heine as the paradigmatic Jewish "pariah" of the nineteenth century, as the embodiment of the Jewish critical spirit. In Kraus's text he belongs mainly to the opposite category.[131] Kraus's Heine is a Jewish parvenu. He deals in the sweet, non-nourishing superficialities of Western culture. But, again, as a Moses, Heine remains a transformative moment for the Jews. Thus Kraus suggests that Heine's feuilletonistic writing, a verbal Eau de Cologne, has a kind of foundational significance in German-Jewish culture, or for the turn-of-the-century Jewish literati, "the consequences." If Heine is a foppish Moses in assimilated Jewish culture, his textual legacy, feuilletonism, would amount to its saccharine sacred text.

Kraus's fanciful scenario gives his readers a satirical emblem of what he perceives to be a real problem: the proclivity of assimilated Jews for the feuilleton. Assimilated Jews follow Heine and "swindle" their way into German culture through the feuilleton, where they exhibit—since the feuilleton tries to be at once literature and reportage—both an apparent artistic intimacy with the German language and their cultural erudition. And it is all so easy. Every "Itzig Witzig" can rhyme with great speed. By applying antisemitic language to their idol, Heine, Kraus dramatically distinguishes himself from them. From there he distinguishes his analysis of the "Jewish feuilleton" and his *Fackel* from antisemitic constructions of journalism, including the antisemitic constructions that introduce his text. He does so, again, by aligning his hypermimetic anti-journalism with an innovative set of *counter*-ideals and practices, with ideals and practices that run directly counter to the guiding ones in the discussions that made the feuilleton into a privileged marker of Jewishness.

Yet there are more twists in the text. In assuming the perspective of a sovereign, playful observer who sees Heine as a coxcombical Moses, Kraus puts space between himself and Heine. At the same time, Kraus's humor evokes Heine's. More specifically, Kraus's Heine-Moses calls to mind Heine's cultural reports from his Parisian exile. Ruminating on his physical breakdown in 1848, Heine also travestied a mythical figure whose powers had abated. The epilogue to *Romanzero* stages his collapse in front of the statue of Venus de Milo in the Louvre. Heine looks up at Venus and knows that she wants to help him. However, much like Kraus's diminished modern Moses, Venus cannot save anyone now because she has no arms.[132] In a text in which oppositions between French and German culture, between cognitive effeminacy and linguistic success, between Jewish pretenders and real German artists, and between journalism and real art melt away, at least for one moment, so too does the distance between the ironic author and the subject of his irony.

This move is part of a larger pattern. For example, in the essay "He's Still a Jew" ["Er ist doch e Jud," 1913], Kraus's most comprehensive statement about his attitude toward "Jewish things," identification with Jewish culture gets the last word. And it gets that word after much deconstructing and disavowing. Having asserted that he does not know what Jewish characteristics are, Kraus insists that he does not have any, whereupon he allows that he has a crucial one. Precisely the linguistic sensibilities that set him apart from fast rhyming Jewish feuilleton writers are, he implies, a kabbalistic inheritance.[133] No doubt such self-portraiture facilitated those panegyrics in which Kraus appears as an "arch-Jew." But, of course, in order to understand how "Jewish significance" accrued to Kraus's writing—and especially to its mimetic features—we need to look closely at his style itself. My next chapter attempts to do just that.

CHAPTER THREE

Mirror-Man

I am perhaps the first case of an author who simultaneously experiences his writing as an actor. —Karl Kraus

One of the best-known evocations of German-Jewish literature comes from a letter by Franz Kafka. Addressing his friend Max Brod in June 1921, Kafka remarked: "Most Jews who began to write in German wanted to get away from Judaism, generally with the vague approval of their fathers (it was the vagueness that was so infuriating). But with their back legs they stuck to the Judaism of the fathers, and with their front legs they found no new ground. Their despair over this was their inspiration."[1] Less well known is that Kafka arrives at these ideas through reckoning with Kraus.[2]

"Quite awhile ago, I read Kraus's *Literature,* you must be familiar with it?" Kafka asks Brod as he turns from daily affairs, e.g., the weather and his health, to the topic of German-Jewish writing (*KB* 1:61.335–36). *Literatur oder man wird da sehn* (1921) is a satirical drama in which Kraus mocks another of Kafka's friends, Franz Werfel, who had recently published a drama that satirized Kraus: *Mirror-Man* [*Spiegelmensch,* 1920].[3] There Werfel creates a Kraus cipher, "Mirror-Man," whose chief talent is "acoustic mirroring," and whose foibles include crass self-aggrandizement and acidulous Jewish self-hatred.[4] In his reply Kraus lampoons the would-be mythopoeic character of Werfel's expressionism, in part by trying to show how the grand sweep of Werfel's writing results from a very local process of Jewish assimilation.[5] Thus *Literature* resembles Kraus's polemics against Harden and Heine. As he does in those texts, Kraus attempts to connect stylistic overreaching with an overdetermined Jewish desire to exhibit stylistic mastery in the German language.[6]

But *Literature* probes an added dimension of this dynamic. It suggests that generational conflict underlies the stiltedness of German-Jewish expressionism. The young authors in Kraus's play stylize themselves as myth-making German *Dichter* and promote a neo-romantic, antibourgeois ideal of authentic "experience" [*Erlebnis*] as a way of flouting their fathers, who are at a different stage of assimilation. Although the fathers evince no real affinity for Jewish ritual life and have given their sons names from the pantheon of German classicism—for example, "Johann Wolfgang"—they are self-consciously Jewish figures. Their speech abounds with Yiddish, and they often advert to their Jewish heritage.[7] Moreover, for the fathers, acculturation means achieving wealth or straightforwardly distancing themselves from a ghetto existence. So the sons' mystagogic airs and disdain for practical activities leave the fathers feeling miffed—that is, until the sons' writing turns out to be lucrative. *Literature* ends with the fathers placated and the grandfather, who sits silently during the play, opening his eyes and emitting a plangent "Oy."[8] Through this line Kraus offers what could well be his own view on such intergenerational reconciliation. In his letter to Brod, in fact, Kafka likens Kraus's perspective to the grandfather's. And Kraus's climactic "Oy" further ridicules Werfel's drama. For Werfel concludes *Mirror-Man* by having Thamal, the *positive* foil against which Mirror-Man seems so depraved, "bring forth, with the last strength of his soul, the holy, world-encompassing syllable, Om!!!!!"[9]

Where Kafka calls *Literature* "extraordinarily accurate," and lauds the "truth" in Kraus's "writing hand," he appears to be alluding to the critique of German-Jewish writing I just described (*KB* 336). After wondering why "Jews are drawn so irresistibly to German literature," and noting that German literature has become "less multifarious" [*mannigfaltig*] since the "emancipation of the Jews" (337), Kafka observes: "And that these two things hang together with Judaism as such, and more precisely, with the relation of young Jews to their Judaism, with the terrible inner state of these generations, Kraus recognized that particularly well" [*das hat doch besonders Kraus erkannt*]. Furthermore, Kafka prefaces the famous verbal image I cited above—in which the "front legs" of German-Jewish authors "find no new ground"—with an approving reference to the "father complex" in Kraus's play: "More than psychoanalysis, what appeals to me in this case is the idea that the father complex, from which some [Jews] nourish themselves intellectually, does not have to do with the innocent father, but rather with the Judaism of the father" (337).

Kafka seldom praised univocally; and in his letter to Brod he does not depart from his personal norm. For instance, Kafka maintains that Kraus writes "boring poems" (*KB* 337), though he adds that Kraus has a "certain justification" for doing so. Some elements of *Literature* are, for Kafka, "pitifully lamentable" (336). Harsher still is the intimation that Kraus suffers from the very syndrome—the bad "relation to Judaism" and the attendant "terrible inner state"—which he diagnoses with special perspicacity: "Kraus recognized that particularly well." Having credited Kraus with bringing German Jewry's literary discontents to light, Kafka suggests that these problems also "became visible through him." Elsewhere Kafka supposedly remarked: "Karl Kraus locks Jewish authors in his hell, watches over them, disciplines them strictly. However, he forgets that he also belongs in this hell."[10] Kraus is, it seems, part of the tormented scene that *Literature* portrays. His work too "hangs together with Judaism." According to Kafka, Kraus's "boring poems" are analogous to the grandfather's "Oy." They are an *insider's* response to the German-Jewish cultural debacle, a "boring" response that at least breaks with the turgidity of its impetus. Hence, perhaps, Kraus's "certain justification" for writing them.

Kafka's most striking comments about Kraus are at once similar to, and appreciably more flattering than, his reading of Kraus's poetry: "No one can speak *Mauscheln* like Kraus, even though in this German-Jewish world there is scarcely someone who can do anything except speak *Mauscheln*" (*KB* 336). If Kraus's *Mauscheln* is unique—"no one can speak *Mauscheln* like Kraus"—his use of *Mauscheln* puts him squarely "in this German-Jewish world," since what one does there is precisely speak *Mauscheln*.[11] But how is Kraus's *Mauscheln* so singular? And what does Kafka mean when he writes, "there is scarcely someone who can do anything except speak *Mauscheln*"? What is this *Mauscheln?* Kafka defines *Mauscheln* unconventionally. Whereas the term, which derives from the Hebrew-Yiddish word for Moses, generally connoted German-Yiddish dialect, or *Jargon,* Kafka proposes that *Mauscheln* is not characterized by solecisms and Yiddishisms.[12] Rather than having to do with grammatical deviance, the problematic nature of *Mauscheln* turns on the issues of legitimacy and true vitality: "*Mauscheln* taken in its broadest sense, which is the only sense in which it should be taken, is a boisterous or furtive or self-lacerating appropriation of someone else's property, something not earned, but rather stolen through a (relatively) hasty hand, and something that remains foreign property, even when it cannot be shown to exhibit a single grammatical mistake" (336). That *Mauscheln* "remains *foreign* property" and originates in a "hasty hand" or "gesture," as Kafka's word, *Griff,* has also been translated, seems to determine its constitution. For Kafka proceeds to claim: "It [*Mauscheln*] is an organic coupling of paper German and a language of gestures [*Gebärdensprache*]."

Despite its enduring estrangement from the fluidity of colloquial German—despite its status as part "paper German," that is—*Mauscheln* can be "beautiful," according to Kafka. Yet it is also a "linguistic middle position" [*sprachlicher Mittelstand*] that exists in a no man's land between the two things that "still live" in language: "dialects" and "the most personal high German" (*KB* 337). Indeed, *Mauscheln* is ultimately "nothing but ashes." *Mauscheln* has only the "appearance of life" [*Scheinleben*], thanks to the "hyperactive Jewish hands" [*überledendige Judenhände*] that "stir" it (337). In contrast to this frenetic hollowness, Kraus's "writing hand" is as "frighteningly physical" [*beängstigend körperlich*] as Kafka's (336). Thus Kafka's hand metaphors form a paradox, a paradox whose conspicuousness has not prevented it from being overlooked in scholarly accounts of the letter to Brod. How can Kraus produce *Mauscheln* when his "writing hand" differs saliently from the "hyperactive Jewish hands" that "stir" *Mauscheln,* as well as from the larcenous, "(relatively) hasty hand" that sets *Mauscheln* into motion?[13] The reason appears to be as follows: like his "boring" poetry, Kraus's *Mauscheln* is a Jewish *response* to the verbal deeds of those "Jewish hands." Kafka speaks of how Kraus "has so admirably *subordinated himself*" (my emphasis) to the dominant "principle" in "this small world of German-Jewish literature" (336). Shortly thereafter he makes the observation that "the humor" in *Literature* "is mainly the *Mauscheln*" (336). And given the play's focus on *mimicking* Jewish expressionist voices, which, as Kraus depicts them, correspond to Kafka's unusual definition of *Mauscheln,* it seems fair to infer that in Kafka's letter Kraus's *Mauscheln* is a satiric mirroring of German-Jewish literature. "Admirably," and with singular effectiveness, Kraus has "subordinated himself" to its governing "principle." Again, "no one can speak *Mauscheln* like Kraus." For Kafka, then, *Literature* offers a simulacrum of *Mauscheln* that facilitates "recognition" (337) of where German-Jewish literature stands—and of where its authors "stick." As Kraus himself once declared, "In art what matters is *who* speaks *Mauscheln.*"[14]

Of course, with this line Kraus did not mean to imply that he himself spoke *Mauscheln.* Yet when Kafka attached that term to Kraus's mimetic exploits, he was not exactly labeling them against the grain. No doubt

Kraus sought for himself a central place in German letters. But he did so in complex, paradoxical, daringly counterintuitive ways. For example, he positioned his anti-journalism over against a series of *dominant* cultural values, or over against the ideals of authenticity and originality that Werfel mobilizes against him in *Mirror-Man*. Kraus also explicitly aligned his radical mirroring with the cultural margins—with "minor" forms that were in some cases close to conventional notions of *Mauscheln*. I touched on this aspect of his self-stylizing in the previous chapter. My focus, however, lay elsewhere. So here, in a chapter that will eventually show how Kraus's mimetic practices hang together with his difficult "Jewish question," I want to expand my analysis of his self-fashioning. Once again I will concentrate on that formative moment in his career: the years before the First World War. Moreover, as I proceed I will at times compare Kraus to Kafka, who famously valorized Yiddish literature as a "minor literature," locating in it a great vitality, one that contrasts directly with the lifeless *Mauscheln* he would attribute to Kraus's German-Jewish antagonists.[15] My hope is that considering certain (neglected) affinities between Kraus and Kafka will help us to situate Kraus's anti-journalism, or rather to re-situate it, within the world of German-Jewish modernism.

OF MAUSCHELN AND MIMESIS

Not long after he had published "Heine and the Consequences," and in the same year in which Kafka delivered his "Lecture on the Yiddish Language" ["Rede über die jiddische Sprache"], Kraus wrote a particularly suggestive piece about a theater troupe that performed in Jewish dialect. Originally entitled "My Proposal" ["Mein Vorschlag," 1912], the article was reprinted under a more dramatic heading: "The Last Actors" ["Die letzten Schauspieler," 1922]. Both titles warrant discussing. "My Proposal" refers to an assertion that Kraus had hazarded in June 1911, the upshot of which is that Vienna's prestigious and periodically unused Burgtheater should be leased to the Budapester Orpheumgesellschaft.[16] Why this move surprised some of Kraus's readers, including the eminent theater director Alfred von Berger, is hardly puzzling. Kraus, who liked to point out small grammatical mistakes and stylistic infelicities in the press, had a reputation for being a language "purist," for being a protector of his beloved German language. And while the Budapester Orpheumgesellschaft seems to have enjoyed considerable popularity in fin-de-siècle Vienna, it was ultimately regarded as an un-German *shtetl* institution.[17] In his novel *The Road into the Open*

[*Der Weg ins Freie*, 1908], for example, Arthur Schnitzler has an antisemitic aristocrat wish that he could ghettoize German-Jewish playwrights through the rule: "Only the Budapester Orpheumgesellschaft would be allowed to stage dramatic works by Jews [dürften Stücke von Juden überhaupt nur von der Budapester Orpheumgesellschaft aufgeführt werden]."[18]

Yet Kraus's "proposal" did not simply function as a vehicle through which to shock his audience and denigrate Viennese theater, though part of his message is that Vienna's theater community has sunk into a bad state. By writing that the Budapester Orpheumgesellschaft is "the only real theatrical pleasure offered by a Vienna that no longer has [Alexander] Girardi" (*F* 324–25:23), Kraus colorfully stressed Vienna's theatrical impoverishment. The other part of Kraus's message, however, is that the Budapester Orpheumgesellschaft is a "real theatrical pleasure," and that, as he would imply with his titular homage, a theater troupe that operates in *Mauscheln* provides the city's "last actors."

Kraus might not have displayed quite the kind of searching enthusiasm for Eastern Jewish culture that Kafka exhibited, yet he does seem to have genuinely enjoyed the antic farces of the Budapester Orpheumgesellschaft. Often accompanied by his friends Oskar Kokoschka and Adolf Loos, he went repeatedly to see "the Budapester" perform.[19] Moreover, this practice corresponds to a larger pattern of behavior, one that his worth sketching out in some detail. Kraus championed "minor" forms elsewhere too, both ardently and circumspectly. Indeed, if he adulated Shakespeare and Goethe, he embraced Offenbach's operettas and Nestroy's comedies, neither of which counted as art for the ages, at least as energetically. Late in Kraus's career, Offenbach even became a kind of mission: Kraus devoted a large chunk of his time and energy to "rescuing" Offenbach and to promoting an Offenbach revival.

After witnessing, in 1924, what he deemed to be an "unworthy" performance of *Bluebeard* at the Carl-Theater, Kraus retranslated Meilhac and Halévy's libretto, rearranging the dialogue to fit his style of dramatic reading (*F* 717–23:99). He performed the text on stage in February 1926. It would prove to be the first of many readings. In fact, during the last decade of his life Kraus dedicated more than a third of his stage performances to Offenbach: 123 of 346, by Kari Grimstad's reckoning.[20] He was so successful in generating interest in Offenbach that he soon felt the need to save Offenbach again, this time from the famous German-Jewish director Max Reinhardt and the official "Offenbach Renaissance" that he, Kraus, had done more than anyone to create (*F* 757–58:38–48). The problem here, according to

Kraus, is that by assimilating Offenbach to its standards, conventional theater denatured him. For whereas conventional theater offers its audience meanings they can process, the great power of operetta lies in its being "nonsense." Operetta at its best conveys something of the world's absurdity. So to domesticate it, to make of operetta "Salonoperetta," as Reinhardt does, is to operate against the spirit of the form. Operetta was for Kraus what it was for Siegfried Kracauer: an outsider form, an "exile genre."[21]

If Kraus began to perform Offenbach's works late, he developed an investment in them early on. This investment had to do, apparently, with an erotic one. Shortly after founding *Die Fackel,* Kraus saw a production of Offenbach's *Tales of Hoffmann.* In it was a young actress named Annie Kalmar, with whom Kraus fell in love, immediately and deeply: she died two years later, leaving him devastated.[22] And, as Edward Timms has noted, Kraus formed a lasting association between the adored actress and the stage role in which he first beheld her.[23] More relevant for us, however, is that Kraus laid the theoretical groundwork for his attack against Reinhardt's "Offenbach Renaissance" just around the time during which he wrote "The Last Actors." Indeed, in "rescuing" operetta from Reinhardt, Kraus extensively cited an essay he had published in 1909, "Grimacing over Culture and the Stage" ["Grimasse über Kultur und Bühne," 1909].[24] It is here that Kraus first celebrated the "thought-provoking" nonsense in operetta, how out of its nonsense serious thought about the world emerges. And it is here that he first distinguished between operetta's real and domesticated forms. In doing so Kraus decries the alliance between the banal "Salonoperetta" and the feuilleton writers who have supported it (*F* 289:4). He thereby links his predilection for what he constructs as, in effect, unassimilated operetta to his hostility to the aesthetic values of acculturated feuilleton writers. "Grimacing over Culture and the Stage" thus directly suggests, among other things, that Kraus's passion for Offenbach's operettas reinforces his status as an anti-journalist. Written almost contemporaneously with that text, "Heine and the Consequences" (1910) contains a similar gesture. After all, Kraus plays Offenbach off against the essay's main target: the feuilleton.

So Kraus goes far beyond casually appreciating operetta as a boisterous alternative to more conventional, more staid cultural offerings. He prizes and parses its core virtues, trying to uncover its "essence." While integrating operetta into his critique of the feuilleton, he attempts to differentiate, to show in exact ways that not all operettas have Offenbach's strengths. And he asserts for operetta a provocatively special place in the world of theater. According to Kraus, operetta is "the only dramatic form that is completely equal to the possibilities of theater," because in it music and theatricality merge into a "'Gesamtkunstwerk'" (*F* 270-71:8-9). By putting the term "Gesamtkunstwerk" between quotation marks, Kraus heavily accentuates the iconoclastic character of his claim. He makes clear that he is ascribing to operetta, a genre whose very name connotes diminutive standing, a position traditionally associated with that superlatively major form, Wagner's operas. His point that operetta is the true "Gesamtkunstwerk" becomes clearer still when, on the next page, he compares the sublime nonsense of operetta to "a Wagner opera's exercises in worship, which are theatrical nonsense."

During the same period, Kraus advanced analogous ideas about vaudeville, or "Varieté." "Vaudeville is given only a narrow space to set up its mirror," an essay from 1909 begins (*F* 289:17). Yet within that space it too reveals much more about the difficult truths of our existence than do most theatrical forms. "Theater tickles. Vaudeville whips" (*F* 289:17). Sounding very much like the French theorist Henri Bergson, Kraus comments on the key figure in vaudeville: "The knockabout—that is the triumph of mechanical culture. He represents us all. His humor is groundless, just as we ourselves are. He has effect without cause, just as we ourselves come from nowhere in order to move on again. His violent humor encompasses the whole tragedy of our enslavement to goals, and the huge dimensions of his gestures have no model in a single human type" (*F* 289:19). Though consigned to a "narrow space," vaudeville, like the improbable "Gesamtkunstwerk" of operetta, expands into something large, into a mirror of the world: the knockabout "represents us all" with his "gestures of huge dimensions." What they reflect is deeper than surface-level phenomena—what they reflect has "no model in a single human type." Vaudeville at its most forceful is, in addition, "violent." "Vaudeville whips." In some slightly earlier thoughts, Kraus indicates that when vaudeville becomes tamer, when it provides its audience with comfort, its artistic value dissipates (*F* 279-80:12). Once again the most effective modern art comes from the margins and exhibits the sort of disturbing "undomesticated mimesis" that Adorno would later attribute to Kraus.[25]

Similarly, in the essay "He's Still a Jew" (1913) Kraus resolutely exalts two borderline indigent, decidedly noncanonical authors. There he claims, "the works of the Jews Peter Altenberg and Else Lasker-Schüler stand closer to God and to language than anything Germanic writing [*deutsche Schrifttum*] has brought forth in the fifty years since Herr [Hermann] Bahr has been alive."[26] Thus it is simply misleading to contend, as quite a few critics have, that Kraus campaigned for a chauvinistic version of linguistic purity, "a good language." Not only did he mock the idea of "purifying language," as well as the pedantry of Eduard Engel, a German Jew who tried to deliver his fellow German Jews from the blight of *Mauscheln,* Kraus also argued *for* using foreign words in German. When Alfred Kerr accused him of employing "Austrianisms," and when Werfel captiously spotted a Yiddishism in his prose, his defense was to question the narrow standards on which those charges rested.[27] For Kraus, all linguistic elements, even the most quotidian and the most cacophonous, have the potential to be poetry. What matters is how they are used, and therefore who uses them. "In art what matters is *who* speaks *Mauscheln.*"

But what conveys the seriousness of Kraus's views on the Budapester Orpheumgesellschaft is not only how they connect with a larger trend in his works. Just as important is the character of the encomium itself, its analytic character. In "The Last Actors" Kraus responds to the bemusement his original "proposal" caused and *explains* why the Budapester Orpheumgesellschaft—and especially its leader, Heinrich Eisenbach—have his respect. He focuses on Eisenbach's mimetic skills. With Eisenbach, the "repeated word" takes on "the power of recreated life" ("LS," 153). Eisenbach is, moreover, capable of a "complete metamorphosis of the soul" (154). Nowhere is this talent more evident than in a skit that entails imitating an English artist who has to imitate the movements and demeanor of a chimpanzee. Eisenbach's uncanny "metamorphosis," which "belongs to the most moving impressions" that Kraus "has taken from the theater" in "twenty-five years" (155), would "send a shudder down the spine of the dullest audience" (154). And so, it seems, would another instance of Eisenbach's hypermimesis, of his ability to portray someone copying someone—or something—else. By "having an ur-Viennese locksmith apprentice imitate Jewish *Jargon,*" Eisenbach produces "a full, old image of the outer Vienna" (154).

I described "The Last Actors" as "particularly suggestive" for a number of reasons. Like Kafka's contemporaneous "Lecture on the Yiddish Language," through which Kafka introduced to an audience of German-speaking Jews a Yiddish theater troupe that he fervently admired, Kraus's essay inverts an established hierarchy. Yiddish culture, whose lowly status in the turn-of-the-century German imagination scholars have abundantly documented, is rehabilitated in both texts. But Kraus's inversion might be even more radical than Kafka's, despite certain appearances to the contrary. After all, it is Kafka's text that attributes mysterious powers to the Yiddish language. Kafka enthuses: "Once *Jargon* [Yiddish] has touched you—and *Jargon* is everything, word, Hasidic melody and the very essence of these Eastern Jewish actors—then you will no longer recognize your earlier peace

[*Ruhe*]. Then you will feel the true unity of *Jargon*, so strong that you will be afraid, not of *Jargon*, but rather of yourselves."[28] With its mystical "unity"—"*Jargon* is everything"—Yiddish holds out transformative, even redemptive, possibilities. Experiencing "the true unity of *Jargon*" means, for the Western Jews in Kafka's audience, becoming drastically and productively alienated from their former selves. It means no longer being able to "recognize" a "peace" that stands over against the "true unity" and strength of Yiddish, and thus seems false and superficial.

As numerous commentators have emphasized, Kafka's projection of an inspiring "unity" onto Yiddish has to do with the discontent that he ventilates in his letter to Brod. More precisely, it has to do with the sense that Jews who wrote in German—or in *Mauscheln*—were precariously suspended between two cultures. Kafka's "Lecture on the Yiddish Language" is, in other words, an expression of longing on the part of a writer who once apostrophized himself as "the most Western-Jewish of all Jews." Ernst Pawel makes this point eloquently: "What he [Kafka] sought in Judaism was not so much faith as a living community, one in which he could himself be a living part. And therein resided the seductive magic of [the Eastern Jewish actor] Yitzhak Levi [*sic*] and his players: eight messengers from the world in which his own father had been a son, kindred spirits to a spirit that was stirring within him, speaking his own lost language, rooted and secure in their unassailable identity as Jews, Jewish in the way the Czechs were Czech, the Germans German—and he himself was nothing."[29] Of course, Kafka was not the only German-speaking Jew who sought a redeeming existential fullness in Eastern Jewish folkways and in an organic connection to an ur-language that had been "lost" but not forgotten. (Kafka begins his lecture by telling his audience: "You understand much more Yiddish than you believe.") To prepare for his talk, Kafka discussed Yiddish culture with members of Prague's Bar Kochba Verein. And several other figures with ties to that Zionist organization, e.g., Nathan Birnbaum, Fritz Mordecai Kaufmann, and Martin Buber, found mystical depth and creative force in the lifestyle and language of *Ostjudentum*.

That Kraus dismisses the importance of the language spoken by Eisenbach and his troupe is therefore remarkable. Simply bringing *Mauscheln* into the Burgtheater would "prove nothing" ("LS," 155), he contends. "What matters," for Kraus, is the mimetic talent with which Eisenbach "speaks *Mauscheln*." Instead of locating in Yiddish culture qualities that assimilated German Jews were supposed to *lack*—for example, an authentic relation to a living language—Kraus sees and venerates in the Budapester Orpheumgesellschaft a capacity that was insistently and damningly *imputed to* German Jews. He sees and venerates a capacity that both Germans and German Jews framed as the very mechanism behind the Jews' putative foreignness to cultural authenticity: their "reproductive" intelligence. Consider the derision that Kraus's mimetic talent prompted, or how Werfel, for instance, selected it as his chief target in parodying Kraus as a self-hating and cognitively debilitated Mirror-Man. In the same year Franz Blei, another expressionist writer, gave Kraus the following entry in his *Great Bestiary of Modern Literature* [*Das große Bestiarium der modernen Literatur*]: "The Fackelkraus.... Characterized by its ability to imitate human voices.... It imitates the voices of prophets and poets in order to be like them and in order to be confused with them. It imitates other voices in order to lambaste and destroy them."[30]

What sort of meaning did Kraus find in the mimetic abilities that, for Blei, help one to become "*confused with* prophets and poets" and that by extension should not be mistaken for prophetic or poetic depth? Unlike Kafka, Kraus does not write of mystical unities in revering dialect-speaking actors. But as in "Heine and the Consequences," where he mandates a complete coming together of form and content, in "The Last Actors" Kraus operates in a charged, modernist discourse on form that complained about a growing disjunction between form and content and that longed for the highest possible unity, where form would be nothing less than the visible manifestation of Geist. Kraus's idealized notion of form—which he elsewhere calls "the very flesh of the mind"—and his panegyric to Yiddish theater evoke one of the most influential modernist meditations on form, Georg Lukács's *Soul and the Forms* [*Die Seele und die Formen*, 1911].[31] Taking up the preferred modernist theme of the fragmented modern self, Lukács develops various speculations as to how "forms" might help palliate that problem. Form allows for an overcoming of the alienation between "the inside and the outside." In his introductory piece on the essay form—which he addressed to Leo Popper, who published a long article on the *Formfrage* in Kraus's *Fackel*—Lukács writes: "The critic's moment of truth is that where things become forms; the moment when all feelings and experiences that used to be on this and that side of form receive a form themselves, fuse and condense into form. It is the mystical moment of union of the outside and the inside, of the soul and the form."[32]

In Kraus's writings the moment of true mimetic transformation constitutes as forceful a synthesis. Only here the "complete metamorphosis" of one "soul" enables another to be revealed. A subject becomes "merged" [*verschmolzen*],

Kraus claims, with what it is representing and thereby produces a revelatory *formal* unity.[33] Eisenbach, who possesses a kind of "mimetic genius" and effects "mimetic disclosures," to use two phrases that Benjamin attached to Kraus, gives the "repeated word" the "power of recreated life" ("KK," 364). And if the principle of revelatory mimesis is most perspicuous in the realm of acting, it can apply to criticism too. Indeed, Kraus lays out the idea of mimetic *Verschmelzung* in an article that discusses his "new journalistic form." He also foregrounded the affinity between acting and his literary work, the bulk of which consists of critical prose. Witness his pronouncement: "I am perhaps the first case of an author who simultaneously experiences his writing as an actor."[34] It seems, then, that in his account of the Budapester Orpheumgesellschaft Kraus offers an immanent hermeneutics, an interpretive justification for his own emphasis on the "repeated word."

But I am not suggesting that Kraus thought of—or that we should think of—his vaunted mimetic techniques as an Eastern Jewish inheritance.[35] Nor are they simply a response to what Kraus saw as the hazardous excesses in German-Jewish writing, or a formal vehicle through which he stylized himself against the foil of such writing. Many factors shaped the mimetic aspect of Kraus's anti-journalism. A crucial one is his linguistic turn. Kraus's muckraker's goal, "write down what exists," remained in place. Yet, having become increasingly concerned with how mass media affect the popular imagination, he shifted his focus away from exposing the corruption that existed in the form of political and journalistic graft. Kraus started to undertake the more ambitious task of showing how the press creates a swirling shadow world of mass-marketed phrases and images, which invade the minds of readers and thus help to determine the course of the "real" world.[36] Only after 1910 did he remark on the "ghostly" correspondence between "reality" and his "satires" of the press.[37] Only after 1910, furthermore, did he assert that "the newspaper talks like the world because the world talks like the newspaper"[38] and speak of how his style "shrieks" with "all the noises of the world."[39] Reproducing "all the noises of the world" demands sophisticated "acoustic mirroring." Accordingly, Kraus's mimetic activities intensified appreciably during the period of his linguistic turn.[40] The first of the fictional dialogues in which Kraus mimics journalists' voices appeared in *Die Fackel* after 1910, the first of his photomontages in 1911.[41] Of the essays by Kraus that are made up mostly of quotations, few predate his decennial watershed.[42]

When thinking about the evolution of Kraus's mimesis, we also should take into account the impact of specific historical events, such as the First

World War. Kraus understood the war to be the ineluctable result of an imaginative disorder for which he held the press responsible.[43] So the catastrophe made the need to demonstrate how the press assaulted the minds of its readers even more urgent. Kraus's augury that the "black magic" of newspaper ink would cause the "destruction of the world" was, it appeared, coming true; and he felt a new pressure to reveal compellingly how that magic worked. Moreover, the war confronted Kraus with an epochal mimetic challenge. How to reproduce "all the noises of the world" *war* in all their horror and absurdity? In *The Last Days of Mankind* [*Die letzten Tage der Menschheit*, 1919], his first dramatic work, Kraus both details the carnage of the battlefield and portrays at length Austrians' alternately benighted and sinister responses to their military demise. Very often he does so by having a whole parade of cultural types speak for themselves: his list of characters alone takes up thirteen pages. And not only do direct quotations of the press and vernacular speech comprise much of the play, but Kraus also elaborated on his innovative uses of visual media. He wrote propaganda films into his massive drama, for example, calling for them to be projected as occasional scenic backdrops.[44]

The expansive, page-long first sentence of Kraus's most famous essay about the war, "In This Great Time," mirrors the rhetorical swollenness of the moment. Yet the conflict also drove Kraus toward a mimetic minimalism. More frequently than he had before, he cited compact images and texts that, he believed, would effectively represent the utter disgrace of "mankind." For instance, during the war Kraus printed a picture of a Christ statue in Belgium whose cross, or symbol of redemption, a bomb had blown off. A photograph from the same period shows a woman and a child cozily ensconced in a rocking chair—wearing gas masks. The essay that ends with this image begins with one of a unit of flame-throwers saluting Kaiser Wilhelm with a giant, fiery "W." It carries the title "The Mirror of the World" ["Der Weltspiegel," 1918].[45] With little commentary, Kraus artfully arranged excerpts from various forms of propaganda, from Hermann Bahr's fulsome "Open Greeting to Hugo von Hofmannsthal" to war poetry that appeared in schoolbooks, literary representations of the war, and, of course, newspaper articles.[46] An unadorned double quotation from 1918, "A Kantian and Kant" ["Ein Kantianer und Kant"], lays bare the fatuity of the Kaiser's propagandistic appropriation of Kant's categorical imperative. In a two-column format Kraus juxtaposes the Kaiser's belligerent words with excerpts from Kant's essay on eternal peace.[47]

Still, Kraus's investment in mimesis has key additional points of reference. In his analysis of how the press transforms the world and colonizes the popular imagination, Kraus singled out the feuilleton, as we have seen. He argued that in mixing fiction and fact, in disseminating easily consumable "impressions" along with the news, feuilletonists make the world correspond to their poetic "tone" while obviating imaginative responses to the news. And although wartime mimetic challenges certainly helped animate the essays I described above, those pieces often read like critical reactions to, and innovative attempts to assert distance from, the "feuilletonism" of Kraus's Jewish rivals. By entitling one such essay "The Austrian Face" ["Das österreichische Anlitz," 1917], Kraus evoked both his own technique of concisely quoting emblematic material and the work of a well-known Jewish feuilletonist. Kraus evoked the work, that is, of Felix Salten, whose journalistic style and assimilationism he, Kraus, would later connect and castigate together.

Not only had Salten published an anthology of essays—several of which first appeared in the *Neue Freie Presse*—under the very same heading (*Das österreichische Anlitz*, 1909), but the book's eponymous article conveys a rather patriotic version of Austria's countenance. Salten's "The Austrian Face" sketches Kaiser Franz Joseph's features with respect, affection, and the smooth, descriptive strokes of an accomplished feuilletonistic style. "Wherever we turn, the venerable head smiles from behind a white beard, and from its eyes, which are thickly covered by white brows, comes a peaceful smile."[48] In Kraus's "Austrian Face" the assimilated Jewish feuilletonist is no longer the sovereign observer of Austria's characteristics. He has become the visage of Austria. The first half of Kraus's article belittles the social climbing of Mendel Singer, a prominent Jewish feuilletonist. The second half consists almost entirely of an obituary by Singer: Kraus quotes Singer using his journalistic medium, and the death of an influential count, as a way of flaunting his intimacy with Austria's arch-aristocracy. So through alternative formal means, Kraus draws a radically alternative "Austrian face." His stark critical mirroring yields an inverted image of Salten's picture of stately, well-meaning eminence and venerability.[49] As Kraus disrupts the conventions of feuilletonistic portraiture, he indicates that a kind of assimilationist mentality drives such journalistic forms and, with them, the dangerous surreality in Austrian culture. Hence the status of that mentality as Austria's *real Anlitz*.

During the years before the war, as his mature style was taking shape, Kraus put forth similar messages. "Heine and the Consequences" suggests that German Jews use the feuilleton as a handy, easy way of putting their "talent," their ability to rhyme with great "speed" in German, on display. Indeed, Kraus blames this impulse for the rise of the genre. In doing so he deploys *against* Heine an antisemitic discourse that equates stylistic prowess with phallic power, then, citing Heine's ideal of linguistic mastery as a virile writing "without hesitation," he accuses Heine of having adopted *those* chauvinistic standards. Thus Kraus provocatively sets his *Fackel* apart from such values. And he aligns it with very different ones. Where the feuilletonists of Vienna subscribe to the conceit that they are putting forth original impressions, Kraus will win lasting significance for *Die Fackel* by "gathering" thoughts that he did not design.[50] Where Jewish feuilletonists have made the dandyish Heine into their "Moses" and his verbal "Eau de Cologne" into their model, Kraus praises the bedridden Heine of the "Hebrew Melodies" and the ribald operettas of the French Jew Offenbach.

Consider also how "He's Still a Jew" connects with this mode of self-fashioning. Kraus actually published two essays under that title, the second of which was originally titled "I and Judaism" ["Ich und das Judentum," 1913].[51] Both articles have as a starting point letters that readers had sent to Kraus. In fact, he reproduces the full text of these notes, which query him about his Jewishness, at the beginning of each essay. Theorists of race had been interested in Kraus's relation to Judaism. The Aryan supremacist linguist Jörg Lanz von Liebenfels, who admired Kraus and whom Kraus deprecates in the second "He's Still a Jew" essay, had even labeled Kraus a "special type of Jew, the blond Jewish type."[52] Now, it seems, everyday readers too had become intrigued. Under a *general* pressure to "declare his racial colors," as Kraus himself put it, he offered more paradoxes, yet also gestured toward identifying with venerable Jewish traditions.

At first, however, Kraus avoided speaking to the matter of his Jewishness. The earlier of the two letters asks Kraus how he, a Jew, could be so critical of Jewish culture, especially given that his Jewish auditors were saying about him after his lectures: "He's still a Jew!" In his response Kraus theorizes that his personal identity is suspended during his performances. He wryly adds that he has heard his listeners make comments far more damaging than "He's still a Jew," for example, "I know him [Kraus] personally."[53]

When, shortly thereafter, a second reader challenged Kraus to address his "Jewish characteristics," Kraus wrote the later "He's Still a Jew" piece. In it he anathematizes the materialistic "language of the world" and asserts that this language is particularly rampant among, if not exclusive to, Jews. It is here that Kraus offers the damning partial syllogism I discussed at the start of chapter 1: "If I am someone who writes a lot, and someone for whom every letter is the mark of a wound, who could say that I am a journalist? It would have to be a Jewish characteristic to have no Jewish characteristics." But in the same essay he claims that "the language of the world" is not simply worldly or materialistic. It is also global—it is a language of the world because it has been "divided equally among all peoples of the world." And he elevates the beleaguered "Jews" Altenberg and Lasker-Schüler to a stratum of accomplishment high above the last fifty years of "Germanic writing." He also gives a distinctly kabbalistic flavor to his own, anti-inflationary linguistic ethics, to his deeply sensuous experience of linguistic detail. At the very end of "He's Still a Jew," Kraus writes: "What remains that could be a Jewish characteristic is this: I have destroyed a double issue of *Die Fackel* because I discovered a question mark grimacing at the world, where the punishing rod of an exclamation point should have threatened it."[54]

Published between "Heine and the Consequences" and "He's Still a Jew," "The Last Actors," in which revelatory power resides in the ability of an actor speaking *Mauscheln* to mimic an Englishman mimicking a chimpanzee, is part of the pattern those texts make up. When we read "The Last Actors" alongside such essays, we see how the text—and the mimesis it celebrates—serves to reinforce both Kraus's harsh critique of acculturated German-Jewish authors and the radical self-fashioning that goes along with his critique. Like Kafka, Kraus aspired to be a major author and appears to have felt that in a "hyperactive" literary milieu, getting to this goal would entail, among other things, identifying with small forms.[55]

TOWARD A MINOR JOURNALISM?

"You think that I read newspapers?" asks the father shortly before he condemns Georg, his son and interlocutor, to death in Kafka's breakthrough story "The Judgment" ["Das Urteil," 1912]. After posing this question, the father "throws at Georg a page of newspaper that he had somehow carried with him into bed. An old newspaper whose name Georg had never seen."[56] Georg, a reader of modern newspapers, has misread the father, having thought that the father occupied himself with the same kind of newspapers.[57] Of course, the father's statements are no more reliable than those made by Georg, about whom we know that he lies by omission in his letters to a wayward friend. The father is part righteous patriarch, part deranged old man, who in a taunting, "flute-like tone" speculates about Georg's weakness and about the lubricity of the woman to whom Georg is engaged. Not only that, pulling up his nightshirt, the father acts out how the fiancé must have "lifted her skirts" for Georg. But in the case of the father's newspaper reading, material evidence, i.e., a page from an old newspaper, supports his assertion. He does not read newspapers, at least not the sort known to Georg. What had been, for Georg, one of the few activities that the father and he shared—after eating dinner separately, "they would sit for a little while, most often each with his newspaper, in the common living room"—turns out to be a crowning disparity.[58] For we learn of this difference at the end of a scene driven by the revelation of profound incongruities between father and son, and, again, just before "the judgment."

As in Kafka's *The Metamorphosis* [*Die Verwandlung*, 1913], where Gregor the provider reads the newspaper aloud at the table to his passively listening family, and Gregor the "monstrous vermin" eats his first meal of table scraps off of newspaper, in "The Judgment" newspapers punctuate a shift in power.[59] When we first encounter the father of "The Judgment," he is sitting in a dark, fusty room, squinting at a large sheet of newspaper that he holds crosswise, "as if to compensate for some visual defect."[60] This image of frailty makes Georg think that the father has become utterly helpless, and that he, Georg, must take care of him. And so the sight of the feeble father with his newspaper corresponds, contrastively, to the scene in which the father hurls an old page of a newspaper at Georg, forcing the cowed son to realize that he had inaccurately assessed the father's mental life.

There is also the possibility that reading modern newspapers has damaged Georg's mind. Like the press in Kraus's contemporaneous accounts of it, Georg fails to report the news effectively. His missives to his friend "contain no real communication" [*keine eigentlichen Mitteilungen*].[61] The friend, who has relocated to the mythic expanses of Eastern Europe that so intrigued Kafka, comes back with stories worthy of being "told again." Georg's memory, on the other hand, seems to operate according to the rhythms of a culture in which the evening edition's headlines blot out those of the morning edition. At one point in the text, he remembers a decision that he had forgotten, only to lose the memory once more, "like one pulls a short string through the eye of a needle."[62] Toward the conclusion of the story, Georg experiences a mnemonic meltdown. He holds his thought "only for a moment, from then on he forgot everything."[63]

We find further critical commentary on journalism in Kafka's "A Report to an Academy" ["Ein Bericht für eine Akademie," 1917]. Red Peter, the ape protagonist who recounts his passage "into the world of men," maintains an attitude of extreme forbearance toward his captors. He is even ready to ascribe good intentions to a teacher who has evidently tortured him: "And to the credit of my teacher, he was not angry; sometimes he would hold his burning pipe against my fur until it began to smolder in some place I could not easily reach, but then he would extinguish it with his own kind, enormous hand."[64] Only once does Red Peter grow irate. What enrages him is a different hand, a journalist's hand, about which he has violent fantasies. According to Red Peter, one of the "the ten thousand windbags who discuss me in the newspapers" has proposed that "my ape nature is not yet under control, the proof being that when visitors come to see me, I like to take down my trousers to show them where the shot went in." "The hand that wrote this," he continues, "should have its fingers shot off one by one."[65] Because Red Peter was shot during his capture, the offending article implies that in order to be part of human society, Red Peter must literally cover up the violence through which he was brought into human society. In a sort of ironic twist, the journalistic contention that Red Peter has not assimilated himself fully "to the world of men" so angers him that, for a moment, he becomes truly like the men who scarred him with a "wanton shot." Red Peter wantonly calls for every digit of the author's writing hand to be shot off, "one by one." If, as critics have long contended, "A Report to an Academy" (which first appeared in Martin Buber's journal *The Jew*) is on some level about Jewish acculturation, then in Kafka's story as in Kraus's critical writing, journalism plays an important, complex, troubling role in that process.

But neither "A Report to an Academy" nor "The Judgment" merely allegorizes a Kraus-like critique of the press. The latter story, indeed, is one of the most radically indeterminate of Kafka's works. With good reason, scholars often appeal to Kafka's claim that he could not "find any coherent, straightforward meaning in it."[66] Certainly Georg, who undergoes a sudden transformation from successful businessman to auto-executioner, is if nothing else an enigmatic figure. So it would be silly to reduce the cause of his bad writing and his bad memory to his habit of perusing the newspaper. Furthermore, I am not concerned with the issue of influence, though we might note that by the time of his breakthrough Kafka had become familiar with *Die Fackel*. He also had been an auditor, in 1911, at one of Kraus's readings in Prague. Years later, Kafka's friend Robert Klopstock spoke of the private "orgies" of *Fackel* reading that Kafka and he "knew."[67]

For us, what is of immediate relevance is how Kafka embeds newspapers and journalistic language in a nexus that connects it with the themes of power, Jewish acculturation, misapprehension, flawed ethics, communicative emptiness, and, quite possibly, cognitive impairment. A very similar thematic constellation represents perhaps the leitmotif of Kraus's criticism. And tracking newspapers in Kafka's fiction therefore gives added depth and specificity to significant parallels between Kafka and Kraus, to the ones that come to light in the 1921 letter to Brod. It gives added depth and specificity, that is, to parallels between the ways in which Kafka and Kraus constructed an *inflated* "world of German-Jewish literature" as they constructed their own resolutely maverick, "frighteningly physical" styles. In comparing Kafka and Kraus, Adorno equated the chief injunction in their respective works: "Read every word."[68] Just how that imperative "hangs together with Judaism" is, in Kraus's case, never a simple matter. But, as I have been arguing, he seems to have developed signature features of his style in opposition to what he perceived to be the problem of a "hyperactive," fatally anti-mimetic German-Jewish writing—a problem that he "recognized particularly well," according to Kafka. It is in "Heine and the Consequences," which insistently links the feuilleton to Jewish acculturation, that Kraus most directly diagnoses the feuilletonist as "an observer who compensates himself with indulgent adjectives" for what he lacks "in nouns."[69] There too Kraus articulates the counter-ideal of keeping his style uninflated by using mostly nouns, or mostly *Hauptwörter*, "main words," as they are called in German. Kafka's works contains less explicitly oppositional self-stylizing, to be sure. Yet his pursuit of verbal economy—a pursuit that was radical even by modernist standards and helped drive his iconoclastic "minor" style—appears to have emerged in part out of a similar, similarly severe critical confrontation with German-Jewish culture. Thus when, in writing to Brod, Kafka pointed to the affinities between himself and Kraus, he was doing much more than riling his friend, who despised Kraus and hoped that Kafka's "Jewish commitments" would become greater, or at least more tangible, than they ever did.

There are, however, notable differences between Kafka's and Kraus's experience of being a Jewish author in the German language. For Christoph Stözl, "Specifically Jewish fear was the dominant motif of Kafka's life: fear of anti-Semitic threats whose danger was that once they had been uttered, one was compelled to carry them out against oneself."[70] This claim may be something of an overstatement. But Kafka was no doubt extremely sensitive to antisemitic stereotypes, and, as Sander Gilman has shown, he worried about the extent to which his work and that other corpus, his body, conformed to them.[71] Moreover, Kafka was also anxious about and famously bitter toward his father over what he felt to be his profound deracination, his status as the "most Western-Jewish of all Jews." And while he sometimes displayed great confidence in the force of his art—e.g., when he adverted to the "truth" in his "writing hand"—Kafka brooded over whether his alienation from Jewish ritual life might have somehow compromised his strengths. Accordingly, he idealized the evocative power of the Yiddish language, set about learning Hebrew, suggested that the German word for mother could not adequately convey what a Jewish mother was, and spoke of the "impossibility of writing in German" (KB 337).

Nowhere, by contrast, did Kraus question his ability to be as at home as anyone *auf deutsch*. As a physically deformed, effusively vitriolic Jewish writer who worked mostly in the sphere of journalism, Kraus was, unsurprisingly, repeatedly subjected to antisemitc ridicule. Yet he seems to have maintained considerable equanimity in the face of such derision. In 1913, for example, Kraus coolly reprinted in his *Fackel* a cartoon that depicts him with exaggeratedly "Jewish features," using the image as an occasion for drawing intricate theoretical distinctions between caricature and satire.[72] Only major catastrophes appear to have given Kraus pause, or to have led him to doubt the adequacy of his language: he notoriously fell silent at the beginning of the First World War, and again when Hitler became chancellor. But these doubts had to do with the adequacy of language in general, not with his language as a Jew writing in German. And Kraus's doubts did not last long. In fact, they soon became a topic in his writing, or material for more paradox-building. Breaking his silence in November 1914, Kraus called for silence through the long and highly stylized essay, "In this Great Time." His voluminous invective against the Nazis begins with the sentence: "I have nothing to say about Hitler."

More than antisemitic scorn, what set Kraus off were attempts to associate him with precisely the acculturated German-Jewish literati in opposition to whom he was formulating dynamic parts of his anti-journalism. Such attempts occurred with some frequency. For instance, in 1910 a member of Freud's Psychoanalytic Society argued that the enmity Kraus felt toward Moriz Benedikt derived from *filial* tension, from a father complex.[73] The ferocity with which Kraus tried to annihilate Benedikt stems, in this reading, from Kraus's delicate psychic economy and from Benedikt's status as the great patriarch of Viennese journalism, rather than from honest reservations about a corrupt press. Not long thereafter, the same critic, Fritz Wittels, struck again, suggesting that Kraus's criticisms of Jewish journalists were propelled by social greed.[74] These charges irritated Kraus, who, in addition to being sensitive to that sort of accusation, was deeply skeptical of psychoanalysis. He famously complained that "psychoanalysis is that disease of the mind for which it believes itself to be the cure."[75] But in the same text, "Longing for Aristocratic Company" ["Sehnsucht nach aristokratischem Umgang," 1914], Kraus also responds violently to the idea that the motive behind his "satires of Jews and journalism" is an assimilationist desire to make common cause with aristocrats.[76] Instead of being merely instrumental, he emphasizes, his hatred of the Jewish literati is deep and even murderous, at least on the level of metaphor. Kraus concludes his essay by wishing for a very particular kind of aristocrat: "a king with a bomb for these all-too clever subjects." That is, he wishes for a king who could wipe out the "life-threatening" "plague" of the German-Jewish literati.[77]

In "He's Still a Jew," tellingly, Kraus interprets his reader's call for clarification with regard to his Jewish identity as a challenge to explain not only the upshot of his critical attitude toward German Jewry but also its underlying causes. Hence his avowal that he has never, and would never, "deny the Jewry" from which he "stems."[78] And Kraus vigorously reproaches those Jews who "with a cold heart betray their own heritage [*Stamm*]" in order to gain cultural advantages.[79] Once again Kraus stresses that his animus toward assimilated Jews is something utterly apart. Next to it, he declares, the "aversion against Jewish things" in antisemitic "circles" is "merely child's play."

"He's Still a Jew" is by far Kraus's most comprehensive statement about his relation to Jewish culture. As such, it has a unique place in his work. Yet we find in *Die Fackel* abundant passages in which Kraus distances himself in similarly aggressive and explicit ways from forms of acculturation whose linguistic effects he regarded as catastrophically harmful. Many of these passages come from the same period: the years before the First World War. In 1911, for example, when a Berlin-based Jewish professor of literature grouped Kraus's polemical style together with Harden's, Kraus reacted by attacking the professor's style of assimilation. His essay "The New Kind of Cursing" ["Die neue Art des Schimpfens"] begins by mocking the professor for seeing in Harden's deprecatory use of terms like "prostitute" and "eunuch" a forceful "new type of cursing." Then Kraus draws a connection between the professor's practice of abbreviating as "M." his middle name, which was Moses, and his stylistic foibles.[80] Ironically, a professor who likes how "eunuch" can be employed as an insult has "castrated his name."[81] Along with this truncation goes a grating stiltedness. Kraus "will not look away from the most horrible details" of the professor's absurdly "respectable language" [*salonfähiger Sprache*].[82] Here, in effect, Kraus applies his critique of Harden to the professor who had linked him to Harden. Just as he does in lambasting Harden, whose turgidities, in Kraus's reading, result from his fear of being a "Schmock," Kraus stresses how much language suffers when it is made to serve as a vehicle for social advancement, for becoming "salonfähig." At the same time, Kraus, who by implication is insisting on the "undomesticated" status of his antistyle, emphasizes his own suffering. That someone could blithely describe him as just another "Viennese critic," that he could be viewed as a Harden acolyte by a Jewish professor who "missed his journalistic calling," has incensed him. Seething, Kraus exclaims: "I can write three thousand sentences a month, the last one of which surpasses the life's work of a successful reporter—and yet I still have not made it into the University of Berlin."[83] When, just one year later, Kraus published his first major fictional dialogue, these concerns—i.e., the stylistic problems that attend Jewish acculturation and the place of his own writing in the "world" of German-Jewish letters—were manifestly on his mind. Indeed, they are the dialogue's main themes.

"THE DIALECT OF THE WORLD"

Originally published in October 1912, "Harikari und Feuilleton" was reissued in 1922, right next to "The Last Actors." The former piece directly precedes the latter in the volume *The Destruction of the World Through Black Magic* [*Untergang der Welt durch schwarze Magie*]. And together they form a block of writing in which Kraus introduces his mode of mimetic representation, mimics the "dialect" of German-Jewish journalists, and praises the "power" of the "repeated word" in a dialect-speaking theater troupe. I say "introduces" because the 1922 version of "Harikari und Feuilleton" gives some methodological self-analysis before proceeding to imitate journalistic "dialect." In his forward Kraus writes: "The persons acting and suffering here speak in a dialect. But this representation [*Darstellung*] does not want to create the impression that the real persons who live in the milieu being evoked speak the same dialect, or that they speak it with the same clarity. Because this narrow milieu is simultaneously the broadest milieu in the world, the author who seeks to represent it must have these persons speak the dialect that their souls speak. I confess that I wouldn't have other persons, whose race or upbringing lies far from the possibility of such a dialect, speak any differently. Their souls too speak dialect. It is the dialect of the world" ("HF," 140).

Kraus's goal is not an exact reproduction of the language that the "real persons"—after whom he models "the persons who act and suffer here"—

actually speak. Rather, he is pursuing a revelatory mimesis, a mimetic reproduction of "the dialect that their souls speak." Later in his forward Kraus again stresses that "realistic" mirroring is not at stake in his dialogue: "The details, which might seem to be realistic and which have been borrowed from local events, are only there for the sake of that natural truth which is a symbol" ("HF," 142). Here Kraus is working with a paradoxical idea that pervades his journalistic self-stylizations. Like conventional journalists, he writes "about the day," but readers should not think that he writes "for the day." Whereas conventional journalism ages quickly, Kraus's "actuality" will only grow over time, the reason being that in his accounts "of the day" he finds "symbols" of a general fate. A "destiny," not a "contingency," "plays itself out" in his dialogue, he claims (142): "Hier waltet kein Zufall, sondern ein Schicksal." Or as Kraus puts it—in the passage that Adorno used as the epigraph for an essay on Benjamin—his aim is "to listen to the noises of the day as though they were the chords of eternity."[84] In "Heine and the Consequences" Kraus is even more concise. He states about his reportage: "The event was near, but the perspective was far."

But the dialect Kraus wants to evoke is not simply a local dialect whose far-reaching significance can be uncovered at its core. The dialect that concerns him has a more radical paradoxicality. It comes out of a "narrow milieu" that is "simultaneously the *broadest* milieu in the world." With the line, "I confess that I wouldn't have others, whose race or upbringing precludes the possibility of such a dialect, speak any differently," Kraus informs his readers that this narrow-wide, dialect-speaking "milieu" has an ethnic coloration. "Race or upbringing" appears to determine the "possibility" that one belongs to the milieu, that one speaks its dialect. Shortly thereafter Kraus makes the identity of his dialect speakers even more explicit—by referring to the dialect in question with the label "Jargon" ("HF," 141), which, as we know, connoted both "Yiddish" and "Mauscheln." And so it comes as no surprise when the interlocutors in Kraus's dialogue turn out to be Jews. One is "an older editor." His conversation partner is "Zifferer," or an undisguised cipher for Paul Zifferer, a correspondent whose coverage of the conflict between Bulgaria and Turkey Kraus would soon execrate. Only a few weeks after "Harikari und Feuilleton" had appeared, in fact, he printed in *Die Fackel* a whole series of quotations from Zifferer's articles on the battle of Adrianople. These dispatches dwell on the city's exotic beauty and, Kraus argues, thereby make a scene of war into the sort of material needed for a picturesque, not-too-disquieting feuilleton.[85]

Now if the dialect Zifferer and the older editor speak is bound to a specific "race or upbringing," if it comes from a "narrow milieu," how can it be "the dialect of the world"? Kraus's answer is that their dialect is the language of all strivers, of all "people who stretch themselves toward the ceiling." Despite his allusion to "Jargon," moreover, Kraus is not trying reveal that the language of Jewish strivers contains a current of Yiddish-German dialect, or of *Mauscheln*. In "He's Still a Jew" the venal language of Jews—a language in which "the rolling of money" is supposedly perceptible—is the Jews' only identifiable "characteristic" and, paradoxically, a property of the whole world.[86] Similarly, in "Harikari und Feuilleton" local parvenus have analogues everywhere who speak in their souls the same dialect.

Yet although the "dialect of the world" is thus the "one means of communication among the different languages," as dialect it remains "untranslatable." Furthermore, the striver mentality that Jewish journalists symbolize does not exist apart from the dialect their "souls speak." Kraus maintains, indeed, that his dialogue "shows how these figures [e.g., Zifferer and his anonymous interlocutor] cannot deny how they originate in their language [*den Ursprung aus ihrer Sprache*]." Hence the need for a mimetic representation of the "dialect of the world" as it manifests itself in a *particular* style. And hence, in turn, Kraus's concern that his dialogue will be read merely as a satire of local idiom. His "representation does not want to create the impression that the real persons who live in the milieu being represented speak exactly the same dialect." It is perhaps for this reason that Kraus is relatively sparing in his use of the dense vernacular of characters from this "narrow" world. For example, the play *Flink und Fliederbusch*, (1917), Arthur Schnitzler's send-up of the same journalistic "milieu," reproduces colloquialisms much more extensively. So does Hermann Bahr's novelistic parody of Viennese journalism, *The Bird Brain* [*Das Tschaperl*, 1898].

At the same time, Kraus tells us that his "representation" consists of quoted "phrases," that it is "a collection of phrases out of which those who speak them have grown a face." He adds: "They [these phrases] are quotations, which go into motion and make up a dramatic life." Whereas Schnitzler and Bahr both lampoon the German-Jewish journalistic scene in Vienna by creating risible characters and a picaresque story, mimetic language is the star of Kraus's conversation, as well as the source of its "dramatic life." His dialogue is not framed within a plot structure; nor does it have any real internal narrative development. And because Kraus puts all the speech into a single, intricately arranged, nine-page-long paragraph—and generally does not say who is speaking, or what his characters are doing as they speak—the language itself seems always to be performing in the foreground. Thus "the author who seeks to represent dialect" in this way is, as Kraus writes, "der Darsteller," or author *and* actor: The German word "Darsteller" has both meanings. In the end, Kraus suggests, his dialogue exists in an ambiguous discursive space. "Is it a drama?" he asks ("HF," 141). Where he responds to the question, he describes his radical quoting with an oxymoronic neologism: "nachschöpferisch," or "creatively imitative" (142).

This "creatively imitative" mode has a pointedly oppositional relation to the views and linguistic practices of Kraus's protagonists. For Kraus's paradigmatic German-Jewish journalists—i.e., Zifferer and the older editor—cling, in contrast to *Die Fackel*, to the ideal of "original" writing ("HF," 147). Moreover, the end of Kraus's "creatively imitative" style is to uncover large and uncomfortable truths, the sound of the "dialect of the world." The older editor and Ziffer simply hunger for conventionally juicy stories that will further their project of social advancement. So even if they are the speakers of dialect, Kraus is the one whose mimetic activity comes across as "undomesticated," or as radical in much the same way as Offenbach's frenetic and funny but ultimately hard-hitting operettas. Indeed, a chief topic of the discussion between older editor and Zifferer is how the latter will successfully exploit a gruesome act of harikari, how he will get out of it a feuilleton that will be "interesting on Sunday." Their strategizing is both mercenary and platitudinous. That a Japanese general, General Nogi, has committed harikari by slashing his throat is cause for complaint. A "proper" goring of the stomach would have fit in better with a feuilletonistic account of Japanese rituals, it seems.

Still, when the older editor asks Zifferer how he will sketch the "physiognomy" of the suicide, Zifferer's reply indicates that Nogi's harikari will provide the material for a graceful feuilleton full of engaging images: "A coarse beard, made pale by the years, framed his chin and cheeks." Nogi's real appearance is of little importance. He is fodder for the feuilletonistic "mood." What matters, for Kraus's journalists, is not how they can adequately represent their subject but rather how often they can use the feuilletonistic devices that will produce the desired atmospheric effects. Upon being queried about Nogi's mustache, Zifferer ripostes: "Small and brushed down, but I need that for when Pavlik comes to Vienna." The older editor then accuses Zifferer of having forgotten "the slanted eyes," causing the latter to intone: "You might think so. Yet I say to you, 'with wonderful intelligence and vitality, the small black eyes looked out from their narrow, slanted openings. . . . the entire figure, the entire face, the entire essence of the

General seemed to shine forth from those eyes.'" Thoroughly excited, the editor compares the "plasticity" of Zifferer's portraiture with that of Felix Salten's. And, like "The Austrian Face," Kraus's apparent response to Salten's "The Austrian Face," "Harikari und Feuilleton" directly inverts what Kraus saw as the structure of the feuilletonistic profile.[87] Zifferer imposes his phrases on Nogi's face. Kraus, on the other hand, presents us with "a collection of phrases out of which those who speak them have grown a face" ("HF," 147).

But only a small part of this "collection" consists of feuilletonistic "phrases." More often Zifferer and the older editor speak the more private dialect that, Kraus's dialogue implies, lies behind such public utterances. Its movement is very different from the deliberate cadences of Salten's literary journalism. In fact, Zifferer and the older editor communicate in a frenetic, desultory manner. Each repeatedly loses track of the other's line of conversation. "'You're speaking about the telephone?' 'I'm speaking about harikari'" ("HF," 143) runs one exchange. Later we read: "Who's talking about Nogi? I'm talking about Mendel Singer" (144). These moments give the dialogue a farcical feel, yet Kraus seems also to be earnestly emphasizing the cognitive restlessness of journalists "who stretch toward the ceiling," of strivers who want, above all, to get ahead. Petty jealousies and potential story topics constantly distract Zifferer and the older editor. With nonsequiturs veering away from "harikari and feuilleton," the discussion takes on an antic quality. Apropos of nothing, for instance, the focus of the dialogue shifts to the ennoblement of Mendel Singer, the Jewish journalist whom Kraus derides in "The Austrian Face." The motif of Singer returns several times, each time drawing attention to the link between journalism and Jewish assimilationism and away from another theme. As a result, Zifferer and the older editor wind up considering none of their subjects in detail.

There are further distractions. By having the "the voice of the Lord" [*die Stimme des Herrn*] intrude menacingly on the dialogue ("from the next room"), Kraus spoofs Moriz Benedikt, the mighty publisher of the *Neue Freie Presse,* and his heavy-handedness. Kraus also intimates that the journalists who work for Benedikt are craven in addition to being ambitious. For the older editor "cowers" upon hearing the "voice of the Lord" threaten to "throw everyone out" ("HF," 142). Moreover, Kraus himself is a distraction. The older editor repeatedly adverts to apocryphal news items that Kraus had duped the *Neue Freie Presse* into printing. And he worries that the report of Nogi's harikari and the news of Singer's noble status might actually be "a trick by Kraus" (144).[88] On the issue of Kraus's success, the two interlocutors trade statements whose clipped and phrase-like character seems to preclude sustained reflection. The older editor exclaims: "What would have become of him [Kraus] if he hadn't become independent! Today he could be the boss! If only you could talk with him! A made man! Can write, intelligent, and a Jew!" (144-45). Zifferer replies by speaking skeptically of Kraus's abilities: "You overestimate him [Kraus] greatly. What can you do with the writing when the attitude is worthless? But is he one of us? Now he says he's an artist!" (145).

These remarks elicit another round of staccato utterances from the older editor: "Artist! He's gone far! That comes from his need to be different! The whole world is for Heine—he has to be against Heine! The horrible antisemite!" ("HF," 145) Here, needless to say, Kraus has made the gap between himself and his characters into the topic of his dialogue. The older editor seems unable to fathom why Kraus did not use his talent, as well as a certain loyalty among Jews in journalism, to go farther. Kraus "can write," is "intelligent," and is also a "Jew." If only he had not been so strangely bent on being "independent," he "could be the boss," the older editor reasons. Zifferer's lines too prompt us to think about the differences between Kraus and the figures in "Harikari und Feuilleton." After all, using a phrase that is utterly foreign to Kraus's just-mentioned ethos of independence, Zifferer wonders: "But is he one of us?" His next observation—"Now he says he's an artist!"—further puts into the foreground the theme of Kraus's ambiguous status. Having characterized Kraus as a journalist who does not quite fit in ("But is he one of us?"), Zifferer cites Kraus claiming to be an "artist."

By having Zifferer treat that claim suspiciously, or as just a claim ("Now he *says* he's an artist"), Kraus also picks up on the topic of how journalists understood his complex and often paradoxical self-stylizing. Elsewhere he deals explicitly and critically with the sense that his desire to stand apart, to distance himself aggressively from German-Jewish journalists and their model (Heine), is a vain psychological need rather than a serious literary program. More precisely, Kraus has the older editor interpret key aspects of his undertaking with the sort of reductionism of which he was violently contemptuous when he encountered it in readings of his life and work. The older editor sees Kraus's critique of Heine as nothing more than the effect of a psychological trait, of an overlarge "need" to seem unique. Indeed, he attributes no weight at all to the actual argument in the reckoning with Heine that Kraus's had recently published, "Heine and the Consequences."

The hypermimetic moment in "Harikari und Feuilleton"—its representation of the older editor's and Zifferer's representations of Kraus—expresses another emblematic disparity. Just as *Literature* does, the text dramatizes a generational divide. Like the fathers in Kraus's play, who utter Yiddishisms in the verse form of the classical German drama, the older editor at once identifies with the culture of German classicism and liberalism and retains a self-consciously Jewish identity. He reveres Goethe and wistfully tells Zifferer: "You don't know those days in which we [an older generation of Jews, presumably] still struggled, grown up with the ideas of Germanness" ("HF," 144). In other words, Zifferer, whose model—Paul Zifferer—was born in 1879, did not experience the time in which the liberal dream was alive in Austria and Jews "struggled" to bring that dream to fruition. Though disillusioned, the older editor remains combative. He is quick to denounce Kraus as a "horrible antisemite." Yet the older editor also acknowledges Kraus's talent and states, again, what Kraus believed to be a key truth about the *Neue Freie Presse:* that being Jewish would help one advance through its ranks. "If only you could talk with him! A made man! Can write, intelligent, and a Jew!" Zifferer, the author of feuilletons, is sweepingly dismissive of Kraus ("'You overestimate him greatly!'") and seemingly unconcerned with social causes. Neither character could be called favorable. But the older editor and his language come across as less pernicious. As Kraus writes in his forward, the two interlocutors relate to each other like "the lead article relates to the feuilleton." It was the latter genre, he believed, that was destroying the popular imagination and thus the world. So in this respect too "Harikari und Feuilleton" resembles *Literature:* both texts have the generation of assimilated Jewish "sons" as the *primary* object of their satirical mirroring. Clearly, Werfel's conceit of linguistic mastery disturbed Kraus much more than did the Yiddishisms of the "half-assimilated" fathers.

Kraus's use of generational juxtapositions extends well beyond "Harikari and Feuilleton" and *Literature*. In "The Destruction of the World though Black Magic" (1912), for instance, he sets next to each other citations from feuilletonistic accounts of the ongoing crisis in the Balkans and passages from soberer, mid-nineteenth-century war journalism. His aim is to reveal, through "startling citations," the dangerous swelling in the feuilletonistic language that he vehemently attacks in his commentary. This language, he once again emphasizes, "hangs together with Judaism," with a certain "Jewish mentality" [*Judengeist*].[89]

To a significant extent, Kraus constructed the problem of journalism as the problem of an antimimetic style that is, paradoxically, driven by mimesis—by the overreaching mimesis of *a particular* form of Jewish assimilationism. As German-Jewish journalists "stretch toward the ceiling," their language becomes distended. And as is the case when operetta becomes "Salonoperetta"—or perhaps whenever form is only an instrument, "only clothing for the body and not the very flesh of mind"—vacuity is the result. But with the feuilleton there is a crucial additional issue. Its mimetic impoverishment causes the popular imagination to become deformed. Responding to this "destruction," Kraus exalted the power of a "creatively imitative" form that can convey a dialect spoken by the soul. His style, which he associated with the noninstrumental, revelatory imitation of the Budapester Orpheumgesellschaft, is thus presented as a modernist antistyle, as a direct counterpoint to the writing German-Jewish feuilletonist "sons."

It also presented as a truly radical counterpoint. For, again, Kraus did not fashion himself as possessing the qualities that deracinated Jewish intellects supposedly lacked, i.e., the mystical unity and authenticity that some German Jews sought in the culture of *Ostjuden*. Rather, he lionized, and developed an extreme form of, what was commonly regarded as a symbol of German Jewry's "terrible inner state": journalistic mirroring. Kraus's "creatively imitative" style is paradoxical and steadfastly "undomesticated," yet it is not exotic. Conspicuously out of sync with dominant aesthetic values, anti-journalism is thus, in a certain sense, a small form. But, as with vaudeville—which has "only a narrow space to set up its mirror" and still adequately "represents us all"—Kraus claims for his anti-journalism the greatest evocative power. Like the improbable "Gesamtkunstwerk" of Offenbach's operettas, it activates all the possibilities of its medium. So in mirroring the dialect of a "narrow milieu," Kraus's anti-journalism manages to represent "the dialect of the world."

That Kraus's mimetic commitments appealed to certain younger German-Jewish writers, writers who were at once critical of significant trends in German-Jewish acculturation and the rhetoric of authenticity in alternatives like cultural Zionism, should not be all too surprising. I have in mind here, above all, Benjamin's and Scholem's dramatic interpretations of *Die Fackel*. However, there are other such readings, some of which I have discussed, for example, Kafka's. It seems appropriate to conclude this chapter by citing a little-known reference that I will not be able to address in the following chapter, and that places Kraus in the intellectual lineage of another maverick

German-Jewish thinker. For the present chapter began and has ended with the theme of generational movement in German-Jewish culture. So here is how Max Horkeimer, who together with Adorno saw an essential honesty in a Jewish "undisciplined mimesis,"[90] positioned Kraus in his "Intellectual Family Tree" ["Geistiger Stammbaum," undated]: "Schopenhauer (Kant), Marx. Freud, Nietzsche (as corroboration). Voltaire, Karl Kraus. Judaism."[91]

CHAPTER FOUR

Messianic Journalism? Benjamin and Scholem Read *Die Fackel*

*That this man [Kraus], one of an evanescent few who have a sense of what freedom is, can serve it only by being the highest prosecutor—that is the purest expression of his dialectics. A being [*Dasein*], which—precisely here—is the hottest prayer for redemption that passes through Jewish lips today.*
—Walter Benjamin

The Zionists blocked Kraus's path to Zionism. —Gershom Scholem

Walter Benjamin's writings abound with dramatic phrases and superlative forms. But his use of such devices is seldom as concerted as it is in his essays on Kraus. Witness the last two sentences of "Karl Kraus" (1928), the first of those works. There Kraus is the "*highest* prosecutor," while the "*purest* expression" of his "dialectics" is the "*hottest* prayer for redemption that passes through Jewish lips today" (*BGS* 2:2.625). Also striking is the content of these claims. For "redemption" is a crucial idea in the blend of apocalyptic historiography and utopian longing that has been called Benjamin's "modern Jewish messianism," as well as his "most abiding intellectual and emotional commitment."[1] And Benjamin associated very few authors with genuinely redemptive impulses. Beyond being the "hottest" one among Jews "today," Kraus's "prayer for redemption" is the only one Benjamin named.

His friend Gershom Scholem was more ready to identify that sort of significance in the writings of Jewish contemporaries. Scholem's portrayal of

Kraus as a "messianic movement of language" (*ST* 2:462) is therefore not quite as conspicuous as is Benjamin's remark about what "passes through" Kraus's "Jewish lips." Yet Scholem too ascribed to Kraus an arrestingly singular position within German-Jewish culture. In 1919, or at a time when he was intensely concerned with the fate of Jewish tradition in Western modernity, Scholem credited Kraus with finding "the most unexpected Jewish provinces in this [German] language" (*ST* 2:468).

If Benjamin's and Scholem's utterances about Kraus stand out, their readings of him also cohere with several major patterns in their respective lives and works. First, both thinkers disdained the path of acculturation taken by the Jews among whom they grew up in turn-of-the-century Berlin (Benjamin was born in 1892, Scholem in 1897). "During my childhood," Benjamin recollected, "I was a prisoner of the old and the new West. In those days, my clan inhabited these two districts with an attitude of stubborness mingled with self-confidence, turning them into a ghetto that it regarded as a fiefdom" (BGS 4:1.287). Second, both Benjamin and Scholem had an enduring interest in the "relation of Jews to language," as Scholem put it. And, finally, both attached great value to locating "within tradition" noncanonical sources of vitality.[2] Indeed, Scholem is famous for having produced a "counter-history" of Judaism. Here the Kabbalah, which earlier German-Jewish historians of Jewish culture had frequently marginalized and deprecated, became part of a fecund "dialectic of rationalism and mysticism."[3] According to Scholem, it is looking for such counterintuitive moments, or "brushing history against the grain," that makes for a dynamic interaction with tradition.[4] "There is such a thing," he wrote, "as a treasure hunt within tradition, which creates a living relationship to tradition and to which much of what is best in current Jewish consciousness is indebted, even where it was—and is—expressed outside the framework of orthodoxy."[5] So in averring that Kraus, a language-obsessed satirical journalist and vituperative critic of acculturated Jews, "finds the most unexpected Jewish provinces" in the German language, Scholem was drawing on some of his most basic sensibilities. As I suggested in the previous chapter, Benjamin's and Scholem's largely unexamined interpretations of Kraus's meaning for Jewish culture should not be all too surprising.[6]

That point says little about how their interpretations took shape. Just how did Kraus's "journalism in its most paradoxical form," as Benjamin once labeled it, become the most Jewish writing in German for two of German Jewry's most influential critics? Under what circumstances could Kraus's *Fackel* become "the greatest breakthrough" of Jewish tradition into "the mass of the German language," to cite yet another of Benjamin's superlatives? What, more generally, do the vivid acts of signification at issue here tell us about the process to which they belong? What do they tell us about German-Jewish self-fashioning during one of its most storied, most dialectical moments, namely, the Weimar-era "revival" of Jewish culture?[7]

This chapter seeks to answer these questions by considering Benjamin's and Scholem's reactions to Kraus against the discursive context whose importance I have been stressing all along: fin-de-siècle couplings of journalism and German-Jewish intellectuality. Doing so will enable us to see how Benjamin and Scholem frame Kraus's style as being profoundly Jewish precisely where it reworks elements of journalistic writing that were inscribed—and that in some cases *they* inscribe—as being emblematic of German Jewry's spiritual condition. At the same time, looking carefully at how Benjamin and Scholem creatively appropriated a larger discourse will reveal something about that larger discourse. Benjamin's and Scholem's readings of Kraus powerfully underscore how complex the discourse linking journalistic writing and Jewishness could be, and also how much it mattered during the turbulent war and Weimar years.

But I want to begin with the prewar event that was my point of departure in chapter 1, "the *Kunstwart* Affair." For it was in response to the *Kunstwart* exchange that Benjamin started to write about the special mission of Jewish intellectuals. He started to write, that is, about the special mission of a figure closely related to the much-maligned Jewish journalist, the Jewish "literatus."[8]

BENJAMIN'S "ZIONISM OF THE SPIRIT" AND THE DIALECTICS OF GERMAN-JEWISH IDENTITY

The *Kunstwart* controversy began in March 1912, with the appearance of Moritz Goldstein's essay "The German-Jewish Parnassus." In it, to recapitulate, Goldstein offers a provocatively bleak account of German-Jewish assimilation. He maintains that anti-Jewish hostility and willful self-delusion on the part of German Jews have compressed Jewish intellects. Hence "there are so many Jewish journalists" who can only act as "mirrors," catching the "images of the day" and throwing them back. German Jewry's affinity for journalism thus illustrates its lack of creative power and, ultimately, of full selfhood, the source on which creativity depends, according to Goldstein. For all their education and refinement, for all their prominence in the cultural sphere, German Jews are less than well-formed human beings.

They are debilitated "hermaphrodites." And a drastic existential change is in order.

Goldstein's text is often characterized as though it contained only this exhortatory message. But "The German-Jewish Parnassus" also searchingly addresses the question of how German Jews might overcome their unfortunate "half-ness." In fact, rather than proposing a straightforwardly Zionist answer, Goldstein thinks in several directions, gesturing most ardently at the possibility of an alternative German-Jewish symbiosis, of a *real* symbiosis. At the center of these thoughts is the issue of what role Jewish authors should play in German Jewry's spiritual renewal. It is just this theme that Benjamin made his focus as he brought further, even more dramatic twists into *Kunstwart* exchange.

Benjamin's intervention came in epistolary form. In August 1912, Ferdinand Avenarius, the nationalist editor of *Der Kunstwart,* published over ninety responses to Goldstein's article. Writing under the pseudonym Franz Quentin, Ludwig Strauss—a twenty-one-year-old student and Martin Buber's future son-in-law—contributed one of the longest and certainly one of the most incisive of them. Strauss's commentary is itself an essay, *the* essay that elicited from Benjamin a series of claims about the topic noted above.[9] As Paul Mendes-Flohr has put it, "After reading . . . [Strauss's] reply Benjamin dashed off an enthusiastic letter to its author, dated September 1912. A brief but intense correspondence ensued regarding the Literatenjuden, their place in German culture, and the nature and obligations of their Jewish identity."[10]

Strauss's "reply" to Goldstein is generally quite critical. While Strauss commends him for attempting to foster greater Jewish self-awareness, he challenges what is perhaps Goldstein's basic premise: that external forces, i.e., antisemitism, have prevented Jews from integrating into German culture. Like Goldstein, to be sure, Strauss emphasizes that many Jews wanted to assimilate. He even goes so far as to blame Jews for bringing about the "decimation" of Jewish culture in Germany.[11] But he insists that Jews have remained apart, and that their apartness stems, in the end, from a "distinctively Jewish sensibility."[12] If assimilation has yielded a mostly eviscerated "new type" of Jew, it has not been able to wash away a core Jewish "substance" and special Jewish "inner strengths." Here Strauss is explicitly drawing on Buber and his recently published *Three Addresses on Judaism* [*Drei Reden über das Judentum,* 1911], which state and stress these ideas.[13] By Strauss's and Buber's logic, Goldstein not only errs in holding antisemitism responsible for the persistent outsider status of German Jews. He is also misguided where he intimates that a new Jewish identity needs to be imaginatively constructed by those Jewish authors who have managed to transcend journalistic mirroring. Jewishness has subsisted, according to Strauss. The task of German-Jewish writers is to find a way to access it.

Yet there are various moments of agreement between Goldstein and Strauss. Toward the end of his essay—in a rare instance of optimism—Goldstein notes that certain German Jews have begun to pursue a higher level of self-consciousness. Strauss makes a similar point somewhat more expansively. He surmises that a self-preservation mechanism sets in wherever Jews attempt to divest themselves of their Jewish soul. Intense assimilation has led, paradoxically, to the "reaffirmation" of Jewish substance that appears to be unfolding in Germany. This substance is, Strauss admits, quite possibly indefinable. That it can "be felt" is "sufficient," however. But Jewish intellectuals still have a "duty to clarify" the perception of Jewishness through their "work."[14] Thus Strauss, like Goldstein, advocates the founding of a "central journal for Jewish literature in the German language."[15]

In his second letter to Strauss, Benjamin follows suit and approves of the journal proposal. Indeed, he lauds *Der Kunstwart* for taking up the "Jewish question" from "the literary side" (*BB* 1:61). For "general cultural observations" are too often scattered and intellectually dubious. What is needed is an "area in which the Jewish mind can be isolated and show itself in its nature" (61). Concurring with both Goldstein and Strauss again, Benjamin proceeds to reflect: "If we are bifurcated [*zweiseitig*], Jewish and German, then until now we have given all our affirmation [*Bejahen*] to the German. The Jewish was perhaps often only a foreign, strange (even worse: sentimental) aroma" (61). As is the case with Strauss, moreover, Benjamin believes that "highly valuable strengths in Judaism" are being "lost though assimilation" (61). But he cannot fathom how one gets from that insight to Zionist commitments. "I do not understand how, from here, one arrives at Zionism" (61).

At this point in the letter, Benjamin's thinking begins to diverge rather sharply from Strauss's. Benjamin opines that Zionism seems necessary only for persecuted *Ostjuden*. Then, veering away from Strauss's desire for a separate Jewish culture within Germany, he asks: "Is one sufficiently familiar with the Jewish intellect to be able to build upon it an emergency empire, a culture empire [*Kulturreich*]?" (*BB* 1:61) The distance between Benjamin and Strauss only grows in the succeeding paragraphs, as Benjamin tells his interlocutor: "The very best Western European Jews are no longer free *as Jews*. They cannot become part of the Jewish movement in the sense in which your letter suggests because they are bound to the literary movement" (62). And not only is the "literary movement" "international," so are the other movements to which the most precocious Jews belong. Wherever Western European Jews are "the leaders"—in "science, commerce and literature"—they are "bound to internationalism" (62).

In such statements the idiosyncratic, dialectical character of Benjamin's early relation to Jewish culture comes to light. Benjamin wants to see a rise in Jewish "self-consciousness" and worries that otherwise "valuable strengths in Judaism" will "be lost." Yet he is also convinced that "the best Western European Jews" are not free to give themselves over to a "Jewish movement." Rather, they are "bound to the literary movement" and, with it, "to internationalism." It turns out that not knowing whether "the Jewish intellect" is ready to produce a "cultural empire" is only part of the problem with the goal of an autonomous Jewish culture in Germany. A greater difficulty is that Western European Jews appear to be better suited for, and to have thrived in, different sorts of cultural "movements." More or less fated for internationalism, these Jews "are no longer free *as Jews.*" Thus they "cannot become part of the Jewish movement" in Strauss's "sense." They cannot be cultural Zionists of Buber's ilk.

As we have seen, Benjamin mentions several ways in which Jews are affiliated with internationalism. But their connection to the international "*literary* movement" is clearly his chief concern. After introducing the idea of internationalism, he expatiates at length on the Jews' place in modern letters. He begins with an avowal of the importance of the Jewish literati. Benjamin writes: "I want to speak about the literati because their striving appears to me to be the most promising and most significant culturally, yes! religiously. . . . In most circles the word 'literatus' [*Literat*] has a pejorative undertone. And yet these circles stand before him [the literatus] with exactly the helplessness that we feel before someone who is totally superior to us in an area we hardly know. One feels that it is the literati who occupy themselves with today [*mit Heute*] as earnestly as Tolstoy once did with Christianity. . . . They have their serious mission in extracting from the art they cannot make themselves spirit [*Geist*] for the present" (*BB* 1:62).

The literati who Benjamin is lionizing, and from whom he derives what he calls "the idea of the literatus," are not an exclusively Jewish group. In a later missive to Strauss, Benjamin states that finding a "German among intellectuals" gives him "extraordinary joy" (*BB* 1:75). But, of course, that qualification further shows how closely Benjamin associated Jews with critical intellectual culture. That he feels "extraordinary joy" upon meeting a German among intellectuals is a measure of the extent to which such encounters are anything but ordinary occurrences. Benjamin soon speaks to this point directly. He contends that Jews "represent an elite party of intellectuals," which one can justifiably refer to as "culture Jewry." It is his actual empirical "experience" [*Erfahrung*] of this Jewish "elite," rather than an inner "Jewish experience" [*jüdisches Erlebnis*], that has shaped his "position on Judaism" (75). Accordingly, the cosmopolitan "literati-Jew" [*Literaten-Jude*] is "much more important" to him than the "National-Jew" [*National-Jude*] of "Zionist propaganda" (83).

As he valorizes the "literati-Jew" Benjamin extends his rejection of Strauss's thought. Jews, he implies with his remark about "empirical experience," can do without the "inner Jewish experience" Strauss found so crucial. And the "serious mission" of Jewish intellectuals is not to advance a distinctively Jewish culture, as Strauss would have it. Instead Benjamin prescribes that they mediate works not of their own design, or "the art" they "cannot make themselves." Because Strauss's letters are not extant, it is impossible to know just how he replied to Benjamin's confutations. But in all likelihood he asked Benjamin to clarify his ideas, for this is what Benjamin undertakes to do in his subsequent missives. It is there that he analyzes his "empirical experience" of the Jewish literati and offers the most famous phrases of the correspondence. More specifically, Benjamin writes that solidarity with Jewish intellectuals, not religious belief or practice, makes him a "National-Jew" [*Nationaljude*] (*BB* 1:72). He is, as such, a Zionist. Yet the Zionism to which he adheres is a special sort of esoteric Zionism, a "Zionism of the spirit" [*Zionism des Geistes*] (82). If this Zionism centers on shared Jewish values, it has no cultural or geographic center. For the Zionist of the spirit sees "Jewish values everywhere" (72).[16] Benjamin's provocative move, then, is to give the name "Zionism" to a way of thinking that opposes organized Zionism and celebrates the ties of Jewish intellectuals to "internationalism."[17]

Yet it would be wrong to characterize Benjamin's letters as polemical. Indeed, his attitude toward Strauss is often quite solicitous. Consider that in the final installment of the exchange, which is dated February 6, 1913, Benjamin eagerly excuses Strauss for not answering his previous letter. In addition, Benjamin stresses that were Strauss to move to Berlin, he, Benjamin, would find it easier to stay there. He also makes an effort to reconcile the Wickersdorf youth movement, the movement that has his "primary loyalty" (*BB* 1:70), with the texts by Buber that Strauss cites so energetically.[18] "What Buber in his second and third addresses labels the essence of Judaism applies very well to Wickersdorf" (71). When we take into account that, in a later letter, Benjamin emphatically dismisses the pursuit of a Jewish essence, this friendly invocation of Buber begins to read like an attempt to propitiate Strauss.

According to that later letter, Judaism must remain "thoroughly esoteric" (*BB* 1:83). It should be undefined—and yet self-evident. Drawing an analogy with morality, which is supposed "to understand itself by itself," Benjamin asserts that Judaism too "should understand itself by itself" (75). German Jews might need more "self-consciousness" and to allow their Jewishness to "show itself"; however, formal attempts at clarification, one of the stated ends of Strauss's journal, would be destructive. "For me," Benjamin writes, "all that which is Jewish and seeks to go beyond the self-understood is dangerous" (76). Similarly, Zionism is attractive but only as a paradoxical "Zionism of the spirit" whose bearers are cosmopolitan "Western European" Jewish literati. These "best" Jews further "Jewish values everywhere," largely, it seems, by distilling the "Geist" from "the art they cannot make themselves." So what appears to be "self-evident" in Benjamin's letters is that Jews have the "serious mission" of acting in different cultures as "the leading carrier and representative of the spiritual." Their Jewish calling, again, is to be international.

As several scholars, e.g., Anson Rabinbach, Gary Smith, and Irving Wohlfarth, have pointed out, here, at the age of twenty-one, Benjamin is manifesting tendencies that would persist throughout his career.[19] Benjamin's highly ambivalent attitude toward Zionism, his unease about formal definitions of Judaism, his preference for maverick theories of Jewish culture, and his inability to commit fully to Judaism, despite actively "discovering as Jewish" the "ideas and people" that are "highest" to him—these early complexities are in basic ways continuous with later ones. During the mid-1920s, for example, Benjamin expressed a desire to learn Hebrew and kept promising Scholem that he would study in Jerusalem. He even arranged to receive financial support for his venture. But he could not get himself to go to, let alone settle in, the "homeland."

Especially noteworthy for our purposes is how, already in his correspondence with Strauss, Benjamin seems determined to resist making the ideals of elemental originality, "inner experience," and cultural autonomy and authenticity a part of Jewish identity. To be sure, he seconds Strauss's claim that Judaism is "the core-like" [*das Kernhafte*], or a kind of essence. But Benjamin also vigorously challenges Strauss's talk of the "inner powers" of Jews, the word "powers," "Mächte," being the focus of Benjamin's opprobrium. Moreover, in *rehabilitating* the Jewish literatus—as Benjamin observes, the term "literatus" had a "pejorative undertone"—he directly questions the standard of Jewish creativity that figures so prominently in Goldstein's text. Goldstein treats the inability of Jewish journalists to do more than "mirror" images of the day as a compelling sign of existential impairment. And he was, as I tried to show in chapter 1, hardly alone in doing so.

Let me offer a further example of such thinking. In his contribution to *On Judaism* [*Vom Judentum*, 1913], an anthology of cultural Zionist writings in which both Goldstein and Strauss published essays, Jakob Wassermann makes precisely the Jewish literatus into the negative foil for the productive Jew: "The Jew as a European, as a cosmopolitan, is a literatus; the Jew as an Oriental, not in the ethnographic sense, but rather in the mythic sense . . . can be a creator."[20] Wassermann, a well-known novelist, adds that he stands by his earlier description of the Jewish literatus "as the person who has been separated from myth."[21] This literatus is *the* paradigmatic rootless, desiccated, assimilated Jew, and therefore *the* antipode of the existentially whole and potent "Oriental" Jew. The literatus is *the* figure who, stripped of all myth and creativity, best emblematizes the need for change, for Jewish renewal. Written at just about the same time as Wassermann's essay, Benjamin's letters, by contrast, frame the ideal Jewish literatus as a daunting, somehow pious figure ("yes! religiously"), before whose intellectual authority we feel "helpless." Benjamin's Jewish literati "cannot make" art. Yet rather than being spiritually hollow, fatally deracinated characters, they carry out an invaluable "mission," presumably through citing, transmitting, and criticism.[22] Thus in his correspondence with Strauss Benjamin articulates strongly revisionist views on the identity of "two-sided" German Jews, views that his later ideas about the exalted status of quotation seem to justify retroactively. Indeed, the classic expression of those ideas is an essay on that most radical Jewish literatus, Kraus, whom Benjamin saw as pursuing a deeply Jewish critical project.

SCHOLEM, KRAUS, AND THE LAST DAYS OF MANKIND

In 1913 Benjamin had not yet begun to reckon with Kraus. That process of reception apparently commenced in the middle of the First World War. In *Walter Benjamin: The Story of a Friendship* [*Walter Benjamin: Die Geschichte einer Freundschaft*, 1977], Scholem informs us: "I no longer know when Walter Benjamin began to occupy himself with Kraus, but I believe it was around 1916, under the influence of Werner Kraft's boundless enthusiasm."²³ Scholem himself had started to read Kraus a little earlier. His initial impressions of the satirist are typically emphatic and also quite mixed. For example, a passage from a diary entry dated December 16, 1915 contains the following lines: "Was able to spend some time with Kraus's *Fackel*, which in places annoys me but, for the most part, gives me great pleasure, e.g., in its fight against the press [*das Zeitungswesen*]. On details about particular people, one could well disagree [with Kraus]. Also, he should not curse at 'the Jews.' It is an unfair way of fighting" (*ST* 1:204).

A passage written on the following day evinces a more derogatory tone. Scholem complains: "Kraus fackels on [*fackelt*] for too long. By doing so he accomplishes nothing. 'Is the *Fackel* a useful member of human society?' No, because it tries to negate 'human society.' Paradox: The *Berliner Tageblatt* offers a favorable discussion of Kraus's public readings. The angels laugh" (*ST* 1:206). The paradox that amused the eighteen-year-old Scholem (and his angels) is this: one of the targets of Kraus's scorn, the liberal *Berliner Tageblatt*, reviewed Kraus's public readings positively. But there is also a subtler paradox here. In lambasting Kraus's prolixity Scholem uses a weapon that evokes Kraus's style of word play. Kraus liked to build jokes on surnames, after all; and he did not shy away from such shenanigans when dealing with even the most obvious material, e.g., Max Brod ("Brod" is pronounced the same way as, and thus sounds identical to, the German word for bread).²⁴ Moreover, Kraus was thought to have done to the words "Kafka" and "Werfel" what Scholem did to "Fackel": make verbs out of them in such a way that they would call to mind popular terms for cacophonous jargon, for instance, *jüdeln* and *mauscheln*. Thus it appears that if the young Scholem found the imprecations Kraus employed against Jews to be "unfair," he at least felt some affinity for Kraus's polemical style.

Another diary entry—from about six months later—refers to Kraus's notorious "Heine and the Consequences" (1910) without implying that the text is at all distasteful. In fact, in an admiring misreading Scholem praises Kraus's claims about the "Erlebnisse," or the "inner experiences," of "today's youth" (*ST* 1:227). As the editors of Scholem's diaries point out, no sentence in "Heine and the Consequences" corresponds directly to Scholem's gloss of the text. And, contrary to Scholem's suggestion, Kraus did not counterpose *mere* "literary" inner experiences to more authentic, more primordial ones. Kraus was generally suspicious of that latter category, as Scholem would eventually acknowledge. In "Heine and the Consequences" Kraus simply underlines a problem with youthful literary experiences. They are often shallow, he stresses.

Having laid out his desire to attain to an entirely different order of experience, to properly mystical experience, Scholem goes on to consider how one might write a history of mysticism. His climactic thought here is that it would be important to have Martin Buber stand as the subject of the final chapter of such a history. Buber belongs in that position for two reasons: "Through him [Buber] Jewish mysticism could be taken into account." Also, "he is the specifically mystical phenomenon, the *essentially* mystical" (S*T* 1:228). Scholem's attitude toward Buber soon changed. And the factors behind this shift, as well as the shift itself, help to explain why Scholem subsequently—or in 1917—warmed to Kraus further still. The years between 1916 to 1918 represent an extraordinarily fruitful and disruptive time in Scholem's development, a period that he himself later deemed to be of "decisive" significance for his "whole life."[25] A major causal agent in this moment was the dominant event of the era: the war. Before its outbreak, Scholem had been critical of the Zionist youth group to which he belonged, "Jung Juda." He had been suspicious, that is, of its neo-romantic emphasis on communing with nature; Scholem thought the actual study of Judaism would be more beneficial for young Zionists. Since the official organ of German Zionism supported the war and Scholem vehemently opposed it, the First World War had the effect of solidifying his "position on the radical fringe of the German Zionist movement," to use David Myers's apt phrasing.[26] Scholem's oppositional stance, and his willingness to express his iconoclastic views, had other consequences as well. In 1915, his epistolary broadside against the war got him expelled from the gymnasium he had been attending. Two years later, Scholem offended his father, a staunch patriot, by propounding antiwar beliefs at the dinner table, with the result that he was subjected to a second expulsion. By registered mail, apparently, Scholem's father notified him on the day after the row that he, young "Gerhard," as he was then called, was to move out of the family home. In this way Scholem wound up at the Pension Struck, a Berlin hostel in which a number of Eastern European Jewish intellectuals resided. There he could and did discuss Judaism with real *Ostjuden*. While continuing his university studies in mathematics, he exchanged ideas about Jewish tradition with Jews who were regarded by many young Western Jews as being the living repositories of a deep Jewish spirituality.

At just this time, Scholem broke with Martin Buber, whose "Hasidic writings," e.g., *The Stories of Rabbi Nachman* [*Die Geschichten des Rabbi Nachman*, 1906] and *The Legend of Baal Schem* [*Die Legende des Baal Schem*, 1908], had done much to promote such favorable, romanticized images of *Ostjuden*. Not only that, as the "reigning leader of the Zionist youth movement," Buber, according to David Biale, had "turned into a virtue the liberal antisemitic accusation that Judaism is not suited to modern Western society: the alien 'Oriental' spirit of Judaism made it a relevant belief for youth in full revolt against nineteenth-century liberalism and Western civilization."[27] When Buber praised the war effort, in the very idiom through which he embraced Jewish otherness and the related ideal of mystical inner experience, *Erlebnismystik,* Scholem began to see Buber's whole prewar philosophy in a new and darker light. Soon after he had written the diary entry in which Buber appears as "the *essentially* mystical"—and shortly after reading Buber's article on the war, "The Solution" ("Die Lösung," 1916)—Scholem began to deride Buber. For example, he mocked Buber's philosophical discourse, labeling it "empty talk" [*Geschwätz*] in a note to his friend Erich Brauer (*SB* 1:122). In a November 1917 letter to another friend, Werner Kraft (the Kraus enthusiast), Scholem goes so far as to anathematize Buber as "the absolutely anti-Jewish" [*das Antijüdische schlechtin*] (*SB* 1:93).

Meanwhile, Kraus, one of a handful of high-profile German-Jewish intellectuals who condemned the war from its early days on, was meeting with better treatment in Scholem's diaries and correspondences. In a letter to Kraft dated November 30, 1917, Scholem reports: "In German one simply cannot describe what I feel when reading the Hebrew Bible. It is what Kraus calls the experience of the old word [*das Erlebnis des Alten Wortes*]" (*SB* 1:126–27). Kraus, then, is able to articulate a Jewish literary experience that is otherwise not to be conveyed *auf deutsch*. As Scholem distanced himself from the "anti-Jewish" Buber and his rhetoric of *Erlebnismystik*, he implied for the first time that there is something *exceptionally* Jewish about what a literary *Erlebnis* meant to Kraus.

But Kraus hardly became an idealized figure. Scholem, in fact, never embraced him uncritically. Consider Scholem's wartime avowal of how *Die Fackel* is the "only 'magazine' anyone needs to read." Characteristically, it ends with the unexplained qualifying claim: "I reject Kraus." Also worth mentioning is that Scholem spent more time thinking about Buber than about Kraus. While Buber was often, even constantly, on his mind, references to Kraus do not occur with great frequency in Scholem's diaries during the crucial 1916–18 period. But despite this incongruity, Kraus and his relation to language appear to have filled at least some of the space opened up by Buber's abrupt departure from Scholem's gallery of Jewish models. A diary entry dated October 24, 1917 strengthens that impression. Scholem, who was making a sort of study of the prewar *Fackel,* begins by citing a 1911 issue in which Kraus simultaneously criticizes both radical Jewish acculturation and what he perceived to be Zionist nationalism. Without fully endorsing Kraus's two-pronged objection, Scholem contends: "'the Zionists' blocked Kraus's path to Zionism." He thereby indicates that Kraus *should* be part of Zionist culture, and likely would be, were it not for "the Zionists," who evidently stand in the way of truly Zionist developments. As Benjamin had done just a few years earlier, Scholem contrasts organized Zionism with a deeper "Zionism of the spirit," whose chief bearers seem to be radical Jewish literati. Kraus, the programmatically unaffiliated commentator on literary experience, comes across here as the "real" Zionist. Accordingly, the type of Zionist that Scholem aspires to be turns out to be one who "does not flee toward Zionism." Then Scholem asks what actual Zionists should flee from. His answer is: "Above all, from Buber and the 'Zionists'" (*ST* 2:64).

Only later, in the company of Benjamin, a harsher and shriller critic of Buber's vitalist discourse, did Scholem become a regular reader of Kraus and his *Die Fackel*. That, at least, is what Scholem's book on Benjamin suggests. In it Scholem notes that Benjamin and he analyzed *Die Fackel* together "routinely" during the last year of the war, when they lived next to each other in Switzerland. And given that until 1918 Scholem alludes in his writings almost exclusively to back issues of *Die Fackel*, it is likely that he was pulled into Benjamin's pattern of serious Kraus consumption, which had begun in 1916. The pattern would stay with Scholem. After his emigration to Palestine in 1923, he faithfully subscribed to *Die Fackel* until Kraus stopped publishing it.[28] More important, however, is that Scholem's interest in the Jewishness of Kraus's style intensified dramatically in Switzerland. Indeed, it was toward the end of his stay in Bern and Muri, or in June 1919, that he enthused: Kraus is a "messianic movement of language."

Scholem makes this statement twice, once in a letter to Kraft (*SB* 1:207) and again in a diary entry (*ST* 2:462). In neither setting does he explicate comprehensively why the term "messianic" should be applied to Kraus. Instead he offers the schematic, and somewhat circular, idea that one cannot fight against Kraus, the "messianic movement of language," because the defining quality of a messianic movement of language is that one cannot fight against it. "A messianic movement of language is at its deepest level irresistible [*unbekämpfbar*]" (*ST* 2:462). But if the precise reasoning behind Scholem's terminology is not transparent, the general stakes of his thinking are clear enough. At a moment of world-historical upheaval, Scholem was probing in newly creative ways the encounter of tradition and modernity.

Remarking on Kraus's messianic authority, as well as on the "purity of the Krausian word," Scholem portrays Kraus as a kind of vestige of Jewish tradition in a hostile and unreceptive modern environment. "Hostile," because the diary entry at issue begins by reproaching Franz Werfel for having attacked what is "unbekämpfbar," i.e., Kraus. And "unreceptive," because Scholem conjectures that Kraus, "a messianic movement of language," can have "no consequences in language" [*keine Folgen in der Sprache haben*].

"No consequences in language" is in this context a suggestive phrase. For it evokes the title of, and a governing theme in, Kraus's famous polemic against Heine, "Heine and the Consequences." There, as we know, Kraus argues that Heine is a dandified Moses who produced for his people "Eau de Cologne" rather than life-sustaining water. He is a Moses who led Jewish literary talents into German culture by way of the feuilleton. Hence Kraus's title: it refers to the notion that (German-Jewish) feuilleton writers are Heine's "consequences." By contrast, in Scholem's diary entry Kraus, who "discovers the most unexpected Jewish provinces" in the German language, will have "no consequences in language." So not only does Kraus's style have profoundly Jewish qualities, it appears by virtue of an intertextual link as Kraus himself often presented it—as a direct counterpoint to a more mainstream and consequential mode of German-Jewish journalism. If this link seems thin, it will appear less so once we take into account that Scholem soon made the adversarial relationship between Kraus and "Jewish journalism" more explicit. "Both: Journalism and Kraus," Scholem wrote, "are children of the Jewish middle ages. *But* Kraus is an unhappy and therefore worthy child" (*ST* 2:468, my emphasis).

The concept whereby Scholem connects "both" journalism and Kraus to the "Jewish middle ages" is the "Musivstil," or the "musive style." According to the Israeli scholar Dan Pagis, in such writing Hebrew poets typically wove biblical verses and verse fragments into their poetry, often transforming the significance of the citations they employed. These allusive techniques involved a particular, meaning-bearing intimacy with tradition. As Pagis defines it, the musive style depended on the audience's recognition of verse fragments, its knowledge of traditional literature, its ability to supply the missing parts of the verse, and its ability to appreciate how their context was changed. Turning to the matter of reception, he states: "Nineteenth-century scholars called this style *Musivstil*, i.e., a mosaic of verses. In our day there have been some objections to that term and its underlying assumption because the result is not simply a collection of citations but a new and dynamic creation."[29]

Scholem was on the side of the revisionists. In an unpublished series of notes, which carry the heading "The Musive Word" ["Das musivische Wort"] and which were probably written in July 1919, he adverts to a "misunderstanding" of the "development" that led to the musive style.[30] He then prizes the musive style in strong language, writing, for example, that in the "efflorescence [*Blütezeit*] of the musive style," the "musive word became the medium of an endless reflection of words." From this idea Scholem quickly works his way to the claim: "The musive word expresses the highest purity of language."[31] As he concludes his celebration, he maintains: "The guarantee of the greatness and effect of this poetry lies in the earnestness and severity with which the positive foundation of an absolute, unalterable word is recognized as the medium of poetry."

Having exalted the musive word in terms (e.g., "purity") that overlap with his ongoing evocation of Kraus, Scholem addresses the "musive style's period of decline [*Verfallszeit*]." Here he limns a dialectical process of change and continuity. Scholem hypothesizes that the "dissolution" of the musive word occurred when the "musive tendency," or musive formal techniques, "began to be applied" in a "negative" way. The "musive tendency" began to be appropriated, that is, in a manner that goes against the searching spirit of the musive style, against its ethos of "the absolute" and of endless reflection. It began to be used "mechanically." According to Scholem's compact narrative, this process resulted in an "impure poetry," which, in turn, "leads in a straight line to journalism."

Implicit in such utterances is the question that Moritz Goldstein poses at the center of his "German-Jewish Parnassus" essay: "Why are there so many journalists?" After all, Scholem is attempting to make sense of what he sees as the outsized role of Jews in the journalistic sphere. His *answer* is that journalism descends directly, or "in a straight line," from the medieval musive style. Thus journalism is a child of "the Jewish middle ages." But it is, in Scholem's view, an illegitimate child. In the essay fragment "On Journalism, Modern Hebrew Poetry, and the Musive Style" ("Über Journalismus, neuhebräische Dichtung und Musivstil," 1919?), he writes: "The great gift of the perverted Jews of the nineteenth-century and of the present for journalism rests, from a linguistic standpoint, on the perversion of the musive style. The danger of this mode of expression is that when its religious basis is removed, it will become journalism" (*ST* 2:586).

But what links journalism with the musive style? What justifies seeing journalism and the musive style as so intimately related? Scholem's theory is that both modes of writing work heavily with citation and linguistic reproduction. For him, quoting is the shared feature—the crucial formal affinity—that explains how perverting the musive style yields journalism. He speculates that modern Jews have inherited the medieval Jewish drive to "say everything twice." But they have used their linguistic inheritance without any spiritual "basis," thereby desacralizing and deforming it. It was Kraus, apparently, who most effectively identified the problem. "What Karl Kraus objects to in 'Heine and the Consequences' is just this inversion: the application of the musive without applying it to an *absolute* object" (*ST* 2:586). Whereas in truly musive writing quotation has force and "purity," in journalism it is eminently unproductive, even debauched. Invoking Kraus again, Scholem asserts that in journalism one "'rubs oneself against the word.'" One no longer quotes in order to open up "the absolute, and at the same time meaningless word" by placing it in "a new context of relations" [*Relationszusammenhang*]. Rather, one cites venally—for profit. More than once, Scholem accuses acculturated Jewish journalists of prostituting the word, of displaying in their writing "prostitute-like" qualities. He speaks, indeed, of the Jewish journalist's "whorish, unproductive relation to language" [*dirnenhafte, unschöpferische Verhältnis zur Sprache*]. And he also speaks of the Jewish journalist's "whorish copulation with the word" [*hurerische Beischlaf am Worte*] (587).[32] Through journalism, then, the "musive" relationship with the word is enacted in modern society in an utterly "perverted" manner. As Scholem puts it, "Jewish journalism is a demonic breakthrough of the objectless musive linguistic spirit into the German language" (587).

Like Goldstein and Wassermann—and a spate of fin-de-siècle writers, including Kraus—Scholem presents "unproductive" journalistic writing as an especially important agent and emblem of German-Jewish assimilation. According to Wassermann, the Jewish literatus is *the* person who has become "separated from myth" and thus from intellectual fecundity. According to Scholem, "the worst journalism" (*ST* 2:587) results from, and mirrors, spiritual diminishment on the part of assimilated Jews, their losing touch with "the absolute." Scholem's rhetoric, however, is even more aggressive than what we find in most of the philippics against "Jewish journalism" that come from German-Jewish circles. Next to his slashing use of sexual imagery, Kraus's lines about Heine's illicit affair with the German language look almost like jocular needling. But it is not only Scholem's vocabulary that breaks with convention. Scholem's historical narrative is, of course, highly original. In his account German Jews have thrived as journalists because of formal connections between journalistic writing and the medieval musive style he so admires. Both forms of writing turn on quoting and configuring verbal material that already exists. It is the Jews' traditional musive tendency to "say everything twice" that propels them, as they fall out of contact with "the absolute," into the journalistic sphere.

Yet Scholem's argument does not simply go off into an uncharted area. On a basic level it runs counter to Goldstein's and Wassermann's ideas about what the plethora of Jewish journalists means. Goldstein and Wassermann set up a dichotomy between the uncreative mirroring of assimilated journalists and a desired elemental creativity. That Jews succeed in journalism reflects, for them, a crisis of German-Jewish identity. The prodigious accomplishments of Jewish journalists are at least as depressing to Scholem, but he does not cast autogenetic originality as an existential imperative. Instead he juxtaposes two "Jewish" forms of quoting. The first, the musive word, is the "highest expression of linguistic purity." The second, journalism, exploits and degrades that tradition of citing. What Scholem wants is not mythic originality but rather a better appropriation of the musive inheritance.

He finds it in Kraus, who counterposed his *Fackel* to the journalism of Heine's "consequences," quoted radically, venerated language as his dominating mistress, and proudly stylized himself as "one of those epigones who dwell in the old house of language." According to Scholem, "this Jew," this "unhappy and worthy child" of "the Jewish middle ages," has somehow forged a "legitimate" connection to the musive word. And he therefore "discovers the most unexpected Jewish provinces in this [German] language." Strikingly, Scholem goes on, in the July 1919 diary entry from which I have been quoting, to insist that Kraus "never had an original thought [*keinen eigenen Gedanken*] in his life" (*ST* II: 2:469). To this remark he appends the statement, "and that is meant here infinitely more as a compliment than as a criticism." Scholem's dialectical logic might be described with the formulation: the way down is also the way up. Journalism represents the "breakthrough" of a spiritually bankrupt musive style "into the German language." But the same formal linkages, e.g., quoting, that Scholem uses to read journalism as a sullying of Jewish tradition lead *him* to "discover the most unexpected Jewish provinces" in that same discursive field, or rather, in its most radical part. A "legitimate" modern connection to the musive style persists, above all, in Kraus's "journalism in its most paradoxical form," his "anti-journalism."

After the war, Scholem continued to regard Kraus as a sort of dialectical turn in the journalistic enactment of Jewish tradition. "For a long time

I had been thinking about how Kraus's style ultimately might derive from the Hebrew prose and poetry of medieval Jewry, from the language of the great halakhic writers and the 'musive style,' from rhymed prose, in which pieces of sacred texts are mixed together kaleidoscopically, journalistically, polemically, descriptively, and are also profaned erotically," writes Scholem as he recounts some of his more memorable postwar conversations with Walter Benjamin.[33] Scholem adds that these discussions were quite "passionate," and also that around the same time (1921) Benjamin and he experienced "choking fits of laughter" while reading Kraus's play *Literature*. In that work, as I mentioned in chapter 3, Kraus responds satirically to Franz Werfel's attempt to caricature him as a lowly, unoriginal "Mirror-man." It was during this moment of collective enthusiasm, and as Kafka was ruminating on how "no one can speak *Mauscheln* like Kraus," that Benjamin began to engage in earnest with Kraus's "investment in language."[34]

THEORIES OF QUOTATION: READING KRAUS WITH AND BEYOND SCHOLEM

In 1921, Benjamin had the intention of founding a literary journal, which was to have the title *Angelus Novus*. He never realized his goal. But while his plan was still alive, Benjamin hoped to publish in his journal Scholem's theories of Kraus's prose. Alluding to his own ideas about Kraus, Scholem recollects in *Walter Benjamin:* "Benjamin often demanded that I put these thoughts into writing, no doubt for *Angelus*."[35] Benjamin later (repeatedly) asked Scholem for his notes on Kraus and Jewish tradition. Whether he ever got them is unclear, but the interpretations I adumbrated in the preceding paragraphs do seem to echo through the essays on Kraus that Benjamin eventually produced. In one of those works, "Karl Kraus" (1928), Benjamin forcefully activates the association Scholem had drawn between "Kraus and the Halakah." More specifically, Benjamin makes Kraus out to be "the greatest breakthrough of halakhic writing into the mass of the German language." Here he adopts also the rhetoric of Scholem's commentary, which attempts to track "the breakthrough" of the musive style "into the German language." To be sure, in "Karl Kraus" (1931), Benjamin develops his own idiosyncratic positions. Yet he seems to work with the logic of Scholem's claim about how Kraus, the "worthy child" of "the Jewish middle ages," stands over against a "bad" child who effects a "whorish copulation with the word." After all, in Benjamin's essay Kraus's language represents a messianic *separation* of "Geist" and "Eros," a separation that is at once related to, and opposes, the feuilleton.

Then there is the motif of citation. Writing about that central theme in both his and Scholem's reading of Kraus, i.e., the spiritual power of "the repeated word," Benjamin posits that quoting can result in a rare and felicitous "consummation" of language. It can bring human language to the point where our words resemble "the angelic tongue" and "mottoes from the Book of Creation." These lines, it is worth noting, might well have emerged directly out of Benjamin's dialogue with Scholem. Indeed, Robert Alter has observed that "the Book of Creation" is both "an old Christian cliché" *and*, "as Benjamin surely would have known through Scholem, the precise translation for the title of a classic kabbalistic text, *Sefer Yetsirah*."[36]

But, again, Benjamin does much more than borrow from Scholem as he attributes "Jewish significance" to Kraus's quoting. In "Karl Kraus" (1931) quotation takes on such meaning within an elaborate network of intratextual references, many of which have little to do with what we find in Scholem's notes on the "Musivstil." Let me offer two examples. Before Benjamin celebrates quoting he distinguishes Kraus's style from the "hieratic" language of Stefan George, a hugely influential, turn-of-the-century German poet whose verbal atavisms Kraus had criticized in 1926. Sharpening his distinction, Benjamin indicates that the difference between the two authors derives, at least in part, from Kraus's affinities with Judaism. He suggests that Kraus's "language" is a "theater for the sanctification of names," and that with "Jewish certainty" Kraus's language "resists" George's particular linguistic mysticism—George's "theurgy of 'word's body'" [*Theurgie des 'Wortleibs'*] ("KK," 376). So when Benjamin subsequently argues that "to quote a word is to call a word by its name," and that "in it [quotation] is mirrored the angelic tongue," he appears to be picking up on the part of "Karl Kraus" where Kraus *sanctifies* names with "Jewish certainty."

Benjamin also sets up the essay's famous passage on quoting by linking language, Jewishness, and justice: "One has said about Kraus, he had 'to subdue his inner Judaism,' and, he has 'traveled from Judaism to freedom'; nothing refutes this better than that, for him too, justice and language remain founded in each other" ("KK," 380). Later we learn: "In the rescuing and punitive quotation language reveals itself as the *Mater* [matrix] of justice" (380). Thus it is only after connecting citation to a loaded nexus of justice and language, to a nexus whose Jewishness has been "established," that Benjamin identifies in quoting resonances of the Kabbalah and of messianic completion.

The messianic character of quoting is, at the same time, typically violent. According to Benjamin's "Theses on the Philosophy of History" ["Über den Begriff der Geschichte," 1940], the "Messiah comes not only as the redeemer, he comes also as the subduer of Antichrist."[37] And in "Karl Kraus" (1931), similarly, quotation entails both calling the word to "its origin" and "destructively tearing" it from its immediate context. In quotation "origin and destruction" at once stand out *and* "interpenetrate each other," producing a rare consummation of language, a consummation in which mundane words, now "freed from the context of meaning," resemble the language of angels.

But not all quoting carries such connotations. Benjamin had far-reaching and broad-ranging interests in mimetic activity, and it would be unfair to treat those interests—and therefore his reading of Kraus's quoting—as though they were determined only by "Jewish issues." For example, Benjamin wrote in an anthropological vein about how "the mimetic faculty" affects all human development.[38] And his unfinished final book, *The Arcades Project* [*Das Passagen-Werk,* 1982], "constellates" a vast array of citations. Moreover, the significance of quotation in Benjamin's works is quite multifarious. In "Karl Kraus" (1931) quoting coheres with, and seems even to revivify, what Benjamin perceives to be hoary elements of Jewish culture. The "Theses on the Philosophy of History" thicken the link between quotation and messianic redemption, bringing into it Benjamin's much-discussed and radical ideas about historical memory. There he predicts: "Only for a redeemed humanity will the past become citable in each one of its moments."[39] Yet the very fin de siècle sense of rupture that made the power and authority of traditional motifs so alluring and so elusive gave quotation a very different meaning as well.

Indeed, Benjamin sometimes treated "destructive" quotation as an important *post-traditional* critical device. Hence Hannah Arendt's remark about his "discovery of the *modern* function of quotation" (my emphasis).[40] Arendt continues: "Walter Benjamin knew that the break in tradition and the loss of authority which occurred in his lifetime were irreparable, and he concluded that he had to discover new ways of dealing with the past. In this he became a master when he discovered that the transmissibility of the past had been replaced by its citability and that in place of its authority there had arisen a strange power to settle down, piecemeal, in the present and to deprive it of its 'peace of mind,' the mindless peace of complacency." Fittingly, though certainly not in order to "deprive" Benjamin's words of "complacency," Arendt appends to these points a quotation by Benjamin: "Quotations in my works are like robbers by the roadside who make an armed attack and relieve the idler of his convictions."[41] As in Benjamin's later Kraus essay, quotation has the effect of startling. But in the passage Arendt cites there is no talk of "the angelic tongue" and of linguistic "consummation"—there is no messianic coming together of "origin and destruction." Quotations are imagined only as marauding agents of critical disabusal. While "armed" to "attack," they seem to be ill-equipped for "messianic violence."

Still, Benjamin became attracted to Kraus's particular mimetic techniques through a text that deals centrally with the matter of mirroring in German-Jewish culture. Like Scholem and Kafka, that is, he was deeply affected by the postwar experience of reading Kraus's *Literature*, where Kraus discerns among assimilated German-Jewish authors what Scholem would later call "Originalitätssucht," or a "compulsion to be original."[42] Not only do the expressionist "sons" in Kraus's play try to use hypertrophied poetry as a means of rebelling against "the Judaism of their fathers," these sons have a correlative, overdetermined contempt for imitation. In the play Werfel's fictional acolytes exclaim that the Kraus cipher engages in "Jewish copying" ["Alles was er kann, ist uns nachjüdeln!"], and that he is therefore an "Epigone!" These assertions are preceded by their cry, "Jewish self-hatred!"[43] The immediate juxtaposition of the phrases "Jewish self-hatred" and "Jewish copying" [*nachjüdeln*] implies that, for Werfel and writers of his ilk, "Jewish copying" stems from Jewish self-hatred. But, as Werfel's followers appropriate it here, the charge of "Jewish self-hatred!" interlocks with an anti-Jewish slur about creatively deficient Jewish mirroring: "nachjüdeln." Thus Kraus suggests that in Werfel's *Mirror-man*—where he is depicted as a self-hating Jew—the accusation of Jewish self-hatred has an anti-Jewish component.[44] "All" the self-hating Kraus figure "can do" is "nachjüdeln," which is what makes him such a pathetic character, an abject Jewish Mirror-Man. Kraus, moreover, goes beyond parodying the contradictions behind Werfel's Mirror-Man figure.[45] He performatively distances himself from Werfel. As Kafka observed, the "humor" in *Literature* is Kraus's mimetic reproduction of expressionist idiom. So Kraus flaunts his imitative abilities as he lampoons Werfel's disparagement of "acoustic mirroring."

That this humor would appeal to Benjamin too is certainly understandable. For he had been, as we saw, a champion of the imposing Jewish literatus who mediates "the art" he "cannot make." Also worth recalling here is Benjamin's analogous tendency to be stridently, even viciously, critical of German-Jewish invocations of the kinds of aesthetic-existential ideals that Werfel deploys against Kraus's abject "mirroring." These are the ideals of mental potency, of elemental creativity, and authentic inner experience, all of which were popular among both expressionists and cultural Zionists, two groups that often overlapped. With such "rhetoric of authenticity" in mind, Benjamin once said of Buber that he "seamlessly imported the terminology of National Socialism into debates about Jewish questions" (*BB* 5:402).[46] We can view Benjamin's similarly dramatic claim that "everything Kraus achieved as a literary critic lies in his reckoning with [Werfel's] expressionism" (*BGS* 2:3.1090) as a related pronouncement, animated by the same distaste.[47]

But Kraus's reply to Werfel is not the only reason why, in wake of the war, *Die Fackel* elicited greater interest from Benjamin. Kraus's pacifism must have resonated with Benjamin, who fervently opposed the war. Indeed, in "Karl Kraus"(1931) Benjamin cites "In This Great Time" ["In dieser Großen Zeit," 1914], Kraus's most famous antiwar essay, at length. And it was during the war that Benjamin began to work with the motifs of messianic destruction that play such an important role in his thoughts about how Kraus, the "apocalyptic satirist," treats language.[48] As Rabinbach has put it, "Missing in the writings of [Ernst] Bloch and Benjamin before August 1914 is the radical and apocalyptic aspect of modern messianism. In this regard the war obliged them. After 1914 we see in both Bloch's and Benjamin's writings an attempt to find a secular and theological philosophy that can embody the messianic impulse in relation to a *real* apocalypse and to translate the promise of European culture into the promise of political redemption."[49]

However, it would be wrong to argue that by 1921 Benjamin was well on his way to the superlative statements about Kraus he would make in 1928 and 1931. Some of the features in Benjamin's "modern Jewish messianism" with which Kraus's style connects most poignantly were, after all, still quite inchoate in the early 1920s. The crucial notion of "origin" [*Ursprung*] is such a feature. In fact, only in his very last text does Benjamin quote Kraus's motto "origin is the goal," or the phrase that, for Rabinbach, "captures this idea ['the messianic idea' of restoration] most succinctly."[50] Even more noteworthy is that several events that took place in the mid-1920s decisively affected Benjamin's attitude toward Kraus.

STYLES OF THE RADICAL WILL IN THE WEIMAR PUBLIC SPHERE

It was in 1925 that the first of these events occurred. Frustrated by academic protocol, Benjamin withdrew his application for a habilitation from the

University of Frankfurt. This inability to work within certain institutional constraints is more than simply well known; it has become part of Benjamin's hallowed outsider mystique. Less widely acknowledged is that as he dropped out of academe, Benjamin was busily establishing himself in the field of literary journalism, a burgeoning part of the Weimar public sphere.[51] His debut piece for the prestigious magazine *Die Literarische Welt* [*The Literary World*], for which he would write over one hundred articles, was actually published in the very year of his departure. What matters, however, is not the brute fact of Benjamin's new career but rather its effects. When Benjamin moved from the one path to the other, his vocational self-image shifted. To be sure, many of basic concerns and theoretical proclivities remained intact. Yet his goals and points of identification changed. Having produced a dissertation on romantic literary criticism and a redoubtably recondite study of baroque tragic drama, Benjamin set for himself the aim of becoming "the preeminent critic of German literature."

By 1930, he could speak of being close to fulfilling that aspiration. "The problem," as he put it, "is that literary criticism is no longer treated as a serious genre in Germany and has not been for more than fifty years. If you want to make a name for yourself in criticism, this ultimately means that you must recreate criticism as a genre. Others have made significant progress here, but I have gone especially far."[52] Twelve years after rehabilitating the Jewish literatus in theory, Benjamin became one in practice. His doing so meant, as his letter indicates, dealing with the stigma that continued to cling to his "disreputable" essayistic genre, as well as keeping a watchful eye on the activities of (seemingly less successful) colleagues. In this altered situation Benjamin's ties to Kraus grew substantially. Not only was it only after 1925 that Kraus began to occupy considerable space in Benjamin's correspondences, but what Benjamin tended to focus on initially is how Kraus asserted himself in hostile exchanges with other German-Jewish critics. With a new attentiveness, Benjamin addressed an old concern, commenting in detail on how Kraus attacked the failings of the "literati-Jew."

In a 1926 letter to his friends Alfred and Grete Cohn, for example, Benjamin laments Kraus's ineffectiveness in an essay on Friedrich Gundolf, a member of Stefan George's circle whom both he and Kraus had long despised, and who had reached a broad audience with his biography of Goethe (*BB* 3:202). A subsequent missive to Cohn, which is dated March 27, 1928, discusses a second event of importance for Benjamin's thinking about Kraus: the lecture by Kraus that Benjamin had just attended in Berlin. There, apparently, Kraus was in top form in castigating Alfred Kerr, who was the sort of moderate acculturated critic whom Benjamin scorned almost as vehemently as he did Buber. Benjamin seems to have thought that, as the author of elegant, graceful, often easy-to-digest feuilletons, Kerr too betrayed the *radical* calling of the cosmopolitan Jewish literatus. And so he was thrilled to see Kerr skewered. Obviously taken with Kraus's performance, Benjamin claims that Kraus "has made a larger impression than ever before." He adds that Kraus has "found an adequate object" and "grown into the greatest stature." Finally, in relating how Kraus exposed Kerr's wartime attempt to denounce him "to the military authorities as a subversive and defeatist author," Benjamin pledges that he, Benjamin, "definitely" wants to write about Kraus (*BB* 3:358–59).

A slightly later letter to Cohn describes the most recent issue of *Die Fackel* (*F* 781–86) as "something for the heart" (*BB* 3:387). One reason why is that Benjamin's name is listed in its "bibliographical section." With palpable delight, he alludes to the "mentioning of my name in *Die Fackel*"—in both his note to Cohn and in a contemporaneous letter to Scholem. Kraus consistently announced the publication of works about him; and in the spring of 1928, not long after Benjamin had heard Kraus lecture in Berlin, the first two of his five pieces on the satirist appeared. Hence that "mentioning" of Benjamin's name in the "bibliographical section" of *Die Fackel*. The short pieces listed there, "Karl Kraus Reads Offenbach" ["Karl Kraus liest Offenbach"] and "Warrior Monument" ["Kriegerdenkmal"], are generally quite positive and at times almost panegyric-like, even if the latter text intones, "nothing [is] more futile than Kraus's fight against the press." In his private correspondences Benjamin maintains a more varied stance. After labeling *Die Fackel* "something for the heart," he allows that Kraus has lost another round to Kerr. Kraus's response to Kerr's very public lyrical barb "The Polemicist" ["Der Polemiker," 1928]—the poem came out in the mass-circulation *Berliner Tageblatt*—simply "lets up" in Benjamin's view.

But Benjamin persisted in offering unreserved public attestations to Kraus's critical intensity. "Warrior Monument," for instance, contains the phrase: "nothing more godforsaken than his [Kraus's] opponents" (*BGS* 4:1.121). And the long "Karl Kraus" essay of 1931 dwells on how Kraus the "cannibal" [*Menschenfresser*] consumes his adversaries ("KK," 361). Furthermore, while some letters do qualify such pronouncements, Benjamin's charged reception of Kraus's polemical fervor appears to have extended even into his dreams. According to Soma Morgenstern, a fellow critic, in 1931 Benjamin recollected having had a Kraus nightmare. In it Kraus is at first sitting at a desk "covered with revolvers." Then without any warning he shoots everyone in the line of people walking by him, "each with a different revolver." Benjamin woke up from the dream, in Morgenstern's account, "deeply horrified" (*SB* 3:318).

Among other things, this oneiric experience implies that where "Karl Kraus" (1931) characterizes Kraus in sanguinary terms—e.g., as having blood dripping from his lips after he mimics someone—Benjamin is drawing on deeply felt impressions. Certainly we might infer from the dream episode that he had a disturbing sense of the violence of Kraus's main polemical instrument: his language. Benjamin would not have been alone with that feeling. Don't the dream-images of Kraus taking pistols into his hand and firing at his human targets recall Kafka's graphic remarks about how Kraus's "writing hand" is just as "frighteningly physical" as his own?

In the typescript of his 1931"Karl Kraus" essay, Benjamin points to a different connection between Kafka and Kraus, or to the analogous way in which "divine justice" and language and law and language come together in the works of both writers.[53] A trace of this gesture remains in the printed version of the piece, where Benjamin insists: "One has said about Kraus, he had 'to subdue his inner Judaism,' and, he has 'traveled from Judaism to freedom'; nothing refutes this better than that, for him too, justice and language remain founded in each other [*in einander gestiftet*]."[54] A trace remains because the "for him *too*" phrase, which has no antecedent here, goes with a deleted sentence, one that is present in the typescript of Benjamin's essay but not in the published version. And the missing lines liken the architecture of Kraus's "Gedankengebäude" to the "labyrinthine" structures that "the law" prefers in Kafka's *The Trial*. According to Benjamin, "Kraus knows no system. Every thought has its own cell. But every cell can turn, in a flash and apropos of nothing, into a room, into a courtroom over which language presides. Thus Kraus's *Gedankengebäude* is identical to the demonic, labyrinthine apartment house in which, in Kafka, K.'s trial is carried out."

The final sentence in this passage is the one that was excised. It is to Benjamin's very next sentence that the phrase "for him [Kraus] too" belongs. So we read in the typescript of "Karl Kraus" (1931): "Thus Kraus's *Gedankengebäude* is identical to the demonic, labyrinthine apartment house in which, in Kafka, K.'s trial is carried out. One has said about Kraus, he had 'to subdue his inner Judaism,' and 'he has 'traveled from Judaism to freedom'; nothing refutes this better than that, for him too, justice and language remain founded in each other." Had his reference to Kafka not been deleted, Benjamin would have suggested that, for Kafka and for Kraus *too*, "justice and language remain founded in each other." Benjamin would have made a further suggestion as well. If Kraus's attitude toward "justice and language" is comparable to Kafka's, and Kraus's attitude entails taking "the authentically Jewish *salto mortale*," Kafka *too* must have made that "authentically Jewish" leap.[55]

Clearly, the thematic nexus of language, justice, and Judaism was also on Benjamin's mind in 1928, when he wrote the first "Karl Kraus" piece. That essay, indeed, concertedly emphasizes the relationship between Kraus's investments in law and language. Benjamin writes: "One will understand nothing about this man [Kraus] until one recognizes that, for him, everything, without exception everything, language and thing [*Sprache and Sache*] necessarily play themselves out in the sphere of law [*Recht*]" (*BGS* 2:2.624). Using this linkage, Benjamin pursues another of his aims in the piece: "to draw Kraus's Jewish physiognomy." In fact, he depicts the radical encompassing of "everything" within the "sphere of law" as a superlatively "halakhic" moment in German, the Halakah being a body of discourse that deals with Jewish law.[56] What precedes the formulation about law and language I just cited is the statement: "In him [Kraus] the greatest breakthrough of halakhic writing into the mass of the German language takes place." From there Benjamin goes on to extol Kraus's prosecutorial activities, framing them as well as a Jewish phenomenon: "That this man [Kraus], one of an evanescent few who have a sense of what freedom is, can serve it only by being the highest prosecutor—that is the purest expression of his dialectics. A being [*Dasein*], which—precisely here—is the hottest prayer for redemption that passes through Jewish lips today" (*GS* 2:2.625).

"Karl Kraus" (1928) is, as far as I can tell, the first text, apart from his letters, in which Benjamin discerns a notable link between Jewish tradition (i.e., "halakhic writing") and the style of a modern German-Jewish author (i.e., Kraus's dialectics). In doing so he brings together longstanding and new concerns. We can hear in the essay echoes of the conversations Benjamin had with Scholem in 1919 and 1921, conversations in which they collectively pondered "the relation of Jews to language," and, more specifically, "Kraus and the Halakah." Where some of Scholem's letters and diary entries from that period attribute a "messianic" character to Kraus's writing, Benjamin's essay portrays it as a uniquely hot "prayer for redemption." Similarly, in both Scholem's outlines and Benjamin's text the appearance of Jewish tradition in the German language has a "breakthrough" character. And, of course, that "event" occurs through the "unexpected" medium of a literatus's prose. Here, again, Benjamin's account of Kraus's superlative

Jewishness is in a general way continuous with his response to the *Kunstwart* debate, which locates the "serious mission" of the Jews among the "religiously" earnest literati.

Yet in "Karl Kraus" (1928) Kraus is also praised for exhibiting qualities that Benjamin does not mention in his exchanges with Strauss. What the essay holds up for acknowledgement is how Kraus acts as the "highest prosecutor," or the combative thrust that Benjamin had been following eagerly, and would continue to take stock of, in his correspondences. Moreover, in connecting that aspect of Kraus's writing to Jewish tradition Benjamin leans heavily on a set of juridical terms (e.g., "Recht," "Ankläger") that play no role in Scholem's reading of *Die Fackel*. These terms also have a prominent place in Benjamin's one other extensive reckoning with the status of Jewish tradition in the work of a German-language writer, namely, his 1934 article on Kafka, whose fictional "law" Benjamin began to analyze in 1928.[57] So if the schematic 1928 "Karl Kraus" text reads like the articulation of long-held ideas, it also reads like an experiment, like an initial foray into meditating on the transmissibility of tradition amidst its modern "sickening," as Benjamin would put it. That the prospect of this undertaking excited Benjamin is recorded in his letters to Scholem. For his part, Scholem seems to have shared that excitement. Displeased by Benjamin's increasingly Marxist vocabulary, he vigorously encouraged Benjamin, in 1928, to let the Jewish dimension of his thought come out from its "latency."[58] Soon after the first "Karl Kraus" piece had appeared, and months before he began working on its lengthier namesake, Benjamin obliged his friend. He asked Scholem for his outlines on "Kraus and the Halakah" (*BB* 3:439). Several weeks later, or in March 1929, Benjamin repeated his request, this time specifying that he wanted to see Scholem's notes on "how Kraus's language derives from the musive style" (*BB* 3:455).

BENJAMIN'S "KARL KRAUS"

"Karl Kraus" was published in the *Frankfurter Zeitung* in four installments. The first appeared on March 10, 1931, the last a little over a week later. As its serialized status implies, the essay is a work of considerable size. It is also rather dense. Indeed, Sigrid Weigel recently described "Karl Kraus" as "this at times cryptic and generally perhaps least accessible text by Benjamin."[59] She continues her account in a more figurative key: "The text juts out like a hermetic block into the midst of the more fluid mode of writing of Benjamin's late works, which are increasingly characterized by thought-images and miniatures, juxtaposed quotations, detail-readings, or single scenarios from the history of culture or the subject."[60] What explains the essay's forbidding difficulty, according to Weigel, is that it attempts "to set out a conclusive *systematic* argument concerning the connection between sexuality and intellectual production."[61] Otherwise put, her claim is that Benjamin's long article has several layers, one of which is rarified. While drawing a nuanced portrait of Kraus and his work, Benjamin seeks to arrange a series of some of his more abstract ideas into a "systematic" constellation. "Karl Kraus" represents "an analysis of the different textual practices of Kraus the writer." And, "at the same time, it is a masked reflection on and a rewriting of Benjamin's own earlier statements on this topic"—on the topic of how "Eros," "Geist" and "Sprache" interact.[62]

No doubt there is merit to these assertions. As Weigel's analysis artfully shows, the dialectical structure of the essay "only becomes decipherable in its larger context when read in relation to concepts from [Benjamin's] early work." For Benjamin traces Kraus's "textual practices" through three enigmatic positions, *Allmensch* ("Cosmic Man"), *Dämon* ("Demon"), and *Unmensch* ("Nonhuman Being"). And all three have to do with those early concepts, e.g., "Eros of the creative" [*Eros der Schaffenden*] and the "Fall of Language-mind" [*Sündenfall des Sprachgeistes*]. In the text's climactic third part, for instance, "Unmensch," Benjamin sees—alongside a true "humanity" that "proves itself by destruction"—the possibility of a redeemed, "consummated" language.

But it is not only paradoxes like the "Unmensch" who is the bearer of "real humanism," and also Benjamin's attempt to bring forth an argument that is both systematic and guided by a pattern of "masked reflection," that make "Karl Kraus" so exegetically challenging. When Benjamin first voiced his intention to write about Kraus, he spoke of being beset by "a mass of ideas" over which he had trouble maintaining a coherent "perspective" [*Überblick*] (*BB* 3:202). The essay itself and the voluminous notes Benjamin compiled while working on it give us an indication as to why. Kraus's writing connects with an array of issues that were of importance to Benjamin and that were in some cases tightly interlinked for him. Here are just a few of those themes: Shakespeare; the baroque rant; the press in the age of "high capitalism," "the destructive character," the convergence of opposing tendencies (e.g., "reactionary theory and revolutionary practice"), *Sprachkritik,* the ideology of form, Judaism, quotation, mimesis, apocalyptic thinking. So I want to add to Weigel's somewhat narrow point about the intertextual character of "Karl Kraus" the following qualification. The structure of, and major theoretical claims in, the essay are informed by *various* strands of thought that stretch back to the start of Benjamin's career, including the ones with which I have been dealing in this chapter.

Benjamin begins by depicting *Die Fackel* as a "newspaper" [*Zeitung*], but an extraordinary one: "In old etchings the messenger who has come screaming—his hair standing on end, and in his hands a paper [*Blatt*] full of war and pestilence, of death cries and woe, of fire and drought—this messenger spreads the 'Newest Newspaper' [*Neueste Zeitung*]. *Die Fackel* is a newspaper [*Zeitung*] in that sense, in the sense the word has in Shakespeare" ("KK," 353). Taking up how the issue of *Die Fackel* relates to other newspapers, Benjamin explores the extent and nature of Kraus's animus toward "the press." The "hatred" with which *Die Fackel* pursues modern newspapers is, he contends, analogous to the enmity an "ur-progenitor [*Urahn*] casts upon the line [*Geschlecht*] of degenerate dwarves that have sprung from his seed" (353). Much like Scholem, Benjamin colorfully puts Kraus and the press at different ends of the same lineage. They are once again members of the same family. Not only that, Kraus remains "worthy" as the irascible "ur-progenitor," while journalism, which Scholem viewed as "perverted," is again a "degenerate [*entarteter*] child."

Benjamin proceeds to reinforce this play of dissimilarity and blood connections. As he does so, he addresses in more detail that crucial issue in early twentieth-century debates about Jewish identity and journalism: the existential stakes of journalistic writing. He argues: "A hatred of the type Kraus heaps on the journalists can never be rooted simply in what they do, however vile that may be. Such hatred must have its basis in their being [*Sein*], whether it is opposed or related to his. In fact, it is both" ("KK," 353). How so? To explain his point, Benjamin cites a conventional definition of "the journalist," a definition similar to some of those that we encountered in chapter 1 (e.g., Adolf Jellinek's). Here the journalist is a person "'who has little interest in his own existence and in the sheer existence of things, but who first senses things in their relation to other things, and, above all, where these relations come together in events'" (353–54). This sentence, Benjamin proposes, "is nothing other than Kraus's negative image." After all, "could anyone display a more burning interest in his own existence than Kraus, who never tires of that theme? Who has a more attentive eye for the sheer existence of things, for their origin?" (354). These ideas, which place Kraus over against relational perception and align him with origins, anticipate the famous passage on quoting that appears in the third part of Benjamin's essay. For there the redemptive mechanism in quotation is precisely that it tears words out of a relational context—or a "context of meaning"—and delivers them back to an "origin." And the foreshadowing continues. After defining Kraus as a journalistic paradox, Benjamin goes on to examine Kraus's "struggle against" those reified words though which "the topicality in journalism achieves domination over the world of things": the journalistic "empty phrase." Just as he does "in quotation," in combating the phrase Kraus attempts, in effect, to redeem fallen words.

In evoking Kraus's "struggle" against journalistic reification, Benjamin's portrait closely mirrors Kraus's self-image. Indeed, the language with which Benjamin outlines Kraus's opposition to Heine's "feuilletonism" recalls the very terms with which Kraus distanced himself from German-Jewish journalists. Kraus, according to Benjamin, stands over against "the Schmock," who blurs "the boundaries between journalism and literature" ("KK," 354). But Benjamin does not simply adopt Kraus's ideas about himself and his work. Whereas Scholem affirmed Kraus's reading of the linkage between the feuilleton and German-Jewish assimilation, Benjamin leaves his attitude somewhat more open. He synthesizes the argument of "Heine and the Consequences" with a certain tone of approbation but withholds a definite imprimatur. Furthermore, Benjamin then offers a loosely Marxist analysis of "the function" of the journalistic "empty phrase" in the "high capitalist world" and notes that *Die Fackel* contains this critique only in "blueprint form," not as a "theory" (355).[63]

Having subsequently touched on Kraus's "biblical pathos," on how his "tact" is "destructive and critical" and "theological," and on how in *Die Fackel* the "polemical possibilities of every situation are utterly exhausted," Benjamin returns to the theme of paradoxical anti-journalism as he concludes the essay's first part. That is, Kraus again appears as "journalism in its most paradoxical form," to use a formulation from Benjamin's notes for the essay. Benjamin writes that Kraus "opposes to the unchanging sensations—with which the daily press serves its audience—the eternally new 'newspaper' whose task is to report on the history of creation: the eternally new, continuous complaint." Yet if Benjamin, in contrast to Scholem, emphasizes how Kraus resists the press as "an instrument of power," the basic structure of reversal resembles what we find in Scholem's diary entries and essay fragments. Journalism is the language of an ethnically tinged cultural diminishment and linguistic degradation. It is the language that "the Schmock" authors. And it is Kraus's "newspaper," a discursive phenomenon from the same "line," that sets for itself the opposing, neo-biblical "task" of reporting "on the history of creation" and delivering an "eternally new, continuous complaint" (363).

Under his next heading, "Demon," Benjamin almost immediately takes up the specific feature of Kraus's writing that Scholem valorized: mimesis and quotation. To be sure, Benjamin's account is hardly a straightforward encomium. He begins it, tellingly, by distancing his approach to Kraus from the "apologetic perspective" of Leopold Liegler, Kraus's first biographer ("KK," 363). Moreover, dark forces animate the "Demon." "The light from the day of creation falls onto him [Kraus], and so he emerges from this night. Yet not every part of him does; and some remain sunk in night more deeply than one would suspect" (363). But dark is not necessarily bad. And the radical, often brutal mimetic techniques on which Benjamin focuses in the "Demon" section receive at least as much sustained praise as any other component of Kraus's style. Benjamin lauds Kraus's practice of destructive, bloody "self-mirroring" as having the "hidden" goal of being "the highest critical organ," while likening that process to Kierkegaard's "martyrdom." After noting Kraus's "mimetic genius" (364), Benjamin imputes to the "quotations in *Die Fackel*" a kind of "revelatory" force. He also links the polemical, prosecutorial activities that he had long been tracking, and that he had, in 1928, associated with Kraus's Jewishness, to Kraus's mimetic exploits. "But also in his [Kraus's] relation to the objects of his polemics the mimetic plays a decisive role" (365). In addition, Benjamin pursues Kraus's quoting into his attitude toward "law," or into the primary locus of his Jewishness in "Karl Kraus" (1928). Writing of how with Kraus "the sphere of law" is ubiquitous, Benjamin stresses that here too Kraus "takes the words of others into his mouth" (367).

Quoting himself, or rather, a line from his first "Karl Kraus" essay, Benjamin reestablishes the connection between Kraus and law, this time without using the term "halakhic." He again declares that, "for him [Kraus], everything, without exception everything, language and thing play themselves out in the sphere of law" ("KK," 367). But a deeper "proof" of Kraus's Jewishness in the 1931 essay is that, "for him [Kraus] too, language and justice are founded in each other." For having that perspective *entails* worshipping "the image of divine justice in language," which, in turn, is the "authentically Jewish *salto mortale*." "To worship the image of divine justice in language—yes, even in the German language—that is the authentically Jewish *salto mortale* with which he tries to break the spell of the demon" (367). As I mentioned above, the "too" in "for him too" links Kraus to Kafka, whose attitude toward the co-foundational status of language and justice Benjamin equates with Kraus's in the typescript of "Karl Kraus" (1931). Kafka and Kraus are, again, Benjamin's two "authentically Jewish" jumpers. Both see "language and justice" as co-founded. Both therefore perform, "even in the German language," the "authentically Jewish" death-defying leap. They perform a Jewish leap that is a potential means of breaking a demonic "spell," which, it becomes increasingly clear, Benjamin sees as a function of "law" and "mind." And if "Karl Kraus" (1931) elaborates on, and thus looks back to, "Karl Kraus" (1928), it also looks forward to "Franz Kafka" (1934), where Benjamin's reflections on "tradition" in Kafka culminate in complex claims about "law" and "justice."

In reworking—and radicalizing—an argument by Kraft, Benjamin proposes that it is through "justice" *rather than* "law" that Kafka "fights against myth."[64] He adds that Kafka does not "attach to study," which is "the gate to justice," the "promises tradition has attached to the study of the Torah." About Kafka's parables, Benjamin later wrote: "They do not lie modestly at the feet of doctrine, as the Haggadah lies at the Halakah. Though apparently reduced to submission, they unexpectedly raise a mighty paw against it" (*BB* 6:113). Benjamin was manifestly fascinated by the way in which "the classic Jewish triad of revelation, law and commentary virtually defines" Kafka's "imaginative world," to use Robert Alter's phrasing.[65] Yet what struck a more sonorous chord with him is how, amidst such thematic constellating, Kafka refuses not only the allure of myth—a point that might well have had a special urgency in 1934—but also any kind of forced sublation. Kafka refuses the "promises" of a "tradition" in which he could not feel himself to be grounded. Thus he stood out, on the German-Jewish Parnassus, against the alternatives of assimilationism and the "pieties" and "self-indulgent pose of the professional Jew," as Irving Wohlfarth puts it in examining Kafka's appeal for Benjamin.[66] According to Benjamin, Kafka makes vivid loss, the loss of "truth in its haggadic consistency" (*BB* 6:112). His work is an "ellipse" whose divergent chief coordinates are "mystical experience (in particular, the experience of tradition)" and "the experience of modern urban-dwellers [*Großstadtmenschen*]" (110). And Kafka "raises a mighty paw" at the ethos of law and "doctrine"—at least in part, it seems, because of his attachment to "justice." Again, Benjamin specifies that through "justice," rather than "law," Kafka flouts "myth."

Benjamin does not offer anything like formal definitions of his key "Jewish" categories. Still averse to fixing "the essence of Judaism," and also lacking in expertise, he proceeds intuitively. In his uses of Jewish culture Benjamin himself clearly knew "no system." "He was deeply attracted," writes Michael André Bernstein, "to a cluster of powerful images and ideas in Judaism, but for him these were completely detached from their original context in Jewish collective experience and religious practice."[67] Yet we can infer from various usages that a reverence for "justice" is, for Benjamin, a kind of Jewish third way. It is a way of connecting with tradition that combats "myth" and avoids the rigidity of "law" and the Halakah, both of which demand "submission." To worship divine *justice* in language is the "authentically Jewish death-defying leap" through which Kraus and Kafka attempt to "break the spell" of a "demon" whom, again, Benjamin aligns with law. Of course, what complicates this point is that in the 1928 "Karl Kraus" essay Kraus's subsuming of "everything" under the sphere of "law" helps make his "dialectics" the "hottest prayer for redemption that crosses Jewish lips today." Benjamin's position changed, it appears. In one respect he moved closer to Scholem, his teacher in Jewish matters. For although Scholem's utterances about the Halakah by no means add up to a univocal message, he could be quite critical of the idea that "Halakhic Judaism" constituted the core of Jewish tradition. Speaking of his attitude toward the Halakah during the 1920s and 1930s, Scholem stated in a late interview: "I was interested in the question: does Halakhic Judaism have enough potency to survive? Is the Halakah really possible without a mystical foundation? Does it have enough vitality of its own to survive for two thousand years without degenerating? I appreciated the Halakah without identifying with its imperatives. . . . This question was tied up with my dreams about the Kabbalah, through the notion that it might be the Kabbalah that explains the survival of the consolidated force of Halakhic Judaism."[68]

Up until almost the end of his life, to be sure, Benjamin argued with Scholem over Kafka's place in Jewish culture as well as over Kafka's indebtedness to Jewish tradition. Yet Scholem found considerable value, and resonances of his own thought, in his friend's readings. And he offered one of the most effective formulations of those readings. In November 1938 he wrote to Benjamin: "If you were to succeed in representing the borderline case of wisdom, which Kafka does indeed represent, as the crisis of the sheer transmissibility of truth, you would have achieved something absolutely magnificent."[69]

Kraus, whose "demonic" spirit contrasts with the "radiant serenity" Benjamin ascribed to Kafka, is not the same kind of "borderline case of wisdom" in "Karl Kraus." But he is an uncompromising, formally rigorous outsider figure, a "messenger" who possesses self-evidently Jewish sensibilities—"the Jewish" still ultimately "understands itself by itself." Through the prism of these sensibilities, which centrally involve law, justice, language, and the relationship among them, Kraus records the experience of urban modernity. In all of this he is close to Benjamin's Kafka. What I am suggesting is as follows: Benjamin's (deleted) comparison of Kafka and Kraus alerts us to look for further affinities between the ways in which Benjamin positioned the two writers, and these affinities are illuminating. Given Kafka's importance for Benjamin, they shed further light on why Benjamin was so decisively invested in the idea of Kraus's Jewishness, on why he rejected with such adamancy the proposition that Kraus "suppressed his Judaism." Moreover, there are significant additional similarities between Benjamin's portrayals of Kafka and Kraus. Benjamin's notes for the "Karl Kraus" essay, for example, attribute to the "Unmensch" stage the characteristic that it entails an "overcoming of myth" (*BGS* 2:3.1106). The "Unmensch" is, apparently, "therefore an angel," a "new angel."

Benjamin repeatedly works with the theme of angels in the text of "Karl Kraus." But first he returns to the topic of anti-journalism. Here Benjamin indicates that journalism constitutes a "betrayal of the literati [*Literatentum*], of mind [*Geist*], of demon" ("KK," 370). Operating rather loosely with genre categories, Benjamin appends to his claim the remark that "empty chatter" [*Geschwätz*] is the "true substance" of the "feuilleton" (370). Conversely, the real "literatus" is "pure mind." Benjamin soon restates his point: "The literati [*das Literatentum*] are being [*Sein*] under the sign of pure mind [*des bloßen Geistes*]" (370). Hence the "solidarity" between Kraus and prostitutes, who embody "pure sexuality." These extreme opposites have a natural bond, Benjamin asserts. Hence also the fact that the demon "banishes the literatus into the courtroom." As "pure mind," the literatus belongs to—and thrives in—the sphere of law. The courtroom has thus been "the forum" of "the great journalists," i.e., of the journalists whose work stands over against the mindless "chatter" of the feuilleton. Kraus and Lassalle—a Jew who was on uneasy terms with both Judaism and his journalistic medium—are the most prominent of the "great journalists" whom Benjamin names as examples (371).

These emphatic statements have a direct antecedent in Benjamin's writings, namely, his utterances about the literati in his response to the *Kunstwart* debate. After all, there too Benjamin casts the literati as the true "representatives of mind [*das Geistige*]." They are the ones who carry out German Jewry's "serious mission" of extracting "Geist" from "the art they cannot make themselves." In "Karl Kraus," however, Benjamin takes this discussion to an entirely different level of possibility. After defining the nature of the "Literatentum," he activates the vocabulary of his "modern Jewish messianism" and gestures at a realm of linguistic activity—"yes, even in the German language"—beyond "the spell of the demon." Indeed, Benjamin's final characterization of Kraus as a "great" journalist, and as an anti-feuilletonist, sets up the essay's most dramatic reversal, as well as an addendum to Benjamin's early thinking about the linguistic potential of German-Jewish culture.

The third, vaguely redemptive "Nonhuman Being" section of the essay again assigns *Die Fackel* to the category "journalism." Benjamin contends that "from its first number on" one would have to have read this "aesthetically oriented journalism" [*ästhetisch ausgerichtete Publisistik*] completely "literally" in order not to see that it was "destined to become the political prose of 1930" ("KK," 373). But then Kraus, the radical Jewish literatus and demonic, polemical agent of "pure mind," becomes *the* superlative anti-journalist in a new and higher sense, in the sense of bringing about *the* greatest separation of language and mind. "Never has language been more perfectly separated from mind, never has it been more tightly bound to eros," writes Benjamin about an epigram by Kraus, after citing Kraus's line about how he is "merely one of those epigones who dwell in the old house of language" (379). In key places, furthermore, Benjamin treats the linguistic practices that go along with this mentality, or writing beyond all "intellectual creation," as Weigel puts it, as having distinctly Jewish qualities.

Naming, for example, belongs under the aegis of "Nonhuman Being." And Benjamin maintains that in divesting "his language of all hieratic moments" Kraus makes it into "a theater for the sanctification of names," and that "with this Jewish certainty" he, Kraus, resists the "theurgy of the word's body." Benjamin associates the latter linguistic mode, we might note once more, with Stefan George, a poet known for emphasizing the Germanness of his style ("KK," 376). There is also the famous passage on quoting—on Kraus's quoting. Building off of his utterances about naming, Benjamin writes: "To quote a word is to call it by its name. . . . In the rescuing and punitive quotation language reveals itself as the *mater* [matrix] of justice. Quotation calls the word by its name, tearing it destructively from its context. Yet quotation also calls the word back to its origin. . . . In quotation both territories [*beide Reiche*], origin and destruction, show themselves before language. And vice versa: Only where these territories interpenetrate each other, in quotation, is language consummated [*vollkommen*]. In it is mirrored the angelic tongue in which all words, startled from the idyllic context of meaning, have become mottoes in the Book of Creation."

Here the "authentically Jewish *salto mortale*" through which Kraus "tries to break the spell of the demon"—i.e., worshipping "the image of divine justice in language"—seems to have reached a kind of completion.

For in quotation language "*reveals* itself as the matrix of justice." Moreover, the destruction of such revelatory citing effectively "calls the word back to its *origin*." And this movement "*back*" to an origin, this idea of redemptive "restoration," is, as Rabinbach stresses, a dominant theme in Benjamin's "messianic" thinking. Thus the calling back to an origin through destruction results in a rare consummation of language, in which the nonhuman, near-divine language of angels is mirrored. As I stated above, furthermore, the phrase "the Book of Creation" evokes the mystical world of the Kabbalah (or the title of the "classic kabbalistic text," *Sefer Yetsirah*).

Also worth repeating is that with its connotations of the linguistic "absolute," Benjamin's climactic homage to quoting (under the sign of "Unmensch") echoes Scholem's notes on the quotation-centered, "pure" Musivstil, which Benjamin had asked for in 1930. Of course, where Scholem's "musive" quoting serves to put words *into* a new context of meaning, Benjamin's redemptive citation does the opposite, startling them *out of* a meaningful context. But my aim has not been to find exact continuities in Benjamin's and Scholem's imaginative exegetical logic. By now it should be clear that I have been tracking *patterns* of association and signification, and their underlying *cultural* logic. What interests me is how—with varying degrees of explicitness, and in different, idiosyncratic ways—Benjamin and Scholem invoke and drastically reinscribe the idea of "Jewish journalism" in their readings of Kraus. Positioning Kraus as a paradoxical anti-journalist, both Benjamin and Scholem carry out, in effect, dialectical reversals. Both discover "the most unexpected Jewish provinces" in the German language by having Kraus discover "the most unexpected Jewish provinces" in the German language—*as a journalist*. Precisely journalism, the reified, "mechanical," derivative, deracinated, "whorish" discourse of Scholem's "perverted Jew," takes on "messianic" significance and tells "the eternally new history of creation." And this anti-journalism is at its most redemptive and intensely Jewish in just that formal area where, for Scholem, Moritz Goldstein, and Richard Wagner too, Jewish journalists enact assimilated German Jewry's intellectual bathos: in verbal mirroring and quoting. Scholem execrates the "unproductive" writing of assimilated Jewish journalists who trade on the musive drive "to say everything twice," and he "compliments" Kraus, the other child of "the Jewish middle ages," for never having had a "single original thought." Benjamin disparages the "epigonic character" of the journalists who betray the "mission" of the radical literati, and subsequently celebrates Kraus's self-characterization as "one of those epigones" who are able to separate "Geist" from language. Here a paradigmatically modern language, *the* language that most forcefully emblematizes the ills of acculturation and stands in the same "line" as that of the "Schmock," comes closest to the language of angels.

At the very end of his essay, Benjamin again emphasizes the paradoxical status of Kraus's writing. Speculating about what kind of "new angel" the "Nonhuman Being" represents, he claims: "Perhaps one of those [angels], who, according to the Talmud, are created anew in huge numbers, only to disappear into nothingness after speaking before God. Complaining, accusing, or shouting joyously? Whatever the case might be, Kraus's ephemeral work is modeled on this evanescent voice" ("KK," 384). Benjamin then refers back to his initial definition of Kraus's "ephemeral work." That is, he reiterates the point that *Die Fackel* is a special sort of messenger/newspaper, linking it now to the theme of angels. The final sentence of "Karl Kraus" reads: *"Angelus—*that is the messenger of the old etchings" (384).

Benjamin's article left Kraus unenthused, so unenthused, in fact, that he derided it as an instance of "abyssal feuilletonism" [*abgründigem Feuilletonismus*]. Also among Kraus's cursory, tepid comments are the lines: "I have been able to gather from this well-meaning and well-conceived essay merely that it deals with me, and that the author appears to know things about me of which I had been unaware, and which I cannot comprehend even now. I can only express the hope that other readers will understand the essay better than I have" (*F* 852–56:27). Agreeing with the latter part of these remarks, Scholem dismissed Kraus's verdict as being "without understanding" [*verständnislos*]. Benjamin could not brush it aside so easily. Clearly embittered, he swore that he would never write another word about the satirist (*BB* 4:34). By the winter of 1934, however, Benjamin's resentment had abated. Indeed, he disclosed to Bertolt Brecht plans for a cycle of lectures on "avant-garde Germany" in which Kraus was to be the subject of the talk on innovative "journalism" (*BB* 4:362). Later that year, Benjamin expressed some dismay over Kraus's decision to support Engelbert Dollfuß, the right-wing leader, as "the lesser evil" in Austrian politics (*BB* 4:467). Yet Benjamin continued to display an interest in Kraus's work, which he addresses quite a few times in his late correspondences. And when Kraus died in 1936, in letters to friends Benjamin repeatedly ventilates his indignation over the treatment Kraus's life received in the press—something Scholem would do more publicly several years later.

In 1939, Scholem reacted balefully to an article about Kraus that appeared in *Davar,* a Hebrew-language newspaper. Its author, Moshe Ungerfeld, accused Kraus of Jewish self-hatred, which led Scholem to challenge

Ungerfeld's "information about Kraus's hatred for Judaism." Scholem's letter-to-the-editor states that Ungerfeld has belittled a "great and tragic chapter" (presumably in the story of Jews in German culture), and that Ungerfeld has mistaken for broad Jewish antisemitism Kraus's "hatred for a particular type of Jew." This "type of Jew," Scholem continues, was "unfortunately widespread" (*SB* 1:278–79). Today, Scholem's and Kraus's construction of such Jews—i.e., the acculturated, fin-de-siècle, German-Jewish literati who appeared to be so abundant—seems overly dismissive. Certainly Scholem is far from judicious where he applies the draconian critique of "Heine and the Consequences" to generations of Jewish journalists, and thus to authors of eloquent and astute feuilletons, like Heine. But my concern has not been to assess the accuracy of Scholem's, Kraus's, and Benjamin's constructions of German-Jewish journalists. Rather, I have tried to show how, as they established their respective critical voices, these writers engaged thoroughly and innovatively with the discourse that made German-Jewish journalists especially salient emblems of a "crisis of modernity." In the case of Kraus, I have attempted to demonstrate how this critical interaction helped to foster new journalistic forms. And I have tried to bring to light how answering the question—"Why are there so many Jewish journalists?"—shaped the searching responses of all three authors to an even larger "Jewish question," one whose immediacy belongs to the past, but whose poignancy endures in the present. What kind of Jewish writing can there be in the German language?

CONCLUSION

The Afterlife of Anti-Journalism

Kraus's living voice has become eternalized in his prose. It gives his prose style its mime-like quality. His power as a writer is close to that of an actor.
— Theodor Adorno

Three years after Kraus's death, Walter Benjamin wrote what is surely the saddest tribute to his particular talent as a social critic. The impetus was some chilling news about Vienna's Jewish population, news that has become, in the meantime, chillingly ironic. In a letter dated June 4, 1939, Benjamin informs a friend that he has heard the following "story from Vienna": "There the gas in Jewish households has been cut off, at least temporarily. It was too expensive for the gas company to supply its Jewish customers. They were using too much. And because they were often doing so to commit suicide, in many cases the bill went unpaid afterward" (*BB* 6:288). According to Benjamin, the "Historie" his letter relates "would have had its true chronicler in Karl Kraus."

Benjamin changes the topic of his missive rather abruptly and without offering any further commentary, almost as if he were deferring, hastily and hopelessly, to the late "true" teller of his tale. But why he assigned that role to Kraus is no great mystery. Kraus, to be sure, was not exactly known for rushing to defend the victims of antisemitic hostility. As we have seen, he aggressively denounced Alfred Dreyfus's journalistic supporters, though he never actually suggested that Dreyfus should have been convicted. Similarly, in 1902 Kraus complained about the sympathy Leopold Hilsner, a

Jew charged with the crime of ritual murder, was receiving from the liberal press. And when, shortly after the assassination of Walther Rathenau, right-wing fanatics nearly beat to death Maximilian Harden, Kraus condemned the violence but persisted in attacking Harden, his longtime German-Jewish rival. In Kraus's view Harden had been foolish not to watch out for his safety, especially given that he had been repeatedly threatened. Harden had, in effect, let a misguided investment in appearing to be courageous jeopardize his ability to exercise his courage productively. Where a critic can make good use of bravery is at a desk. The second a writer like Harden stops writing, how he comports himself in the face of danger begins to matter much less, or so Kraus maintained.[1]

But *Die Fackel* also abounds with passionate and colorful interventions on behalf of people who were suffering as a result of bigotry or chauvinism or the systemic hypocrisy in fin-de-siècle Austrian society or, as it often happened, as a result of all three. What moved Kraus, and what he excelled at "chronicling," are moments in which large mechanisms of injustice bore down on individuals whom he saw as defenseless. These included women, prostitutes, disgraced homosexuals, the poor, and, eventually, Jews. A long essay from 1908 bitterly tells of a prostitute who committed suicide after her stepfather had been caught soliciting clients for her.[2] With more humor but no less ardently a later piece inveighs against a legal system that doubly failed a prostitute who had been given a fake iron cross instead of real payment. Outraged, Kraus reports on how the system did nothing to protect the prostitute and then fined her for wearing the costume medal.[3] Or recall the event over which Kraus's rift with Harden appears to have begun: the "Hervay Affair." In 1904, Kraus took up the cause of Donna Hervay, a woman who had been accused of bigamy and was being defamed as a sexually deviant "Jewish vampire." Here, tellingly, Kraus spoke out *against* some of the very same claims that he had made during the Hilsner trial just two years earlier. Having execrated the liberal press for preaching "Jewish solidarity between the lines" in its coverage of Hilsner, he dismissed precisely the idea that "Jewish solidarity" had skewed the liberal press's accounts of Hervay.

Yet there is also a very basic continuity between Kraus's responses to Hilsner's and Hervay's persecutions. Indeed, if his attempt to discredit the liberal "Jewish press" for defending Hilsner seems like a low point in his criticism, it nonetheless has a broadly representative character. For Kraus thought that he saw in Hilsner's journalistic supporters the coming together of a powerful modern institution, i.e., authoritative mass-circulation daily newspapers, and an old parochialism, i.e., ethnic loyalties. And ultimately at issue in his writings on the Hervay Affair is something quite similar. Beyond objecting to the misogynistic spectacle of a "witch trial," Kraus tries to expose an analogous colluding of new and old tendencies. In *Ethics and Criminality,* the volume in which he anthologized his essays on the Hervay case, he strives to reveal how the modern push to administer rationally the most intimate social space, the sexual sphere, incites—and draws energy from—the most barbaric prejudices. The book diagnoses a kind of a "dialectic of Enlightenment," while at the same time providing an extensive and forcefully concrete record of that process. Understandably, then, it was the postwar reissuing of *Ethics and Criminality* that served as the impetus for Theodor Adorno's tribute to Kraus's intellectual accomplishments.

More recently, the sociologist Pierre Bourdieu emphasized the "actuality" of Kraus's media criticism.[4] Certainly this gesture too is understandable. Bourdieu turned his attention to the social role of mass media in the late 1990s, or during a moment that famously witnessed the emergence of a new virtual world. Writing at a time when a truly mass press first took shape, Kraus trenchantly laid bare the structure of the virtual reality it created. "He was a critic of ideology in the most precise sense," as Adorno stresses in his essay on *Ethics and Criminality.*[5] Thus *Die Fackel* offers contemporary media theory both historical perspective and analytic insight.

Kraus argued that the language of the feuilleton, and especially of the heavily ornamented Viennese feuilleton, acts upon the imagination of readers in such a way that the virtual reality of journalistic reportage determines the external reality it should cover. The result is a dangerously uncanny situation. "Shadows throw bodies," and the press can make happen whatever it wants to. It can bring about the sorts of events that sell newspapers, like wars. Above all, the Viennese press is what made turn-of-the-century Austria into "the laboratory of world destruction."

This view of causality is narrow, needless to say. But despite that narrowness, as well as Kraus's apocalyptic fervor, there is a balance to his analysis of the cognitive effects of journalism and their political consequences. As he does in his reports on sex trials, Kraus combines large-scale theoretical pronouncements with the most exact sampling and parsing of local culture. With their copious citations and verbal mimicry, his works track the big developments they diagnose into particular manifestations, giving an artfully selected and constructed material record of such trends. That might well be why historians too have acknowledged Kraus's value at *our* turn of the century. Witness what Niall Ferguson, a leading scholar of the First World War, recently claimed: "One of the most compelling of all critiques of the press at war was advanced by Karl Kraus in his one-man magazine *Die Fackel* and his epic postwar drama *The Last Days of Mankind*."[6]

Still, Kraus evidently failed in his attempt to produce a paradoxical antijournalism whose actuality would only grow over time. He failed to do what Benjamin, in a utopian aside, once suggested he had done: author an "eternally new newspaper." For if important thinkers regularly rediscover Kraus, and if both the significance of his major themes and his skill at chronicling them have been vigorously underlined, he is not widely read today. Of course, popularity and actuality are two different things. And no doubt some of the reasons for Kraus's lack of popularity have more to do with the demands he makes of present-day readers than with whether or not he connects with their interests. Not only is his prose often syntactically complex and difficult, it can be vexingly allusive. Many of the figures who appear in Kraus's micro-accounts of world decline have become obscure. Hence, unlike scholars of fellow language-obsessed central European modernists (e.g., Rilke and Kafka), Kraus scholars—a shrinking group—talk about the kinds of resource materials that could render their subject more accessible. Also worth noting is how Kraus's use of idiomatic language can make his writing hard to translate and his satirical humor hard to enjoy. But I suspect that more is at work here, that on one level Kraus's failure to achieve the actuality of, say, Benjamin represents a measure of his success as an anti-journalist.

Let me be more precise. That *Die Fackel* seems to feel less immediately relevant than many other instances of modernist thought does not necessarily mean Kraus's anti-journalism, as a form of cultural reportage, has a built-in ephemerality. Rather, Kraus's status in contemporary culture might be a function of the radical character of his modernism. As he never tired of pointing out, Kraus operated in a medium in which, to a particularly extreme degree, literary language was made exchangeable and consumable, and was assimilated into various projects of social advancement. *His* project of internecine resistance took him, correlatively, particularly far in the direction of developing a style that would not be easy to assimilate—that would not have "consequences" in the way he believed Heine's literary journalism had. So it is not simply that one needs to be familiar with the fin-de-siècle feuilleton, the negative referent of the innovative "anti" features in Kraus's style, in order to appreciate his work. The overwhelming prominence of those features poses a challenge for readers today because it blocks standard processes of reception. By tying the shape of his writing so actively and so relentlessly to a specific discursive context, Kraus disrupts our ability to pull him toward ours and thus to effect the satisfying hermeneutic move that

Hans-Georg Gadamer labeled a "fusing of horizons." When Kraus ventured into drama and wrote an "epic" war play that could not possibly be performed (or formally appropriated), he was, among other things, acting on the drastic commitments he forged as an anti-journalist.[7] Hermetic elements, more than enduring newness, make *Die Fackel* something like "journalism in its most paradoxical form."

But if Kraus's anti-journalism alienates contemporary readers, tracing its formation prompts us to rethink issues that have immediate actuality in ongoing discussions of German-Jewish culture. Indeed, we can even say that it prompts us to rethink some of those issues with unique force. Like no other mode of writing, journalism functioned as a marker of modern German-Jewish identity, generally as a pejorative one. Critics have therefore treated a conspicuous pattern in Kraus's work as a privileged symptom of Jewish self-hatred: his use of stereotypes that link the feuilleton with German Jewry's intellectual deficiencies. Yet just the charged dynamic of a Jewish journalist mobilizing important stereotypes about Jews and journalism gives the complexities that come to light through Kraus a special vividness. Here, after all, we have a "case" rebelling against the theories of Jewish self-hatred that cite it as their ultimate evidence. For when we pursue Kraus's anti-Jewish utterances rigorously, we see how in the decades before the Shoah a German-Jewish author could manipulate antisemitic discourse strategically, or as a "cultural code," and also in the service of a highly reflective critique.

If Kraus linked the ills of the feuilleton with the ill effects of Jewish assimilation, he often did so in a dramatically paradoxical way. In texts like "Heine and the Consequences," the place where we are supposed to have *the* surest signs of Jewish self-hatred, Kraus activates familiar anti-Jewish tropes and concertedly undermines their logic. What emerges is a critique of the feuilleton that provocatively distances Kraus and his *Fackel* from *both* German-Jewish feuilleton writers and the values of their antisemitic antagonists, values that he believed German-Jewish feuilleton writers had adopted. What emerges also is a set of creative counterprinciples, which subvert the main tenets of the very discourse that made the feuilleton into a crucial emblem of Jewishness. Where that discourse centered on the ideals of autogenetic creativity and phallic mastery over language, Kraus prized opposing, mimetic tendencies: i.e., mirroring and quoting language. And in various ways he associated these tendencies with an unassimilated and "undomesticated" Jewish culture. As I have stressed, it is as if establishing a truly radical position as a Jewish journalist had to entail what amounted to a radical performance of German-Jewish identity.

The fact that Kraus's style was essentially read as such adds to our understanding of the dialectical character of German-Jewish self-fashioning during the late Wilhelmine and Weimar eras. Much attention has been paid to certain salient reversals, such as the valorization of Yiddish culture by young Jews exhibiting a new "Jewish consciousness." But in their largely neglected interpretations of Kraus's Jewishness Benjamin and Scholem go farther, at least in a certain sense. Whereas Kafka, for example, located in Yiddish culture what German Jews supposedly did not possess—e.g., an authentic relationship with a living language—Benjamin and Scholem extolled as profoundly Jewish the traits in Kraus's style that were damningly attributed to Jews. They extolled the "minor" traits that Kraus himself counterposed to the stylistic practices of acculturated Jewish feuilleton writers: the eagerly reproductive or mimetic aspects of his writing, its *lack* of originality, as Scholem once put it. Indeed, Benjamin and Scholem seem to have been inspired by Kraus's dialectical self-presentation. Benjamin, again, called "Heine and the Consequences" the "high point in Heine criticism." Moreover, in their readings of Kraus's style Benjamin and Scholem extrapolate imaginatively from his ideas about the problem of the German-Jewish feuilleton.

Benjamin and Scholem framed Kraus's "unoriginal" anti-journalism as an unlikely locus of superlative Jewishness against another foil as well: the rhetoric of authenticity and elemental originality in Weimar-era cultural Zionism. This they did in ways that today seem to be blithely essentialist and therefore curiously contradictory. Kraus, who had little knowledge of Jewish tradition, is seen to be the authentic transmitter of the Halakah and the medieval "musive style." Through him the "greatest breakthrough" of these traditions into the German language supposedly occurs. The result is that Benjamin's and Scholem's claims about Kraus's style come across as alternately probing and dogmatic, a combination we encounter in their writings elsewhere too. In a single address from 1966, for instance, Scholem proposes that "not all 'Jews' were Jews," and also that there was something constitutively Jewish about almost every German thinker with Jewish heritage, including Kraus.[8]

But Kraus plays only a small role in Scholem's later thoughts about German-Jewish culture. As was the case with Scholem's reading of Kafka, in Benjamin's absence sustained reflection ceased. Still, in the postwar period we can find echoes of Benjamin and Scholem's conversations about how Kraus's anti-journalism redeems deeply Jewish and powerfully ethical modes of mimetic writing, of "saying everything twice." Some of those echoes have produced significant echoes of their own. I am thinking, above all, of Adorno's ideas about a particularly Jewish mimesis, which he first expressed in *The Dialectic of Enlightenment*. Like Scholem and Benjamin, whose work on Kraus he admired, Adorno sketched out the relationship among Jews, assimilation, and imitation in complex and sometimes unflattering ways. But, for him, the Jews in the end managed to preserve a valuable "undisciplined mimesis," which resists the leveling of difference that occurs in the dominant mode of Western understanding: conceptual subsumption.[9] Adorno further develops key aspects of these meditations in his famous essay on the essay, "Der Essay als Form" (1954–58). There he alters Lukàcs's high modernist injunction for the essayist, which was: Bring about a unity of the inner and outer, or of "soul and form." Nazism, Adorno believed, was in large part an outgrowth of subsumptive understanding and an attempt to destroy all particularity. Accordingly, in the postwar era he continued to stress the importance of preserving difference through mimetic intellectual activity. His idealized essay, which is apparently made to wear "the yellow star" [*der gelbe Fleck*], interprets objects but also assimilates itself *to* them.[10] It contains the sort of "undomesticated mimetic moment," to use a phrase from Adorno's reading of Kraus, that Kraus exalts in his article on the Budapester Orpheumgesellschaft and calls for in speaking of his "new journalistic form." So perhaps we could trace lines of influence running from Adorno's celebration of a marginalized, metaphorically Jewish mimesis back to Kraus's fiercely performative anti-journalism and the seminal fin-de-siècle culture wars from which it emerged.

In strong terms Adorno encouraged us to try. The "undisciplined mimicry" of *The Dialectic of Enlightenment* is a "mark" in the "living substance" of Jews, or something nonverbal. It was Kraus, Adorno maintained, who brought the force of such mimesis into critical *discussions*. Indeed, in 1964 he credited Kraus, "in whom the inheritance of the persecuted and pleading Jew has become intellectualized," with a great ethical-linguistic accomplishment: reconciling a potent "minor" mimesis with "written language."[11] I want to let Adorno's claim stand here as a suggestive last word: "The convicted took refuge in written language [*im Geschriebenen*] . . . in just that language which was ashamed of the mimetic moment, and which was its enemy, until Kraus."[12]

NOTES

INTRODUCTION

1. Siegfried Kracauer, *The Mass Ornament: Weimar Essays,* trans. and ed. Thomas Levin (Cambridge, Mass.: Harvard University Press, 1995), 5.

2. Richard Wagner, "'Modern,'" in Wagner, *Richard Wagners Gesammelte Schriften,* vol. 13, ed. Julius Kapp (Leipzig: Hesse und Becker, 1911), 178.

3. Friedrich Nietzsche, *Menschliches, Allzumenschliches: Ein Werk für freie Geister,* in Nietzsche, *Werke in Drei Bänden,* vol. 2, ed. Karl Schlechta (Munich: Hanser, 1955), 983.

4. Robert Musil, *Der Mann ohne Eigenschaften* (Hamburg, Rowohlt, 1988), 1:13. "Kakania" was the name Musil gave to his fictional version of the Austro-Hungarian Empire. The term plays off of both the German term for the dual monarchy, kaiserlich und königlich, and a slang term for excrement, Kacke.

5. On this point, and also on the diverse significance of journalism in turn-of-the-century German culture, see Peter Fritzsche's illuminating and informative study, *Reading Berlin 1900* (Cambridge, Mass.: Harvard University Press, 1996).

6. Quoted in ibid., 55. My analysis of the short text differs, however, from Fritzsche's. His emphasizes the extent to which readers "craved" the newspaper and leaves open the question of the mechanism behind their (manic) craving.

7. Of course, religious identities prior to the Enlightenment were hardly stable. There was, in fact, a great fear of heresy and conversion in the early modern era, as historians such as Richard Popkin have emphasized. Also worth noting is that the very idea of modernity as being characterized by increasing secularization has come under attack. In speaking of a "crisis of modernity" among modernist authors, however, what is at issue is really subjective experience or *perception*—the perception that society was becoming increasingly disenchanted and destabilized. For an insightful recent discussion of this general topic, and one that relies heavily on Weber's

diagnosis, see T. J. Clark, *Farewell to an Idea: Episodes from a History of Modernism* (New Haven: Yale University Press, 1999), 7–10. The classic text on the "experience of modernity" in different cultural settings is Marshall Berman's *All That Is Solid Melts into Air: The Experience of Modernity* (New York: Simon & Schuster, 1982). There exists one monograph that deals extensively with the theme of modernity in the feuilleton, Hildegard Kernmayer's *Judentum im Wiener Feuilleton (1848–1903): Exemplarische Untersuchungen zum literarästhetischen und politischen Diskurs der Moderne* (Tübingen: Niemeyer, 1998). Kernmayer's study contains a wealth of bibliographical information, as well as an extensive survey of what has been said about the modernity of the feuilleton. I am indebted to her research.

8. G. W. F. Hegel, *Jenaer Schriften, 1801–1807*, in Hegel, *Werke*, vol. 2, ed. Eva Moldenhauer and Karl Markus Michel (Frankfurt/M: Suhrkamp, 1971), 547. As to the Hegel quotation, in his study *Imagined Communities*, which contains a seminal discussion of the effect of newspapers on national identity formation, Benedict Anderson suggests that, for Hegel, reading the newspaper "serves modern man as a substitute for morning prayers." This summary strikes me as misleading. For what seems to concern Hegel is the *transformation* of the mode through which "one orients oneself" each day. What concerns him is the becoming "realistic" of the primary mode of self-orientation. So instead of being a "substitute for prayer," journalism signals and furthers a dramatic shift toward secularization. Anderson, moreover, is not alone here. In a recent article Derek Jonathan Penslar formulates Hegel's point in just the same way, using the word "substitute," that is, to describe how Hegel saw the relation of prayer and journalism. See Anderson, *Imagined Communities: Reflections on the Origin and Spread of Nationalism* (New York: Verso, 1983), 35; and Penslar, "Transmitting Jewish Culture: Radio in Israel," *Jewish Social Studies* 10, no. 1 (Fall 2003): 2.

9. On Benjamin's reverential attitude toward language, see Susan Handelman's chapter "Language and Redemption," in Handelman, *Fragments of Redemption: Jewish Thought and Literary Theory in Benjamin, Scholem, and Levinas* (Bloomington: Indiana University Press 1991), 15–61.

10. Cited in Kernmayer, *Judentum im Wiener Feuilleton*, 37. On the issue of reenchantment in the Weimar Republic and beyond, see Brett Wheeler, "Aesthetic Reenchantments: The Work of Art and the Crisis of Politics in German Modernism" (Ph.D. diss., University of California, Berkeley, 1998).

11. Theodor Lessing, *"Ich warf eine Flaschenpost ins Eismeer": Essays und Feuilletons (1923–1933)*, ed. Rainer Marwedel (Damrstadt: Luchterhand, 1986), 314.

12. In his *Handbuch der literarischen Fachbegiffe*, Otto Best claims that the concept of the feuilleton was "introduced within the framework of the industrialization of literature," and he calls the feuilleton section of the newspaper "the entertainment section, which means that it was dedicated to art and culture in the broadest sense." Best, *Handbuch der literarischen Fachbegiffe: Definitionen und Beispiele* (Frankfurt/M: Fischer, 1990), 159. There were also, it worth noting, "po-

litical feuilletons." For example, a volume of Ferdinand Kürnberger's feuilletons appeared under that heading. As Best maintains, the word "feuilleton" gained currency—as a literary category—in France at the beginning of the nineteenth century. Abbé Julien Louis de Geoffrey provided the impetus. On January 18, 1800, he began offering observations about general cultural events in the space that remained on the loose sheet of advertisements that contemporary newspapers, and, in particular, the newspaper for which he wrote, the *Journal des Débates,* included. ("Feuilleton" literally means "small sheet.") Even after newspapers had begun to make the feuilleton part of their main body, the name persisted. And most major German-language newspapers today offer a feuilleton section. Here you will find reviews, essays on culture and politics, short fiction and travel reports under the rubric "Feuilleton." On the history of the feuilleton, see Kernmayer's book; Wilmont Haacke's sometimes antisemitic three-volume *Handbuch des Feuilletons* (Emsdetten: Lechte, 1953), which was originally submitted as a *Habilitationsschrift* in 1943; Ulrich Weinzierl, "Typische Wiener Feuilletonisten? Am Beispiel Salten, Blei, Friedell, Polgar, Kuh," *Literatur und Kritik* 20 (1985); Erhard Schütz, *Kritik der literarischen Reportage* (Munich: Fink, 1977); Arno Maierbrugger, "Das 'historische' Zeitungs-Feuilleton: Forschungsprobleme aus der Sicht der Kommunikationsgeschichte," in *Zeitungen im Wiener Fin de Siècle: Eine Tagung der Arbeitsgemeinschaft 'Wien um 1900' der österreichischen Forschungsgemeinschaft,* ed. Sigurd Paul Scheichl and Wolfgang Duchkowitsch (Vienna: Verlag für Geschichte und Politik, 1997), 148–56.

13. Hugo von Hofmannsthal, "Franz Stuck," *Das junge Wien: Österreichische Literatur und Kunstkritik 1887–1902,* vol. 1, ed. Gotthard Wunberg (Tübingen: Niemeyer Verlag, 1976), 430.

14. Alfred Polgar, *Sperrsitz,* ed. Ulrich Weinzierl (Vienna: Löcker, 1984), 36.

15. Carl Schorske, *Fin-de-Siècle Vienna: Politics and Culture* (New York: Vintage, 1981), 9.

16. Rudolf Strauß's review is of Peter Altenberg's *Wie Ich Es Sehe* [*How I see it*]. See *Das junge Wien,* 607.

17. Schorske, *Fin-de-Siècle Vienna,* 9.

18. Peter Pulzer, *The Rise of Political Anti-Semitism in Germany and Austria* (Cambridge, Mass.: Harvard University Press, 1988), 13. Otto Best, suggestively enough, names four writers of Jewish descent and one non-Jew (the Viennese critic Hermann Bahr) in giving examples of "masters of the feuilleton in Germany." His list reads: "Heine, Börne, A. Polgar, H. Bahr, Tucholsky, among others." Best, *Handbuch der literarischen Fachbegiffe,* 160. A question that Best ignores here is that of the regional flavor of the feuilleton. Helpful in regard to the issue of regional variety is Christian Jäger and Erhard Schütz, *Städebilder zwischen Literatur und Journalismus: Wien, Berlin und das Feuilleton der Weimarer Republik* (Wiesbaden: Deutscher Üniversitätsverlag, 1999).

19. Antisemitism as a perverse response to modernity has been and continues

to be the focus of diverse scholarly analyses, from classic discussions such as Jean-Paul Sartre's *Anti-Semite and Jew,* trans. George Becker (New York: Grove Press, 1948) and Hannah Arendt's *The Origins of Totalitarianism* (New York: Harcourt, Brace, and World, 1951) to penetrating more recent works like Zygmunt Bauman's *Modernity and Ambivalence* (Ithaca, N.Y.: Cornell University Press, 1991); Paul Lawrence Rose's *German Question/Jewish Question: Revolutionary Antisemitism from Kant to Wagner* (Princeton: Princeton University Press, 1990); Michael Mack's *German Idealism and the Jew: The Inner Anti-Semitism of Philosophy and German Jewish Responses* (Chicago: University of Chicago Press, 2003); and Matti Bunzl's *Symptoms of Modernity: Jews and Queers in Late-Twentieth-Century Vienna* (Berkeley and Los Angeles: University of California Press, 2004).

20. This is not to suggest, of course, that anticapitalist attacks on the feuilleton were necessarily antisemitic. For such a suggestion would go too far. And yet historians do sometimes conflate anticapitalism and antisemitism. Witness Jacques Kornberg's claim about those two dispositions in turn-of-the-century Vienna: "Anti-capitalism and antisemitism were thus synonymous in Austria." Kornberg, *Theodor Herzl: From Assimilation to Zionism* (Bloomington: Indiana University Press, 1993), 96.

21. "Karl Kraus als Erzieher," in *Studien über Karl Kraus* (Innsbruck: Der Brenner Verlag, 1913), 72.

22. See, for example, the story of Bismarck's banker Bleichröder, the classic account of which is Fritz Stern's *Gold and Iron: Bismarck, Bleichröder and the Building of the German Empire* (New York: Knopf, 1977).

23. Drawing on Clifford Geertz's theories about why bad metaphors can be successful, Shulamit Volkov makes this point in *Germans, Jews, and Antisemites: Trials in Emancipation* (Cambridge and New York: Cambridge University Press, 2006), 89.

24. Heinrich von Treitschke, "Unsere Aussichten," in Walter Boehlich, ed., *Der Berliner Antisemitismusstreit* (Frankfurt/M: Insel, 1988), 9.

25. Treitschke, *Ein Wort über unser Judenthum* (Berlin: G. Reimer, 1880), 3.

26. Treitschke, "Der souveräne Feuilleton," in Treitschke, *Bilder aus der Deutschen Geschichte,* vol. 2 (Lepizig: Hirzel, 1908), 154. As far as I know, this essay was first published posthumously (Treitschke died in 1896). My surmise is that it was written around 1890, which was when Treitschke concerned himself with Heine most intensively. Hereafter cited parenthetically as "SF."

27. By associating Heine's writing with France, Treitschke was not simply smearing it as being foreign and decadent, he was also activating longstanding ideas about the Jews' lack of German patriotism, which is a point that his antisemitic writings repeatedly stress. For although German Jews had fought and died in the wars of liberation against Napoleon, some prominent German Jews (e.g., Heine) had embraced Napoleon and his reforms, thereby bringing upon themselves the wrath of German nationalists. And even three-quarters of a century after Napoleon had put an end to the first German Reich and forever altered Germany's political

landscape, to align Jews with French culture was, in context's such as "The Sovereign Feuilleton," to question their loyalty to Germany.

28. Heine pioneered his formally intricate, though hardly vacuous, style of feuilleton writing very early in his career, in his "Letters from Berlin" ["Briefe aus Berlin," 1822]. Later, during his time in Paris, he wrote dispatches about cultural and political life in Paris for several German newspapers, especially the *Morgenblatt für Gebildete Stände,* whose title sounds impossibly awkward in English translation, *Morning Paper for the Educated Classes.*

29. I do not want to imply that the stereotype of the Jews' inability to produce art is a modern phenomenon. Kalman Bland offers a useful history of that trope in his recent study *The Artless Jew: Medieval and Modern Affirmations and Denials of the Visual* (Princeton: Princeton University Press, 2000), 3–36. For reasons that will become clear below, I disagree with Bland's suggestion that German Jews generally believed themselves to be capable of poetry but not of visual art. See also Margaret Olin, *The Nation without Art: Examining Modern Discourses on Jewish Art* (Lincoln: University of Nebraska Press, 2001).

30. See Kernmayer, *Judentum im Wiener Feuilleton,* 28.

31. George Mosse, *German Jews Beyond Judaism* (Bloomington: Indiana University Press, 1985), 11. The notion of Bildung, and the matter of what it meant to German Jews, are complex issues, which I will take up in greater detail in chapter 1 of this study. For now, let me simply say that there have been penetrating attempts to refine Mosse's theory of Bildung in German-Jewish culture. Perhaps the most important of them is Shulamit Volkov's essay "The Ambivalence of Bildung," which makes a strong case for the idea that Bildung functioned among Jews not only as a means of integration but also as a vehicle of dissimilation, of distinction and separation. The essay has been published in several places, including Volkov's *Germans, Jews, and Antisemites,* 248–55.

32. Stefan Zweig, *Die Welt von Gestern: Erinnerungen eines Europäers* (Frankfurt/M: Suhrkamp, 1996), 123.

33. Schorske, *Fin-de-Siècle Vienna,* 152.

34. Hitler was apparently one of the *Neue Freie Presse*'s non-Jewish readers. In *Mein Kampf* he claims the following about what he read during the years he spent in Vienna (1906–13): "I zealously read the so-called world press (*Neue Freie Presse, Wiener Tageblatt,* etc.) and I was astonished at the scope of what it offered its readers in general and at the objectivity of the representation in detail. I respected the dignified tone, though the extravagance of its style sometimes did not quite satisfy me and at times displeased me." It is important to note that Hitler is, ostensibly, recreating his youthful perception of the liberal press here. His later diagnosis is less favorable. See Hitler, *Mein Kampf* (New York: Reynal and Hitchcock, 1939), 69.

35. Karl Kraus, *Die letzten Tage der Menschheit,* ed. Christian Wagenknecht (Frankfurt/M: Suhrkamp, 1986), 107.

36. Adolf Bartels, *Jüdische Herkunft und Literatur Wissenschaft: Eine gründ-

liche Erörterung (Leipzig: Bartels Verlag, 1925), 7. Here Bartels is citing his study *Die Alten und die Jungen,* which appeared in 1897 in *Die Grenzboten.* Kernmayer's book alerted me to this and other citations, and she provides a useful overview of Bartels's invectives against the feuilleton. See Kermayer, *Judentum im Wiener Feuilleton,* 45–46.

37. Sander Gilman, *Jewish Self-Hatred: Anti-Semitism and the Secret Language of the Jews* (Baltimore: Johns Hopkins University Press, 1986), 226–27. German Jews are not Gilman's exclusive focus, and we should note that what he stresses above all is the role of language as a *general* indicator of civilization. According to Gilman, in all modern societies linguistic defects were key markers of difference. Since, as is customary, I am including Austrian Jews under the heading "German Jews," we should also note that the relation of language and culture and national identity was in the Austro-Hungarian Empire not the same as it was in Germany, which had a different political history and a vastly different linguistic constitution. Yet culture and language played a crucial role in national identity-formation in the Habsburg territories too. Gilman addresses this point on the pages to which I referred above. It was also the case that German discussions of German-Jewish identity (such as Wagner's) profoundly informed discussions of German-Jewish identity in Austria. In any event, see also Scott Spector's excellent study of the meaning of culture for the young German-speaking Jews in the "Prague Circle": *Prague Territories: National Conflict and Aesthetic Innovation in Franz Kafka's Fin de Siècle* (Berkeley and Los Angeles: University of California Press, 2000).

38. It might be argued that in his essay "Judaism in Music," which was published in 1850, Wagner attributes to Jewish musicians the capacity to produce "deceptively similar" replicas of German culture. After all, and as is well known, he uses precisely that phrase in the essay. But the accent is elsewhere. With just a bit of reflection, Wagner suggests, "Jewishness" in music becomes easy to identify, almost as easy to identify as it is in speech and writing, where it is gratingly conspicuous. As I will show in chapter 1, Wagner's attitude on this matter changed. He seems, over the ensuing decades, to have grown afraid that "Jewish journalism" would produce an entirely different and altogether more menacing order of confusion. For Wagner, the crisis of modernity entailed a crisis of authenticity.

39. I have put these phrases (e.g., "deceptively similar," "solid sensibilities") in quotation marks because they are all quotations, ones that I will discuss in the body of my text.

40. On the stereotype of Jewish copying, see Mark Anderson, "'Jewish Mimesis'? Imitation and Assimilation in Thomas Mann's 'Wälsugenblut' and Ludwig Jacobinski's *Werther, Der Jude,*" *German Life and Letters* 49 (1996): 193–204.

41. For a discussion of how mimicry on the part of a different cultural "other" made the ideal of authenticity difficult to sustain and, in doing so, caused anxiety, see

Homi K. Bhabha, "Of Mimicry and Man: The Ambivalence of Colonial Discourse," in his *The Location of Culture* (London and New York: Routledge, 1994), 85–92.

42. For a colorful and stimulating recent account of the relation of Jewish identity and modernity, see Yuri Szelkine, *The Jewish Century* (Princeton: Princeton University Press, 2004). Szelkine implies, in effect, that the figure of the journalist does accurately evoke Jewish identity. For he emphasizes that Jews were disproportionately mobile, literate, and urban. Then, flipping around the traditional model of assimilation, he argues that Jews were not the paradigmatic assimilationists. Rather, it was the rest of the modern world that assimilated itself to the Jewish model of mobility. Hence the idea of the twentieth century being the *Jewish* century. Here, of course, Szelkine is intimating that antisemitic fears about the dominance of a Jewish modernity were well-founded. For this reason, and others as well, his book has been controversial. The particular cultural dynamisms generated by the German-Jewish encounter with modernity is at the center of a rich and diverse and burgeoning scholarly literature, one that includes, to name just a few titles, David Sorkin's *The Transformation of German Jewry, 1780–1840* (New York and Oxford: Oxford University Press, 1987); Klaus Berghahn's *Grenzen der Toleranz: Juden und Christen im Zeitalter der Aufklärung* (Cologne: Böhlau, 2000); Michael Meyer's *Response to Modernity: A History of the Reform Movement in Judaism* (Detroit: Wayne State University Press, 1988); Shulamit Volkov's edited volume *Deutsche Juden und die Moderne* (Munich: Oldenbourg, 1994); Willi Goetschel's *Spinoza's Modernity: Lessing, Mendelssohn, Heine* (Madison: University of Wisconsin Press, 2003); and Jonathan Hess's *German Jews and the Claims of Modernity* (New Haven: Yale University Press, 2002).

43. Moritz Goldstein, "Deutsch-jüdische Parnaß," *Der Kunstwart: Halbmonatsschau für Ausdruckskultur auf allen Lebensgebieten* 25, no. 11 (March 1912): 281–94. With its biological connotations, "assimilation" is an unsavory term for describing a process of social and cultural integration. I use it here because it corresponds to Goldstein's views—he repeatedly uses biological metaphors to evoke the cultural and spiritual situation of German Jews. For example, the failure of acculturation has turned them, in Goldstein's account, into "hermaphroditic beings." In this book I use the term "assimilation" where I am reconstructing a perspective that, directly or indirectly, works with the idea of assimilation. Elsewhere I will use the word "acculturation," which I think more effectively designates the actual process of German-Jewish integration, a process that, as scholars have been emphasizing, was not generally characterized by a complete giving up of traditional identity, but rather entailed increasing participation in German and Austrian cultural and political life. Hence the aptness of "acculturation." On the issue how Austrian Jews lived with multiple identities, see Marsha Rozenblit, *Reconstructing a National Identity: The Jews of Habsburg Austria during the First World War* (New York and Oxford: Oxford University Press, 2001). It is worth noting here that historical fig-

ures who in some places advanced the idea of "assimilation" often turn out to have had complex and countervailing attitudes about the nature of German-Jewish integration. Goldstein is, as we will see, one of these figures.

44. Theodor Gomperz, "Über die Grenzen der jüdischen intellektuellen Begabung," in Robert Kann, ed., *Theodor Gomperz: Ein Gelehrtenleben im Bürgertum der Franz-Josephszeit* (Vienna: Verlag der österreichische Akademie der Wissenschaften, 1974), 384–92.

45. Cited in Zweig, *Die Welt von Gestern,* 131. Of course, Herzl is implying here that doing anything other than pursuing the Zionist cause would be a sign of his Jewish inability to focus on a great task. But his juxtaposition—or really, opposition—of writing feuilletons and Zionism is revealing. It conveys the sense that writing feuilletons is not a truly worthy pursuit, that it is part of the Jewish culture of distraction and failure that Zionism should help Jews to overcome. That possibility is never entertained, needless to say. Indeed, Herzl frames writing feuilletons as a temptation. He knows that he should put his mind and his pen to a higher use. Yet, as a Jewish intellectual who has not yet learned what "dedication means," he cannot help himself and still works in the lower form. "I continue to write feuilletons." Also worth noting is that Herzl does not mention the possibility of writing feuilletons in support of the Zionist cause, something he in fact did for the Zionist newspaper *Die Welt*. Instead he lets the form stand as an emblematic Jewish distraction.

46. The Kraus scholar Edward Timms translates the term "Literat" as journalist, for example. See Timms, *Karl Kraus, Apocalyptic Satirist,* vol. 1: *Culture and Catastrophe in Habsburg Vienna* (New Haven: Yale University Press, 1986), 183. As we will see, moreover, in his "Karl Kraus" (1931) essay Benjamin explicitly treats journalists as literati of a certain kind.

47. Jakob Wassermann, "Der Jude als Orientale," in *Vom Judentum: Ein Sammelbuch* (Leipzig: Kurt Wolff Verlag, 1913), 5. On the topic of Jewish "orientalism," see Paul Mendes-Flohr, "Fin de Siècle Orientalism, The *Ostjuden* and the Aesthetics of Self-Affirmation," in Mendes-Flohr, *Divided Passions: Jewish Intellectuals and the Experience of Modernity* (Detroit: Wayne State University Press, 1991), 77–132.

48. The idea of *Mauscheln* was similarly reinscribed, as we will see in chapter 3 of this study.

49. Since Benjamin is talking about a group of writers who, he notes, have been insistently maligned, and who concern themselves with the "affairs of today," it seems reasonable to call their medium "journalistic." At the same time, it is not easy to identify just whom Benjamin has in mind here. For he claims that he is speaking of the "idea" of the literati. I will discuss this complexity in chapter 4, where I examine the place of journalism in Benjamin's thoughts on Jews and Jewishness.

50. On the links between questions about Jewish identity and aesthetic innovation in turn-of-the-century central Europe, see Steven Beller, *Vienna and the Jews: A Cultural History, 1867–1938* (Cambridge: Cambridge University Press, 1989); Leon Botstein, *Judentum und Modernität: Essays zur Rolle der Juden in der öster-*

reichischen Kultur, 1848 bis 1938 (Vienna: Böhlau, 1991); Michael Steinberg, "Jewish Identity and Intellectuality in Fin-de-Siècle Vienna," *New German Critique* 43 (Winter 1988): 3–33; and also Spector, *Prague Territories*.

51. Benjamin's line about Kraus's "prayer for redemption" comes from W.B., "Karl Kraus" (1928), in W.B., *Gesammelte Schriften,* vol. 2.2, ed. Rolf Tiedemann (Frankfurt/M: Suhrkamp, 1977), 625. Hereafter I will cite Benjamin's *Gesammelte Schriften* as *BGS*. Benjamin wrote two essays entitled "Karl Kraus," the first in 1928, and the other, more substantial one reprinted in *Illuminationen,* in 1931. His note about Kraus being "journalism in its most paradoxical form," or a kind of anti-journalism, can be found in *BGS* 2.3:1114. As Benjamin's phrase suggests, the genre status of Kraus's writing is a difficult question, and not only because he worked with a variety of forms (e.g., aphorisms, poems, dramas, etc.). I take up the matter of whether Kraus should be called a journalist in chapter 2.

52. Karl Kraus, *Aphorismen,* ed. Christian Wagenknecht (Frankfurt/M: Suhrkamp, 1986), 334. Hereafter I will cite Kraus as K.K.

53. K.K., "Selbstbespiegelung," in K.K., *Die chinesische Mauer,* ed. Wagenknecht (Frankfurt/M: Suhrkamp, 1987), 195.

54. On the availability of sources, see Leo Lensing, *Brief über den Vater: Ein Brief des Jungen Karl Kraus* (Warmbronn: Ulrich Keicher Verlag, 2005), 5–22, and Edward Timms, *Karl Kraus, Apocalyptic Satirist,* vol. 2: *The Post-War Crisis and the Rise of the Swastika* (New Haven: Yale University Press, 2005), 168.

55. Fritz Wittels, a member of Freud's circle, presented such a reading of Kraus and his "neurosis" to the Vienna Psychoanalytic Society in 1910, effectively beginning this line of interpretation. As Timms notes, Wittels, who knew Kraus personally but was given to polemical excesses, is "not the most of reliable of witnesses." Yet Timms goes on to suggest that Kraus and Wittels "may well have exchanged confidences," or, in effect, that Wittels is a valuable witness, after all. For Timms too wants to demonstrate that Kraus's familial life was a highly fraught affair. Here Timms misrepresents Kraus's correspondence with his mother and sisters, making it sound much graver than it is. See Timms, *Karl Kraus,* 2:169. I am grateful to Leo Lensing for pointing out to me the disjunction between the actual content Kraus's early correspondence and the idea that he was an angry adolescent who made life difficult for his entire family.

56. This letter is housed in the Kraus collection in the Vienna Stadt und Landesbibliothek (i.n. 171.276).

57. Lensing offers an extremely meticulous account of the relationship between Kraus and his father in *Brief über den Vater*.

58. Kraus's correspondence about his father is the focus of Lensing's book *Brief über den Vater*. In addition, Timms discusses and cites the 1897 letter in *Karl Kraus,* 2:170.

59. Timms repeatedly makes this point in both volumes of *Karl Kraus, Apocalyptic Satirist*.

60. Cited in ibid., 1:53.

61. K.K., "I and the *Neue Freie Presse*," *Die Fackel* no. 5 (Mid-May 1899): 11.

62. This is not to imply that Kraus's newspaper had no models. It did, and I will discuss its relation to the main one, Maximilian Harden's *Die Zukunft* [*The Future*] in chapter 2.

63. The phrase "one of the most expensive puns in literary history" is Timms's. See his account of this affair in *Karl Kraus*, 1:52. The basis for the pun is the double meaning of the word Ground: It can mean reason, as in "good reason," and also ground, as in earth or land.

64. Siegfried Kracauer, *Das Ornament der Masse: Essays* (Frankfurt/M: Suhrkamp, 1977), 50.

65. For Kraus, it is worth noting, it was not the case that there were two cultures existing next to, and in opposition to, each other in Vienna: mainstream and modernist culture. As we will see, Kraus rejected the claims of most Viennese modernists to genuine innovativeness and tried to show how they remained stuck in the morass of Viennese culture, of its culture of kitsch.

66. Hermann Broch, *Hofmannsthal und seine Zeit: Eine Studie* (Frankfurt/M: Suhrkamp, 1974), 69.

67. K.K., "Die Handelssprache," in K.K., *Die Sprache,* ed. Wagenknecht (Frankfurt/M: Suhrkamp, 1987), 266–67.

68. K.K., *Aphorismen,* 146.

69. See Helmut Andics, *Die Juden in Wien* (Vienna: Böhlau, 1988), 318: "No one except the Jewish feuilletonist in Vienna managed to produce this mixture of viciousness and charm, hardness and invective."

70. Simmel wrote his famous essay on "the essence" of fashion fairly early, but he continued to revisit the topic and refine his ideas on it, and my account, accordingly, draws on a number of his works, especially the essays: "Wandel der Kulturformen," "Großstädte und Geistesleben," and "Das Individuum und die Freiheit," all of which are anthologized in Simmel, *Das Individuum und die Freiheit: Essais* (Frankfurt/M: Fischer, 1993). I have also drawn on Kracauer's helpful profile of Simmel and his work ("Georg Simmel"), as well as David Frisby's *Georg Simmel* (New York and London: Routledge, 2002).

71. Not all of these quotations come from Simmel, it should be noted. Some are from Kracauer's profile, and some are from contemporaries who effectively formulated similar notions about the modern condition, like Robert Musil.

72. K.K., *Aphorismen,* 112.

73. Ibid., 110.

74. Ibid., 86.

75. K.K., "Pretiosen," in *Die Sprache,* 260–61.

76. Oskar Kokoschka, *My Life,* trans. David Britt (New York, Macmillan, 1974), 40.

77. K.K., Die Sprache, 261.

78. See J. P. Stern, "Karl Kraus's Vision of Language," *Modern Language Review* 61 (1966): 71–84.

79. See Timms, *Karl Kraus*, 2:135. As Timms points out, Kraus's criticisms of punctuation problems were not "mere pedantry." Indeed, his account of Kraus's seemingly fanatical investment in clean punctuation is characteristically informative and generally accurate. The problem occurs where Timms likens that investment to Lynne Truss's "zero tolerance" approach to language, which is really a sustained, mostly trivial gripe about the inconveniences poor punctuation can cause. This problem is, unfortunately, a recurring one in *The Rise of the Swastika*. As should be clear, I have benefited greatly from Timms's research. But while this latest volume is as learned and incisive as the first volume of *Karl Kraus, Apocalyptic Satirist*, it presses much too hard in trying to make a case for Kraus's relevance and prescience. Without offering the necessary qualifications, Timms credits Kraus with being a precursor to a whole panoply of thinkers, from Derrida to, well, Lynne Truss. As a result, numerous misleading elements creep into his image of Kraus.

80. See, for example, Simon Ganahl, *Ich gegen Babylon: Karl Kraus und die Presse* (Vienna: Picus, 2006).

81. This is a rather complicated point, because Kraus, in effect, accused those people who wanted to regulate the irrational through rational systems of knowledge of acting on irrational impulses themselves—tawdry, lecherous ones. I discuss this complexity and its place in Kraus's thought in the conclusion.

82. K.K., "Sehnsucht nach aristokratischem Umgang," in K.K., *Untergang der Welt durch schwarze Magie*, ed. Wagenknecht (Frankfurt/M: Suhrkamp, 1989), 339.

83. K.K., *Aphorismen*, 350.

84. Ibid., 134.

85. Elias Canetti, *Die Fackel im Ohr: Lebensgeschichte 1921–1931* (Franfurt/M: Suhrkamp, 1996), 66–73.

86. An audio CD is available: *Karl Kraus liest aus eigenen Schriften* [Karl Kraus Reads from His Own Works], Hörsturz, 1989.

87. K.K., "Das ist der Krieg—C'est la Guerre—Das ist die Zeitung!," *Untergang der Welt durch Schwarze Magie*, 365.

88. K.K., "In dieser großen Zeit," in K.K., *Weltgericht*, 2 vols., ed. Christian Wagenknecht (Frankfurt/M: Suhrkamp, 1988), 1:173.

89. The critic is Nike Wagner; cited in Lensing, "Karl Kraus Writes 'He's a Jew after All,'" in Sander Gilman and Jack Zipes, eds., *The Yale Companion to Jewish Writing and Thought in German Culture, 1096–1996* (New Haven: Yale University Press, 1997), 313.

90. Leopold Liegler, *Karl Kraus: Sein Leben und sein Werk* (Vienna: R. Lanyi, 1920), 87.

91. K.K., "Verbrecherische Irreführung der *Neuen Freien Presse*," *Untergang der Welt durch schwarze Magie*, 280.

92. K.K., *Aphorismen*, 223.

93. K.K., "Das Hexen Prozeß von Leoben," *Die Fackel* no. 168 (November 1904): 16. Hereafter cited parenthetically as *F*.

94. Cited in Jacques Le Rider, *Modernity and Crises of Identity: Culture and Society in Fin-de-Siècle Vienna*, trans. Rosemary Morris (New York: Continuum, 1990), 253.

95. K.K., "Heine and the Consequences" ("Heine und die Folgen") was first published as a pamphlet in 1910. Kraus reprinted it in *Die Fackel* in September 1911 (*F* 329-30:6-33).

96. K.K., "Zum Prozeß Rutthofer," in K.K., *Sittlichkeit und Kriminalität*, ed. Wagenknecht (Frankfurt/M: Suhrkamp, 1987), 223.

97. Mechthild Börries, *Ein Angriff auf Heinrich Heine: Kritische Betrachtungen zu Karl Kraus* (Stuttgart, Berlin, Mainz, Cologne: Kohlhammer, 1971); Dietmar Goltschnigg, *Die Fackel ins wunde Herz: Kraus über Heine. Eine "Erledigung"? Texte, Analysen, Kommentar* (Vienna: Passagen Verlag, 2000).

98. Gilman, *Jewish Self-Hatred*, 240.

99. Mark Anderson, *Kafka's Clothes: Ornament and Aestheticism in the Habsburg Fin de Siècle* (New York: Oxford University Press, 1992), 201-206.

100. Le Rider, *Modernity and Crisis of Identity*, 264.

101. Theodor Adorno, "Sittlichkeit und Kriminalität," in Adorno, *Noten zur Literatur*, ed. Rolf Tiedemann (Frankfurt/M: Suhrkamp, 1989), 375.

102. Here Kraus is not using the familiar Yiddishism "schmuck." Rather, he is alluding, as he often did, to the name of a disreputable, inept, and conniving Jewish journalist character ("Schmock") in Gustav Freytag's well-known play *Die Journalisten* (1852). One widely used German dictionary, it is worth noting, lists Freytag's character Schmock and the traits he exhibits as the *primary* meaning of the word "Schmock." See the (Wahrig) *Deutsches Wörterbuch* (Munich: Bertelsmann Lexikon Verlag, 1992), 1132.

103. See Harry Zohn, "Karl Kraus: 'Jüdischer Selbsthasser' oder 'Erzjude,'" *Modern Austrian Literature* 8 (1975): 20-37; Robert Wistrich, *The Jews of Vienna in the Age of Franz Joseph* (London and New York: Oxford University Press, 1990), 497-536; Timms, *Karl Kraus*, 1:237-49; see also Lensing, "Karl Kraus Writes 'He's a Jew after All.'"

104. Let me emphasize that I am not questioning the value of biographical criticism. Indeed, I will be dealing at length with what might be considered biographical factors in this study. But my main aim, in the end, is not to develop new insights into Kraus's "relation to Judaism." Rather, I am interested in offering a fresh reading of the development and meaning of his journalistic style, of how these processes of development and signification seemed to be shaped by the discursive links between journalism and "Jewishness." That, among other things, is what separates my study of his "Jewish Question" from the work of more biographically oriented scholars.

105. Leo Lensing's work represents a very important exception to the trend I

have outlined here. In an article written after his contribution to the *Yale Companion* had appeared, Lensing proposes an artful, conceptually ambitious approach to the question of Kraus's self-fashioning as a Jewish critic. Drawing on Judith Butler's constructivist reading of cultural identity formation, he suggests that we might understand Kraus's convoluted claims about his Jewishness as a sort of provocative performance of Jewish identity rather than merely as the "symptom" of a deep psychic conflict. This reading has had a significant influence on the one I will be developing, and I want to acknowledge my debt to it. What Lensing does not undertake to do in his article, however, is explicate in detail how Kraus's performance of Jewish identity connects with his stylistic evolution and the cultural significance of his style. Illuminating this connection is, as I have said, the main goal of the present study. See Lensing, "Tiertheater: Textspiele der jüdischen Identität bei Altenberg, Kraus und Kafka," *Das jüdische Echo* 48 (October 1999): 79–86.

106. K.K., *Aphorismen,* 361. In another aphorism Kraus takes stock of how the significance of self-critical humor changes not simply according to context, but also from mood to mood: "Jews practice a sort of incest of humor. Among themselves they are permitted to make fun of themselves. But woe, if in doing so they wind up falling out with each other." *Aphorismen,* 361.

107. Shulamit Volkov, "Antisemitism as a Cultural Code: Reflections on the History and Historiography of Antisemitism in Imperial Germany," in Michael Marras, ed., *The Nazi Genocide: Articles on the History of the Destruction of European Jews,* vol. 2 (Westport and London: Meckler, 1989), 307–30.

108. Quoted in Harry Zohn, *Karl Kraus and the Critics* (Columbia, S.C.: Camden House, 1997), 25. Zohn's book extensively surveys writings on Kraus's Jewish identity; see, for example, 19–26.

109. Canetti, "The New Karl Kraus," in Canetti, *The Conscience of Words,* trans. Joachim Neugroschel (New York: Farrar, Straus and Giroux, 1976), 214.

110. In her excellent study of Kraus's "eroticism," Nike Wagner, who also emphasizes how paradoxes functioned as a means of self-stylization for Kraus, offers what I believe to be a slight misreading of this passage. Here, according to her, Kraus conveys the idea that "only the most positions extreme were possible" for him. That seems not to be so. After all, Kraus speaks of the necessity of "defending an idea against those who claim to stand for it." The actual positions held do not need to be extreme. What needs to be extreme—or beyond the pale of established "parties"—is the writer himself. Indeed, precisely in the area of sexual policies and practices Kraus was in basic ways a liberal. He may have flirted with valorizing sexual libertinism, but when Kraus fought for sexual freedom, he did so in the language of classical liberalism. He pushed to keep unregulated (by "ethics laws") private, intimate spaces because in his view those are the spaces in which consenting adults make decisions about how to treat vulnerable others, and thus develop key ethical faculties—ethical faculties crucial for political life. Again, what the passage cited here expresses is that it was impossible for Kraus to *identify* straight-

forwardly with legible social and political positions. The passage expresses that Kraus did not want to be associated with *the people* who occupied those positions. The positions themselves were not always unpalatable to Kraus; some were worth "defending." See Wagner, *Geist und Geschlecht: Karl Kraus und die Erotik der Wiener Moderne* (Frankfurt/M: Suhrkamp, 1982), 19.

111. In Germany and Austria, where Kraus is known as a modernist master, his reputation is better than it is in the U.S. But in the former countries too he is often strongly associated with Jewish antisemitism. The two monographs on "Heine and the Consequences" were produced in those countries, and, as I mentioned, both see the text as an instance of Jewish self-hatred (see note 100 above). Moreover, Kraus's German admirers do not necessarily absolve him of antisemitism. In a recent essay in *Merkur,* for example, Jens Malte-Fischer takes pains to note that in 1938 the official newspaper of the Nazi party (*Die Völkische Beobachter*) strongly associated Kraus with Jewish antisemitism. And if Malte-Fischer's profile of Kraus is generally positive, he does not challenge the idea that Jewish self-hatred was part of Kraus's outlook. See Malte-Fischer, "Der Haß ist Fruchtbar noch: Karl Kraus— Der Nörgler als Rechthaber," *Merkur* 665–66 (Fall 2004): 847–56.

112. This critique is *A Crown for Zion* [*Eine Krone für Zion,* 1898], which I discuss in chapter 2. Kraus, it is worth noting, emphasized the notion of Zionism as radical assimilationism elsewhere too. For example, the famous aphorism that criticizes assimilationists for creating " pseudonymous culture" links the urge to change "Samuel to Siegfried" to the impulse behind "Jewish nationalism." See K.K., *Aphorismen,* 215.

113. To be sure, Kraus accuses German-Jewish feuilletonists of sounding alike and thus of parroting each other, but he does not set up a dichotomy between copying and authentic cultural productivity.

114. K.K., *Aphorismen,* 241. Kraus, it should be noted, did not categorically embrace imitation. Indeed, he denounced what he took to be the unimaginative reproduction of journalistic formulas, and so we can also find in his work critical remarks about the ubiquity of imitation and the lack originality in journalistic culture.

115. Whether Kraus provides a serviceable critique of Heine's prose here is not at issue in this study. For a thoughtful analysis of how journalistic language could connect with the project of Jewish acculturation, see the section entitled "Die Sprache der Assimilation" in W. G. Sebald's study of the critic Carl Sternheim, *Carl Sternheim: Kritiker und Opfer der Wilhelminischen Ära* (Stuttgart; Kohlhammer, 1969), 90–94.

116. K.K., "Die letzten Schauspieler," in *Untergang der Welt durch Schwarze Magie,* 152–56. Kraus was not alone in holding up Eastern Jewish culture as a positive alternative to the general cultural tendencies of assimilated German Jewry. But there are considerable differences among such readings (and uses) of *Ostjuden.* And in chapter 3 I show how Kraus's deviates from some others. Neither was Kraus alone in finding value in a sort of traditional, and also radical, "Jewish mimesis."

In the conclusion, I discuss how Adorno, who developed certain analogous ideas, understood Kraus's mimetic activities as a Jewish phenomenon.

117. See Rathenau's "Höre, Israel!," first published under a pseudonym in Harden's *Die Zukunft* in 1897. I am citing from the version reprinted in *Deutschtum und Judentum: Ein Disput unter Juden aud Deutschland,* ed. Christoph Schulte (Stuttgart: Reclam, 1993), 33.

118. It is interesting to note that Kraus was perhaps the first critic to link Heidegger's celebration of authenticity with his dubious politics. For a detailed reading of Kraus's critique, see Gerald Stieg, "Kraus gegen Heidegger," in Amy Colin and Elisabeth Strenger, eds., *Bridging the Abyss: Reflections on Jewish Suffering, Anti-Semitism and Exile* (Munich: Fink, 1994), 159–83.

119. As I hope I have made clear, in speaking of Kraus's writing as a "radical performance of Jewish identity," I am not trying to locate in it an actual, "radical" model of Jewish identity. And I certainly do not want to imply, as, say, Scholem and Benjamin did, that I have found in Kraus some kind of extreme Jewishness, or mysteriously transmitted links to Jewish traditions. My point, again, is that for complex reasons Kraus's writing activated and disrupted what were in his context crucial *markers* of Jewish intellectuality. That is the sense in which his style can be read as a radical performance of Jewish identity. Also worth emphasizing is that other factors—factors beyond "Jewish issues"—were at work in the development of Kraus's style. Indeed, his views on language and his innovative mimetic techniques emerged out of a whole matrix of circumstances and influences. Many of them are intimately tied to his most immediate context: Vienna. And generations of commentators, from Hans Kohn, Erich Heller, J. P. Stern, and Paul Schick, through Kurt Krolop, Sigurd Paul Scheichl, Allan Janik, Wilma Iggers, and Timms, to Nike Wagner, Leo Lensing, and Burkhard Müller, have effectively linked key aspects of Kraus's work to his Viennese setting. His work has been linked, for example, to particularly Viennese and Hapsburg modes of strident oratory, of linguistic hyperconsciousness, of satirical theatricality, of moral rigorism, and of eroticism. In addition, without Vienna's extraordinary culture of verbal and visual ornamentation, it is hard to imagine that Kraus's "anti-style" would have developed as it did. Of similar importance for his writing are the complicated fault lines and dichotomies within the modernist movement in Vienna (Adolf Loos's crusade against ornamentation as over against the aesthetics of the Wiener Werkstatte). The voices Kraus famously mimicked were, moreover, for the most part Viennese. He endlessly discussed Vienna's political, social, and journalistic problems. So with some justification Kraus has been called (by Arthur May) "the most Viennese of all Viennese authors." As much as any Viennese author, and much more than most, Kraus was a palpably Viennese phenomenon. But if minimizing the significance of Vienna makes little sense, so does neglecting other contexts. In short, and needless to say, this study does not seek to bring forth the last word on Kraus's style. Rather, I hope to add to our understanding of Kraus's anti-journalism by

reading it against a discursive context that has not been sufficiently taken into account in discussions of it.

120. Gershom Scholem, *Tagebücher, 1917–1923*, vol. 2, ed., Herbert Kopp-Oberstebrink et al. (Berlin: Jüdischer Verlag, 2000), 469. Hereafter cited as *ST*. Most of Scholem's claims about Kraus are to be found in his recently published early diaries, which, as Steven Aschheim forcefully suggests in a long review essay on them, enable us to see just how many of Scholem's important views emerged out of his first struggles with the "Jewish Question." See Aschheim, "The Metaphysical Psychologist: On the Life and Letters of Gershom Scholem," *The Journal of Modern History* 76 (December 2004): 903–33.

CHAPTER 1

1. Moritz Goldstein, "Deutsch-jüdische Parnaß," *Der Kunstwart: Halbmonatsschau für Ausdruckskultur auf allen Lebensgebieten* 25, no. 11 (March 1912): 281–94, at 288. Hereafter cited parenthetically as "DJP."

2. "True creativity," "the productive character," and "to be a mirror" are Goldstein's phrases, which is why I have put them in quotation marks. See Goldstein, "DJP," 288–89.

3. Hitler, *Mein Kampf* (New York: Reynal and Hitchcock, 1939), 334.

4. Ibid., 330–31.

5. Ibid., 335.

6. This strategy of argumentation was often used in the early rhetoric of political Zionism. For example, after his turn to Zionism Herzl blamed all manner of stereotypical Jewish weakness on antisemitism with more vigor than he had during his assimilationist phase. See Jacques Kornberg, *Theodor Herzl: From Assimilation to Zionism* (Bloomington: Indiana University Press, 1993), 131. Such an approach to the "Jewish Question" could, of course, be seen as corroborating basic anti-Jewish ideas. Indeed, overlooking the complexities in Goldstein's essay, antisemites received it positively, both in 1912 and also during the Third Reich, when propagandists invoked Goldstein as a Jewish authority on Jewish excesses. On this point, see Gary Smith, "'Das Jüdische versteht sich von selbst': Walter Benjamins frühe Auseinandersetzung mit dem Judentum," *Deutsche Vierteljahresschrift* 65, no. 2 (1991): 324–25.

7. On one level Goldstein was stating the obvious. For Jews were disproportionately represented in the journalistic world of turn-of-the-century Germany and Austria. As noted, the historian Peter Pulzer has even asserted about that time and those places: "There was no profession that was more completely dominated by Jews than journalism." See Pulzer, *The Rise of Political Anti-Semitism in Germany and Austria* (Cambridge, Mass.: Harvard University Press), 13. Memoirs by well-known contemporaries, e.g., Stefan Zweig and Jakob Wassermann, support Pulzer's claim, as do the membership lists of Concordia, the Viennese journal-

ists' association. Steven Beller suggests that in 1909, when they made up 10 percent of Vienna's population, Jews comprised 60 percent of Concordia's membership. See Beller, *Vienna and the Jews: A Cultural History, 1867–1938* (Cambridge: Cambridge University Press, 1989), 39. Furthermore, journalists who had some kind of Jewish heritage, who were "Jews" by the standards of the day, did not only become conspicuous through sheer force of numbers. They seemed also to preponderate among the cynosures of literary and political reportage. Daniel Spitzer, Ludwig Hevesi, Bertha Zuckerkandl, Theodor Herzl, Maximilian Harden, Alfred Kerr, Felix Salten, Siegfried Jacobsohn, Julius Bab, Victor Adler, Kurt Tucholsky, Alfred Polgar, Siegfried Kracauer, Egon Erwin Kisch, Joseph Roth, and Kraus all fell into the category "Jewish journalists." Also worth noting here is that in his history of the radical journal *Die Weltbühne*, István Deák underlines the dramatically disproportionate representation of Jews there. See Deák, *Weimar Germany's Left-Wing Intellectuals: Political History of "Die Weltbühne" and its Circle* (Berkeley and Los Angeles: University of California Press, 1968), 24.

8. Theodor Lessing, *Der jüdische Selbsthaß* (Berlin: Jüdischer Verlag, 1930), 43.

9. Ibid.

10. In discussing the Musivstil the scholar Dan Pagis speaks of the medieval Hebrew poets' technique of interweaving biblical verses and verse-fragments into their poetry, and of how the new context often transforms the meaning of the citation. He also notes that, to be effective, this allusive technique relies on the audience's recognition of the verse fragments, their ability to supply the missing portion of the verse, and to appreciate how the context has changed. Pagis writes: "In the 19th century scholars called this style *Musivstil*, i.e., a mosaic of verses. In our day there have been some objections to this term and its underlying assumption, because what results is not simply a collection of citations, but a new and dynamic creation." Dan Pagis, *Ḥiddush u-masoret be-shirat ha-ḥol ha'ivrit: sefared ve-Iṭalyah* [Change and Tradition in the Secular Poetry: Spain and Italy] (Jerusalem: Keter, 1976), 70. I am grateful to my colleague at Ohio State Adena Tanenbaum for translating this passage from the Hebrew. I discuss Scholem's notion of the *Musivstil* in detail in chapter 4.

11. In German Scholem's sentence reads: "Beide: der Journalismus und Kraus sind Kinder unseres Mittcralters, Kraus aber ein würdiges und darum unglückliches Kind" (*ST* 2:468). I have translated the phrase "unseres Mitteralters" freely—as "medieval Jewish culture"—in order to convey its meaning. In the diary passage from which I am quoting, Scholem discusses styles of writing and thinking, and how with respect to some of these *cultural* practices hardly any Jews have "overcome the middle ages." Hence my translation of "middle ages" as "medieval culture." Equally clear is that Scholem is addressing the influence of *Jewish* culture. Speaking as a Jew, Scholem is attempting to identify improbable links between contemporary and medieval Jewish uses of language. It is for these reasons that I rendered the possessive adjective "our" as "Jewish."

12. As we can infer from the epigraph that introduces this chapter, Kraus resisted the label "journalist." And because critics who categorized him as a journalist often did so in the same spirit as Lessing, or to devalue Kraus's writing, Kraus scholars generally prefer appellations such as satirist or dramatist—Kraus's most renowned work, *The Last Days of Mankind* [*Die letzten Tage der Menschheit*, 1919] is a drama. But on the first page of the first issue of *Die Fackel* (April 1899), Kraus refers to his journal as a "newspaper."

13. See, for example, Jacques Le Rider, *Modernity and Crises of Identity: Culture and Society in Fin-de-Siècle Vienna*, trans. Rosemary Morris (New York: Continuum, 1990), 264.

14. For a concise account of Jellinek's cultural significance, see Robert Wistrich, *The Jews of Vienna in the Age of Franz Joseph* (London and New York: Oxford University Press, 1990), 111.

15. On the migration of Austro-Hungarians to Vienna, see Marsha Rozenblit, *The Jews of Austria, 1867-1914: Assimilation and Identity* (Albany: State University of New York Press, 1984), 22. The secondary literature on the general topic of Jewish assimilation is too large to list here, but a good place to start is Jacob Katz's classic study *Out of the Ghetto: The Social Background of Jewish Emancipation, 1770-1880* (Cambridge, Mass.: Harvard University Press, 1973).

16. Adolf Jellinek, *Der jüdische Stamm* (Vienna: Herzfeld und Bauer, 1869), 89.

17. See, for example, John Hoberman, "Otto Weininger and the Critique of Jewish Masculinity," in Nancy Harrowitz and Barbara Hyams, eds., *Jews and Gender: Responses to Otto Weininger* (Philadelphia: Temple University Press, 1995), 141-54; see also Sander Gilman, *The Jew's Body* (New York and London: Routledge, 1991), 104-27.

18. There are scholars of Jewish culture who agree with Jellinek. That is, there are scholars who believe that Jewish culture has traditionally evinced more "femininity" than other Western cultures, and that this femininity counts as a Jewish ethical strength. And such scholars might argue that rather than trying to negotiate an entrenched antisemitic stereotype, Jellinek was pointing out a basic truth about Jewish culture. See, above all, Daniel Boyarin, *Unheroic Conduct: The Rise of Hetereosexuality and the Construction of the New Jewish Man* (Berkeley and Los Angeles: University of California Press, 1997).

19. Elias Canetti emphasizes how intensely Viennese intellectuals discussed Weininger's work after the First World War. Canetti, *Die Fackel im Ohr: Lebensgeschichte, 1921-1931* (Frankfurt/M: Suhrkamp, 1982), 115. Lessing deals with Weininger in his *Der jüdische Selbsthaß*, 80-100. The quotation here comes from Otto Weininger, *Geschlecht und Charakter: Eine prinzipielle Untersuchung* (Vienna, 1903), 436. I will offer further references to secondary literature on Weininger in the following chapter, where he plays a slightly greater role.

20. Jellinek, *Der jüdische Stamm in Sprichwörtern* (Vienna: Herzfeld und Bauer, 1882), 91.

21. Authors who wanted to make a case for the Jews' value for literary culture very often stressed analogous qualities, i.e., the Jews' acumen for criticism and commentary. See, for example, Julius Bab, *Goethe und die Juden* (Berlin: Philo, 1926). Bab argues that Jewish theoretical thought, in particular Spinoza's, made Goethe's elemental art possible. Thomas Mann made very similar claims just around the same time (1921), that is, at a moment of burgeoning antisemitism. Indeed, Mann too emphasized the salutary effect of Jewish interlocutors on Goethe. See Mann, "Zur jüdischen Frage," in Mann, *Politische Aufsätze* (Frankfurt/M: Fischer, 1972), 68–70.

22. On the stereotype of Jewish mobility—both Weininger and Jellinek use a form of the word "beweglich"—see the chapter dedicated to that stereotype in Gilman, *The Jew's Body*, 48–63.

23. K.K. "Er ist doch e Jud," in K.K., *Untergang der Welt durch Schwarze Magie*, ed. Wagenknecht (Frankfurt/M: Suhrkamp, 1989), 333.

24. Of course, it is possible to claim that in the very act of mirroring, Jews effectively expressed an ethical, *Jewish* characteristic and were indeed being themselves, insofar as anyone can be oneself. Max Horkheimer and Theodor Adorno make this argument in their *Dialectic of Enlightenment*. See Adorno and Horkheimer, *Dialektik der Aufklärung: Philosophische Fragmente* (Frankfurt/M: Suhrkamp, 1988), 189–92.

25. K.K., "Selbstbespiegelung," 195.

26. Ibid., 191.

27. For an overview of *Bildung*, see Franz Rauhut, "Die Herkunft der Worte und Begriffe: 'Kultur,' 'Civilization,' und 'Bildung,'" *Germanisch-Romanische Monatsschrift* 111 (1953): 83–91; Wilhelm Vosskamp, "Bildung ist Mehr als Wissen," *Zeitschrift der Alexander von Humboldt Stiftung* 76 (2000): 2–19; Rudolf Vierhaus, "Bildung," in Otto Brunner, Werner Conze, and Reinhart Koselleck, eds., *Geschichtliche Grundbegriffe: Historisches Lexikon zur politisch-sozialen Sprache in Deutschland* (Stuttgart: Klett-Cotta, 1972), 508–51. On the particular importance of *Bildung* for German Jews, and on Herder's radical notion of *Bildung*, see Paul Mendes-Flohr, *German Jews: A Dual Identity* (New Haven: Yale University Press, 1999), 9–10. On the importance of *Bildung* for German Jews, see also George Mosse, *Germans and Jews Beyond Judaism* (Bloomington: Indiana University Press, 1985), 10, and David Sorkin, *The Transformation of German Jewry, 1780–1840* (New York and Oxford: Oxford University Press, 1987). More colloquially, *Bildung* meant, and means, simply cultural education.

28. Cited in Vosskamp, "Bildung ist mehr als Wissen," 13.

29. Weininger, *Geschlecht und Charakter*, 445.

30. Werner Sombart, *Die Juden und das Wirtschaftsleben* (Munich and Leipzig: Duncker and Humboldt, 1911), 325.

31. Sombart, *Die Juden*, 328. On the previous page, Sombart writes of the Jews' "pronounced talent for journalism." Sombart also calls Jellinek's *Der jüdische*

Stamm "one of the best books ever written about the essence of the Jews." Sombart, *Die Juden,* 496.

32. See, for example, Felix Theilhaber's *Der Untergang der deutschen Juden: Eine volkswirtschaftlische Studie* (Berlin: Jüdischer Verlag, 1911), which appeared contemporaneously with Sombart's book.

33. A further paradox here, of course, is that the dissolution of Jewish identity—or total assimilation—would put an end to the Jews' important assimilatory capacities, or so Sombart seems to suggest.

34. Gary Smith discusses the impact of Sombart's book—and also the series of lectures Sombart held on "the Jewish Question"—in his essay "'Das Jüdische versteht sich von selbst,'" 320–21. To describe Sombart as an antisemite is to read him against the grain of his self-understanding, since he regarded himself as a friend of the Jews. On Sombart's complex cultural politics, see Jeffrey Herf, *Reactionary Modernism: Technology, Culture and Politics in Weimar and the Third Reich* (Cambridge and New York: Cambridge University Press, 1984), 36–54.

35. See *Judentaufen,* intro. Arthur Landsberger (Berlin: Müller, 1912). Other contributors include: Hermann Bahr, Paul Natorp, Ferdinand Tönnies, Max Weber, Richard Dehmel, and Fritz Mauthner, or, in short, a whole series of eminent minds.

36. Sombart, *Die Juden,* 320.

37. Ibid., 318.

38. Ibid., 327. In listing journalism as one of the professions for which Jews have a special "talent," Sombart is, of course, invoking the perception that Jews had actually done well at journalism.

39. On the *Kunstwart* debate, see Mendes-Flohr, *German Jews,* 36–50 and 129, and also Steven Aschheim, "The Publication of Moritz Goldstein's 'The German-Jewish Parnassus' sparks a debate over assimilation, German culture and the 'Jewish Spirit,'" in Gilman and Zipes, eds., *The Yale Companion to Jewish Writing and Thought,* 299–305.

40. Scholem, "Jews and Germans," in his *On Jews and Judaism in Crisis: Selected Essays,* ed. Werner Dannhauser (New York: Schocken, 1976), 91.

41. This issue of how Jews can better their situation is, as we will see, a complicated one in Goldstein's essay.

42. This point warrants emphasizing because there has been a tendency among scholars to describe Goldstein's text as a screed lacking in subtlety and inner tension. For example, Noah Isenberg has portrayed "The German-Jewish Parnassus" as "arguably the sharpest invective ever launched against German-Jewish assimilation." This statement strikes me as a rather extreme misrepresentation. After all, self-identifying antisemites inveighed against the perils of assimilation much more brutally than Goldstein, who repeatedly celebrates all that German Jews have given to German culture. And, as we will see, in the end Goldstein does not really call for

Jews to stop participating in the project of building up European culture. Clearly, this is a far cry from Nazi calls for racial purity, which are where the "harshest" philippics against "assimilation" are to be found. See Isenberg, *Between Redemption and Doom: The Strains of German-Jewish Modernism* (Lincoln: University of Nebraska Press, 1999), 8.

43. Hannah Arendt, "The Jew as Pariah: A Hidden Tradition," in Arendt, *The Jew as Pariah: Identity and Politics in the Modern Age,* ed. Ronald Feldman (New York: Gove Press, 1978), 67; *KB* 336.

44. I am not trying to suggest that Goldstein was some kind of protopoststructuralist, only that *a* certain aspect of his thinking corresponds to *one* important aspect of poststructuralist thinking about identity formation. I make this point not to say something about the origins of poststructuralist theory, but rather to underline the highly multifarious character of Goldstein's ideas about identity.

45. This point is worth stressing because scholars sometimes characterize Goldstein's essay as a call for a return to a "traditional Judaism." Here we see that his desideratum is not nearly so straightforward.

46. Theodor Gomperz, "Über die Grenzen der jüdischen intellektuellen Begabung," in Robert Kann, ed., *Theodor Gomperz: Ein Gelehrtenleben im Bürgertum der Franz-Josephszeit* (Vienna: Verlag der österreichische Akademie der Wissenschaften, 1974), 384–92. Hereafter cited parenthetically as "JIB." See Michael Stanislowski's artful sketch of Gomperz in Stanislowski, *Zionism and the Fin de Siècle: Cosmopolitanism and Nationalism from Nordau to Jabotinsky* (Berkeley and Los Angeles: University of California Press, 2000), 10–12.

47. Quoted in Stanislowski, 10.

48. Weininger, Goldstein, and Gomperz all use the verb *fehlen,* which is more pejorative than the English "to lack." For another form of *fehlen* means mistake (*Fehler*), and the prefix *fehl* roughly corresponds to the strongly negative English prefix "mis."

49. Ray Monk, *Ludwig Wittgenstein: The Duty of Genius* (London and New York: Penguin, 1990), 315.

50. Quoted in ibid., 316.

51. See Ritchie Robertson, *The 'Jewish Question' in German Literature: Emancipation and its Discontents, 1749–1939* (Oxford: Oxford University Press, 1999), 112.

52. I certainly do not mean to imply that Gomperz, Wittgenstein, and Schnitzler *simply* internalized antisemitic ideas about Jewish intelligence. In most cases they seem to carry on a kind of dialogue with such ideas and to have taken on only *certain* elements of them.

53. Gerson Cohen, "German Jewry as a Mirror of Modernity," *Leo Baeck Institute Yearbook* 20 (1975): xi. As Mendes-Flohr points out in glossing Cohen's claims,

"German Jewry's articulate struggle to live with a plurality of identities and cultures—which is increasingly recognized to be a salient feature of Western modernity—is a mirror of a larger phenomenon beyond the specifics of Jewish existence." Mendes-Flohr goes on to emphasize that the German-Jewish "response to modernity" intertwined with German responses. See Mendes Flohr, *German Jews*, 3–5.

54. Adorno and Horkheimer, *Dialektik der Aufklärung*, 191.

55. Ibid. On Adorno and Horkheimer's conception of an ethical Jewish mimesis, see Anson Rabinbach, *In the Shadow of Catastrophe: German Intellectuals between Apocalypse and Enlightenment* (Berkeley and Los Angeles: University of California Press, 1997), 166–98.

56. See Adorno and Horkheimer, *Dialektik*, 181–89.

57. Adorno and Horkheimer use the term "scapegoat" in this context. Ibid., 183.

58. See Saul Friedländer, *Nazi Germany and the Jews, 1933–1939* (New York: Harper Collins, 1997) and Jean-François Lyotard, *Heidegger and the Jews*, trans. Mark Roberts (Minneapolis: University of Minnesota Press, 1991).

59. In what follows I am interested in showing how, rather than why, journalism was attacked in antimodern, antisemitic discourse. But certainly worth mentioning here is that, as I stressed in my introduction, journalism was a modernizing force—in the sense that newspapers facilitated the rise of such modern developments as bourgeois nation states and "national consciousness." See Jürgen Habermas, *Strukturwandel der Öffentlichkeit* (Frankfurt/M: Suhrkamp, 1972) and also Benedict Anderson, *Imagined Communities: Reflections on the Origin and Spread of Nationalism* (New York: Verso, 1983), 33–46.

60. See Paul Lawrence Rose, *German Question/Jewish Question: Revolutionary Antisemitism from Kant to Wagner* (Princeton: Princeton University Press, 1990), 360.

61. Cited in ibid., 360.

62. Cited in ibid., 361.

63. See, for example, Wagner, "Was ist deutsch?," in Wagner, *Gesammelte Schriften*, 13:163. Unless otherwise indicated, the Wagner quotations in this book come from volume 13 of Wagner's *Gesammelte Schriften*. Hereafter cited parenthetically as *WGS*.

64. The scholarship on Wagner's antisemitism is too large to review in detail. I found most helpful the chapter on Wagner in Rose's *German Question/Jewish Question* (358–80), Jakob Katz, *The Darker Side of Genius: Richard Wagner's Anti-Semitism* (Hanover, N.H.: University Press of New England, 1986) and, by virtue of the mass of information it provides, Marc Weiner, *Richard Wagner and the Anti-Semitic Imagination* (Lincoln: University of Nebraska Press, 1995).

65. Here Wagner might be referring to the fact that the Jewish figures in Heine's works are often unprepossessing. See S. S. Prawer, *Heine's Jewish Comedy: A Study of his Portraits of Jews and Judaism* (Oxford: Clarendon Press, 1981).

66. Cited in Paul Peters, *The Poet as Provocateur: Heinrich Heine and his Critics* (Rochester: Camden House, 2000), 43.

67. See my essay, "Heinrich Heine and the Discourse of Myth," in Roger Cook, ed., *A Companion to the Works of Heinrich Heine* (Rochester: Camden House, 2002), 201–28.

68. In his monograph, *Richard Wagner and the Anti-Semitic Imagination,* Marc Weiner emphasizes the significance of another "mirror metaphor." Weiner writes: "His [Wagner's] superior, Total Works of Art will reject the modern commercial theatrical institutions and will hold up a mirror to a different society yet to come, one characterized by the familiarity of community of—literally—*anti*-Semitic, like kind.... When discussing the mirror metaphor in conjunction with Wagner's anti-Semitism, it is important to realize that for the discussion of the Jew, the physiological dimension of that metaphor is of paramount importance: Wagner's model of recognition guarantees for the German the demarcation, and hence the preservation, of racial and national boundaries precisely because in his culture the Jew was understood to be endowed with a corporeal iconography that distinguished him from the non-Jew" (55–56). Perhaps, as Weiner maintains, in Wagner's operas an "iconography" of Jewish alterity—the physical foreignness and inferiority of Jewish figures—goes beyond symbolic representation and over into proto-racist ideology. But in Wagner's essays the category of ethnicity remains opaque. It has more to do with collective historical experiences than with biology. Wagner's writings about Germanness and Jewishness focus on *cultural* characteristics—on a dichotomy of German originality and Jewish imitation. Here Wagner does not foreground how he will capture racial Jewish deviance in the mirror of his art with anything like the energy with which he thematizes how Jews mirror Germans. This is the mimetic relationship that matters in Wagner's antisemitic texts, and far from guaranteeing a stable "demarcation" of "national boundaries," it disturbs them.

69. Kraus makes this point after claiming that reality conforms to his satire of the press. In other words, the press has created a real parody of the world.

70. Wagner refers to the antisemites Constantin Franz and Lagarde as able and even sagacious thinkers in the final paragraph of "Was ist deutsch?" (176).

71. Hegel, *Jenaer Schriften,* 547.

72. Peter Fritzsche, *Reading Berlin: 1900* (Cambridge, Mass.: Harvard University Press, 1996), 2.

73. See Richard Grunberger, "The Jews in Austrian Journalism," in Josef Fraenkel, ed., *The Jews of Austria: Essays on their Life, History and Destruction* (London: Vallentine and Mitchell, 1967), 83–96.

74. Pulzer, *The Rise of Political Antisemitism,* 13.

75. Wilhelm Marr, *Der Sieg des Judenthums über das Germanenthum: Vom nicht confessionellen Stanpunkt aus betrachtet* (Bern: Costenoble, 1879), 25. Of course, Marr does name Jewish characteristics. The most important of them is,

for him, the Jews' innate materialism. Germans are concerned with rarified ideas, by contrast. According to Marr, Germany is "das Land von Denker und Philosophen" (23).

76. Haacke, *Handbuch des Feuilletons*, 2069.
77. See *F* 890–905:46 (July 1934).
78. Cited in Peters, *The Poet*, 112.
79. Cited in *F* 88:21.
80. See Werner Kraft's comments on Treitschke in Kraft, *Karl Kraus: Beiträge zum Verständnis seines Werkes* (Salzburg: Müller Verlag, 1956), 163.
81. See Hans Liebschütz, *Das Judentum im deutschen Geschichtsbild von Hegel bis Max Weber* (Mohr: Tübingen, 1967), 170. Liebschütz's chapters on Treitschke's antisemitic views (157—219) offer a detailed account of their development.
82. Treitschke, "Unsere Aussichten," 9.
83. Ibid., 11.
84. Treitschke, *Ein Wort über unser Judenthum*, 3.
85. Cited in Karl Holz, ed., *Heinrich Heine: Wirkungsgeschichte als Wirkungskritik: Materialien zur Rezeptions- und Wirkungsgeschichte Heines* (Stuttgart: Klett-Cotta, 1975), 116.
86. Ibid., 117.
87. Adolf Bartels, *Heinrich Heine: Auch ein Denkmal* (Dresden und Leipzig: Koch, 1906), 297.
88. See *F* 217:29.
89. Hannah Arendt attaches that modifier to *Der Kunstwart* in Arendt, "Walter Benjamin," in W.B., *Illuminations*, trans. H. Zohn (New York: Harcourt Brace Jovanovich, 1968), 30.
90. See *F* 329–30:31.
91. Mann "Zur jüdischen Frage," 56.
92. Bartels, *Heinrich Heine*, 375.
93. Bartels, *Jüdische Herkunft und Literatur Wissenschaft*, 7.
94. Ibid., 37.
95. Bartels, *Heinrich Heine* 95.
96. Ibid., 366.

CHAPTER 2

1. Following Edward Timms's translation, I have rendered the word "Literaten" here as "journalists." See Timms, *Karl Kraus Apocalyptic Satirist*, vol. 1: *Culture and Catastrophe in Habsburg Vienna* (New Haven: Yale University Press, 1986), 183. Lassalle's formulation reads: "Zwei Dinge in der Welt kann ich nicht Leiden: Juden und Literaten." The problem with Timms's rendering, and mine, is that "Literat" has a range of meanings wider than "journalist." And so elsewhere I

will translate the term as "literatus." But it seems important not to dull the apodictic character of Lassalle's statement through using a term that is more ambiguous in English than "Literaten" was in German. Hence the logic of changing "Literaten" to "journalists" in this case. The quotation by Lassalle comes from *Klärung: 12 Autoren über die Judenfrage* (Berlin: Verlag Tradition Wilhelm Kolk, 1932), 13.

2. Steven M. Lowenstein, "Self-Rejection and Self-Hatred," in Michael A. Meyer et al., ed., *German-Jewish History in Modern Times,* vol. 3 (New York: Columbia University Press, 1996), 288–92. The heading "Prophets of Doom" is Robert Wistrich's. See his *The Jews of Vienna in the Age of Franz Joseph* (Oxford: New York and Oxford University Press, 1990), 497.

3. *Die Fackel* appeared three times per month, at least in its early years. Over thirty-seven years, Kraus published nine hundred and twenty-two "numbers," whose topics range from sex trials to preposition usage. *Die Fackel* had a circulation of about thirty thousand copies—at its high point, that is. Many of Kraus's readers were cultural luminaries, for example, Arnold Schönberg, Sigmund Freud, Ludwig Wittgenstein, Thomas Mann, Alban Berg, and Bertolt Brecht. For a survey of the cultural impact of *Die Fackel,* see Martina Bilke, *Zeitgenossen Der Fackel* (Munich: Löcker, 1981).

4. K.K., *Untergang der Welt durch schwarze Magie,* ed. Christian Wagenknecht (Frankfurt/M: Suhrkamp, 1989), 339.

5. Ibid., 330.

6. Ibid., 336.

7. It is worth noting that Kraus called for the dissolution of Judaism in 1899, during one of his socialist phases and just after he had become "confessionless," which was an official category in the Austria of his day. Jewish critical intellectuals who were generally hostile to religion could and did oppose Judaism for reasons other than antisemitism. Indeed, in an illuminating essay on Jewish self-hatred, Paul Mendes-Flohr observes that assimilated German-Jewish intellectuals often criticized Jewish culture not so much because they had internalized antisemitic ideology as out of secularist conviction. For them, Jewish religious and ethnic loyalties impeded social progress, just as did other such loyalties. See Paul Mendes-Flohr, *Divided Passions: Jewish Intellectuals and the Experience of Modernity* (Detroit: Wayne State University Press, 1991), 67–76. See also Alfred Pfabigan, *Karl Kraus und der Sozialismus: Eine politische Biographie* (Vienna: Europaverlag, 1976).

8. Theodor Lessing, *Der jüdische Selbsthaß* (Berlin: Jüdischer Verlag, 1930), 43. It is worth noting that Lessing's diagnosis of Kraus focuses on what Kraus was, namely a journalist, rather than what he actually said about Jews.

9. See, for example, Werfel's portrayal of the eponymous Kraus cipher in his *Spiegelmensch: Magische Trilogie* (Munich: Kurt Wolff, 1920). See also Max Brod, "Der Selbsthaß von Karl Kraus," *Aufbau* (1967): 1–22. During the First World War,

Schnitzler called Kraus a "paragon of renegade cowardice" and claimed that Kraus "blames the Jews for the war." Schnitzler, *Tagebücher, 1913–1916* (Vienna: Österreichische Akademie der Wissenschaften, 1983), 298. There are many further instances of this reception of Kraus. For example, in 1917 Anton Kuh, a well-known Austrian journalist, castigated Kraus as a "Jewish antisemite." See Kuh, *Juden und Deutsche*, ed. Andreas B. Kilcher (Vienna: Löcker, 2003), 32.

10. Ritchie Roberston, one of the more prominent figures in Austrian studies today, explicitly endorses Lessing's assessment of Kraus. See Roberston, "'Jewish Self-Hatred'? The Cases of Canetti and Schnitzler," in Robert Wistrich, ed., *Austrians and Jews in the Twentieth Century: From Franz Joseph to Waldheim* (New York: St. Martin's Press, 1992), 85. See also Robertson's "The Problem of 'Jewish Self-Hatred' in Herzl, Kraus and Kafka," *Oxford German Studies* 16 (1985): 81–108. Robert Wistrich, perhaps the leading historian of Jewish life in modern Austria, has written: "Like Weininger, Kraus equated Judaism with the materialistic degradation of his age which for him was symbolized not so much by sexuality as by the power of the press and the corruption of language." See Wistrich, *Socialism and the Jews: The Dilemmas of Assimilation in Germany and Austria-Hungary* (Rutherford, Madison, and Teaneck, N.J.: Fairleigh Dickinson University Press, 1982), 216. We find such characterizations of Kraus in popular intellectual works as well. See Ray Monk, *Ludwig Wittgenstein: The Duty of Genius* (London and New York: Penguin, 1990), 316, and Anthony Heilbut, *Thomas Mann: Eros and Literature* (New York: Knopf, 1996), 192. Ernst Pawel's account of Kraus's self-hatred is the harshest of the lot, by far. See Pawel, *The Labyrinth of Exile: A Life of Theodor Herzl* (New York: Farrar, Straus and Giroux, 1989), 395–97.

11. See Walter Kaufmann, "On Karl Kraus," *The New York Review of Books* 20 (August 9, 1973): 18; Sander Gilman, *Jewish Self-Hatred: Anti-Semitism and the Secret Language of the Jews* (Baltimore: Johns Hopkins University Press, 1986), 233–43; Mark Anderson, *Kafka's Clothes: Ornament and Aestheticism in the Habsburg Fin de Siècle.* (Oxford and New York: Oxford University Press, 1992), 201–206; Jacques Le Rider, *Modernity and Crises of Identity: Culture and Society in Fin-de-Siècle Vienna*, trans. Rosemary Morris (New York: Continuum, 1991), 254–69; Lowenstein, "Self-Rejection and Self-Hatred," 288–92. Many other recent scholarly responses to "Heine and the Consequences" frame the essay as an example of Jewish self-hatred. See Paul Peters, *Heinrich Heine "Dichterjude": Die Geschichte einer Schmähung* (Frankfurt: Anton Hain, 1990), 131–72; Hildegard Kernmayer, *Judentum im Wiener Feuilleton (1848–1903): Exemplarische Untersuchungen zum literarästhetischen und politischen Diskurs der Moderne* (Tübingen: Niemeyer, 1998), 32–36; and Dietmar Goltschnigg's *Die Fackel ins wunde Herz: Kraus über Heine. Eine "Erledigung"? Texte, Analysen, Kommentar* (Vienna: Passagen Verlag, 2000). Some such accounts are not at all polemical, it should be noted. I have in mind here the section on "Heine and the Consequences" in George Peters's *The Poet as Provocateur: Heinrich Heine and his Critics* (Rochester: Camden

House, 2000), 112–14. Leo Lensing has written two persuasive alternative readings of "Heine and the Consequences." In both cases Lensing emphasizes the text's complexities, though not the same ones that I will be attempting to illuminate. See Lensing, "Heine's Body, Heine Corpus: Sexuality and Jewish Identity in Karl Kraus's Literary Polemics against Heinrich Heine," in Marc Gelber, ed., *The Jewish Reception of Heinrich Heine* (Tübingen: Niemeyer, 1992), 95–111, and Lensing's review of *Die Fackel ins wunde Herz* in *wespennest* 120 (September 2000): 114–16.

12. Kraus's general respect for Weininger has facilitated this kind of reading. See *F* 144:15–21. Kraus, in defending Weininger against his critics, worked with Weininger's idea that Judaism is a way of thinking that is not particular to Jews. More precisely, in an article in which he denies that the message of *Die Fackel* is shaped by "Jewish" interests, Kraus proclaims that Weininger was "more German than many Germans with a Jewish mind-set" (*F* 165:19). But elsewhere Kraus seldom operated with such ideas, which suggests that he might have used them more to underscore his esteem for Weininger than out of conviction. In his more recent defense of Weininger, Allan Janik stresses the very same aspect of Weininger's thought. Janik points out that Weininger's "investigation" of identity, *Sex and Character*, does run counter to racist antisemitism, since it proposes that Jewishness is a cultural principle, which both Jews and non-Jews exhibit. See Janik, "Viennese Culture and the Jewish Self-Hatred Hypothesis: A Critique," in Ivar Oxaal et al., eds., *Jews, Anti-Semitism and Culture in Vienna* (New York and London: Routledge, 1987), 75–88. But Weininger, in contrast to Kraus, goes on to pummel every aspect of this principle. He also insults every Jew whom he discusses. And so Weininger earned the admiration of Nazi leaders, including Hitler himself, who applauded him for doing what socially responsible Jews were obliged to do, according to the perverse logic of eliminationist antisemitism: commit suicide. See Dietrich Eckhart, "Das Judentum in und außer uns," in Barbara Miller Lane and Leila Rupp, eds., *Nazi Ideology before 1933: A Documentation* (Austin: University of Texas Press, 1978), 18–26; and Adolf Hitler, *Monologe im Führer-Hauptquartier, 1941–1944*, ed. Werner Jochmann (Hamburg: A. Knaus Verlag, 1980), 148. Weininger (1880–1903) famously killed himself in the house where Beethoven had lived.

13. Le Rider, *Modernity and Crises of Identity*, 264. A rather striking measure of how entrenched this position has become is Todd M. Endelman's recent essay "Jewish Self-Hatred in Britain and Germany," in Michael Brenner et al., eds., *Two Nations: British and German Jews in Comparative Perspective* (Tübingen: Mohr Siebeck, 1999), 331–64. In a learned call for greater rigor in the study of Jewish self-hatred, Endelman designates "Heine and the Consequences" to be an *actual instance* of Jewish self-hatred, and suggests that Kraus derides Heine's writing as *Mauscheldeutsch*, or as German-Jewish dialect: "For [Jakob] Wassermann and other self-hating Jewish writers, Heine was a frequent and convenient target. Attacking his work allowed them to demonstrate their ability to recognise what was and was

not authentically German. The Viennese critic Karl Kraus, for example, also took aim at Heine, accusing him of lacking a feeling for nature, failing to shed a mercantile outlook, repudiating moral seriousness and 'talking Jewish [*mauscheln*].'" But, as we will see, not only was Kraus suspicious of categories like "authentic Germanness," his polemic contains no such assertions about Heine's German. Bluntly put, Endelman is wrong, for Kraus did not accuse Heine of exhibiting *Mauscheldeutsch.* Yet this not to negate the general value of Endelman's larger argument, which is as follows. Endelman insists that there is a difference between shrill self-criticism and pathological self-hatred. "Moses Mendelssohn," he writes, "was not a self-hating Jew because he believed that Yiddish was a 'repulsive,' 'corrupt,' 'deformed' language of 'stammerers' that had 'contributed more than a little to the uncivilized bearing of the common man.'" Why not? Because Mendelssohn was clearly "committed to the collective well-being of the Jewish people," as were most early Zionist leaders, according to Endelman. And thus "it would make no sense to describe" such figures "as self-hating Jews." Furthermore, "because all westernised or acculturated Jews internalised some Gentile standards, it would be a mistake to treat Jewish self-hatred as an isolated pathology, a mental illness that afflicted only the maladjusted, the disaffected and the disturbed." Some degree of Jewish self-hatred was, in other words, a *normal* condition for Jews who had integrated into antisemitic societies. Indeed, Endelman claims that this everyday self-hatred is a concomitant or "outgrowth" of the "fundamental transformation" that occurred in the "political status" of Jews in the eighteenth and nineteenth centuries. Yet he also perceives a less common—but, in Germany, fairly widespread—pathological self-loathing. Hence the need for a concept like Jewish self-hatred. "By this definition, self-hating Jews were converts, secessionists, radical assimilationists who, not content with disaffiliation from the community, felt compelled to articulate how far they had travelled from their origins by echoing antisemitic views, by proclaiming their distaste for those from whom they wished to dissociate themselves. What set them apart from other radical assimilationists was that, having cut their ties, they were unable to move on and forget their Jewishness." Refining the category of Jewish self-hatred, so that only properly self-hating Jews belong to it, seems fair. But there are significant problems with Endelman's definition. How can an inability to forget one's Jewishness be a feature of self-hatred in a society in which forgetting one's Jewishness was not an option? As Endelman's main examples—Rahel Varnhagen, Jakob Wassermann, and Walther Rathenau—demonstrate, Jews who tried to dissociate themselves from Judaism frequently met with *external* resistance. Moreover, how do we identify obsession? How might we distinguish it *precisely* from what Endelman himself describes as German Jews' normal, understandable, often witheringly censorious preoccupation with how their fellow Jews comported themselves? Finally, how might we do all this while heeding Endelman's admonition to shift "the focus away from the internal to the external, from psychology to history"? Here Endelman's approach begs crucial methodological questions. Who actually corresponds to his definition of self-hatred? Rathenau, whom Endelman profiles at length, eventually embraced Jewish culture and, before that, had seen himself as engaging in well-meaning, if also slashing, self-criticism. Weininger might be a better fit. But he is, by all accounts, an extreme case. In short, Endelman imposes an overly neat division on a fluid phenomenon. One of the most difficult questions that students of Jewish self-hatred face—or should face—is that individual German-Jewish authors often displayed very different attitudes toward Jewish culture more or less simultaneously. What do we do with instances of rabid self-hatred that come from Jews who did not consistently dissociate themselves from Judaism? It is hard to say, of course. Moreover, what about the variety we find in the use of antisemitic language by German Jews? Since conversion was not a sure sign of self-hatred, and antisemitic Jews did not join antisemitic parties and commit violent acts against other Jews, language is what we have to go on here. So if we want to understand the full complexity of Jewish self-hatred, then we need to take into account the complexities of self-hating *discourse*. We need to go beyond paying close attention to fluctuations in the social pressures that bore down on German Jews, which Endelman does very effectively. Reckoning with the complexities of Jewish self-hatred should entail an attempt to track and understand historically the different types and functions of antisemitic language in the writings of Jews. Endelman's claim about the normal character of Jewish self-hatred certainly makes sense, as does his argument that, given this normal character, not all Jews who employed some antisemitic stereotypes should be labeled as self-haters. But, like Gilman, Endelman moves from utterance to psychological state without pausing to consider why *public* Jews such as Mendelssohn might have used harshly anti-Jewish stereotypes in public debates. That Mendelssohn worked with antisemitic tropes does not mean that he was a self-hater. However, contrary to Endelman's assumption, neither does it necessarily imply that Mendelssohn had internalized a "normal amount" of antisemitism. In examining Jewish self-hatred, we should scrutinize not only large contextual factors, such as the level of antisemitic sentiment in Germany, but also the immediate *rhetorical exigencies* under which Jews operated, and which—*some* of the time—help explain why critically minded intellectuals, such as Mendelssohn, Heine, and Kraus, laced their writing with crude antisemitic stereotypes. In his well-known discussion of Hermann Levi's "self-hatred," Peter Gay notes the variety and strangeness of uses of antisemitic discourse by Jews and non-Jews alike. But he does not undertake to analyze this rhetorical variety. See Peter Gay, *Freud, Jews and Other Germans: Masters and Victims in Modernist Culture* (Oxford and New York: Oxford University Press, 1978), 189–230.

14. Gilman, *Jewish Self-Hatred*, 242.

15. As I mention below, Kraus, who seems to have been raised without much religious instruction, formally left Vienna's Jewish community in 1899. But because he conceived of Judaism as an ethnicity, as a *Stamm*, he continued to regard himself as a Jew. See K.K., *Untergang der Welt durch schwarze Magie*, 330. Also

worth noting here is that it is possible to be harshly critical of Jewish culture while identifying with Jewish culture through the very form of the criticism used to convey such an annihilating verdict. And, indeed, Kraus often presented himself as an apocalyptic, modern-day Old Testament prophet as he inveighed against assimilated Jewry. Consider the titles of some of his most significant works: *Judgment Day, The Last Days of Mankind,* "Apocalypse," "The End."

16. Moreover, Benjamin emphatically rejected the claim that Kraus had to "suppress the Judaism in himself" in order to achieve intellectual success ("KK," 367). Benjamin speaks of Kraus's "Jewish physiognomy" in a 1928 letter to Scholem, which is cited in *BGS* 2.3:1433.

17. When, in 1939, a journalist writing for the newspaper *Davar* derided Kraus as a Jewish antisemite, Scholem fired off a scathing letter to the editor (*SB* 278-79).

18. See Erich Heller, *In the Age of Prose: Literary and Philosophical Essays* (New York: Cambridge University Press, 1984), 94; Berthold Viertel, *Karl Kraus: Ein Charakter und die Zeit* (Leipzig: Kaemmerer, 1921), 55 (Viertel, who was also a poet, called Kraus an "arch-Jew"); and Werner Kraft, *Franz Kafka: Durchdringung und Geheimnis* (Frankfurt/M: Suhrkamp: 1966), 201.

19. Adorno, "Sittlichkeit und Kriminalität," in Adorno, *Noten zur Literatur,* ed. Rolf Tiedemann (Frankfurt/M: Suhrkamp, 1989), 371.

20. Of course, there have been important shifts in the theoretical discourse about Jewish self-hatred. As Gilman points out, for early theoreticians of Jewish self-hatred, being Jewish meant belonging to the Jewish race. And so for early commentators on Jewish self-hatred, that problem and the neuroses associated with it resulted from futile, tortured attempts to deny an inescapable racial difference, and not only from the internalization of antisemitic stereotypes. More recent students of Jewish self-hatred, such as Gilman himself, do not regard Jewishness as a racial category and attempts at thorough assimilation as necessarily self-destructive and self-hating. See Gilman, *Jewish Self-Hatred,* 286.

21. Timms, *Karl Kraus,* 1:237-49.

22. See Harry Zohn, "Karl Kraus: 'Jüdischer Selbsthasser' oder 'Erzjude,'" *Modern Austrian Literature* 8 (1975): 20-37; Lensing, "Karl Kraus Writes 'He's a Jew After All,'" in Sander Gilman and Jack Zipes, eds., *The Yale Companion to Jewish Writing and Thought in German Culture, 1096-1996* (New Haven: Yale University Press, 1997); and the section on Kraus and Weininger in Robert Wistrich's *The Jews of Vienna.*

23. Again, Lensing's sophisticated "constructivist" reading of Kraus's Jewish identity—in his "Tiertheater: Textspiele der jüdischen Identität bei Altenberg, Kraus und Kafka," *Das jüdische Echo* 48 (October 1999): 79-86—tries to get at the deep cultural logic of Kraus's claims about Jews and Jewish culture, and it thus represents an exception to the interpretive tendency I have been adumbrating.

24. Le Rider, *Modernity and Crises of Identity,* 264.

25. Gilman writes: "Self-hatred results from the outsiders' [the Jews'] acceptance of the mirage of themselves generated by the reference group—that group in society which they see as defining them—as a reality." Gilman, *Jewish Self-Hatred*, 2. Le Rider works with the same model.

26. Volkov, "Antisemitism as a Cultural Code: Reflections on the History and Historiography of Antisemitism in Imperial Germany," in Michael Marras, ed., *The Nazi Genocide: Articles on the History of the Destruction of European Jews*, vol. 2 (Westport and London: Meckler, 1989)." Volkov writes: "By the end of the nineteenth century it [antisemitism] had become a 'cultural code.' Professing antisemitism became a sign of cultural identity, of one's belonging to a specific cultural camp" (317). She goes on to assert that when used "symbolically," antisemitism often had little to do with an actual "dislike of Jews" (318). Volkov herself has expressed reservations about the general tendency to view Jewish self-hatred as a pathology and within a narrowly psychologizing framework. But her alternative reading only reinforces this interpretive structure, oddly enough. For Volkov likens Jewish self-hatred to familial tension, which calls for psychological analysis as do few other things. In addition, Volkov concludes these remarks with the shaky proposition that Kafka is the one true example of a self-hating Jew. Here Volkov emphasizes precisely Kafka's well-known "father complex" and also his claim that German Jews used the German language as "foreign property." But she fails to take into account the context of Kafka's claim. In the same letter in which Kafka suggests that the German of German Jews is somehow a deficient "paper language," he ascribes "truth" to his own writing hand and stresses the "frighteningly physical" nature of both of his style and of Kraus's. I will discuss the letter in question in a later chapter. See Volkov, "Selbstgefälligkeit und Selbsthaß," in Volkov, *Antisemitismus als kultureller Code* (Munich: Beck, 2000), 191–200. In his influential study *Außenseiter* Hans Mayer also claims to be unsatisfied with Lessing's analysis of Jewish self-hatred. However, Mayer too designates Kraus as a "representative" of Jewish self-hatred. And when he redefines this "identity conflict," Mayer does so cursorily and in very general terms. He writes: "Alleged [Jewish] 'self-hatred' merely proves that the Enlightenment failed, and that this failure was recognized." In other words, Jewish self-hatred is an epiphenomenon of a larger process, or the expression of a larger despair. Regardless of how true this assertion might be, in that form it tells us very little about the complexities of Jewish antisemitic discourse. Certainly Mayer brings us no closer to making sense of Kraus's multifarious use of antisemitic language. That self-hating critiques of German-Jewish culture have to do with the difficult course of German-Jewish assimilation has, moreover, been apparent to most commentators. See Hans Mayer, *Außenseiter* (Frankfurt/M: Suhrkamp, 1981), 421.

27. By now it should be clear that I will not be providing an overarching, formal definition of antisemitic discourse. Instead I will evaluate Kraus's remarks on a case-by-case basis. My logic is that there exists no handy model to borrow, and

an original definition of what constitutes antisemitic discourse cannot be confined to footnotes or to a theoretical excursion. That said, let me add that what counts as antisemitic discourse here will be, for the most part, and quite simply, the stereotypes and tropes that self-identifying antisemites preferred in their attacks on Jews.

28. Certainly Janik deserves to be acknowledged for his forceful stand against the use of "the Jewish self-hatred hypothesis" to dismiss a whole body of work. But in trying to show that Otto Weininger's much-maligned *Sex and Character* actually contains ideas that run against the current of antisemitic discourse, Janik does not offer any kind of explanation as to why Weininger, in an anti-antisemitic text, would avail himself so liberally of the most scurrilous antisemitic language. He begs the question I will be taking up here, in other words. Furthermore, Janik seriously distorts the position of the critic who serves in his essay as a negative example—as an example of how not to approach the self-hatred problem, namely, Peter Gay. In doing so, needless to say, Janik weakens his own case. He suggests that, for Gay, as for most critics who invoke the concept of Jewish self-hatred, being Jewish is a destiny, an existential essence of which one cannot divest oneself. The idea here is that critical assessments like the one Gay offers of Weininger are, in the end, motivated by a sort of cultural politics. Gay treats Weininger and his work harshly because Weininger the convert flouted Gay's notion of Jewishness. Otherwise put, Janik accuses Gay not only of simplifying Weininger's work, of reducing it to a symptom of self-hatred, he also charges Gay with "smuggling metaphysics," or a metaphysical conception of Jewishness, into "the history of ideas." The problem is that this complaint turns on a rather egregious misreading of Gay's text. As he discusses Gay's account of Weininger, Janik repeatedly cites Gay's line about Weininger's "'indelible' Jewish identity." For Janik, this line is evidence of how Gay's "metaphysical" notion of Jewishness intrudes on his intellectual historical reading of Weininger. But with the phrase in question Gay means to evoke *Weininger's views* on Jewish identity, not to formulate his own views. Within the context of the essay, the meaning of the phrase is clear. Hence my claim that Janik seriously distorts the position of his antagonist. Moreover, if Gay actually wanted to promote a metaphysical conception of Jewish identity, wouldn't that agenda manifest itself in his writings on other German Jews who had a complex relation to Judaism? Janik omits to ask this question, no doubt because the avenue of inquiry it opens runs counter to his argument. See Janik, "Viennese Culture and the Jewish Self-Hatred Hypothesis: A Critique," 84.

29. At the same time, the large shadow of the Holocaust has created a tendency to view turn-of-the-century self-hating Jews as deranged characters who actively promoted their own demise. On the problem of "backshadowing," of allowing the shadow of the Shoah to inform our understanding of the culture that preceded it, and on the problem of becoming overly judgmental toward the pre-Shoah past,

see Michael André Bernstein, *Foregone Conclusions: Against Apocalyptic History* (Berkeley and Los Angeles: University of California Press, 1994).

30. As Gilman emphasizes, self-hating Jews tend not to "project" antisemitic stereotypes onto themselves, but rather onto other Jews, who seem to conform to antisemitic ideas more closely. See Gilman, *Jewish Self-Hatred*, 3.

31. See, again, the note on Heine and Treitschke in Werner Kraft, *Karl Kraus: Beiträge zum Verständnis seines Werkes* (Salzburg: Müller Verlag, 1956), 163. The strategic use of antisemitism varies widely. While both Germans like Treitschke, and German Jews like Kraus, worked with antisemitic discourse strategically, in doing so, they pursued different ends and, accordingly, their respective tones differ too. (There is much more irony in Kraus's strategic antisemitism.)

32. See Richard Geehr, *"I Decide Who's A Jew": The Papers of Dr. Karl Lueger* (Washington, D.C.: University Press of America, 1982), 322. Geehr notes that Lueger's famous dictum is hearsay; there is no contemporary written record of Lueger making such a remark. But Geehr finds the line plausible enough to name his book after it.

33. In this chapter—as in the other parts of this study—I use the word "discourse" in a non-Foucauldian, nontechnical sense and often as a synonym for "language" and "rhetoric."

34. Franz Kafka would qualify as an example. As we will see, Kraus's critique of German-Jewish culture very often had to do with the linguistic excesses of overzealous assimilationists. Kraus effectively formulated this position in his drama *Literatur: Oder man wird da sehn* (1921). Kafka responded enthusiastically to *Literatur* and, concurring with Kraus, wrote to his friend Max Brod of "hyperactive Jewish hands." In the same letter Kafka dramatically sketches these authors as insects perched over a cultural divide to illustrate his point (*KB* 336).

35. Thus, whereas in Volkov's study Germans use antisemitism to mark their cultural affiliations, Kraus uses antisemitism to assert his independence from cultural affiliations.

36. The critic doing the designating is Werner Kraft; see, Kraft, *Das Ja des Neinsagers: Karl Kraus und seine geistige Welt* (Munich: edition text + kritik, 1974), 115.

37. In this context "conspiracy theories" is a loaded phrase, of course. I employ it because Kraus advanced strikingly incendiary ideas about "Jewish solidarity" in the press, to use one of his formulations. However, I do not wish to imply that Kraus came close to subscribing to conspiracy theories of the order of, say, Alfred Rosenberg's apparent favorite: *The Protocols of the Elders of Zion*.

38. It is interesting to note that in his private correspondence Kraus emphasized his antipathy toward "war profiteers of all confessions," thereby suggesting that, for him, Jews were one group among several that had promoted and exploited the war. I have in mind here Kraus's (unpublished) letter of November 20/21, 1920 to

his friend Mary Dobrenska, which is document i.n. 174.733 in the Kraus collection at Vienna's Stadt und Landesbibliothek. Also worth noting, of course, is that Kraus is replying to Dobrenska's sense that his response to the war is basically antisemitic. After the war, Kraus returned to his earlier complexity with regard to the "Jewish Question." The years between 1899 and 1914 are therefore more representative of his career than the war years are. For Kraus's ideas about the role of Jews in the First World War, see K.K., *Die letzten Tage der Menschheit,* ed. Christian Wagenknecht (Frankfurt/M: Suhrkamp, 1987), 194. Here Kraus has his "Grumbler" castigate Jewish warmongering; the Grumbler's perspective is similar to, but not identical with, Kraus's own. For analogous remarks about the Jews' role in destroying Western culture, see *Die letzten Tage der Menschheit,* 352 and 754. In the play's epilogue Kraus has Naschkatz and Fressack, two "hyenas" whose caricatured Jewish names connote rapacity, gloat over having successfully started the war and over having profited from it. See also "Das Gebet an die Sonne von Gibeon," in K.K., *Gedichte,* ed. Wagenknecht (Frankfurt/M: Suhrkamp, 1989), 201. Also worth noting is that Kraus's critique of Heine became cruder and, in keeping with Kraus's wartime focus on the issue of "Jewish profiteering," more interested in how Heine used language for commercial gain. See Kraus's 1915 essay "The Enemies of Heine and Goethe," in *F* 406-12:58-89.

39. As one of only a few major antiwar voices in Austria, Kraus did not have to worry about bolstering his singularity in 1914, which perhaps helps to explain the decline in his strategic use of antisemitic discourse at the start of the First World War. After the war, as Ritchie Robertson has pointed out, antisemitic language began to play a less prominent role in Kraus's writings. This development might be read as a response to a new, more violent antisemitism in postwar Germany and Austria. See Robertson, *The 'Jewish Question' in German Literature: Emancipation and its Discontents, 1749-1939* (Oxford: Oxford University Press, 1999), 323.

40. K.K., *Die demolierte Literatur,* in K.K., *Frühe Schriften,* vol. 2, ed. J. J. Braakenburg (Munich: Kösel Verlag, 1979), 270-91.

41. Gilman, *Jewish Self-Hatred,* ix.

42. See K.K., "Vom großen Welttheaterschwindel, "in K.K., *Brod und Lüge,* ed. Christian Wagenknecht (Frankfurt/M: Suhrkamp, 1991), 228. There Kraus complains that the church authorities let Max Reinhardt, a German-Jewish director, stage Hugo von Hofmannsthal's play *Das Salzburger große Welttheater* in a church. This, Kraus maintains, is what turned him off Catholicism.

43. See K.K., "Wer ist der Mörder?," in K.K., *Literatur und Lüge,* ed. Wagenknecht, (Frankfurt/M: Suhrkamp, 1987), 302, and Leo Lensing, "Die Fotoportraits," in Heinrich Lunzer, Victoria Lunzer-Talos, and Marcus Patka, eds., *"Was Wir Umbringen": Die Fackel von Karl Kraus* (Vienna: Mandelbaum Verlag, 1999), 54-61.

44. See, for example, K.K., *Literatur und Lüge,* 196. There Kraus explains his

use of dialect and his more radical mimetic techniques, which Benjamin found "revolutionary."

45. Max Horkheimer, *Gesammelte Schriften,* vol. 13, ed. Alfred Schmidt and Gunzlein Schmid Noerr (Frankfurt/M: Fischer, 1989), 21.

46. See Jeffery Herf, *Reactionary Modernism: Technology, Culture and Politics in Weimar and the Third Reich* (Cambridge and New York: Cambridge University Press, 1984),

47. For example, see Kraus's polemics against Gottfried Benn and Martin Heidegger, one of Herf's main reactionary modernists, in K.K., *Die dritte Walpurgisnacht,* ed. Wagenknecht (Frankfurt/M: Suhrkamp, 1989), 71 and 78.

48. The instances of reactionary modernism with which Herf deals all have pronounced nationalistic tendencies. Inveighing against Heidegger, Kraus ridicules his emphasis on cultural authenticity, which he, Kraus, saw as a dangerous ideal.

49. Carl Schorske, *Thinking with History: Explorations in the Passage to Modernism* (Princeton: Princeton University Press, 1997), 135-37.

50. See Nike Wagner, *Geist und Geschlecht: Karl Kraus und die Erotik der Wiener Moderne* (Frankfurt/M: Suhrkamp, 1982).

51. K.K., *Aphorismen,* ed. Christian Wagenknecht (Frankfurt/M: Suhrkamp, 1986), 33. Kraus anthologized his essays on sexism in Austrian courts in K.K., *Sittlichkeit und Kriminalität,* ed. Wagenknecht (Frankfurt/M: Suhrkamp, 1987). See especially the eponymous essay "Sittlichkeit und Kriminalität," 9-29.

52. Quoted in Harry Zohn, *Karl Kraus and the Critics* (Columbia, S.C.: Camden House, 1997), 25.

53. Kraus uses the German word "Publicist," which does not have the same meaning as the English word "publicist." As Kraus employs it, the term denotes a journalist.

54. K.K., "Selbstbespiegelung," 194.

55. *Die Fackel* appeared irregularly; as Scheichl, Lensing and Lunzer point out in a co-written essay, this irregularity separated Kraus's organ from conventional newspapers.

56. Kraus may be the only nominee for the Nobel Prize for literature—he was nominated in 1925—whose main works defy effective historical-critical annotation, precisely because of their journalistic character. The scholarly commentary required would be massive.

57. See BB 4:362. Here Benjamin speaks of wanting to write a cycle of articles on the four figures "in whom the present situation" of four genres "takes decisive shape" [*maßgebend ausprägt*]: the novel, theater, the essay, and journalism. Thus Benjamin dramatically aligns Kraus with journalistic writing—Kraus would be the subject of Benjamin's journalism lecture. See also Scholem, *ST* 2:486-89. Scholem explicitly bases his reading of Kraus on Kraus's status as a journalist, for, again, he suggests that journalism in general—and Kraus's journalistic style in particular—

bears affinities with medieval traditions of Hebrew writing. I will examine Scholem's reception of Kraus in chapter 4. Mann calls Harden a "publicist," then, by grouping together Harden and Kraus, clearly implies that Kraus should subsumed under the same heading. *See Frank Wedekind, Thomas Mann, Heinrich Mann: Briefwechsel mit Maximilian Harden*, ed. Ariane Martin (Darmstadt: Häusser, 1996), 223–24.

58. Pierre Bourdieu, *Homo Academicus*, trans. Peter Collier (Stanford: Stanford University Press, 1984), 5. Here Bourdieu is paraphrasing—and agreeing with—Kraus's early diagnosis of his situation as an "independent journalist." See *F* 1:6. See also Kurt Krolop, "Vom 'Kampfblatt zur 'Kriegsfackel': Die Werdejahre des 'Anti-Mediums,'" in Lunzer et al., eds., *"Was Wir Umbringen": Die Fackel von Karl Kraus*, 8–27.

59. See Helmut Arntzen, *Karl Kraus und die Presse* (Munich: Fink, 1975).

60. By "phrases," Kraus meant the mass-marketed platitudes through which the press reduced a complex reality to easy and entertaining reading. Below I will explain how, for Kraus, such phrases made possible the destruction of the First World War—hence Kraus's formulation "the catastrophe of phrases."

61. K.K., *Aphorismen*, 212.

62. Most Kraus scholars today avoid calling Kraus a "journalist." While this impulse is understandable, given all that has been said so far, I think that programmatically refusing to see Kraus's writing as a radical mode of journalism is a mistake. For Kraus did not only criticize journalism by mimicking its structure, thereby creating an "anti-medium," to use a term currently popular among Kraus scholars, in doing so he produced an *innovative* journalism. Kraus himself expressed this sense when he referred to his writing as a "new journalistic form." But perhaps a more important reason for opening up to the idea that, despite his many imprecations against "journalists" and "newspapers," Kraus brought about a highly unconventional—indeed, anticonventional—"new journalistic form" is as follows: We will thus be able to understand how readers like Benjamin and Scholem were able to see his prose as redeeming a sullied genre from *within* or immanently. Again, they regarded Kraus's writing as a sort of redemptive journalism. In other words, what is important for my argument is not simply accepting that Kraus was a radical journalist, but also recognizing that his status as such—in the eyes of readers—was a crucial component of his significance. I want to add, moreover, that putting Kraus outside journalism diffuses the paradoxicality that was so central to his project. Scholars who read literally Kraus's claims about the vacuity of journalists and keep him neatly apart from the journalist category lose sight of the bigger picture, of how in both theory and practice Kraus's writing deliberately complicates such categories. Contenting ourselves with generalizing neatly from some of his anti-journalistic statements—and working from them to a profession of writerly identity—is just as problematic as is generalizing from his antisemitic statements.

63. K.K., *Aphorismen*, 164.

64. *BGS* 2.3:1114. Benjamin's sentence, which I will discuss in chapter 4, reads: "Denn Journalismus, in seiner paradoxesten Gestalt, ist Kraus." This line comes from a mass of notes that Benjamin took for his essay "Karl Kraus" (1931). In one part of the essay, Benjamin suggests that Kraus's *Fackel* differs from the standard "press" precisely in telling the "eternally new story of creation." There is, however, a countervailing claim in "Karl Kraus." So, like so much else in Benjamin's portrait of Kraus, the issue of how Kraus is "journalism in its most paradoxical form" is complex.

65. Quoted in Lensing, "Tiertheater," 84.

66. See Elias Canetti, *Die Fackel im Ohr: Lebensgeschichte, 1921–1931* (Frankfurt/M: Suhrkamp, 1982), 252. Earlier, Canetti had been a great admirer of Kraus. Aharon Appelfeld, *Badenheim 1939*, trans. Dalya Bilu (Boston: David Godine, 1980), 62. Appelfeld has a character regard Kraus as a "great Jew" who revived satire. Harry Zohn claims to have asked Appelfeld how his personal views about Kraus jibe with those of his character, and to have received an answer to the effect that Appelfeld concurs with his creation. See Zohn, *Karl Kraus and the Critics*, 24.

67. Benjamin suggests that, for Kraus, "idiosyncrasy" functioned as the "highest critical organ" ("KK," 364).

68. Kraus had some allies, such as Ludwig Ficker, the editor of the journal *Der Brenner*. Kraus was friendly with Arnold Schönberg, Egon Friedell, Peter Altenberg, Adolf Loos, and Else Lasker-Schüler. And during the early years of *Die Fackel*, he had collaborators, like Berthold Viertel and Otto Stoeßl. But with the exception of Loos, none of these figures exerted a palpable influence on Kraus. Kraus's modernist connections simply help us to place him within the very general category of Viennese modernism. Given his many feuds with other Viennese modernists (e.g., Hermann Bahr, Hugo von Hofmannsthal, and Arthur Schnitzler), that designation does not go very far toward identifying the precise place of his work within Viennese culture. See Timms, *Karl Kraus*, 1:4–10, and Gerhard Stieg, *Der Brenner und die Fackel* (Salzburg: Otto Müller, 1976).

69. I am drawing on Sigurd Paul Schleichl's summary of "Vom Tage," an article in the *Arbeiter-Zeitung*. Schleichl summarizes it in his essay, "The Contexts and Nuances of Anti-Jewish Language: Were All the 'Antisemites' Antisemites?," in Oxaal et al., eds., *Jews, Antisemitism, and Culture in Vienna*, 89–110.

70. Again, Mendes Flohr offers a helpful discussion of criticism of Jewish culture among Jewish socialists. See Mendes-Flohr, *Divided Passions*, 67–76.

71. For a useful overview of Kraus's attitudes toward Herzl, which changed significantly over time, becoming more favorable, see Gerald Krieghofer, "The Case of Kraus versus Herzl," in Ritchie Robertson and Edward Timms, eds., *Theodor Herzl and the Origins of Zionism* (Edinburgh: Edinburgh University Press, 1997), 107–21.

72. Here Kraus is ironically alluding to the title of a recent play by Herzl, *Das neue Ghetto* [*The New Ghetto*, 1898].

73. In other words, for Kraus, the Zionist call to assimilate European intellec-

tual achievements to Jewish culture, or to "the Jewish mind," represents a mode of Jewish assimilation to European culture, since this kind of cultural nationalism is a European phenomenon.

74. Of course, turn-of-the-century dandyism was not regarded as an exclusively Jewish phenomenon. But many critics did feel that with their rootlessness, Jews had a disproportionate, even a special, inclination to such superficiality.

75. In response to being caricatured in an antisemitic cartoon, Kraus developed an interesting analysis of the differences between satire and caricature. See K.K., *Literatur und Lüge,* 299.

76. See chap. 1, note 7.

77. On the role of Jews at the *Neue Freie Presse,* see Richard Grunberger, "Jews in Austrian Journalism," in Josef Fraenkel, ed., *The Jews of Austria: Essays on their Life, History and Destruction* (London: Vallentine and Mitchell, 1967), 83.

78. On the Kraus-Chamberlain connection, see Timms, *Karl Kraus,* 1:238–40, and Hans-Heinrich Wilhelm, "Houston Stewart Chamberlain und Karl Kraus: Ein Bericht über ihren Briefwechsel," *Zeitgeschichte* 10, no. 11 (1983): 405–34.

79. Schnitzler too suggested that the *Neue Freie Presse* exhibited a tendentious, cloying tone in its support of Dreyfus. And Kraus may well have had a point in objecting to its partisanship. What matters here is not simply Kraus's general objection, but his recourse to ideas about the Jews' indelible ghetto mentality. On Schnitzler's response to the *Neue Freie Presse,* see Le Rider, *Modernity and Crises of Identity,* 253.

80. For a pithy account of the Neue Freie Presse's prestige in turn-of-the-century Vienna, see Zweig, *Die Welt von Gestern: Erinnerungen eines Europäers* (Frankfurt/M: Suhrkamp, 1996), 123–24.

81. Shortly before Easter 1899, Leopold Hilsner, a shoemaker's apprentice in Polna, was accused of murdering a Christian girl for her blood. He was found guilty and condemned to death, but the sentence was commuted in 1916.

82. Kraus probably had other influences, for stereotypes about a Jewish media campaign against German culture circulated widely in his context. As I stated in the previous chapter, in 1879, Treitschke, who is commonly credited with having made political antisemitism acceptable in educated circles, asserted that Heine and his Jewish rival, Ludwig Börne, corroded German civic feeling through their journalistic writings. Treitschke then proclaimed: "The Jews are our misfortune!" ["Die Juden sind unser Unglück!"]. The phrase became a kind of refrain in antisemitic discourse. See Heinrich von Treitschke, "Unsere Aussichten," in Walter Boehlich, ed., *Der Berliner Antisemitismusstreit* (Frankfurt/M: Insel, 1988), 139. We should note that Kraus did not only oppose "Jewish corruption" in the press. He lambasted the "stupidity" of antisemitic journalism.

83. Gilman uses the phrases Jewish self-hatred and Jewish antisemitism interchangeably, as do I.

84. On the Heine monument debates, see Dietrich Schubert, "Frühlinglied?," *Heine-Jahrbuch* 34 (1995): 118–45.

85. See Goltschnigg, *Die Fackel ins wunde Herz,* 46.

86. This is the same Oskar Blumenthal whom Gomperz listed as one of the Jewish "dramatic feuilletonists." See the section on Gomperz in chapter 1.

87. The installments of the "Harden Dictionary" appeared between 1908 and 1911.

88. Harden, we should note, changed his name as a very young man, when he was fourteen and had run away from home and did not want his father to find him. But if Harden's immediate impetus for the name-change had little to do with his Jewish identity, his *choice,* "Harden," might well reflect an early desire to distance himself from his Jewishness. After all, Harden also converted to Christianity as a teenager.

89. See Maximilian Harden, "Sem," in Harden, *Apostata* (Berlin: Georg Silke Verlag, 1892), 146–56.

90. See K.K., *Sittlichkeit und Kriminalität,* 105–22. On the Hervay affair, see Timms, Karl Kraus, 1:64–65.

91. See K.K., *Sittlichkeit und Kriminalität,* 118.

92. Letter of Harden to Kraus, 10.7.1904, Bundesarchiv Koblenz Nachlass Harden 1062/149a, transcribed by Alexander Moulton, who has generously shared his research with me and whose forthcoming dissertation promises to shed significant new light on Kraus's relationship with Harden.

93. Kraus's reading of Harden, which stresses how Harden displays *Bildung* as a vehicle for social climbing, resembles Pierre Bourdieu's theory of symbolic capital. Again, the affinity was not lost on Bourdieu, who repeatedly invokes Kraus's critical insights in his writings.

94. Kraus entered into these two imbroglios, then, for one reason: When Harden and Kerr attempted to expose as sexually immoral an important German cultural figure (Eulenberg and the Berlin chief of police, respectively), Kraus beat his battle drum. In both cases what Kraus objected to was a violation of privacy. The assimilationist journalists Harden and Kerr, he suggests, wanted to penetrate deep into German culture and to present themselves as champions of German moral well-being so badly that they transgressed against the most basic standards of journalistic decency. Just as Harden's attempt to sound nobly hyper-Germanic makes him ridiculous, his overdetermined desire to be known as righteous led him into iniquity. Overzealous assimilation, for Kraus, seems to be a profoundly self-subverting project.

95. When, in 1911, a literary scholar grouped Kraus's writing together with Harden's, Kraus responded with a great show of frustration, which implies that what he wanted to gain through his feuding was, among other things, distance from Harden. See K.K., *Literatur und Lüge,* 310. Soon thereafter (or in 1913), it

is worth noting, Kraus wrote a testy, public response to a letter that accused him of being biased in favor of Jewish authors. More specifically, the letter speaks of Kraus's loyalty to Peter Altenberg, an author he greatly admired, as an instance of the tendency of Jews to "help their racial comrades." In his counterattack Kraus debunks the charge by pointing out that nepotism is hardly particular to Jews, and that Altenberg's talent merits support. But more important than Kraus's actual argument is the fact that he felt moved to reply so energetically. For this suggests that he was indeed sensitive to attempts to portray him as being something other than fully independent and free of compromising cultural alliances. See K.K., *Literatur und Lüge*, 173–75.

96. For a survey of Kraus's Yiddishisms, see Caroline Kohn, "Der Wiener jüdische Jargon im Werke von Karl Kraus," *Modern Austrian Literature* 8 (1975): 240–67.

97. K.K., *Weltgericht*, 1:73.

98. A word search of the CD-ROM version of *Die Fackel* (Hamburg: Sauer Verlag, 2003) lists 249 entries for the word "Schmock," and in many cases Kraus *directly* invokes Freytag's Jewish journalist character, and uses the term "Schmock," as provocative short-hand for the idea "incompetent, scheming Jewish journalist." Indeed, he even speaks of working among "Schmock's descendants [*Schmocks Nachkommen*]" (F 50:9). Also worth noting is that Kraus reproaches Kerr for belonging to an aestheticist "clique" and mentions only its obviously Jewish members, such as Max Brod, a frequent contributor to *Pan*, and the poet Richard Beer-Hoffmann.

99. *Theodor W. Adorno Alban Berg Briefwechsel, 1925–1935*, ed. Henri Lonitz (Frankfurt/M: Suhrkamp, 1997), 57–58. In his well-known essay on Heine, "Die wunde Heine," Adorno calls the "judgment" that Kraus put forth in "Heine and the Consequences" "inextinguishable." He follows Kraus both in suggesting that "the language of assimilationism is one of unsuccessful identification" and in speaking of the "over-eager imitation" of "the one who has been marginalized." See Adorno, "Die wunde Heine," *Noten zur Literatur*, 95–98.

100. In his rejoinder Kraus bragged that his style "teems" also with "Yiddishisms." K.K., *Literatur und Lüge*, 196.

101. K.K., *Literatur und Lüge*, 213.

102. K.K., *Untergang der Welt durch schwarze Magie*, 152.

103. Ibid., 428.

104. See Goltschnigg, *Die Fackel ins wunde Herz*, 50.

105. See Timms, *Karl Kraus*, 1:115.

106. K.K., *Aphorismen*, 341.

107. K.K., *Untergang der Welt durch schwarze Magie*, 427.

108. See Burkhard Müller, *Karl Kraus: Mimesis und Kritik des Mediums* (Stuttgart: Metzler, 1995).

109. George Steiner, "Karl Kraus: Fear and Loathing in Vienna," *The London Sunday Times,* August 12, 1984: 41.

110. For an eloquent and informative discussion of what was new about Heine's feuilletonistic articles of the 1830s and 1840s, which he wrote in Parisian exile and published in German newspapers, see Jeffrey Sammons, *Heinrich Heine: A Modern Biography* (Princeton: Princeton University Press, 1979), 172–74.

111. Cited in Timms, *Karl Kraus,* 1:35. Kraus made this remark very early in his career—in 1897, to be precise—and I certainly do not want to suggest that only during and after his linguistic turn did he have as one of his main targets the shortcomings of feuilletonistic prose.

112. It is in his contribution to an encyclopedia of Jews in German culture that Benjamin calls "Heine and the Consequences" one of the "high points" of discussions of Heine's work (*BGS* 2:2.812). See also *ST* 2:462, where Scholem too refers favorably to "Heine and the Consequences." As I tried to show in the first chapter of this study, it was not just antisemites who dwelled on the notion that Jews were profoundly connected to journalistic forms. We should note that Kraus himself questions the ideas about journalism that Gomperz and Goldstein advance. As we will see, in "Heine and the Consequences" he portrays journalistic writing, which they belittle as a sign of Jewish "limitations," as art.

113. Again, for a survey of responses to "Heine and the Consequences," see Zohn, *Karl Kraus and the Critics,* 13–18.

114. "Heine and the Consequences" ("Heine und die Folgen") was first published as a pamphlet in 1910. Kraus reprinted it in *Die Fackel* in 1911 (*F* 329–30: 6–33). Hereafter cited parenthetically as "HC."

115. Anderson, *Kafka's Clothes,* 201.

116. Ibid., 202.

117. Gilman, *Jewish Self-Hatred,* 240.

118. Adolf Bartels, *Heinrich Heine: Auch ein Denkmal* (Dresden und Leipzig: Koch, 1906), 485.

119. Hermann Bahr, *Wien* (Stuttgart: Krabbe, 1906), 69.

120. Gilman, *Jewish Self-Hatred,* 240.

121. See, for example, Bartels, *Heinrich Heine,* 95. For a catalogue of the antisemitic stereotypes that were hurled at Heine, see Peters, *Heinrich Heine "Dichterjude."*

122. On Heine's conflict with Platen, see Mayer, *Außenseiter,* 207–23.

123. Weininger, *Geschlecht und Charakter,* 300.

124. K.K., *Die Sprache,* 225.

125. K.K., *Aphorismen,* 30.

126. To be sure, in his discussion of a later essay, Gilman registers Kraus's admiration for Jewish writers who developed a "good German." But here too he misrepresents Kraus. He does so in two ways. With its connotations of linguistic conser-

vatism, the category of "good German" is foreign to Kraus. Indeed, Kraus went to great lengths to emphasize that his defense of linguistic integrity had little to do with pedantry or with a desire to insulate German against foreign elements. In the essay "An die Anschrift der Sprachreiniger," for example, Kraus ridicules the attempt to substitute the Germanic word "Anschrift" for the French import "Adresse," both of which mean address. Kraus also lampooned Eduard Engel, a German-Jewish linguistic conservative who exhorted German Jews to "speak German" instead of *Mauscheldeutsch*. And when Alfred Kerr and Franz Werfel accused Kraus of using Austrianisms and Yiddishisms, respectively, Kraus maintained that he had nothing against such words. What matters is how they are used. Accordingly, Kraus names as the Jewish authors whom he esteems Peter Altenberg and Else Lasker-Schüler, two beleaguered, innovative modernists who were anything but icons of linguistic propriety. See K.K., *Untergang der Welt durch Schwarze Magie*, 331. Gilman notes Kraus's admiration for Altenberg and Lasker-Schüler without commenting on its iconoclastic character (*Jewish Self-Hatred*, 236). Kraus anthologized his attack on language purification and his response to Werfel in *Die Sprache*, 12–16 and 27–43. See also K.K., *Literatur und Lüge*, 197. The second level of misconstruing here has to do with an omission. Not only does Kraus avoid categories like "good German," he does much more than claim that Altenberg and Lasker-Schüler are good writers. He insists that the works of these "Jews" in fact "stand closer to God and to language than everything Germanic writers have produced in the fifty years in which Herr Bahr has been alive." It is one thing to propose that some Jewish writers qualify as good German authors. It is quite another to insist that the works of two Jewish writers are superior to all their German contemporaries. The first statement does not seriously belie Gilman's theory about how Kraus regarded "the language of the Jews." For he, Gilman, argues that most self-hating Jews identified exceptions to the rule of the Jews' ubiquitously defective German. But Jewish writers who surpass everything in "Germanic letters" are clearly more than just exceptions. And to assert that position for Jewish authors is to break radically with the antisemitic outlook that Gilman ascribes to Kraus. Furthermore, Gilman takes similar liberties with Kraus's polemics against Felix Salten, a well-known Jewish journalist who frequently contributed to the *Neue Freie Presse*. Referring to Kraus's essay "Hares that Speak with a Yiddish Accent" ("Jüdelnde Hasen," *F* 820–26:44–45), Gilman writes: "Kraus repeats here a motif that he evolves in developing the idea that Jews possess a special, base language: that the language of the Jews is an artificial sign of their separateness from the European cultural community" (*Jewish Self-Hatred*, 234). Kraus's article, in other words, illustrates the main point of Gilman's book. But does it really? As we know, Kraus was not categorically contemptuous of *Mauscheldeutsch*. And in the essay that Gilman treats as instantiating Kraus's long-held beliefs about the Jews' "base language," Kraus actually says nothing negative about the discourse spoken by Salten's rabbits. For, characteristically, Kraus is not simply interested in exposing how Salten's rabbits speak with a Yiddish accent. Rather, he seizes upon the kind of contradiction that he stresses in his exchanges with Harden. Put more directly, Salten's rabbits are ripe for satire because they clash so glaringly with Salten's professed love of hunting, with his effusive, assimilationist participation in activities not conventionally associated with Jewish culture. That is what Kraus finds truly absurd. In fact, he spends much of the piece making fun of Salten's hunting. After quoting an article Salten wrote for an Austrian hunting magazine, and playing with the morphological proximity of "der Moses" and "des Mooses" [Moses and of moss], Kraus writes about Salten and Imre Bekessy, a Hungarian-Jewish publisher who also hunted and whom he, Kraus, despised: "While our kind lie in wait for noble beasts without leaving our writing desks, they [Salten and Bekessy] have often wandered through the woods or stalked the respect that their journalistic activities did not achieve" (45). Like Harden's very public homophobia and overblown archaisms, Salten's and Bekessy's hunting is seen by Kraus as a tortured attempt to gain respect—"tortured," because it is so obviously contrived and therefore will only make them seem *more out* of place. Kraus, meanwhile, identifies with Jewish critics who stay at their writing desks—"while *our kind* lie in wait for noble beasts without leaving our writing desks."

127. K.K., *Untergang der Welt durch schwarze Magie*, 213.

128. Late in his career, Kraus distanced himself from "Heine and the Consequences." But he suggested only that he no longer approved of what he had written and not that what he had written was, at the time of its composition, a frivolous polemical gesture for him. K.K., *F* 890:46.

129. As Ritchie Robertson has pointed out, "Teetisch" here refers to a famous rhyme in one of Heine's poems. See his discussion of "Heine and the Consequences," in Robertson, *The 'Jewish Question' in German Literature*, 315. In the poem "Jehuda ben Halevy" Heine plays with the pair "Itzig-Hitzig." For an incisive reading of how Heine's line represents a critical commentary on a certain mode of German-Jewish assimilation, see Willi Goetschel, *Spinoza's Modernity: Mendelssohn, Lessing, and Heine* (Madison: University of Wisconsin, Press, 2003), 274–75. On the general connections between Heine's rhyming and Kraus's, see Edward Timms, "Topical Poetry and Satirical Rhyme: Karl Kraus's Debt to Heine," in T. J. Reed and Alexander Stillmark, eds., *Heine und die Weltliteratur* (Oxford: Legenda, 2000), 168–81.

130. Heine himself ridiculed Julius Eduard Hitzig for changing his name from Itzig, which has a more obviously Jewish appearance. So, again, Kraus's joke picks up on Heine's own humor, even as it criticizes Heine. See Gilman's informative discussion in *Jewish Self-Hatred*, 183.

131. Arendt, *The Jew as Pariah: Jewish Identity and Politics in the Modern Age*, ed. Ron H. Feldman (New York: Grove Press, 1978). For Arendt, Heine is the one truly successful example of German-Jewish assimilation in the nineteenth century. And yet, interestingly, Arendt assigns Kraus and Heine to the same category of "Jewish revolutionary tradition." See Arendt, *Antisemitism* (New York, Harcourt, 1968), 65.

132. Heine, *Gedichte* (Frankfurt/M: Insel, 1994), 231.
133. K.K., *Untergang der Welt durch schwarze Magie,* 334–35.

CHAPTER 3

1. *KB* 337.
2. There are several useful discussions of Kafka's reading of Kraus. The most extensive of them appeared recently: Leo Lensing's informative essay, "*Fackel*-Leser und Werfel-Verehrer: Anmerkungen zu Kafkas Briefen an Robert Klopstock," in Hugo Wetscherek, ed., *Kafkas letzter Freund* (Vienna: Inlibris, 2003), 265–92. See also Gerald Stieg, "Kafka als Spiegel der Kraus'schen Literaturpolemik," in Josef Worstbrock and Helmut Koopman, eds., *Formen und Formgeschichte des Streitens: Der Literaturstreit* (Tübingen: Max Niemeyer, 1986), 90–110; Harmut Binder, *Motiv und Gestaltung bei Franz Kafka* (Bonn: Bouvier, 1966), 17–25; Werner Kraft, *Franz Kafka: Durchdringung und Geheimnis* (Frankfurt/M: Suhrkamp, 1968), 199–208; Kurt Krolop, "Prager Authoren im Lichte *der Fackel,*" in Krolop, *Reflexionen der Fackel: Neue Studien über Karl Kraus* (Vienna: Verlag der österreichischen Akademie der Wissenschaften, 1994), 119–40; Ritchie Robertson, *Kafka: Judaism, Politics and Literature* (Oxford: Oxford University Press, 1985), 159–60.
3. On the hostilities between Kraus and Werfel, see Binder, *Motiv und Gestaltung,* 23–24 and Edward Timms, "Poetry, Politics, and Personalities: The Kraus-Werfel Controversy," in Joseph P. Strelka and Robert Weigel, eds., *Unser Fahrplan geht von Stern zu Stern: Zu Franz Werfels Stellung und Werk* (Bern, 1992), 111–38.
4. At the very beginning of *Literature,* Kraus cites a polemical exchange in which Werfel writes from Kraus's perspective and speaks of his—i.e., Kraus's—"talent for acoustic mirroring." See K.K., *Literatur,* in K.K., *Dramen,* ed. Christian Wagenknecht (Frankfurt/M: Surhkamp, 1989), 11. In the body of *Literature,* Kraus borrows Werfel's Mirror-Man figure, inserts him into his play, and has the Mirror-Man—i.e., the Kraus cipher—say, "my mirror is acoustic," thereby registering that in *Mirror-Man* the Mirror-Man has a talent for acoustic mirroring (*Literatur,* 65).
5. On Werfel's complex Jewish identity, see Spector, *Prague Territories: National Conflict and Cultural Innovation in Franz Kafka's Fin de Siècle* (Berkeley and Los Angeles: University of California Press, 2000), esp. 123–29.
6. As in those texts, moreover, Kraus sets his mimetic techniques in opposition to what he sees as an assimilationist desire for originality and authenticity. For *Literature* flaunts Kraus's mimetic talents as it derides what Kraus clearly regards as Werfel's *German-Jewish* expressionist affectations.
7. Sigurd Paul Scheichl points out that Kraus makes fun of the fathers' "half-assimilation" by having them speak Yiddish-German dialect in the verse form of German classical drama. See Scheichl, "Der Stilbruch als Stilmittel bei Kraus," in

Scheichl and Edward Timms, eds., *Karl Kraus in a New Perspective / Karl Kraus in neuer Sicht: London Kraus Symposium* (Munich: edition text + kritik, 1986), 128–43.

8. K.K., *Dramen*, 75.

9. Again, Kraus cites this part of *Mirror-Man* as a sort of introduction to *Literature* (*Dramen*, 11).

10. Quoted in Binder, *Motiv und Gestaltung*, 23.

11. In German most nouns begin with a capital letter, and *Mauscheln* is the nominal form of the verb *mauscheln*, which generally meant "to speak German-Yiddish dialect." Clearly, however, *Mauscheln* had different connotations for Kafka. On the meaning and cultural significance of *Mauscheln*, see Sander Gilman, *Jewish Self-Hatred: Anti-Semitism and the Secret Language of the Jews* (Baltimore: Johns Hopkins University Press, 1986), 140–44.

12. "Jargon" functioned as a synonym both for "Mauscheln," or German-Yiddish dialect, and for Yiddish. As we will see below, Kafka used "Jargon" in the latter sense. "Jüdeln" too could be used more or less interchangeably with "Mauscheln." Indeed, whereas in the first version of an essay I discuss in this chapter— "Die letzten Schauspieler" (1912)—Kraus wrote: "In der Kunst kommt es darauf an, *wer* jüdelt" ("In art what matters is *who* speaks *Mauscheln*"). In the second, 1922 version we find the line changed to: "In der Kunst kommt es darauf an, *wer* mauschelt." Among the bold ideas Kraus expresses with his statement is that one could speak *Mauscheln* in true art.

13. I have not found a reading of Kafka's letter that attempts to answer this question. Most readings—e.g., Gilman's—suggest that, for Kafka, Kraus's writing represented the sort of *Mauscheln* he defines in his letter to Brod, even though, as Kafka describes it, Kraus's writing does not conform to that definition of *Mauscheln*. In other words, Kafka confronts us with a contradiction. He claims that "no one can speak *Mauscheln* like Kraus," but does not portray Kraus's writing as consistent with *Mauscheln*. And, to reiterate, I have not encountered an attempt to disentangle this contradiction, which is made even more slippery by the fact that Kraus's play contains language that was commonly regarded as *Mauscheln*: again, the fathers often speak in Yiddishisms. On Kraus's understanding and use of *Mauscheln*, see Lensing, "*Fackel*-Leser und Werfel-Verehrer," 280–87.

14. K.K., "Die letzten Schauspieler," in *Untergang der Welt durch Schwarze Magie*, ed. Wagenknecht (Frankfurt/M: Suhrkamp, 1989), 155. Hereafter cited parenthetically as "LS."

15. Kafka discusses "small literature" and its virtues in a diary entry dated December 25, 1911. As we will see, during this time Kafka was intensely interested in Yiddish culture, and on Christmas Day 1911, suggestively enough, his thoughts seem to have taken shape decisively, even if he expressed them in outline form. On Kafka's relation to "small literature" or "minor literature," see Gilles Deleuze and Félix Guattari's classic account: *Kafka: Toward a Minor Literature*, trans. Dana Polan (Minneapolis: University of Minnesota Press, 1986). Scott Spector offers a

trenchant revision of Deleuze and Guattari's argument, suggesting that Kafka did indeed create a kind of minor literature himself, or a literature that on the level of form subverts basic tendencies of a major literature, but not because that was his goal. Kafka wanted to be a major German author, in Spector's reading. However, because of his position as a Jew in a hostile fin-de-siècle culture, he wound up producing something other than the major literature of his German models. See Spector, *Prague Territories,* 28–29.

16. On Kraus's "proposal," see Leo Lensing, "Tiertheater: Textspiele der jüdischen Identität bei Altenberg, Kraus und Kafka," *Das jüdische Echo* 48 (October 1999): 81–82.

17. On the significance of Yiddish culture among "Western Jews," see Steven Aschheim, *Brothers and Strangers: The Eastern European Jew in the German and German Jewish Consciousness, 1800–1923* (Madison: University of Wisconsin Press, 1982).

18. Arthur Schnitzler, *Der Weg ins Freie* (Frankfurt/M: Fischer, 1995), 44.

19. See Edward Timms, *Karl Kraus, Apocalyptic Satirist,* vol. 1: *Culture and Catastrophe in Habsburg Vienna* (New Haven: Yale University Press, 1986), 179.

20. Kari Grimstad, *Masks of the Prophet: The Theatrical World of Karl Kraus* (Toronto: University of Toronto Press, 1982), 171. For some analysis of, and documents pertaining to, Kraus's readings of Offenbach, see Georg Knepler, *Karl Kraus liest Offenbach* (Vienna: Löcker, 1984).

21. Kraus speaks of disparagingly of Viktor Leon's "Salonoperetta" in an earlier essay (*F* 289:4). Siegfried Kracauer writes about operetta as an exile genre in the chapter on "the home of the homeless one" in his *Offenbach und das Paris seiner Zeit* (Amsterdam: de Lange, 1937), 67–85.

22. It is unclear to what extent Annie Kalmar reciprocated the affection. Kraus and she do seem to have developed at least something of a friendship: he visited her frequently during her stay at a sanatorium in the summer of 1900, and he remained in close contact with her until her death in May 1901.

23. See Timms, *Karl Kraus,* 1:74–75.

24. Willy Haas recalls Kraus lecturing ardently about Offenbach during nights out with his friends in the years *before* the First World War. See ibid., 179.

25. Indeed, Adorno wrote that Kraus's "preference for certain dialect poets [e.g., Eisenbach] and comedians over so-called high literature is animated by an understanding [*Einverständnis*] with the undomesticated mimetic moment." Adorno, "Sittlichkeit und Kriminalität," *Noten zur Literatur,* ed. Rolf Tiedemann (Frankfurt/M: Suhrkamp, 1989), 385. Here, then, Adorno is aligning Kraus with the valuable "undisciplined mimesis" or "undomesticated mimesis" of which he had spoken and associated with Jews in *The Dialect of Enlightenment*. On the complexity of Adorno's notion of mimesis, see Martin Jay, "Mimesis and Mimetology: Adorno and Lacoue-Labarthe," in Jay, *Cultural Semantics: Key Terms: Keywords of our Time* (Amherst: University of Massachusetts Press, 1998), 120–37.

26. K.K., *Untergang der Welt*, 331.

27. See, respectively, K.K., *Literatur und Lüge*, ed. Christian Wagenknecht (Frankfurt/M: Suhrkamp, 1987), 196, and K.K., *Die Sprache,* ed. Wagenknecht (Frankfurt/M: Suhrkamp, 1987), 27-43.

28. Kafka, "Einleitungsrede über Jargon," in Kafka, *Beschreibung eines Kampfes und andere Schrfiten aus dem Nachlaß,* ed. Hans-Gerd Koch (Frankfurt/M: Fischer, 1994), 153.

29. Ernst Pawel, *The Nightmare of Reason: A Life of Franz Kafka* (New York: Vintage, 1984), 240. On Kafka's relation to Yiddish, see also Evelyn Torton Beck, *Kafka and the Yiddish Theater: Its Impact on his Work* (Madison: University of Wisconsin Press, 1971); Giuliano Baioni, "Zionism, Literature and the Yiddish Theater," in Mark Anderson, ed., *Reading Kafka: Prague, Politics and the Fin de Siècle* (New York: Schocken, 1989), 95-115; and Noah Isenberg, *Between Redemption and Doom: The Strains of German-Jewish Modernism* (Lincoln: University of Nebraska Press, 1999), 19-50.

30. Quoted in Lensing, "Tiertheater," 84. Blei's *Bestiary* appeared in 1920 under a pseudonym (Dr. Peregrin Steinhövel). The volume's entry on Kraus was written by the philosopher Carl Schmitt, who chose to remain anonymous. Kraus strikes back at Blei in the final scene of *Literature*.

31. For "the very flesh of the mind," see K.K., *Untergang der Welt,* 188.

32. Georg Lukács, *Die Seele und die Formen: Essays* (Berlin: Luchterhand, 1971), 17.

33. K.K., *Die chinesische Mauer,* ed. Christian Wagenknecht (Frankfurt/M: Suhrkamp, 1987), 195.

34. K.K., *Aphorismen,* ed. Christian Wagenknecht (Frankfurt/M: Suhrkamp, 1986), 334.

35. Adorno surmises in a letter to Scholem that Kraus's extraordinary, almost mystical investment in form derives from his roots as an *Ostjude* (*SB* 2:274). That is not what I am suggesting here, needless to say.

36. Of course, Kraus by no means ceased to expose political and bureaucratic corruption. And even in the first issues of *Die Fackel* Kraus decries what he would later anathematize as the "world of phrases"—or the world of clichés that the mass press builds up. So his "linguistic turn" is not a conversion experience, but rather a shift of emphasis that brought with it key stylistic innovations.

37. K.K., *Untergang der Welt,* 434.

38. Ibid., 74.

39. K.K., *Literatur und Lüge,* 196.

40. On the evolution of Kraus's mimetic activities, see Burkhard Müller, *Karl Kraus: Mimesis und Kritik des Mediums* (Stuttgart: Metzler, 1995).

41. See Leo Lensing, "'Photographischer Alpdruck' oder politische Fotomontage? Karl Kraus, Kurt Tucholsky und die satirischen Möglichkeiten der Fotografphie," *Zeitschrift für deutsche Philologie* 107 (1988): 556-71.

42. It is worth noting here that Kraus's new mimetic intensity carried over into his attempts to expose journalistic corruption. Perhaps the most striking example of this development is an incident discussed in the previous chapter: his success in using of elaborate mimetic trickery to get a letter published in the *Neue Freie Presse*. See *F* 245:21.

43. K.K., *Weltgericht,* 2 vols., ed. Christian Wagenknecht (Frankfurt/M: Suhrkamp, 1988), 1:9.

44. See Leo Lensing, "'Kinodramatisch': Cinema in Karl Kraus's *Die Fackel* and *The Last Days of Mankind*," *The German Quarterly* 55 no. 2 (Spring 1982): 480–98.

45. K.K., *Weltgericht,* 2:68–75.

46. K.K., *Weltgericht,* 1:67–79. In August 1914, Bahr published an effusively patriotic "greeting to Hofmannsthal" in which he, Bahr, suggests that Hofmannsthal was entering into combat ["in Waffen"] somewhere and hopes that the wind will blow his letter to its addressee. Kraus shows that Hofmannsthal was actually in Vienna in August 1914.

47. K.K., *Weltgericht,* 2:92–93.

48. Felix Salten, *Das österreichische Anlitz* (Berlin: Fischer, 1909), 267.

49. K.K., *Weltgericht,* 1:148–51.

50. In "Heine and the Consequences" Kraus complains of the unfounded "Entdeckerton," or airs of original discovery, that feuilletons display. See K.K., *Untergang der Welt,* 190.

51. The first essay, which was originally untitled, appeared in October 1913. See K.K., *Literatur und Lüge,* 180–84. The second essay came out in the same month of the same year.

52. See K.K., *Untergang der Welt durch schwarze Magie,* ed. Christian Wagenknecht (Frankfurt/M: Suhrkamp, 1989), 332–33. In reprinting the essays Kraus gave them both the same title. Like most racist antisemites, Liebenfels believed that Jews could not write well in German. But he esteemed Kraus's prose. And so, in order to reconcile his antisemitism with his almost fanatical admiration, Liebenfels had to engage in some racial gerrymandering. Hitler, in turn, admired Liebenfels, and apparently sought him out in Vienna around the time that Liebenfels wrote his paeans to Kraus. Liebenfels went on to play a significant role in the early Nazi Party. Before that, Liebenfels wrote several essays about Kraus. See, for example, "Karl Kraus und das Rassenproblem," *Der Brenner* 4 no. 5 (November 1913): 180–98.

53. K.K., *Literatur und Lüge,* 183.

54. K.K., *Untergang der Welt,* 334.

55. On Kafka's "major designs," see Spector, *Prague Territories,* 27–30.

56. Kafka, *Ein Landarzt und andere Drücke zu Lebezeiten,* ed. Koch (Frankfurt/M: Fischer, 1994), 51.

57. Several passages, which I discuss below, suggest that in Georg's mind the father reads the newspaper.

58. Kafka, *Ein Landarzt*, 44.

59. Kimberly Sparks makes that observation about *The Metamorphosis* in Sparks, "Drei schwarze Kaninchen: Zu einer Deutung der Zimmerherren in Kafkas *Die Verwandlung*," *Zeitschrift für deutsch Philologie* 84 (1965): 78–79.

60. Kafka, *Ein Landarzt*, 44.

61. Ibid., 40.

62. Ibid., 50.

63. Ibid., 51.

64. Ibid., 243.

65. Ibid., 236.

66. See, for example, Stanley Corngold, *Franz Kafka: The Necessity of Form* (Ithaca: Cornell University Press, 1988), 25.

67. See Lensing, "*Fackel*-Leser und Werfel-Verehrer," 278–80.

68. Adorno, "Sittlichkeit und Kriminalität," *Noten zur Literatur*, 381. Adorno also compares a related feature of Kraus's style, its "singularity," with Kafka's stylistic singularity in Adorno, *Prismen: Kulturkritik und Gesellschaft* (Frankfurt/M: Suhrkamp, 1987), 261.

69. K.K., *Untergang der Welt durch schwarze Magie*, 190.

70. Christoph Stözl, "Kafka: Jew, Anti-Semite, Zionist," in Anderson, *Reading Kafka*, 60.

71. See Sander Gilman, *Franz Kafka: The Jewish Patient* (New York and London: Routledge, 1994). Mark Anderson develops a penetrating reading of Kafka's story "Josephine the Singer," in which he suggests that the text reckons with, or really negotiates, Kafka's anxieties about the Jews' putative inability to produce music. See Anderson, *Kafka's Clothes: Ornament and Aestheticism in the Habsburg Fin de Siècle*. (Oxford and New York: Oxford University Press, 1992), 194–216.

72. See K.K., *Literatur und Lüge*, 299–309.

73. See Fritz Wittels, "The Fackel-Neurosis," in Hermann von Nunberg, ed., *The Minutes of the Vienna Psychoanalytic Society*, vol. 2 (New York: International Universities Press, 1962), 382. See also Wittels, "Kraus and the *Neue Freie Presse*," in Wittels, *Freud and the Woman Child: The Memoirs of Fritz Wittels*, ed. Edward Timms (New Haven: Yale University Press, 1995), 35–44. See Martina Bilke, *Zeitgenossen Der Fackel* (Munich: Löcker, 1981), 180. Kraus also responded directly and disparagingly to Theodor Lessing's claim that he, Kraus, was a self-hater. Kraus assured his readers that his "criticism of Jewry" does not have "the slightest element of the 'Jewish self-hatred' that a certain cultural theorist has recently evoked, and that has always served as a compensatory fable for gossipers and literary failures" (*F* 890–905:36).

74. See Fritz Wittels, *Ezechiel, der Zugereiste* (Berlin: Fleischel Verlag, 1910).

75. K.K., *Aphoristen*, 351.

76. K.K., *Untergang der Welt durch schwarze Magie*, 339.

77. Ibid. It is worth noting that in the more violent antisemitic climate of the

1920s, Kraus distanced himself from his line about wanting a "bomb" (ibid., 340).

78. Ibid., 330.
79. Ibid., 331.
80. K.K., *Literatur und Lüge*, 312–13.
81. Ibid., 313.
82. Ibid., 315.
83. Ibid., 314.
84. Adorno, *Prismen*, 234.
85. See Timms, *Karl Kraus*, 1:154–56. In January 1913, in fact, Kraus wrote a second fictional dialogue about Zifferer.
86. K.K., *Untergang der Welt*, 329.
87. Kraus himself wrote profiles, and it is instructive, I think, to compare them to those that he regarded as instantiating "Feuilletonismus." Indeed, in 1909, both Salten and Kraus published profiles of Peter Altenberg to celebrate the latter's fiftieth birthday. And against this common background the differences between Salten's flowing style and Kraus's much denser prose become manifest with particular starkness. See Salten, "Peter Altenberg," in Salten, *Das österreichische Anlitz*, 97–114, and K.K., "Peter Altenberg," in K.K., *Die chinesische Mauer*, 87–90. Here Salten produced a fifteen-page essay that begins by framing Altenberg as an almost exotic object of contemplation: "Isn't it strange, the way he [Altenberg] wanders on the margins of bourgeois life?" While Kraus too emphasizes Altenberg's eccentricities, he does so without situating himself as a viewer who takes them in from a position that is squarely within "bourgeois life." In fact, Kraus creates and ultimately foregrounds a kind of formal identification between himself and his subject. Whereas Salten does not alter the format of his feuilleton to fit Altenberg, Kraus ends his four-page profile by telling his readers that he has written about Altenberg in the form that Altenberg preferred: the "sketch" [*Skizze*].
88. As Ritchie Robertson points out, Kraus's piece sets up a contrast between Nogi's archaic ethos of nobility and Singer's purchased nobility. See Robertson, *The 'Jewish Question' in German Literature: Emancipation and its Discontents, 1749–1939* (Oxford: Oxford University Press, 1999), 314.
89. K.K., *Untergang der Welt*, 333. It is interesting to note that Arendt, a slashing commentator on the phenomenon of the Jewish parvenu, approvingly referred to the critique of assimilationist culture that Kraus develops in the essay "Untergang der Welt durch schwarze Magie." See Arendt, *Antisemitism* (New York: Harcourt, Brace, and World, 1951), 66.
90. See Adorno and Horkheimer, *Dialektik der Aufklärung: Philosophische Fragmente* (Frankfurt/M: Suhrkamp, 1988), 189. They use the phrase "unbeherrschte Mimesis" and also, on the next page, the phrase "undisziplinierte Mimik."

91. Max Horkheimer, *Gesammelte Schriften,* vol. 14, ed. Gunzelin Schmid Noerr (Frankfurt/M: Suhrkamp, 1988), 391.

CHAPTER 4

1. The first phrase cited here has been used by Anson Rabinbach and Michael Löwy, among others. See Anson Rabinbach, *In the Shadow of Catastrophe: German Intellectuals between Apocalypse and Enlightenment* (Berkeley and Los Angeles: University of California Press, 1997). See also Michael Löwy, *Redemption and Utopia: Jewish Libertarian Thought in Central Europe, a Study in Elective Affinity,* trans. Hope Heaney (Stanford: Stanford University Press, 1988); Richard Wolin, *Walter Benjamin: An Aesthetic of Redemption* (New York: Columbia University Press, 1982); and also the references given in the previous chapter. On the place of "redemption" in the "messianic" thinking of Benjamin, Ernst Bloch, and other Central European Jews, Rabinbach writes: "Second, there is a redemptive utopian aspect that conceives of utopia in terms of a new unity and transparency that is absent in all previous ages which is its central ideal. The utopian vision is that of a future that is the fulfillment of all that which can be hoped for in the condition of exile but cannot be realized within it. Redemption appears either as the *end of history* or as an event *within history,* never as an event produced by history. In every case it is experienced as a decisive and total break with the past and restoration of esoteric truth" (Rabinbach, *In the Shadow,* 32). Also worth noting here is Rabinbach's invocation of Gershom Scholem: "Scholem has emphasized the 'tension between the destructive nature of redemption on the one hand and the utopianism of the content on the other'" (33). The second phrase here comes from Michael André Bernstein's essay "Walter Benjamin: Apocalypse and Memory," in Bernstein, *Five Portraits: Modernity and the Imagination in Twentieth-Century German Writing* (Evanston: Northwestern University Press, 2000), 81. As Bernstein notes on the same page, Benjamin's "messianism" is an eclectic affair, which draws on various elements in *German* culture, including German Romanticism.

2. Witness Benjamin's famous, early, often-invoked claims about how there is utopian possibility "deeply embedded" in "the most endangered, most disparaged and derided" moments of the present.

3. That is how David Biale, who applied to Scholem's work the term "counter-history," describes Scholem's conception of Jewish culture. See Biale, *Gershom Scholem, Kabbalah and Counter History* (Cambridge, Mass.: Harvard University Press, 1981), 7–8.

4. I have inserted Benjamin's famous historiographical dictum (about "brushing against the grain") into this synopsis of Scholem's approach to history in order to foreground their shared revisionism.

5. Cited in Biale, *Gershom Scholem,* 8.

6. There exist only a few readings of Benjamin's understanding of Kraus. And they do not treat in detail the theme that interests me—how Benjamin came to assign a profound "Jewishness" to Kraus's journalism—in detail. See C. J. Thornhill, *Walter Benjamin and Karl Kraus: Problems of a 'Wahlverwandschaft'* (Stuttgart: Heinz, 1996); Christian Schulte, *Ursprung ist das Ziel: Walter Benjamin über Karl Kraus* (Hamburg: Königshausen & Neumann, 2003); and Sigrid Weigel, "Eros and Language: Benjamin's Kraus Essay," in Gerhard Richter, ed., *Benjamin's Ghosts: Interventions in Contemporary Literary and Cultural Theory* (Stanford: Stanford University Press, 2002), 278–98.

7. For an excellent, compact overview of German-Jewish self-fashioning at this time, see Steven Aschheim, "German Jews Beyond *Bildung* and Liberalism: The Radical Jewish Revival in the Weimar Republic," in Aschheim, *Culture and Catastrophe: German and Jewish Confrontations with National Socialism and Other Crises* (New York: New York University Press, 1996), 31–44.

8. Of course, Benjamin had been engaged in conversations about Jewishness and Zionism—with his friend Kurt Tuchler. See Rabinbach, *In the Shadow of Catastrophe*, 36.

9. Strauss's response to Goldstein appeared in *Der Kunstwart* without a title, and under the same heading as the other replies: "Sprechsaal: Aussprache zur Judenfrage," *Der Kunstwart* 25, no. 22 (August 1912): 238–45.

10. Paul Mendes-Flohr, *German Jews: A Dual Identity* (New Haven: Yale University Press, 1999), 48–49. On the Benjamin-Strauss correspondence, see Mendes-Flohr, *German Jews*, 48–56; Rabinbach, *In the Shadow*, 36–44; Itta Shedletzky, "Fremdes und Eigenes: Zur Position Ludwig Strauss in den Kontroversen um Assimilation und Judentum in den Jahren 1912–1914," in Hans Otto Horch, ed., *Ludwig Strauss, 1892/1992* (Tübingen: Niemeyer, 1995), 173–83; Gary Smith, "'Das jüdische versteht sich von selbst': Walter Benjamins frühe Auseinandersetzung mit dem Judentum," *Deutsche Vierteljahresschrift* 65 no. 2 (1991): 318–34; and Irving Wohlfahrt, "Männer aus der Fremde: Walter Benjamin and the 'German-Jewish Parnassus,'" *New German Critique* 70 (Winter 1997): 3–86.

11. Strauss, *Der Kunstwart*, 239.

12. Mendes-Flohr, *German Jews*, 49.

13. Strauss, *Der Kunstwart*, 241.

14. Ibid., 242.

15. Ibid., 243.

16. When, in October 1912, Benjamin made this remark about "standing with" a Zionism that "sees Jewish values everywhere," he had not yet begun to speak of his Zionism as "Zionism of the spirit." He started to use that term a month later, but it can be retroactively applied to the Zionism that he had been sketching out, since it was Benjamin's terminology, not the substance of his ideas, that changed.

17. Of course, there were many self-professed Zionists in Europe who never con-

sidered emigrating or even disengaging from the "majority culture" in the countries where they lived. On this paradox, see Michael Berkowitz, *Western Jewry and the Zionist Project 1914-1933* (Cambridge: Cambridge University Press, 1997).

18. On Benjamin's relation to Wickersdorf, see Rabinbach, *In the Shadow*, 36-50.

19. See ibid., 37; Smith, "'Das jüdische versteht sich von selbst,'" 318-27; and Irving Wohlfart, "Männer aus der Fremde," 20-40.

20. Jakob Wassermann, "Der Jude als Orientale," in *Vom Judentum: Ein Sammelbuch* (Leipzig: Kurt Wolff Verlag, 1913), 5. On the topic of Jewish "orientalism," see Paul Mendes-Flohr, "Fin de Siècle Orientalism, the *Ostjuden* and the Aesthetics of Self-Affirmation," in Mendes-Flohr, *Divided Passions: Jewish Intellectuals and the Experience of Modernity* (Detroit: Wayne State University Press, 1991), 77-132.

21. Wassermann, "Der Jude als Orientale," 6.

22. In this context it is interesting to note that Franz Rosenzweig later deemed the Jews' "fate" to be to "transmit" [*vermitteln*] rather than to "produce." Franz Rosenzweig, *Zweistromland: Kleinere Schriften zu Glauben und Denken*, ed. Reinhold and Annamarie Mayer (Dordrecht: Nijhoff, 1984), 169.

23. Gershom Scholem, *Walter Benjamin: Die Geschichte einer Freundschaft* (Frankfurt/M: Suhrkamp, 1977), 105.

24. See *F* 324-25:56-58.

25. Quoted in Biale, *Gershom Scholem*, 155.

26. David Myers, *Re-Inventing the Jewish Past: European Intellectuals and the Zionist Return to History* (Oxford and New York: Oxford University Press, 1994), 154.

27. Biale, *Gershom Scholem*, 13.

28. Scholem's library contains a set of *Die Fackel* that runs from 1923, the date of his arrival in Jerusalem, to 1936, and it is complete for those years. Scholem also owned anthology editions of Kraus's work, as well as some secondary literature on Kraus. The original editions of *Die Fackel* bear signs of heavy use.

29. Dan Pagis, *Ḥiddush u-masoret be-shirat ha-ḥol ha'ivrit: sefared ve-iṭalyah* [Change and Tradition in the Secular Poetry: Spain and Italy] (Jerusalem: Keter, 1976), 70. Again, I am very grateful to Adena Tannenbaum for translating this passage.

30. G.S., "Das musivische Wort," Jewish National University Library, Arc 4o 1599/277: 139. A small fragment of these notes appears in *ST* 2:586.

31. Here Bernstein's point about German Romanticism and Benjamin's "Jewish thinking" seems to apply to Scholem as well. For Scholem's remarks about endless reflection on the word evoke Friedrich Schlegel and Novalis as much as they do "Jewish thought."

32. If Scholem cites "Heine and the Consequences" in making his case against

"Jewish journalism," he also deviates from Kraus's rhetoric. For, as Kraus himself took pains to point out, he, Kraus, never used the word "prostitute" [*Dirne*] as an insult. See *F* 339–40:51.

33. G.S., *Die Geschichte einer Freundschaft*, 105.

34. Ibid.

35. Ibid.

36. Robert Alter, *Necessary Angels: Tradition and Modernity in Kafka, Benjamin, and Scholem* (Cambridge, Mass.: Harvard University Press, 1991), 81.

37. W.B., *Illuminationen*, sel. Siegfried Unseld (Frankfurt/M: Suhrkamp, 1977), 253. On Benjamin's messianic thinking and its "Jewish aspects," see Michael Löwy, "Jewish Messianism and Libertarian Utopia in Central Europe," *New German Critique* 20 (Spring/Summer 1980): 105–15; Rabinbach, "Between Apocalypse and Enlightenment: Benjamin, Bloch and Modern German-Jewish Messianism," in Rabinbach, *In the Shadow, of Catastrophe*, 27–65. Certainly it is worth noting again here that Rabinbach describes a line by Kraus as the pithiest evocation of "modern German-Jewish messianism." It is a line that Benjamin cited, as Rabinbach observes: "The messianic concept is thus intimately connected to the idea of a return to an original state that lies in *both* the past and the future. Karl Kraus's motto Origin Is the Goal, cited by Benjamin, among others, captures this idea most succinctly" (*In the Shadow*, 31). Michael André Bernstein offers a concise account of Benjamin's "messianic violence" in his *Five Portraits*, 82.

38. In fact, in the notes Benjamin took for his 1931 Kraus essay, he speaks of "the behavioristic moments in Kraus's mimesis" (*BGS* 2:3.1106).

39. W.B., *Illuminationen*, 252.

40. Arendt, "Walter Benjamin," in W.B., *Illuminations*, trans. H. Zohn (New York: Harcourt Brace Jovanovich, 1968), 38.

41. Ibid.

42. In a 1968 letter to Adorno, Scholem applies this term to Arendt (*SB* 2:206).

43. K.K., *Dramen*, 52.

44. Scholem seems to have agreed with Kraus. In his copy of *Literature* he vigorously underlined the sentence through which Kraus has Werfel's followers employ the charge of self-hatred in a self-hating manner. The copy of the play to which I am referring is in the Scholem library at the Jewish National University Library.

45. The contradiction that Kraus identifies is not particular to Werfel. Consider, for example, the following remarks by Arthur Schnitzler: "His [Kraus's] attitude toward antisemites is the most repulsive thing I have ever seen. If it had been inspired by clear sightedness and a concern for fairness—but in all it is nothing but servility. . . . In a word, Kraus's attitude toward the antisemites is . . . *typically Jewish*" (my emphasis). Quoted in Jacques Le Rider, *Modernity and Crises of Identity: Culture and Society in Fin-de-Siècle Vienna*, trans. Rosemary Morris (New York: Continuum, 1991), 253.

46. On Benjamin's critical response to Buber, see Rabinbach, *In the Shadow*, 30–35.

47. Again, Benjamin writes in his notes for the Kraus essay: "Everything Kraus achieved as a literary critic lies in his reckoning with expressionism. Werfel." At the same time, in the actual essay Benjamin likens Kraus to certain strains of expressionism, so it would be unfair to suggest that, for Benjamin, Kraus's relation to expressionism is coextensive with his response to Werfel.

48. In a 1936 letter to Karl Thieme, Benjamin speaks of Kraus as an "Apokalyptiker" (*BB* 5:436).

49. Rabinbach, *In the Shadow*, 47.

50. Ibid., 31.

51. Bernstein, *Five Portraits*, 92.

52. Quoted in Bernstein, *Five Portraits*, 92–93.

53. The typescript to which I am referring is housed in Scholem's Benjamin archive at the Jewish National University Library, Arc 40 1598/92.

54. Ibid.

55. What happened to Benjamin's line about Kafka? Certainly an editor at the *Frankfurter Zeitung*, which published "Karl Kraus" in multiple installments, could have made the change after Benjamin had corrected the galleys. However, the feuilleton editor at the *Frankfurter Zeitung* was Benjamin's friend Siegfried Kracauer, and I doubt that Kracauer would have allowed an allusion to Kafka to be removed without Benjamin's consent. Yet given how long Benjamin had labored on the essay (almost a full year), and, correlatively, how intimate he must have been with his piece, that he would leave dangling an antecedent-less "him too" construction seems unlikely. Nonetheless, the most probable scenario is that Benjamin himself expunged the comparison—for stylistic reasons. *Gedankengebäude* is a metaphor that literally translates as "building of ideas" and connotes "structure of thought." In comparing Kraus's "Gedankengebäude" to the buildings in which K.'s trial occurs, then, Benjamin plays somewhat preciously off a German rhetorical figure. And doing so in an essay that repeatedly applauds Kraus's uncompromising *Sprachkritik* might well have struck him as being a kind of performative contradiction.

56. The Halakah refers to the body of discourse about Jewish law and commandments, about the *path* one is supposed to follow. Indeed, the root of the word, "halakh," means to walk or go. Hence Benjamin proceeds from an assertion of the halakhic character of Kraus's writing to a series of points about Kraus and the law, about how, for Kraus, everything "takes place in the sphere of law." On Benjamin and the Halakah, see Susan Handelman, *Fragments of Redemption: Jewish Thought and Literary Theory in Benjamin, Scholem, and Levinas* (Bloomington: Indiana University Press, 1991), 52–61.

57. In one of his most substantial profiles of Benjamin, Scholem cites his friend's essays on Kraus and Kafka to illustrate Benjamin's interest in Judaism. For

Scholem, in other words, it is in *these* essays that Benjamin's engagement with the question of the Jewishness of German-Jewish culture comes to light most compellingly. See G.S., "Walter Benjamin," in G.S., *On Jews and Judaism in Crisis: Selected Essays*, ed. Werner Dannhauser (New York: Schocken, 1976), 194.

58. At times in his essays on Kraus, Benjamin seems to be trying to show how his Marxist and Jewish commitments could exist side-by-side. It is Kraus's "freedom"-promoting "*dialectics*," after all, that represent the most ardent "prayer for redemption that passes over Jewish lips today." Not only that, in the longer essay on Kraus Benjamin cites Marx's famously anti-Jewish text *On the Jewish Question* to illustrate Kraus's "real humanism," and he then proceeds to adulate Kraus as an authentically Jewish author.

59. Weigel, "Eros and Language," 278.

60. Ibid., 278.

61. Ibid., 279.

62. Ibid.

63. Benjamin extends this analysis of journalism, it is worth noting, in his famous essay "Der Erzähler" (1936). Here Benjamin speaks of how "the press" is "one of the most important instruments" of bourgeois "domination" in the era of "high capitalism." He also counterposes the press's narrow conveying of mostly local "information" to the openness of "storytelling," which relates events from "afar." See W.B., *Illuminationen*, 390.

64. W.B., "Franz Kafka: Zur zehnten Wiederkehr seines Todestages," in W.B., *Benjamin über Kafka*, ed. Hermann Schweppenhäuser (Frankfurt/M: Suhrkamp, 1981), 37.

65. Alter, *Necessary Angels*, 17.

66. Wohlfahrt, "Männer aus der Fremde," 19.

67. Bernstein, *Five Portraits*, 83. Yet where he asserts that—as with Marxism—Benjamin appropriated Judaism as "a network of charged phrases and concepts to which he was already predisposed," Bernstein goes too far. After all, Benjamin was only twenty-one when he began to think seriously about the "mission" of Jewish culture.

68. Quoted in Biale, *Gershom Scholem*, 34. Here, then, Scholem appreciates the Halakah "*without* identifying with its imperatives." Furthermore, he is suggesting that his aim was to invert an established hierarchy—by showing that the Halakah actually depended for its "vitality" on the Kabbalah.

69. W.B., *Benjamin über Kafka*, 89–90.

CONCLUSION

1. See K.K., "Die Affäre Harden," in K.K., *Brod und Lüge*, ed. Christian Wagenknecht (Frankfurt/M: Suhrkamp, 1991), 231–39.

2. See K.K., "Prozeß Veith," in K.K., *Die chinesische Mauer*, ed. Christian Wagenknecht (Frankfurt/M: Suhrkamp, 1987), 9–33.

3. See K.K., "Das Ehrenkreuz," in ibid., 49–51.

4. The Kraus scholar Gerald Stieg, who was a colleague of Bourdieu's in Paris, is the source of this information. According to Stieg, in 1999 Bourdieu planned to teach a seminar entitled "The Actuality of Karl Kraus." The focus of the seminar was to be Kraus's media criticism. Stieg spoke of this at a Kraus conference held in London to mark the centenary of the founding of *Die Fackel*.

5. See Adorno, "Sittlichkeit und Kriminalität," in Adorno, *Noten zur Literatur*, ed. Rolf Tiedemann (Frankfurt/M: Suhrkamp, 1989), 371.

6. Niall Ferguson, "How the Papers Went to War," *The Independent*, October 27, 1998: 15.

7. I am not trying to claim for Kraus a privileged position among modernists, or to suggest that we should attach special value to his work because it resists decontextualization and thus domestication. Rather, I am attempting to go beyond the obvious factors in explaining Kraus's relatively minor cultural standing. And the localizing effects of Kraus's stylistic tendencies do seem to matter. Consider what Peter Gay claimed about turn-of-the-century Vienna's most widely-read modernist thinker: "In truth Freud could have developed his ideas in any city endowed with a first-rate medical school and an educated public large and affluent enough to furnish him with patients." Most historians would disagree, of course; but the important point here is that no one would say anything even remotely similar about Kraus's writing. See Gay, *Freud: A Life for Our Time* (New York, Norton, 1988), 10.

8. See G.S., "Jews and Germans," in G.S., *On Jews and Judaism in Crisis: Selected Essays*, ed. Werner Dannhauser (New York: Schocken, 1976), 71–92.

9. See the "Elemente des Antisemitismus" section in Adorno and Horkheimer, *Dialektik der Aufklärung: Philosophische Fragmente* (Frankfurt/M: Suhrkamp, 1988), esp. 181–89, a section that Adorno is believed to have written. As is the case with Benjamin, Adorno's interest in the "mimetic faculty" is exceedingly eclectic and in based in anthropological and zoological theories. See Martin Jay, "Mimesis and Mimetology: Adorno and Lacoue-Labarthe," in Jay, *Cultural Semantics: Key Terms; Keywords of our Time* (Amherst: University of Massachusetts Press, 1998), 121–28.

10. See Adorno, "Der Essay als Form," in *Noten zur Literatur*, 9–33, esp. 14 and 26.

11. Adorno, "Sittlichkeit und Kriminalität," in *Noten zur Literatur*, 371.

12. Ibid., 385.

BIBLIOGRAPHY

This bibliography lists the most important secondary sources for the preceding study. The notes contain full references for all secondary sources cited, as well as for primary sources and archival material.

Alter, Robert. *Necessary Angels: Tradition and Modernity in Kafka, Benjamin, and Scholem.* Cambridge, Mass.: Harvard University Press, 1991.
Anderson, Mark. *Kafka's Clothes: Ornament and Aestheticism in the Habsburg Fin de Siècle.* Oxford and New York: Oxford University Press, 1992.
———. "'Jewish Mimesis'? Imitation and Assimilation in Thomas Mann's 'Wälsugenblut' and Ludwig Jacobinski's *Werther, Der Jude.*" *German Life and Letters* 49 (1996): 193–204.
———, ed. *Reading Kafka: Prague, Politics, and the Fin de Siècle.* New York: Schocken, 1989.
Arendt, Hannah. *The Origins of Totalitarianism.* New York: Harcourt, Brace, and World, 1951.
———. *The Jew as Pariah: Jewish Identity and Politics in the Modern Age.* Edited by Ron H. Feldman. New York: Grove Press, 1978.
Arntzen, Helmut. *Karl Kraus und die Presse.* Munich: Fink, 1975.
Aschheim, Steven. *Brothers and Strangers: The Eastern Jew in German and German Jewish Consciousness, 1800–1923.* Madison: University of Wisconsin Press, 1982.
———. *Culture and Catastrophe: German and Jewish Confrontations with National Socialism and Other Crises.* New York: New York University Press, 1996.
———. "The Metaphysical Psychologist: On the Life and Letters of Gershom Scholem." *The Journal of Modern History* 76 (December 2004): 903–33.

Bauman, Zygmunt. *Modernity and Ambivalence.* Ithaca, N.Y.: Cornell University Press, 1991.
Beck, Evelyn Torton. *Kafka and the Yiddish Theater: Its Impact on His Work.* Madison: University of Wisconsin Press, 1971.
Beller, Steven. *Vienna and the Jews, 1867–1938: A Cultural History.* Cambridge: Cambridge University Press, 1989.
Berman, Marshall. *All That Is Solid Melts into Air: The Experience of Modernity.* New York: Penguin Books, 1982.
Bernstein, Michael André. *Five Portraits: Modernity and the Imagination in Twentieth-Century German Writing.* Evanston: Northwestern University Press, 2000.
Bernstein, Richard. *Hannah Arendt and the Jewish Question.* Cambridge, Mass.: The MIT Press, 1996.
Biale, David. *Gershom Scholem: Kabbalah and Counter-History.* Cambridge, Mass.: Harvard University Press, 1982.
Bilke, Martina. *Zeitgenossen der Fackel.* Vienna: Löcker, 1981.
Botstein, Leon. *Judentum und Modernität: Essays zur Rolle der Juden in der österreichischen Kultur, 1848 bis 1938.* Vienna: Böhlau, 1991.
Brenner, Michael. *The Renaissance of Jewish Culture in Weimar Germany.* New Haven: Yale University Press, 1996.
Broch, Hermann. *Hofmannsthal und seine Zeit: Eine Studie.* Zurich: Rhein-Verlag, 1955.
Brodersen, Momme. *Spinne im eigenen Netz: Walter Benkamin—Leben und Werk.* Cologne: Elster, 1990.
Cohen, Gershon. "German Jewry as Mirror of Modernity." *Leo Baeck Institute Yearbook* 20 (1975): ix–xxxi.
Deleuze, Gilles, and Félix Guattari. *Kafka: Toward a Minor Literature.* Translated by Dana Polan. Minneapolis: University of Minnesota Press, 1986.
Field, Frank. *The Last Days of Mankind: Karl Kraus.* New York: St. Martin's Press, 1967.
Fritzsche, Peter. *Reading Berlin: 1900.* Cambridge, Mass.: Harvard University Press, 1996.
Gay, Peter. *Freud, Jews and Other Germans: Masters and Victims in Modernist Culture.* New York and Oxford: Oxford University Press, 1978.
Gilman, Sander. *Jewish Self-Hatred: Anti-Semitism and the Secret Language of the Jews.* Baltimore: Johns Hopkins University Press, 1986.
———. *The Jew's Body.* New York and London: Routledge, 1991.
———. *Franz Kafka: The Jewish Patient.* New York and London: Routledge, 1995.
Gilman, Sander, and Jack Zipes, eds. *The Yale Companion to Jewish Writing and Thought in German Culture, 1096–1996.* New Haven: Yale University Press, 1997.

Goetschel, Willi. *Spinoza's Modernity: Mendelssohn, Lessing, Heine.* Madison: University of Wisconsin Press, 2003.
Goldberg, David Theo, and Michael Krausz, eds. *Jewish Identity.* Philadelphia: Temple University Press, 1993.
Handelman, Susan. *Fragments of Redemption: Jewish Thought and Literary Theory in Benjamin, Scholem, and Levinas.* Bloomington: Indiana University Press, 1991.
Heller, Erich. *The Disinherited Mind.* New York: Meridian Books, 1959.
———. *In the Age of Prose: Literary and Philosophical Essays.* New York: Cambridge University Press, 1984.
Hess, Jonathan. *German Jews and the Claims of Modernity.* New Haven: Yale University Press, 2002.
Hohendahl, Peter Uwe. *The Institution of Criticism.* Ithaca, N.Y.: Cornell University Press, 1982.
Iggers, Wilma Abeles. *Karl Kraus: A Viennese Critic of the Twentieth Century.* The Hague: Nijhoff, 1967.
Isenberg, Noah. *Between Redemption and Doom: The Strains of German-Jewish Modernism.* Lincoln: University of Nebraska Press, 1999.
Jäger, Christian, and Erhard Schütz. *Städebilder zwischen Literatur und Journalismus: Wien, Berlin und das Feuilleton der Weimarer Republik.* Wiesbaden: Deutscher Universitätsverlag, 1999.
Janik, Alan, and Steven Toumlin. *Wittgenstein's Vienna.* New York: Touchstone, 1973.
Jay, Martin. "Mimesis and Mimetology: Adorno and Lacoue-Labarthe." In Martin Jay, *Cultural Semantics: Key Terms: Keywords of our Time,* 120–37. Amherst: University of Massachusetts Press, 1998.
Johnston, William. *The Austrian Mind: An Intellectual and Social History, 1848–1938.* Berkeley and Los Angeles: University of California Press, 1972.
Kernmayer, Hildegard. *Judentum im Wiener Feuilleton (1848–1903): Exemplarische Untersuchungen zum literarästhetischen und politischen Diskurs der Moderne.* Tübingen: Niemeyer, 1998.
Kohn, Caroline. "Der Wiener jüdische Jargon im Werke von Karl Kraus." *Modern Austrian Literature* 8 (1975): 240–67.
Kohn, Hans. *Karl Kraus, Arthur Schnitzler, Otto Weininger: Aus dem jüdischen Wien der Jahrhundertwende.* Tübingen: Mohr, 1962.
Krolop, Kurt. *Sprachsatire als Zeitsatire bei Karl Kraus: Neun Studien.* Berlin: Akademie, 1987.
———. *Reflexionen der Fackel: Neue Studien über Karl Kraus.* Vienna: Österreichische Akademie der Wissenschaften. 1994.
Lang, Alexander. *Ursprung ist das Ziel: Karl Kraus und sein "Zion des Wortes"—das jüdisch-eschatologische Konzept in der Fackel.* Frankfurt/M and New York: Peter Lang, 1998.

Langmuir, Gavin. *Toward a Definition of Antisemitism*. Berkeley and Los Angeles: University of California Press, 1990.
Lensing, Leo. "'Kinodramatisch': Cinema in Karl Kraus's *Die Fackel* and *The Last Days of Mankind*." *The German Quarterly* 55 no. 2 (Spring 1982): 480–98.
———. "'Photographischer Alpdruck' oder politische Fotomontage? Karl Kraus, Kurt Tucholsky und die satirischen Möglichkeiten der Fotographie." *Zeitschrift für deutsche Philologie* 107 (1988): 556–71.
———. "Heine's Body, Heine Corpus: Sexuality and Jewish Identity in Karl Kraus's Literary Polemics against Heinrich Heine." In Marc Gelber, ed., *The Jewish Reception of Heinrich Heine*, 95–111. Tübingen: Niemeyer, 1992.
———. "Tiertheater: Textspiele der jüdischen Identität bei Altenberg, Kraus und Kafka." *Das jüdische Echo* 48 (October 1999): 79–86.
———. "*Fackel*-Leser und Werfel-Verehrer: Anmerkungen zu Kafkas Briefen an Robert Klopstock." In Hugo Wetscherek, ed., *Kafkas letzter Freund*, 267–92. Vienna: Inlibris, 2003.
———. *Brief über den Vater: ein Brief des jungen Karl Kraus an seinen Bruder Richard, faksimiliert und erläutert*. Warmbronn: Kiecher, 2005.
Le Rider, Jacques. *Modernity and Crises of Identity: Culture and Society in Fin-de-Siècle Vienna*. Translated by Rosemary Morris. New York: Continuum, 1991.
Liebschütz, Hans. *Das Judentum im deutschen Geschichtsbild von Hegel bis Max Weber*. Tübingen: Mohr, 1967.
Mayer, Hans. *Außenseiter*. Frankfurt/M: Suhrkamp, 1975.
Mendes-Flohr, Paul, *Divided Passions: Jewish Intellectuals and the Experience of Modernity*. Detroit: Wayne State University Press, 1991.
———. *German Jews: A Dual Identity*. New Haven: Yale University Press, 1999.
Meyer, Michael, et al., eds. *German-Jewish History in Modern Times*. 4 vols. New York: Columbia University Press, 1996–98.
Mosse, George. *German Jews beyond Judaism*. Bloomington: Indiana University Press, 1985.
———. *Confronting the Nation: Jewish and Western Nationalism*. Hanover, N.H.: Brandeis University Press, 1993.
Müller, Burkhard. *Karl Kraus: Mimesis und Kritik des Mediums*. Stuttgart: Metzler, 1994.
Myers, David. *Re-Inventing the Jewish Past: European Intellectuals and the Zionist Return to History*. Oxford and New York: Oxford University Press, 1994.
Oxaal, Ivar, et al., eds. *Jews, Antisemitism and Culture in Vienna*. New York and London: Routledge, 1987.
Pawel, Ernst. *The Nightmare of Reason: A Life of Franz Kafka*. New York: Vintage, 1984.
Peters, George. *The Poet as Provocateur: Heinrich Heine and his Critics*. Columbia, S.C.: Camden House, 2000.

Pfabigan, Alfred. *Karl Kraus und der Sozialismus: Eine politische Biographie.* Vienna: Europaverlag, 1976.
Pulzer, Peter. *The Rise of Political Anti-Semitism in Germany and Austria.* Cambridge, Mass.: Harvard University Press, 1988.
Quack, Josef. *Bemerkungen zum Sprachverständnis von Karl Kraus.* Bonn: Bouvier, 1974.
Rabinbach. Anson. *In the Shadow of Catastrophe: German Intellectuals between Apocalypse and Enlightenment.* Berkeley and Los Angeles: University of California Press, 1997.
Reinharz, Jehuda, and Walter Schatzberg, eds. *The Jewish Response to German Culture: From the Enlightenment to the Second World War.* Hanover, N.H.: University Press of New England, 1985.
Richter, Gerhard, ed. *Benjamin's Ghosts: Interventions in Contemporary Literary and Cultural Theory.* Stanford: Stanford University Press, 2002.
Robertson, Ritchie. *The 'Jewish Question' in German Literature, 1749-1939: Emancipation and Its Discontents.* New York and Oxford: Oxford University Press, 1999.
———. "The Problem of 'Jewish Self-Hatred' in Herzl, Kraus and Kafka." *Oxford German Studies* 16 (1985): 81-108.
———. *Kafka: Judaism, Politics and Literature.* New York and Oxford: Oxford University Press, 1985.
Rose, Paul Lawrence. *German Question/Jewish Question: Revolutionary Antisemitism from Kant to Wagner.* Princeton: Princeton University Press, 1990.
Rothe, Friedrich. *Karl Kraus: Die Biographie.* Munich: Beck, 2003.
Rozenblit, Marsha. *The Jews of Austria, 1867-1914: Assimilation and Identity.* Albany: State University of New York Press, 1984.
———. *Reconstructing a National Identity: The Jews of Habsburg Austria during the First World War.* New York and Oxford: Oxford University Press, 2001.
Rürup, Reinhard. *Emanzipation und Antisemitismus: Studien zur "Judenfrage" der bürgerlichen Gesellschaft.* Göttingen: Vandenhoeck und Ruprecht, 1975.
Santner, Eric. *My own Private Germany: Daniel Paul Schreber's Secret History of Modernity.* Princeton: Princeton University Press, 1996.
Sartre, Jean-Paul. *Anti-Semite and Jew.* Translated by George Becker. New York: Grove Press, 1948.
Scheichl, Sigurd Paul, and Edward Timms, eds. *Karl Kraus in a New Perspective / Karl Kraus in neuer Sicht: Londoner Kraus Symposium.* Munich: edition text + kritik, 1986.
Schorske, Carl, *Fin-de-Siècle Vienna: Politics and Culture.* New York: Vintage, 1981.
———. *Thinking with History: Explorations in the Passage to Modernism.* Princeton: Princeton University Press, 1997.
Schulte, Christian. *Ursprung ist das Ziel: Walter Benjamin über Karl Kraus.* Hamburg: Königshausen & Neumann, 2003.

Schütz, Erhard. *Kritik der literarischen Reportage*. Munich: Fink, 1977.
Simmel, Georg. *Das Individuum und die Freiheit: Essais*. Frankfurt/M: Fischer, 1993.
Smith, Gary. "'Das Jüdische versteht sich von selbst': Walter Benjamins frühe Auseinandersetzung mit dem Judentum," *Deutsche Vierteljahresschrift* 65 no. 2 (1991): 318–34.
Spector, Scott. *Prague Territories: National Conflict and Cultural Innovation in Franz Kafka's Fin de Siècle*. Berkeley and Los Angeles: University of California Press, 2000.
Steinberg, Michael. "Jewish Identity and Intellectuality in Fin-de-Siècle Vienna." *New German Critique* 43 (Winter 1988): 3–33.
Steiner, George. *Language and Silence: Essays on Language, Literature, and the Inhuman*. New Haven: Yale University Press, 1970.
Stieg, Gerald. *Der Brenner und die Fackel: Ein Beitrag zu Wirkungsgeschichte von Karl Kraus*. Salzburg: Müller, 1976.
———. "Kafka als Spiegel der Kraus'schen Literaturpolemik." In Josef Worstbrock and Helmut Koopman, eds., *Formen und Formgeschichte des Streitens: Der Literaturstreit,* 90–110. Tübingen: Niemeyer, 1986.Szelkine, Yuri. *The Jewish Century*. Princeton: Princeton University Press, 2004.
Theobald, John. *The Paper Ghetto: Karl Kraus and Anti-Semitism*. Frankfurt/M and New York: Peter Lang Verlag der Wissenschaften, 1996.
Thornhill, C. J. *Walter Benjamin and Karl Kraus: Problems of a 'Wahlverwandtschaft.'* Stuttgart: Heinz, 1996.
Timms, Edward. *Karl Kraus, Apocalyptic Satirist*. Vol. 1: *Culture and Catastrophe in Habsburg Vienna*. New Haven: Yale University Press, 1986.
———. *Karl Kraus: Apocalyptic Satirist*. Vol. 2: *The Post-War Crisis and the Rise of the Swastika*. New Haven: Yale University Press, 2005.
———. "Poetry, Politics, and Personalities: The Kraus-Werfel Controversy." In Joseph P. S. Strelka and Robert Weigel, eds., *Unser Fahrplan geht von Stern zu Stern: Zu Franz Werfels Stellung und Werk,* 111–38. New York and Bern: Peter Lang, 1992.
———. "Topical Poetry and Satirical Rhyme: Karl Kraus's Debt to Heine." In T. J. Reed and Alexander Stillmark, eds., *Heine und die Weltliteratur,* 168–81. Oxford: Legenda, 2000.
Trommler, Frank. "The Social Politics of Musical Redemption." In Reinhold Grimm and Jost Hermand, eds., *Re-reading Wagner,* 119–34. Madison: University of Wisconsin Press, 1992.
Volkov, Shulamit. *Antisemitismus als kultureller Code: Zehn Essays*. Munich: Beck, 2000.
———. *Das jüdische Projekt der Moderne*. Munich: Beck, 2001.
———, ed. *Deutsche Juden und die Moderne*. Munich: Oldenbourg, 1994.

Wagner, Nike. *Geist und Geschlecht: Karl Kraus und die Erotik der Wiener Moderne.* Frankfurt/M: Suhrkamp, 1982.
Weiner, Marc. *Richard Wagner and the Anti-Semitic Imagination.* Lincoln: University of Nebraska Press, 1995.
Wistrich, Robert. *The Jews of Vienna in the Age of Franz Joseph.* Oxford and New York: Oxford University Press, 1990.
———, ed. *Austrians and Jews in the Twentieth Century: From Franz Joseph to Waldheim.* New York: St. Martin's Press, 1990.
Wohlfahrt, Irving. "Männer aus der Fremde: Walter Benjamin and the 'German-Jewish Parnassus.'" *New German Critique* 70 (Winter 1997): 3–86.
Wolin, Richard. *Walter Benjamin: An Aesthetics of Redemption.* New York: Columbia University Press, 1982.
Zohn, Harry. *Karl Kraus and the Critics.* Columbia, S.C.: Camden House, 1997.
———. "Karl Kraus: 'Jüdischer Selbsthasser' oder 'Erzjude.'" *Modern Austrian Literature* 8 (1975): 20–37.

INDEX

Adler, Victor, 78
Adorno, Theodor, 25, 52, 70, 125, 129, 136, 175, 177, 181, 228–29n25, 231n68, 239n9
Altenberg, Peter, 14, 114, 122
Alter, Robert, 155, 168, 236n36
Anderson, Mark, 25–26, 70, 97, 98, 99, 100, 188n41
Angelus Novus (Benjamin), 154
Appelfeld, Aharon, 78, 219n66
Arcades Project, The (Benjamin), 156
Arendt, Hannah, 25, 42, 105, 156–57, 226n131
"Art and Revolution" (Wagner), 54
"Artwork of the Future, The" (Wagner), 54
Aschheim, Steven, 198n123, 234n7
"assimilation," 189–90n44
Austerlitz, Friedrich, 78
Austrian Face, The (Salten), 120

Bahr, Hermann, 14, 15, 17, 23, 75, 98–99, 114, 119, 130
Bartels, Alfred, 8, 63–67, 98, 104
Beller, Steven, 198–99n7
Benedikt, Moriz, 82, 86–88, 126, 131

Benjamin, Walter: on affinities between Kraus and Kafka, 161–62, 167–70, 237n55; on the feuilleton, 3, 5, 165; on the German-Jewish literati, 11–12, 29, 33, 140–45, 234n10; on Kraus, 1, 12, 22, 25, 29–30, 70, 76, 77, 78, 95, 118, 137–39, 155–73, 178, 180–81, 212n16, 218n57, 219n64, 223n112, 234n6, 234–35n16, 237n56, 238n58; on quotation and mimesis, 29, 118, 142, 155–56, 171–72
Berg, Alban, 16
Bergson, Henri, 114
Berliner Tageblatt, 61, 63, 146, 160
Berman, Marshall, 183–84n1
Bernstein, Michael André, 168, 215n29, 235–36n31
Best, Otto, 184–85n12
Bhabha, Homi K., 189n42
Biale, David, 148, 233–34n3
Bildung, 7, 19, 38–39, 44, 47, 58, 187n31, 201–2n27, 234n7
Bird Brain, The (Bahr), 130
Birnbaum, Nathan, 116
Bland, Kalman, 187n29
Blei, Franz, 117

Bloch, Ernst, 2, 158
Bluebeard (Offenbach), 113
Blumenthal, Oskar, 49–50, 88
Bourdieu, Pierre, 77, 177, 218n58
Börries, Mechthild, 194n99
Brauer, Erich, 148
Brenner, Der, 6
Broch, Hermann, 17, 99
Brod, Max, 69, 109, 116, 146
Börne, Ludwig, 6, 57–58, 64
Brecht, Bertolt, 16, 173
Buber, Martin, 29, 69, 116, 124, 140, 147–49, 158
Budapester Orpheumgesellschaft, 111–12, 116, 135

Canetti, Elias, 21–22, 26, 78, 193n86, 195n11
Chamberlain, Houston Stewart, 83, 84, 85, 220n78
Clark, T. J., 183–84n1
Cohen, Gerson, 52, 204n53
Cohn, Alfred, 159, 160
Cohn, Grete, 159
crisis of modernity, 1–3, 183n1, 183–84n7, 186n19

Dialectic of Enlightenment, The (Horkheimer and Adorno), 181, 239n9
Döblin, Alfred, 16
DuBois, W. E. B., 6, 47
Dreyfus, Alfred, 84, 175

Eisenbach, Heinrich, 115, 116, 118
Endelman, Todd, 210–12n13
Engel, Eduard, 116
Eulenberg, Philip, 89

Fackel, Die: early circulation figures, 14; formal features, 12–20, 92–95, 102–6, 111–22, 127–35, 217n55; founding, 14–15; thematic constitution, 16, 19–21, 23, 26, 69–70, 71, 76–77, 83, 92–95, 217n56, 219n68, 229n36
Ferguson, Niall, 177, 239n6
feuilleton: age of, 4; antisemitic attacks on, 5–10, 23, 32, 39–40, 58–67; as avant-garde writing, 1, 12; definition, 4, 5, 184–85n12, 187n28, 223n110
Feuilleton Handbook (Haacke), 62
Flink und Fliederbusch (Schnitzler), 130
Foundations of the Nineteenth Century, The (Chamberlain), 83
Frankfurter Zeitung, Die, 3, 61, 163
Freud, Sigmund, 17, 126, 136
Freytag, Gustav, 62, 91
Friedländer, Saul, 53
Frischauer, Berthold, 84
Fritzsche, Peter, 61, 183n5
Fulda, Ludwig, 49–50
Future, The (Harden), 16, 87, 89–91

Gadamer, Hans-Georg, 179
Gay, Peter, 214–15n28
George, Stefan, 155, 159, 171
"German-Jewish Parnassus, The" (Goldstein), 31–33, 41–48, 139–40, 151, 202n39, 202n42
Germany: A Winter's Tale (Heine), 63
Gilman, Sander, 8, 10, 24, 70, 95, 98, 100, 102, 188n37, 212n20, 224–25n126
Girardi, Alexander, 112
Goethe, J. W. F., 38, 56, 134, 159
Goldschnigg, Dietmar, 194n99
Goldstein, Moritz, 31–33, 34, 35, 41–48, 50–51, 58, 139–40, 145, 151, 152, 153, 172, 189n44, 198–99
Gomperz, Theodor, 11, 49–51, 190n45, 203n46
Great Bestiary of Modern Literature, The (Blei), 117
Grimstad, Kari, 112
Gundolf, Friedrich, 159

Haacke, Wilmont, 62
Harden, Maximilian, 18, 25, 73, 76, 77, 87–91, 99, 104, 105, 107, 127–28, 176, 221n88, 221n92
Hegel, G. W. F., 3, 9, 61, 184n8
Heine, Heinrich, 6–8, 24–25, 27–28, 43, 56–58, 63–67, 87–88, 92, 95–106, 107, 121, 133, 152, 165, 178
Heinrich Heine: Also A Monument (Bartels), 66
Heller, Erich, 20, 70
Herder, Johann, 38–39, 58, 83
Hervay, Donna von, 89–90, 176
Herzl, Theodor, 7, 11, 14, 15, 27, 73, 79–82, 100, 190n46
Hesse, Hermann, 4
Hilsner, Leopold, 85–86, 175, 176
Hitler, Adolf, 32, 70, 126, 187n34, 209n12
Hofmannsthal, Hugo von, 4, 41, 42, 43, 44, 119, 185n13
Horkheimer, Max, 52, 76, 136

Janik, Allan, 71, 214–15n28
Jellinek, Adolf, 35–39, 40, 60, 165, 200n18
Jew, The (Buber), 124
Jews and Economic Life, The (Sombart), 39–40
Jewish Ethnicity (Jellinek), 35
Jewish Ethnicity in Sayings (Jellinek), 36
Jewish Heritage and Literary Criticism (Bartels), 66
"Jewishness in Music" (Wagner), 53, 55–59, 61, 65, 188n39
journalism: as an emblem of Jewish intellectuality, 9–12, 31–41, 43–44, 49–51, 59–61, 63–68, 139, 144–45, 150–55, 202n38; as the embodiment of capitalism, 2, 183n5, 238n63; as modernism, 1, 12, 16, 21, 239n7; modernity of, 1, 8–10, 17–19, 58–63, 127–35, 204n59; as secular worship, 3, 7, 8, 11, 12, 23, 144–45, 150–55
Journalists, The (Freytag), 62, 91, 194n104
"Judgment, The" (Kafka), 122

Kafka, Franz: affinities with Kraus, 25, 29, 42, 78, 115–16, 122–26, 157, 161–63, 167–70, 178; on Kraus's *Literature*, 107–11, 157, 226n2, 227n13
Kalmar, Annie, 113
Kant, Immanuel, 9, 136
"Karl Kraus" (Benjamin, 1928), 137, 154, 160, 163, 167, 168, 191n52
"Karl Kraus" (Benjamin, 1931), 3, 5, 29, 76, 118, 154, 156, 161, 163–73, 191n52
"Karl Kraus Reads Offenbach" (Benjamin), 160
Kaufmann, Fritz Mordecai, 116
Kernmayer, Hildegard, 183–84n1, 188n36
Kerr, Alfred, 7, 18, 73, 91–92, 96, 99, 104, 105, 159–60
Kierkegaard, Søren, 167
Kokoschka, Oskar, 16, 20
Kracauer, Siegfried, 16, 113, 192n65
Kraft, Werner, 70, 145, 148, 215n36
Kraus, Emma, 13
Kraus, Jakob, 14
Kraus, Karl: on Benjamin, 173; childhood, 13; critique of Jewish journalists, 23–25, 27–29, 31, 36–38, 69, 73–74, 75, 79–92, 94–106, 120–22, 125, 127–35, 196n115, 215n34, 221–22n94, 222n98, 225n128, 232nn87–88; critique of Zionism, 27, 79–82, 196n114; eroticism, 21, 76, 193–94n82; familial relations, 12–13, 191n56; general objections to feuilleton, 17–19, 22, 59–60, 92–95; Jewish self-fashioning, 23–29, 36–37, 72–77, 79–91, 94–106, 111–18, 120–22, 127–135, 157, 195n107,

Kraus, Karl (*continued*)
  195n112, 212n15, 216n39, 222n95;
  Jewish self-hatred, 12, 23–29, 69–91,
  94–106, 133–35, 157, 173–74, 179,
  196n113, 207–8n7, 208–9nn10–12,
  210–12n13, 214n27, 216nn37–38,
  224–25n126, 236–37n45; mimetic
  commitments, 16, 27–29, 38, 76–77,
  86–87, 88–89, 92–95, 102–6, 111–35,
  157, 230nn40–42; on Offenbach,
  103, 112–15, 228n21, 228n24; param-
  eters of oeuvre, 12–23, 218–19n62;
  reasons for early success, 14–15;
  Sprachkritik, 19–20, 102–3; stage
  presence, 21–22; typographical
  perfectionism, 20, 193n80; Viennese
  self-hatred, 17, 23, 197–98n122; on
  Yiddish theater, 28, 111–12, 115–18
Kraus, Karl, works by: "Apocalypse,"
  93; "The Austrian Face," 120; *A
  Crown for Zion*, 74, 75, 79–82, 92;
  "The Decline of the World through
  Black Magic," 112; *The Decline of
  the World through Black Magic*, 128;
  Demolished Literature, 74, 75, 82;
  Ethics and Criminality, 177; "Grimacing over Culture and the Stage,"
  113; "Harden Dictionary," 89;
  "Harikari and Feuilleton," 128–36;
  "Heine and the Consequences," 24–
  25, 27–29, 30, 63, 70, 72, 73, 74, 87,
  95–106, 111, 120, 122, 125, 129, 134,
  146, 150, 152, 174; "He's Still a Jew,"
  106, 114, 121–22, 127; "In this Great
  Time," 22, 94, 119, 158; "A Kantian
  and Kant," 119; "The Last Actors,"
  111, 115–18, 122, 128; *The Last Days
  of Mankind*, 119, 178; *Literature*,
  107–111, 134, 154, 157; "Longing for
  Aristocratic Company," 127; "The
  Mirror of the World," 119, "The
  New Kind of Cursing," 127; "Self-
  Mirroring," 38; "Um Heine," 88;
  "The Witch Trial of Leoben," 89

Kraus, Marie, 13
Kraus, Richard, 14

Lagarde, Paul, 61, 205n70
Lang, Fritz, 16, 21
Lasker-Schüler, Else, 114, 122
Lassalle, Ferdinand, 69, 170
Le Rider, Jacques, 25–26, 70, 71, 95
"Lecture on the Yiddish Language"
  (Kafka), 111, 115–16
Legend of Baal Schem, The (Buber), 147
Lensing, Leo, 14, 70, 195n107
Lessing, Theodor, 4, 33, 40, 69, 184n10
Levin, Thomas, 183n3
Liebenfels, Lanz Jörg von, 121, 230n52
Liegler, Leopold, 167
Literatus, 190n47, 190n50, 207n1
Loos, Adolf, 92–93, 112
Lowenstein, Steven, 70
Ludwig, Emil, 19
Lueger, Karl, 27, 72, 215n32
Lukács, Georg, 117, 181
Lyotard, Jean-François, 53

Mach, Ernst, 21
Mahler, Gustav, 17
Mann, Heinrich, 39
Mann, Thomas, 16, 66, 77, 218n57
Marr, Wilhelm, 61, 205n75
Marx, Karl, 1–2, 136
"Mauschel" (Herzl), 80, 81
Mauscheln, 8, 10, 25, 29, 81, 82,
  92, 109–111, 116, 129, 130, 146,
  227nn13–14
Mayer, Hans, 213–14n26
Mein Kampf (Hitler), 32
Mendes-Flohr, Paul, 140, 204n53,
  207–8n7, 234n10
Menzel, Wolfgang, 64
Metamorphosis, The (Kafka), 123
Meyer, Richard M., 127
Meyerbeer, Giacomo, 55, 58
Mirror-Man (Werfel), 107–11, 157,
  208n9

Index   253

"Modern" (Wagner), 54–55, 58–63
modern Jewish messianism, 137, 150–55, 223n1, 236n37
Monk, Ray, 51
Morgenstern, Soma, 160
Mosse, George, 7, 187n31
Müller, Burkhard, 94
Müller, Wilhelm, 81
Musil, Robert, 2, 17, 192n72
Musivstil, 34, 150–52, 155, 172, 199n10
Myers, David, 147

Neue Freie Presse, 7–8, 10, 11, 15, 16, 61, 74, 82, 83, 84, 85, 86–87, 92, 97, 120, 132, 134
"Newspaper Reader's Prayer" (Tucholsky), 3
Nietzsche, Friedrich, 1–2, 26, 136, 183n3

Offenbach, Jacques, 103, 112–15, 135
On Judaism, 11
"On the Limits of the Jewish Intellectual Gift" (Gomperz), 49–51
"Ornament and Crime" (Loos), 93, 103
Our Company (Sessa), 62
"Our Prospects" (Treitschke), 63

Pagis, Dan, 150
Pan (Kerr), 91
Pfitzer, Gustav, 58
Platen, Graf August von, 101
Polgar, Alfred, 4, 17, 185n14
Politzer, Heinz, 78
Popper, Leo, 117
Pulzer, Peter, 5, 61, 185n18

Rabinbach, Anson, 144, 158, 172, 233n1
Rathenau, Walther, 28, 176
Reading Berlin: 1900 (Fritzsche), 61
Reinhardt, Max, 112, 216–217n42
"Report to an Academy, A" (Kafka), 123–24

Rilke, Rainer Maria, 178
Road into the Open, The (Schnitzler), 111–12
Robertson, Ritchie, 208n10, 225n129
Röckel, August, 53
Romanzero (Heine), 104, 106
Roth, Joseph, 7

Salten, Felix, 14, 73, 75, 120, 224–25n126
Saphir, Moritz, 62
Scheichl, Sigurd Paul, 219n69
Schiele, Egon, 17
Schiller, Friedrich, 41, 56
Schnitzler, Arthur, 24, 51, 69, 112, 130, 220n79
Scholem, Gershom: on German Jews and journalism, 29–30, 33–34, 150–55, 174, 180–81; on Kraus, 25, 29–30, 33–34, 76, 77, 95, 137–39, 146–55, 180–81, 173–74, 180–81, 198n123, 199–200n11, 218n57, 235n28, 236n44, 238n57; on quotation and radical mimesis, 29, 34, 149–55, 235n30
Schopenhauer, Arthur, 136
Schorske, Carl, 4–5, 7, 76
Sessa, Alexander, 62
Sex and Character (Weininger), 25, 35–39, 44, 97
Simmel, Georg, 2, 18–19, 192n71
Singer, Mendel, 120, 132
Smith, Gary, 144, 202n34
Sombart, Werner, 39–40, 60, 202n34
Soul and the Forms (Lukács), 117
"Sovereign Feuilleton, The" (Treitschke), 6–7, 8, 64–65, 100
Spector, Scott, 228n15
Spitzer, Daniel, 82
Steiner, George, 94
Stieg, Gerald, 197n121
Stories of Rabbi Nachman, The (Buber), 147
Stözl, Christoph, 125

Strauss, Ludwig, 140–44
Szelkine, Yuri, 189n43

Tales of Hoffmann (Hoffmann), 113
"Theses on the Philosophy of History" (Benjamin), 156
Three Addresses on Judaism (Buber), 140
Timms, Edward, 16, 25, 70, 95, 113
Treitschke, Heinrich von, 6–8, 10, 61, 63–65, 72, 100–101, 186–87nn25–27, 206n80, 215n31, 220–21n82
Trial, The (Kafka), 161
Tucholsky, Kurt, 3

Ungerfeld, Moshe, 173–74

Victory of Jewishness over Germanness, The (Marr), 61
Volkov, Shulamit, 26, 71, 213–14n26

Wagner, Nike, 195n111
Wagner, Richard: on Jews as artists, 42, 54–61; 188n39; on "Jewish journalism," 5, 9–10, 59–61, 205n68; on the ills of journalism, 1, 4; on the ills of modern life, 1, 9–10, 51–63; as a reactionary, 54; as a revolutionary, 53

Walter Benjamin: The Story of a Friendship (Scholem), 145, 154
"Warrior Monument" (Benjamin), 160
Wassermann, Jakob, 11, 28, 145, 152, 153, 190n48
Weber, Max, 3, 40
Wedekind, Frank, 21
Weigel, Sigrid, 163–64, 171
Weiner, Marc, 205n68
Weininger, Otto, 26, 35–39, 44, 50–51, 58, 69, 72, 97, 98, 101, 214–15n28
Welt, Die, 79
Werfel, Franz, 69, 107–8, 117, 134, 146, 150, 157, 158, 226nn4–5
"What is German?" (Wagner), 58
Wieland, Christoph, 43
Wilde, Oscar, 15
Wistrich, Robert, 25, 70, 200n14
Wittels, Fritz, 127, 191n55, 231–32n73
Wittgenstein, Ludwig, 16, 51, 203n49
Wohlfarth, Irving, 144, 168
World of Yesterday, The (Zweig), 7

Zifferer, Paul, 129–34
Zohn, Harry, 25–26, 70
Zweig, Stefan, 7, 19, 20

www.ingramcontent.com/pod-product-compliance
Lightning Source LLC
Chambersburg PA
CBHW021939290426
44108CB00012B/900